A New Introduction to
American Constitutionalism

A New Introduction
to American
Constitutionalism

MARK A. GRABER

OXFORD
UNIVERSITY PRESS

OXFORD

UNIVERSITY PRESS

Oxford University Press is a department of the University of Oxford.
It furthers the University's objective of excellence in research, scholarship,
and education by publishing worldwide.

Oxford   New York

Auckland   Cape Town   Dar es Salaam   Hong Kong   Karachi
Kuala Lumpur   Madrid   Melbourne   Mexico City   Nairobi
New Delhi   Shanghai   Taipei   Toronto

With offices in

Argentina   Austria   Brazil   Chile   Czech Republic   France   Greece
Guatemala   Hungary   Italy   Japan   Poland   Portugal   Singapore
South Korea   Switzerland   Thailand   Turkey   Ukraine   Vietnam

Oxford is a registered trademark of Oxford University Press in the UK and certain other
countries.

Published in the United States of America by
Oxford University Press
198 Madison Avenue, New York, NY 10016

Library of Congress Cataloging-in-Publication Data
Graber, Mark A.
A new introduction to American constitutionalism / Mark A. Graber.
pages cm
Includes bibliographical references and index.
ISBN 978-0-19-994388-3 (alk. paper)
1. Constitutional law—United States. I. Title.
KF4550.G725 2013
342.73—dc23
2013011813

1 3 5 7 9 8 6 4 2
Printed in the United States of America
on acid-free paper

For Howard and Keith:
For all the obvious and some less obvious reasons

CONTENTS

PREFACE

"You remember each other," the elderly hostess in the first scene of the romantic comedy declares. Miriam and Daniel are temporarily speechless. Daniel remembers a scrawny tomboy who regularly pelted her brother's friends with snowballs. Before him is a shapely premedical student at a major state university. Miriam remembers a gawky nerd whose conversation was exhausted by the latest video games. Before her is a dashing political science major. Sparks will fly as Miriam and David are reintroduced.

Americans need a similar reintroduction to their constitutional order. American constitutionalism is more complex and interesting than the fragments citizens are exposed to in their youth. The Constitution most students remember from high school civics consists entirely of limits on government action enforced by the Supreme Court. Constitutional debate is restricted to whether states may ban abortion (updated to whether same-sex couples have a constitutional right to marry), when the president may constitutionally send troops into foreign combat, and other matters of constitutional law. Some students learn the constitutional facts of life from a legalist who insists that constitutional adjudication must be separated from ordinary politics. Others are taught by behaviorally oriented social scientists who repeatedly describe this distinction between law and politics as a childlike fairy tale. Neither perspective fully encompasses crucial elements of the American constitutional order.

Proper introductions to a mature American constitutionalism begin by exploring different theories about the nature and purposes of constitutions, with particular emphasis on the nature and purpose of the Constitution of the United States. Students then become acquainted with different approaches for determining the meaning of constitutional provisions, allocating constitutional authority, and bringing about legitimate constitutional change. Educated citizens acquire a global perspective on the American constitutional order by familiarizing themselves with the distinctive constitutional issues raised by foreign policy, foreign constitutions, and international law. Finally, a basic course in constitutionalism should highlight that constitutions work more by construct- ing and constituting politics than by compelling government officials to do what they might not want to do. Sparks may fly when teachers and pupils engaging in this course of study explore such questions as:

- What means for interpreting the Constitution and allocating constitutional authority best balance American constitutional commitments to popular sovereignty and fundamental law?
- What forms of constitutional change best secure and preserve essential con- stitutional purposes?
- Are the powers and limits on American governing officials derived solely from the Constitution of the United States, or are some legal powers and lim- its essential aspects of sovereignty rooted in international law?
- What sorts of people are presupposed by American constitutional commit- ments and purposes, and do Americans remain that sort of people?
- Might some other constitutional arrangements better suit contemporary Americans?

Americans whose constitutional education is limited to a series of Supreme Court decisions that focus on only a few constitutional provisions are not trained to ask much less answer these vital constitutional questions.

The study of the American constitutional order should encompass the entirety of American constitutionalism, not just the traces that appear on the pages of the *United States Reports*. Persons who have not thought seriously about the nature and purposes of constitutions, the methods for interpreting consti- tutional provisions, alternative schemes for allocating constitutional authority, the legitimate means of constitutional change, and how constitutions work can- not have an intelligent opinion on the merits of judicial protection for abortion rights. Citizens are unlikely to have well-informed answers to the constitutional questions raised during the war on terrorism absent some knowledge of the rela- tionship between constitutional and international law as well as the geographic scope of constitutional authority. More important, the obsession with judicial decisions enforcing constitutional limits obscures numerous dimensions of con- stitutional life. Elected officials and political movements have historically had a far greater influence on official constitutional practices than nine justices sitting in Washington, D.C. The Civil Rights Act of 1964 played as important a role as *Brown v. Board of Education* (1954) securing the equal protection rights of African Americans. Constitutional provisions influence politics even when they are not the subject of political debate. Consider how candidates during presi- dential elections focus their attention on a few "swing states," often foregoing appeals to the large number of voters who live in major metropolitan areas. The Constitution of the United States both constrains and constitutes fundamental American commitments, influencing as well as being influenced by the interests Americans pursue and the values they hold. The ways Americans think about policies toward political dissenters and the best method for staffing a national legislature are better understood as consequences of constitutional socialization than as naked preferences that must be disciplined by some external body that rises above the political fray.

A New Introduction to American Constitutionalism offers a historical–institutionalist perspective on American constitutionalism, but hardly *the* historical-institutionalist perspective. Such leading historical–institutionalist scholars as Rogers Smith, Howard Gillman, and Keith Whittington have pointed out for many years how the academic obsession in both law and political science with whether judges are making decisions based on legal or political factors too narrowly understands the judicial function and far too narrowly construes the central problems of a constitutional order.[1] Notions of law and legality influence judicial understandings of good policy, just as conceptions of good policy influence how justices interpreted the law. Moreover, explaining how justices decide cases in the last week of June typically requires some understanding of the dynamics of party competition that determine which justices sit on the bench, the structure of legal thought in a particular era that determines the various concepts justices bring to their work, and the broader constitutional culture that determines what constitutional issues are thought particularly salient at a particular time. This study of partisan dynamics, general currents of jurisprudence, and constitutional culture, in turn, reveals that important developments in American constitutionalism take place either entirely outside of courts or with limited judicial participation. A central theme of this work and of historical–institutionalism in general is to bring these nonjudicial, often nonlegal features of American constitutionalism into clear view, whether they be presidential influence on American constitutional development,[2] the way various racial orders structure the constitutional practice of equal protection,[3] or, as Sandy Levinson insists we consider, the influences of constitutional structures that are never litigated, such as the presidential veto power, on the capacity of the Constitution of the United States to deliver vital constitutional goods.[4]

A New Introduction to American Constitutionalism both is and is more than a general text. In the manner of a traditional text, this book offers a comprehensive introduction to American constitutionalism. Unlike a general text on chemistry or the standard reader on constitutional law, however, my goal is not merely to describe in accessible form matters well-known to experts in the field. Important constitutional questions are too often slighted in constitutional scholarship and pedagogy. The following pages aim to teach the teachers of American constitutionalism as well as their pupils.

The Vigeland Sculpture Park in Oslo features a Monolith Tower carved out of a single block of granite, which features 121 human beings in a cooperative effort to seek salvation. This book is the product of a similar, if less divine, experience working as a historical–institutionalist on the borders of law, political science, history, and no doubt a few other disciplines. For the past thirty years, I have received nothing but encouragement, boosts, and inspiration from numerous persons whose names can be found in the footnotes that follow but to whom the footnotes do not do true justice. Sandy Levinson, Mark Tushnet, Rogers Smith, Ran Hirschl, and Howard Schweber deserve particular mention for reading various drafts and making very helpful comments.

Members of two other associations also deserve special thanks. The rest are the people at Oxford University Press, most notably David McBride, the editor of this manuscript, Jennifer Carpenter, John Haber, Maegan Sherlock, and Erin Brown, for their commitment to the American constitutionalism project. The others, of course, my wonderful family, who have supported my obsessions throughout the years, Dr. Julia Frank, star of stage and psychiatry, newly minted Dr. Naomi Graber, soon to be Abigail Graber, Esq, Director Rebecca Graber, and my mother, Anita Graber, social worker, professor, Gourmet Cook and everything else.

A New Introduction to American Constitutionalism is dedicated to Howard Gillman and Keith Whittington. As is obvious, this manuscript originally began as part of our American Constitutionalism project. I am grateful to Howard and Keith for letting me hive this off on my own and more important for their incredibly important suggestions and friendship through the years. To truly acknowledge their contribution would require a full book. Instead, I hope the reader recognizes their extraordinary influence (including many language choices) throughout this manuscript as well as the powerful influence of many other historical–institutionalists. I am truly standing on the shoulders of giants, even if I can make no claim to see farther than anyone else.

A New Introduction to American Constitutionalism

Introduction to American Constitutionalism

1. Basic Constitutional Questions

On May 10, 1776, the Second Continental Congress passed a resolution rec-ommending that each colony draft and ratify a state constitution. Citizens were requested to "adopt such government as shall, in the opinions of the representa-tives of the people, best conduce to the happiness and safety of their constitu-ents in particular, and America in general."[1] Reaction was overwhelming. Local citizens paraded in joy on the streets of Philadelphia, eager to get on with the work of self-government. John Adams described this call to establish funda-mental law as "the most important resolution that was ever taken in America."[2] Within a year, every state but Rhode Island had established a new constitution.

This enthusiasm highlights the fundamental American commitment to con-stitutionalism. Government in the United States is constitutional government. Written constitutions, citizens of all political persuasions agree, are fundamental law, higher than ordinary law made by legislatures or common law announced by justices. Federal, state, and local authorities exercise power legitimately only when they have constitutional authorization. The power of government officials to perform tasks as diverse as sending troops on a peacekeeping mission to the Middle East and correcting grammar in the second grade of a public school must be derived ultimately from the Constitution of the United States or from the relevant state constitution. Consider a simple traffic stop. A state police officer is constitutionally authorized to pull a motorist over for speeding only if (1) the state constitution empowers the state legislature to set speed limits on state highways, (2) the relevant provisions of the state constitution and state law are consistent with the Constitution of the United States and all constitutionally valid federal laws, (3) the police officer was appointed consistently with the pro-cedures set out in the state constitution or laws passed under the state constitu-tion, and (4) the stop does not violate any federal or state constitutional rights.

This American commitment to constitutionalism extends far beyond traditional governing institutions. Many institutions in civil society, such as the local chess club and the local parent–teacher association (PTA), have a constitution that creates, empowers, and limits the leadership.

This passionate commitment to constitutionalism masks intense disputes over what a commitment to constitutionalism entails. Some controversies are very familiar. Contemporary candidates for the presidency are routinely asked whether they will appoint justices to the bench who are *strict constructionists* or who support *Roe v. Wade* (1973), which held that the Constitution protects abortion rights. When justices declare popular laws unconstitutional, some politicians and political movements cry "judicial imperialism." When justices sustain other controversial laws, as in the recent health-care case,[3] some politicians and political movements accuse them of bowing to political pressure. When elected officials seek to curb the power of courts to declare laws unconstitutional, some politicians and political movements accuse them of undermining an independent judiciary.

Other constitutional controversies lurk just beneath the surface of these common quarrels. Whether justices should be strict constructionists may depend on the extent to which the primary purpose of the Constitution is to secure rule by law or to establish justice. Common references to *the living Constitution* raise questions about the legitimate forms of constitutional change in the United States. Frequent assertions that constitutional rules and decision-making should be above politics require some understanding of the proper relationship between constitutional law and politics. Justice Robert Jackson, when declaring mandatory flag salutes unconstitutional, famously asserted:

> The very purpose of a Bill of Rights was to withdraw certain subjects from the vicissitudes of political controversy, to place them beyond the reach of majorities and officials and to establish them as legal principles to be applied by the courts. One's right to life, liberty, and property, to free speech, a free press, freedom of worship and assembly, and other fundamental rights may not be submitted to vote; they depend on the outcome of no elections.[4]

Jackson was able to utter these inspiring words only because he was nominated to the Supreme Court by Franklin Roosevelt, who had been elected to the presidency, and confirmed by senators, all of whom had also won elections. Had different officials won elections, the Supreme Court might have sustained mandatory flag salutes in public schools. The flag salute cases and other episodes in American constitutional development suggest that we ought to think about what constitutes good or legitimate constitutional politics rather than about the distinction between law and politics.

What constitutes good or legitimate constitutional politics depends on the best answers to questions about what citizens hope to accomplish by constitution writing and constitutional government. Americans venerate constitutionalism but are consistently reminded that good constitutional law is not necessarily identical to good public policy. Justice Felix Frankfurter's dissent in the flag salute cases famously insisted that the "great enemy of liberalism" is making "constitutionality synonymous with wisdom."[5] Professor Laurence Tribe of Harvard Law School writes, "If the Constitution is law, and if we are trying to interpret that law, then the claim that a particular government practice...is efficacious, is consistent with democratic theory, and is in some popular sense 'legitimate' just doesn't cut much ice."[6] These conventional assertions that constitutionalism may sometimes entail support for stupid, undemocratic, illegitimate, and unjust policies raise normative and practical questions. The normative question is why political leaders should do what they believe is constitutional when they believe an alternative policy is superior. If effective gun control will save many lives, what reason is there for worrying about whether such policies are inconsistent with the right to bear arms protected by the Second Amendment? The practical question is why political leaders will do what they believe is constitutional when they believe an alternative policy is superior or more popular with most voters. If constitutional decision-makers or popular majorities are convinced that women have a constitutional right to a legal abortion or that the president has the power to send troops into combat without a Congressional declaration of war, why should anyone expect that they will worry very much about what a document ratified in the late eighteenth century prescribes?

A New Introduction to American Constitutionalism introduces readers to the basic questions of constitutional government. Constitutionalism is more than the study of constitutional law or constitutional interpretation. Students, teachers, citizens, and even legal practitioners must consider a broader range of questions when thinking about the actual and desirable impact of constitutionalism in the United States:

- What is a constitution?
- What purposes do constitutions serve?
- How should constitutions be interpreted?
- How should constitutional disputes be resolved?
- How are constitutions, ratified, changed, and repudiated?
- What are the universal and distinctive features of a constitution?
- How do constitutions work?
- What is the relationship between constitutional decision-making and ordinary politics?

The next eight chapters survey possible answers to each constitutional question.

An introduction to constitutionalism throughout the world would include a chapter on constitutional design. Political actors in emerging constitutional democracies are actively debating such issues as the relative merits of presidential and parliamentary governments, the best constitutional means for achieving their regime's distinctive constitutional purposes, and what governing institutions are necessary to prevent civil war from breaking out between the particular political factions of that society. The study of American constitutionalism, by comparison, focuses on the merits and consequences of constitutional design questions answered in the past. Constitutionalists in the United States rarely consider the merits of parliamentary government, ponder what constitutional arrangements will best promote Islamic teachings, or worry about the constitutional institutions necessary to prevent violence between different religious sects. Rather than debate the merits of having a life-tenured judiciary interpret the Constitution, Americans dispute how the life-tenured judiciary mandated by Article III should interpret the Constitution. Legitimate questions exist about whether the Constitution of the United States is well designed in light of either the goals that motivated the framers in the eighteenth century or the aspirations Americans deem worthy at the turn of the twenty-first century.[7] Some questions of constitutional design, as well as the possibility that Americans should adopt a new Constitution, are discussed in the chapters on constitutional purposes and constitutional change. Nevertheless, the study of American constitutionalism remains appropriately focused on the study of the Constitution of the United States as ratified in 1789 and subsequently amended.

2. Identifying Basic Constitutional Questions

Many commentators think *McCulloch v. Maryland*[8] is the most important constitutional decision in American history. The case arose when James McCulloch, an employee of the Bank of the United States, refused to pay a state tax on all bank notes issued by banks not incorporated by the Maryland legislature. McCulloch claimed that Maryland had no power to tax an institution incorporated by Congress. Lawyers for Maryland insisted that the Constitution did not permit Congress to incorporate a national bank. The Supreme Court unanimously ruled in favor of McCulloch on both issues. The justices decided that the national government had the constitutional power to incorporate a national bank and that the Constitution forbade state governments from taxing any federal agency or instrument of the federal government. Chief Justice John Marshall's unanimous opinion is frequently thought to have established the principle that the constitutional powers of the federal government should be broadly construed and that states may not interfere in any way with the exercise of legitimate national powers. As important for our purposes, the *McCulloch* opinion identified and provided some possible answers to the fundamental questions of American constitutionalism.

2.1 Constitutional Interpretation

John Marshall began his opinion in *McCulloch* by introducing traditional questions of constitutional interpretation. "The constitution of our country," he wrote, "in its most interesting and vital parts, is to be considered, the conflicting powers of the government of the Union and of its members, as marked in that constitution, are to be discussed."[9] Much of Marshall's opinion interpreted the provisions in Article I, Section 8, which enumerate the powers of Congress. Interpretation was necessary because, as Marshall admitted, the Constitution does not explicitly empower Congress to incorporate a national bank. One crucial interpretive question was whether the constitutional provision that authorized Congress "to make all Laws which shall be necessary and proper for carrying into Execution the foregoing Powers" expanded or restricted the powers of the national government. The disputants in *McCulloch* also contested the correct interpretation of the provision in Article VI, asserting, "This Constitution, and the Laws of the United States which shall be made in Pursuance thereof... shall be the Supreme Law of the Land." Marshall insisted that this clause was best interpreted as forbidding states from taxing the national bank or any other national institution. The lawyers for Maryland insisted that neither Article VI nor any other constitutional provision should be interpreted as withdrawing from state legislatures their longstanding power to tax all corporations that did business in the state.

2.2 The Nature of the Constitution

When considering how to interpret the "necessary and proper" clause and other constitutional provisions, Marshall stated, "We must never forget, that it is *a constitution* we are expounding."[10] The rules for interpreting a constitution, this passage maintains, are different from the rules for interpreting other texts. *McCulloch* emphasized that a constitution is not a legal code. How the words *necessary and proper* are interpreted depends on whether they are found in a constitution, a legal code, a novel, or a love letter. "It is necessary and proper that we marry" in a romance novel may have a different meaning from the same phrase in Article I, Section 8.

    McCulloch interpreted the Constitution in light of Marshall's belief that constitutions are fundamental law. His opinion insisted that persons interpreting the fundamental law of a nation should not expect the minute details they would find in

an ordinary law regulating the sale of chickens. From this understanding of constitutionalism, Marshall deduced the claim that specific constitutional powers, such
as the power to incorporate a national bank, need not be explicitly enumerated.
"Its nature," he declared, "requires that only its great outlines should be marked,
its important objects designated, and the minor ingredients which compose those
objects be deduced from the nature of the objects themselves."[11] Another justice
might have deduced a different conclusion in *McCulloch* from a different understanding of constitutionalism. If constitutions by nature seek to limit government,
then perhaps all government powers should be interpreted narrowly.

2.3   Universal and Distinctive Constitutional Norms

Marshall's claim that "we must never forget, that it is *a constitution* we are expounding" suggests that the Constitution of the United States has certain universal features. All constitutions, his *McCulloch* opinion declared, are "intended to endure
for ages to come" and, for that reason, cannot be interpreted as legal codes.[12] The
second most famous quotation from *McCulloch*, "the power to tax involves the
power to destroy,"[13] invokes a second universal norm. Any institution with the
power to tax an enterprise, Marshall maintained, controls the fate of that enterprise. This truth transcends the American constitutional regime. Governments
in England, India, or China with the power to tax also have the power to destroy.

Marshall derived other conclusions in *McCulloch* from distinctive features
of the American constitutional regime. His justification for national supremacy
relied on the particular processes by which the Constitution of the United States
was ratified. Marshall wrote:

> The convention which framed the Constitution was indeed elected
> by the State legislatures. But the instrument, when it came from their
> hands, was a mere proposal, without obligation or pretensions to it. It
> was reported to the then existing Congress of the United States with a
> request that it might be submitted to a convention of delegates, chosen
> in each State by the people thereof, under the recommendation of its
> legislature, for their assent and ratification. This mode of proceeding
> was adopted, and by the convention, by Congress, and by the State leg-
> islatures, the instrument was submitted to the people. They acted upon
> it in the only manner in which they can act safely, effectively and wisely,
> on such a subject—by assembling in convention. It is true, they assem-
> bled in their several States—and where else should they have assem-
> bled? No political dreamer was ever wild enough to think of breaking
> down the lines which separate the States, and of compounding the
> American people into one common mass. Of consequence, when they

act, they act in their States. But the measures they adopt do not, on that account, cease to be the measures of the people themselves, or become the measures of the State governments.[14]

In Marshall's view, this distinctive ratification process explains certain crucial features of the Constitution of the United States. Constitutions ratified by a different process—for example, a ratification process that relied on subnational units in their corporate capacity—might be interpreted differently.

2.4 Constitutional Purposes

Constitutional interpretation, *McCulloch* suggests, requires an understanding of constitutional purposes. Marshall insisted that constitutional powers were vested in the national government to promote "the welfare of the nation" and that the Constitution "was intended to endure ages to come, and, consequently, to be adapted to the various *crises* of human affairs."[15] From these premises, he concluded that the necessary and proper clause should be interpreted as facilitating Congressional efforts to achieve these constitutional aspirations. Given that the framers could not foresee all future threats to the common good, constitutional clauses should ordinarily be interpreted as enabling the national government to protect the national interest as elected officials see best. Had Marshall emphasized other constitutional purposes, he might have reached a different conclusion. A constitutional commitment to the rule of law or limited national power, for example, might be thought inconsistent with the open-ended grant of legislative power in *McCulloch*.

2.5 Constitutional Change

The *McCulloch* opinion interprets American constitutional history as well as the constitutional text. Marshall stated, "A doubtful question, if put at rest by the practice of the government, ought to receive a considerable impression from that practice."[16] Constitutional meanings may change, the above quotation asserts, even when no formal constitutional amendment has been passed. Perhaps the constitutional status of the national bank was unclear when the Constitution was ratified in 1789 but was settled without an intervening constitutional amendment by 1819. President James Madison in 1815 explicitly took this view when he confessed to having abandoned constitutional objections to a national bank that he opposed while a member of Congress in 1791. Marshall's reference to the practice of the government included constitutional decisions made by the national legislature and national executive. He considered the congressional and presidential decisions in 1791 and 1816 to incorporate a national

bank to be relevant sources for considering the constitutionality of that institution in 1819. This use of precedent in *McCulloch* raises questions about constitutional change. What counts as a doubtful constitutional question that can
be constitutionally settled by means other than a constitutional amendment?
Might a constitution decision-maker who believed that no very good constitutional arguments could be made for a particular practice in 1789 nevertheless
conclude that an unbroken line of practice established the constitutionality of
that practice at present?

2.6 Constitutional Authority

The first paragraph of *McCulloch* asserts that the federal judiciary is the governing institution responsible for settling constitutional controversies. Marshall
insisted that the dispute over whether Congress may constitutionally incorporate a national bank "must be decided peacefully, or remain a source of hostile
legislation, perhaps of hostility of a still more serious nature; and if it is to be
so decided, by this tribunal alone can the decision be made. On the Supreme
Court of the United States has the constitution of our country devolved this
important duty."[17] In other words, other government institutions must accept
a judicial decision even if they believe the Supreme Court made a constitutional mistake. Such assertions of judicial supremacy raise several constitutional
problems. Marshall did not specify the constitutional source for his claim that
constitutional questions in the United States are settled by judicial decree. No
constitutional provision explicitly states that the Supreme Court has the authority to resolve constitutional disputes. Perhaps constitutional disputes are best
settled by elected officials or left for each generation to decide for itself. Marshall
also did not state explicitly the precise issue the Supreme Court in *McCulloch*
was deciding. Read narrowly, he might have been claiming to resolve only the
dispute over whether Maryland could tax the Bank of the United States. On this
view, whether North Carolina could tax the salary of a federal customs official
remained an open question after *McCulloch*. Read broadly, Marshall was insisting that governing officials when making any decision must behave consistently
with the principles underlying past judicial decisions. On this view, *McCulloch*
settled that North Carolina could not tax the salary of any federal official because
that decision was based on the principle that states could not tax federal employees or federal agencies.

2.7 Constitutional Decision-Making and Politics

Some readers may suspect that these seemingly abstract academic questions
mask very ordinary politics. If constitutional decision makers legitimately

dispute whether fundamental constitutional purposes require constitutional powers to be construed broadly or narrowly, then neither constitutional theory nor constitutional law compelled Marshall in *McCulloch* to interpret constitutional powers broadly. The best explanation for his decision may be that Marshall favored a national bank. The chief justice employed constitutional arguments to disguise what was a preexisting partisan policy preference. Marshall was a member of the Federalist Party, and Federalists at the turn of the nineteenth century championed federal power to incorporate a national bank. Such opponents of the national bank as Thomas Jefferson and Judge Spencer Roane of Virginia championed constitutional arguments against federal power to incorporate a national bank that relied on alternative understandings of constitutionalism, constitutional interpretation, constitutional purposes, universal and distinctive constitutional norms, constitutional change, and constitutional authority. Had the Supreme Court in 1819 been staffed by a majority of states rights Republicans, the result in *McCulloch* would have been different.

While ordinary politics help explain the result in *McCulloch*, constitutional norms mattered as well. The justices on the Marshall Court did not seek to realize their policy preferences whenever those preferences were rejected by elected officials. John Marshall did not support the War of 1812, but he thought hostilities had been declared consistently with the provisions laid out in Article I. The justices in 1819 believed that the federal government should fund various internal improvements, most notably roads and canals connecting the different regions of the United States. They wrote a letter to President James Monroe stating that an internal improvements bill recently passed by Congress passed constitutional muster. Nevertheless, when Monroe rejected that measure, the justices did not declare his veto unconstitutional. The justices believed that the Constitution vested the president with the power to veto any law, even those they thought served vital public purposes.

The Constitution structured *McCulloch* in subtler ways. The Constitution of the United States establishes a life-tenured judiciary. Other national constitutions and many state constitutions restrict judicial tenure to a fixed number of years. Had the Constitution limited judicial tenure to ten years, five of the seven justices who decided *McCulloch*, including Marshall, would not have been on the bench in 1819. Different justices might have reached different conclusions when determining whether Congress had the constitutional power to incorporate a national bank. Marshall might not have been chief justice in 1819 had the framers made different rules for impeaching federal officials. Congressional leaders during the first decade of the nineteenth century attempted to remove Federalist judicial appointees whom they feared would unduly interfere with their Jeffersonian constitutional vision.[18] Their first target on the Supreme Court was Samuel Chase, a justice notorious for making partisan speeches when

conducting trials. Marshall was the likely second target. The Chase impeachment failed. Jeffersonian leaders obtained a Senate majority on crucial counts,
but Article I, Section 3, requires a two-thirds majority for an impeachment to
succeed. Had Article I mandated a majority vote, the judicial majority in 1819
would likely have been dedicated to more Jeffersonian constitutional principles.

3. Thinking about Basic Constitutional Questions

Despite clear evidence that these basic constitutional questions structure political life in the United States, some prominent constitutional practitioners and
social scientists insist constitutional theory is trivial, subversive, or meaningless. Distinguished constitutional decision-makers chide professors who spend
their time thinking about *high* or *grand theory* for providing little practical guidance to lawyers and judges. Judge Harry T. Edwards in 1992 complained that
"judges, administrators, legislators, and practitioners have little use for much of
the [constitutional] scholarship that is now produced by members of the acad-
emy."[19] Chief Justice John Roberts recently repeated these common criticisms.[20]
Conversations about the relationships between constitutionalism and ordinary
politics touch raw nerves. Many law professors insist that challenging the distinction between law and politics risks introducing illegitimate partisan considerations into the constitutional decision-making process. Herbert Wechsler, in
perhaps the most influential article published on constitutional law in the second half of the twentieth century, scorned "those among us who...frankly or
covertly make the test of virtue in [constitutional] interpretation whether its
result in the immediate decision seems to hinder or advance the interests or values they support."[21] Good or legitimate constitutional politics, on this common
view, has everything to do with the Constitution and nothing to do with politics.
Prominent political scientists complain that constitutional theory merely reifies
legal mythologies, diverting attention from conclusive evidence that constitutional decision-makers are guided solely by the policy preferences. Professor
Jeffrey Segal of Stony Brook and Professor Harold Spaeth of Michigan State
University speak of "the fairy tale of a discretionless judiciary," a "myth" that fails
to acknowledge how Supreme Court justices exercise "virtually untrammeled
policy-making authority."[22] Actual constitutional politics, on this common view,
has everything to do with politics and nothing to do with the Constitution.

Constitutional theory may also seem an exercise in the obvious. Many
Americans think the basic questions have easy answers. The Constitution of the
United States is the fundamental law of the land. That Constitution limits government and protects basic rights. The Constitution of the United States consists
of the written text ratified in 1787–89 and amendments passed according to the

procedures set out in Article V. Article VII details the procedures for ratifying the Constitution.[23] Article V details the only legitimate means for amending the Constitution.[24] The Supreme Court resolves constitutional controversies. The decisions of that tribunal on constitutional questions bind all other governing officials. Having constitutional controversies resolved by the branch of government with life-tenured members best guarantees that all exercises of government authority rest on sound principles of constitutional law and not merely on short-term political needs or preferences. The constitutional text is the primary source of American prosperity and liberty. Government officials should respect the Constitution because the Constitution is law, although, alas, too many politicians and citizens are prone to substitute their policy preferences for constitutional commands. The only constitutional question open to serious debate is the proper method for interpreting the Constitution.

Basic constitutional questions are more difficult and more important than these common complaints and answers suggest. Many constitutional practices that Americans now take for granted are products of long historical struggles. Most are not adopted by other constitutional democracies. Americans during the eighteenth and nineteenth centuries routinely asserted that unwritten constitutional principles and international law limited governing officials. The Constitution of the United States was intended to empower as well as limit. The text simultaneously expresses national aspirations while providing a framework designed to enable persons with very different political principles to share the same civic space. The framers of the American Constitution thought their handiwork would best be maintained by a well-designed constitutional politics rather than by clear statements of constitutional law. The present near judicial monopoly on constitutional decision-making is the result of political transformation that began in the late nineteenth century. Prominent contemporary constitutionalists reject as simple-minded the notion that Article V prescribes the only legitimate means for constitutional change in the United States. Despite interpreting constitutional provisions for amending their national constitution similar to ours, constitutional courts in India and Germany insist that amendments inconsistent with the general tenor of the constitution are not legally binding. Leading political scientists and constitutional commentators assert that the Constitution of the United States is responsible for many ills of American society.[25] Constitutional defects caused the Civil War.[26]

Particular constitutional controversies are grounded in more general constitutional disputes. Debates over whether affirmative action policies are constitutional turn on whether the Fourteenth Amendment should be interpreted consistently with the plain language of the text or with political practice at the time the equal protection clause was ratified. Whether the Supreme Court in *Planned Parenthood v. Casey* (1992) correctly ruled that the Constitution permitted states to regulate, but not ban, abortion may depend on whether the Constitution of the United States commits Americans to live by certain ideals or provides guidelines that enable persons with very different ideals to live together. The Civil War was fought over questions of constitutional authority. Secessionists insisted that states were constitutionally authorized to determine whether federal policies were unconstitutional. Unionists maintained that permitting individual states to void federal laws deprived national law of necessary uniformity. Constitutions influence politics beyond dictating outcomes in particular cases. New Deal liberals who opposed legislation restricting the power of labor unions did not constitutionally challenge what they believed were the oppressive provisions in the Taft-Hartley Act of 1947 because they had previously committed themselves to the principle that the national government could constitutionally regulate the national economy as the national government thought best. Al Gore refused to challenge the adverse result in *Bush v. Gore* (2000) because he believed the Supreme Court had the authority to settle all constitutional disputes arising out of the 2000 national presidential election.

Practical answers to these constitutional questions must be informed by knowledge of actual political processes. If the vast majority of Supreme Court justices in American history have failed to adopt the "right" theory of the judicial function, a lecture in the *Harvard Law Review* will not change judicial practice. Instead, the historical evidence apparently demonstrates that federal courts are not structured to make decisions consistently with recommendations made by leading law professors. Rather than quoting *Federalist* 51 on the attachment elected officials have to their home institution, constitutional commentators might highlight the increasing tendency for members of the House and Senate to identify with their political party.[27] While some law professors condemn unelected justices who "thwart the will" of the people's representatives,[28] more empirically oriented constitutional theorists focus on the serious constitutional problems that arise when those representatives foster judicial review in part to obscure their complicity with certain policy decisions.[29]

Constitutionalism, properly done, differs from ideal theory. We might all agree that judicial review would be justified if manna fell from heaven every time the justices declared a law unconstitutional. The problem is that this does not happen. Nor have constitutional decision-makers over long periods of time behaved consistently with any other theory of constitutional interpretation, whether that theory has emphasized constitutional obligations to respect original meanings, to promote democracy, or to protect fundamental rights. Constitutionalism is about evaluating, maintaining, and reforming actual constitutions and practices in the light of what we know about political behavior. Thus, a historical-institutionalist American constitutional theory begins with how constitutional institutions have functioned and developed over time. As the prominent legal realist Karl Llewellyn observed, "There is no reaching a judgment as to whether any specific part of present law does what it ought, until you can first answer what it is doing now" (or has been doing for long periods of time).[30]

Constitutionalism is a distinctive form of government. Constitutions structure ordinary politics in ways that framers and their progeny hope will promote justice, stability, and prosperity. Sometimes constitutions promote goals directly. The Constitution of the United States declares that governing institutions may not lawfully impose "cruel and unusual punishments." More often, constitutions structure governing institutions in ways thought to privilege desirable outcomes. Popular elections, Americans think, provide practical guarantees that elected officials will not oppress the vast majority of citizens. Constitutions both shape and are shaped by ordinary politics. Candidates for the presidency in the United States spend inordinate amounts of money and time in a few swing states because Article II requires a majority of the electoral votes rather than a majority of the popular votes. Change the constitutional rules for electing the president, and the politics of presidential elections will change. *Roe v. Wade* was not overruled in *Planned Parenthood v. Casey* in part because the Senate rejected a judicial nominee, Robert Bork, on record as believing that the Constitution did not protect abortion rights. Change the result of the 1986 national elections, in which Democrats gained majority control of the Senate, and the constitutional status of abortion would have changed.

Constitutional controversies are structured in part by constitutional texts, in part by history, and in part by present politics. Those who think constitutional practice is pure law must explain why virtually all conservatives and hardly any liberals thought the Supreme Court in *Bush v. Gore* (2000) correctly decided that George W. Bush won the 2000 presidential election. Those who think constitutional practice is pure politics must explain why no conservative asked the same Supreme Court justices to rule that Robert Dole won the 1996 presidential election.

What Is a Constitution?

Constitutionalism has a long tradition in politics and political theory, but substantial disagreement exists over when that tradition began and what constitutes that tradition. Many commentators believe the constitutional tradition began in ancient Greece. They see Aristotle's *Politics* as the first great work of constitutionalism and identify constitutionalism with the study of political regimes. Others find the first seeds of constitutionalism in ancient Rome and the Middle Ages. Modern constitutional regimes arose as rulers became committed to governing consistently with certain fundamental legal principles and the rule of law. A third understanding of constitutionalism developed in England and the United States during the seventeenth and eighteenth centuries. The liberal constitutionalism of the Enlightenment was committed to limited government and individual liberty. Constitutions prevented governing institutions from interfering with such fundamental freedoms as the free exercise of religion and the right to acquire property. Another wave of constitutionalism emerged in the wake of World War Two and decolonialization. Contemporary constitutions require government to respect liberal constitutional rights but insist that government officials are also constitutionally obligated to ensure that citizens are able to obtain certain basic goods and services.

Modern and contemporary constitutionalism is grounded in law. Governing officials in constitutional regimes are chosen on the basis of preexisting legal standards and act lawfully only when their conduct is sanctioned by preexisting legal standards. A person may claim the constitutional authority as president of the United States only when that person has obtained office following the rules laid down in Article II, is proposing to exercise an executive authority vested by Article II, and is exercising that authority consistently with other rules laid down in the Constitution. Political actors have no legal authority when they take actions inconsistent with these standards. Legitimate debate exists in the United States and other constitutional regimes over the best interpretation of constitutional provisions and who determines whether a governing official has acted lawfully. Some commentators have even suggested that political leaders in times of emergencies may temporarily suspend constitutional norms. Nevertheless, agreement exists that governing officials act *constitutionally* only when their actions are sanctioned by preexisting law.

The precise way constitutions authorize official actions is contestable. The most conventional view is that constitutions consist of rules for official behavior. Government action is legitimate, in this view, if some constitutional rule, properly interpreted, permits a government official to take the action in question. Justice Antonin Scalia, a leading champion of this approach to constitutionalism, writes that "the Rule of Law, the law of rules, [should] be extended as far as the nature of the question allows."[1] Other commentators see constitutions as establishing "discourses of justification" rather than fixed rules. Government action, in this view, is legitimate if the official can offer a plausible constitutional justification of the action. "What is required for the creation of a legitimate constitutional regime," Professor Howard Schweber of the University of Wisconsin declares, "is an initial shared commitment to the creation of a system of constitutional language in a manner consistent with the principle of justification by consent."[2]

Classical, modern, and contemporary constitutionalism is concerned with the governance of a distinctive people. Immanuel Kant maintained that all rational beings should act according to the categorical imperative. The First Amendment, by comparison, legally restricts the behavior only of federal officials in the United States. Governing officials in other countries may have moral obligations to respect religious liberty and are bound by the fundamental law of their polity, but they have no legal obligation to be guided by American constitutional precepts. From the eighteenth century to the present, prominent Americans have insisted Americans are a distinctive people, whose distinctive characteristics explain and justify distinctive constitutional purposes and practices. Questions about who belongs to this distinctive people, the identifiable characteristics that determine membership, and what particular purposes and rules are best for this distinctive people are at the heart of American constitutional politics.

The Constitution of the United States is the paradigmatic example of a modern, liberal constitution. The late eighteenth-century framers and ratifiers sought to establish a higher law that was rooted in popular sovereignty and would constrain government and protect liberty. American constitutionalism also reflects the influence of the classical constitutional tradition. For more than two centuries, political actors have debated the relationships between cultural practices and political institutions as well as the nature of American exceptionalism. The influence of contemporary constitutional practices is more controversial. Many leading commentators insist that modern constitutions framed in the late eighteenth century guarantee only negative liberties. Such liberties as the free exercise of religion and the right against unreasonable searches are safeguarded when government officials refrain from regulation. Other leading commentators insist that modern and contemporary constitutions may share common purposes and may both guarantee positive liberties. Such liberties as the right to certain basic necessities are often secured only when government acts in certain ways. When thinking about political regimes, this debate suggests, genus and species matter. The questions Americans ask about constitutional rights, interpretation, purpose, and authority cannot be answered until we understand the distinctive elements of constitutional government and the distinctive features of the particular form of constitutionalism practiced in the United States.

1. Classical Constitutionalism

Classical constitutionalists sought to describe every important social institution that influenced life in a particular polity. Political thinkers in ancient Greece and Rome used the term *politeia* or *constitutio* when referring to the structure of and relationships between all significant political and cultural practices of a distinctive regime. The way economic and family life were organized was as central to the *politeia* as the procedures for making military decisions. Had Aristotle studied the contemporary United States, he might have thought pop culture and sports as worthy of constitutional analysis as the composition of Congress and judicial decision-making.

This integration of the legal–political and cultural–social raises questions about whether classical thinkers were analyzing what we think of as constitutional phenomena. The proper translation of *politeia* is controversial. While many English versions of Aristotle's work translate *politeia* as "constitution," others do not. Giovanni Sartori writes, "If Aristotle meant by *politeia* the ethico-political system as a whole, we cannot infer from this that 'constitution' has in Aristotle a loose meaning. The only correct conclusion is that Aristotle has been mistranslated."[3] Sartori is right to emphasize that Aristotle did not identify a constitution with judicially enforceable law in the modern sense. Still, classical Greek and Roman politicians consistently made appeals to what they believed were fundamental regime principles when arguing before legislatures and juries. In one famous speech, the legendary Greek orator Demosthenes declared, "As every citizen has an equal share in civil rights, so everybody should have an equal share in the laws: and therefore . . . it should not be lawful to propose a law affecting any individual, unless the same applied to all Athenians."[4]

Contemporary constitutionalists make similar appeals to basic regime principles. Sometimes these appeals are made in legal settings, but they are often made in legislative debates, during political campaigns, in interest group mailings, and during ordinary conversations with neighbors. "Immortal principles fly their standards in judicial opinions," Thomas Reed Powell observed in 1918, "but so they do in the common every-day talk of the butcher and the banker, of the suffragist and the anti-suffragist, the pacifist and the militarist, the Socialist and the individualist."[5] Frequently, these appeals highlight perceived relationships between cultural and social practices and political and legal practices. Justice William O. Douglas in an opinion supporting state accommodations for parochial schools made such an appeal when he insisted, "we are a religious people whose institutions presuppose a Supreme Being."[6] Given the centrality of debates over what constitutes fundamental political and social practices in any constitutional order, classical constitutional thinking has insights that may help us understand and evaluate American constitutionalism.

Classical Constitutional Principles. Classical political thinkers would have endorsed the contemporary feminist assertion that "the personal is political." Aristotle, Plato, Cicero, and their contemporaries recognized that how politics is organized in any regime depends in large part on how the economy, families, religion, and the military are organized. Aristotle would not have agreed with radical feminist attacks on patriarchal families. Nevertheless, he understood that hierarchies in domestic life were likely to be reproduced in political life. Professor Susan Okin in 1991 observed that men socialized to believe they were the head of their households were unlikely to treat women as equals in the public sphere.[7] Aristotle's *Politics* complained that men who fell "under the dominion of their wives"[8] developed a taste for luxury that inhibited a politically more desirable dedication to honor. Plato similarly emphasized the connections between domestic and political life. Politics in a regime where children are raised and socialized in large part by their biological parents, *The Republic* feared, is likely to be more pluralistic than politics in a regime where children are raised and socialized almost exclusively by state officials.[9]

Classical constitutionalism focused on the distinctive telos of a polity, the particular vision of the good life or good state that a particular polity sought to promote. The first sentence of *The Politics* declares, "Every state is a community of some kind, and every community is established with a view to some good."[10] Constitutional analysis consisted of identifying the good states should aim for and the public institutions that best secured that good. Aristotle urged readers to "study what sorts of influence preserve and destroy states, and what sorts preserve or destroy the particular kinds of constitution, and to what causes it is due that some are well and others ill administered. When these matters have been studied we shall perhaps be more likely to see with a comprehensive view which constitution is best, and how each must be ordered, and what laws and customs it must use, if it is to be at its best."[11] The reference to "particular kinds of constitution" acknowledged that many different regimes exist and that the best constitution, all things considered, might not be best for a particular regime. Aristotle and those he influenced recognize that constitutional founders and reformers work within a given regime, determining what is best for that distinctive polity given that polity's distinctive people and distinctive social practices. Consider Professor Steven Elkin's Aristotelian claim with respect to the Constitution of the United States: "I am not claiming that a commercial republican regime is, or is thought to be, the best regime. Our aspirations [as citizens of the United States] point to something more limited—the best regime for the kind of people we are with our history and capacities."[12] An ideal people might be less concerned with material prosperity than Americans, but any political order that fails to "grow the economy" is unlikely to survive in the United States.

Aristotle and other classical political thinkers were particularly interested in political socialization, the processes by which citizens develop political identities, interests, and values. Constitutionalism in Greece and Rome was as concerned with creating and maintaining a distinctive people as with constraining political leaders. Social institutions "molded the characters and tastes of citizens" so that cultural and political life were mutually reinforcing:

> Guided by a "higher-law" standard of natural right that prescribes *virtue* as man's natural end, ancient constitutionalism turns the classification of regimes into an exercise in moral choice, a problem of choosing the regime best suited to make men virtuous—to make them courageous, moderate, just, and prudent. For most of the classical philosophers and historians, this means choosing an aristocracy of wise and virtuous gentlemen in the ideal circumstances, a mixed or middle-class regime in less ideal circumstances, and a democracy tempered by rule of law and public spiritedness as a realistic third choice. In speaking of ancient constitutionalism, then, one is referring to *regime analysis:* the classification of regimes and the prudential choice of which regime or combination of regimes is best suited to mold virtuous citizens.[13]

This commitment to character development and virtue explains the central role education played in classical constitutional thought. "Education," Plato insisted, was the "one great thing" that guaranteed the success of a constitutional order. In his view, "good nurture and education implant good constitutions, and those good constitutions taking root in a good education improve more and more."[14] Lengthy passages in both Plato's *Republic* and Aristotle's *Politics* are devoted to detailing the appropriate forms of pedagogy in a good constitutional regime.

The Classical Constitution of the United States. Constitutional politics in the United States has been explicitly and implicitly influenced by classical elements of constitutionalism. The framers analyzed extensively the relationships between social and political practices when determining what government institutions best preserved republican liberties. Contemporary social scientists raise similar questions when exploring the cultural, economic, and demographic prerequisites of stable constitutional democracies. Political leaders in the United States have insisted that various social practices have constitutional status, even though they are not explicitly mentioned by the text ratified in 1789 or by subsequent amendments. Political leaders rise to power by offering controversial visions of American nationality and America's distinctive constitutional mission. As classical thinkers understood, what happens constitutionally in the United States can be explained and evaluated only in light of other political, social, and cultural phenomena rarely studied under the heading "Constitutional Law."

Prominent Federalists and Anti-Federalists offered Aristotelian analyses of the Constitution drafted in 1787. Proponents and opponents of ratification debated what sort of people were most likely to staff various institutions, the likely relationships between national and state institutions, and the likely good to be produced by constitutional institutions. Following Plato and Aristotle, eighteenth-century Americans were particularly concerned with the character of governing officials. Federalists insisted that the Constitution was designed to promote the selection of distinguished citizens who had incentives to pursue the public welfare when in office. The relatively large legislative election districts mandated by Article I, Madison thought, guaranteed that elections "center on men who possess the most attractive merit and the most diffusive and established characters."[15] Anti-Federalists charged that the Constitution was designed to promote the selection of an elite who would pursue class interests when in office. "The natural aristocracy of the country will be elected," Brutus complained, and they will "be ignorant of the sentiments of the midling class of citizens, strangers to their ability, wants, and difficulties, and void of sympathy, and fellow feeling."[16]

Much contemporary political science analysis, without citing Aristotle explicitly, adopts a classical understanding of American constitutionalism. Many works examine the political, social, and cultural practices necessary to maintain a constitutional democracy. Most scholars believe these practices include a fairly equitable division of property, social pluralism, and an elite commitment to basic democratic ideals. Robert Dahl, a leading democratic theorist, suggests that constitutional democracy rests on the following socioeconomic conditions:

1. "The means of violent coercion are dispersed or neutralized."
2. The country "possesses an MDP [modern dynamic pluralist] society." Such a society is characterized by a "high standard of living," "occupational diversity," "economic growth," and "numerous relatively autonomous groups and organizations."

3. The country is "culturally homogeneous."

    a. If the country is not homogeneous, it "is not segmented into strong and distinctive subcultures"; or

    b. "If it is so segmented, its leaders have succeeded in creating a consociational arrangement for managing subcultural conflicts."

4. The country "possesses a political culture and beliefs, particularly among political activists, that support the institutions of polyarchy."

5. The country "is not subject to intervention by a foreign power hostile to polyarchy."[17]

Consider what might be added or subtracted from this list. Perhaps a free-market society or a certain degree of economic inequality is a crucial prerequisite of American constitutionalism.

Legal arguments in the United States treat various social practices and national aspirations as central to the American constitutional order. Chief Justice Roger Taney claimed that Americans were constitutionally committed to white supremacy.[18] Justice David Brewer thought the United States was a Christian nation.[19] Justice William Douglas spoke of marriage as being central to the American constitutional order.[20] Taney, Brewer, and Douglas thought such assertions were not simply factual claims about American values. They believed the Constitution of the United States could be understood, interpreted, and implemented only in light of background cultural commitments to racism, Christianity, and marriage, respectively.

Two objections are commonly made to these claims. First, constitutional disputes arise over which background principles must inform American constitutionalism. When Taney asserted a constitutional commitment to white supremacy, Abraham Lincoln countered by asserting a constitutional commitment to abolishing slavery.[21] The telos of American constitutionalism remains contested. Consider what background principles of family and economic life should inform constitutional practice at present. Most commentators agree that the United States is a consumer society that requires a strong middle class. Controversies nevertheless rage over whether the common characterization of the United States as the "land of opportunity" means that constitutional political economy should promote opportunities to become rich or to assure the vast majority of citizens access to basic material goods. Second, many commentators insist that Americans are constitutionally committed only to values and principles explicitly mentioned by the constitutional text. In the absence of explicit constitutional declaration, racism, abolition, Christianity, and marriage have no special constitutional status. These and related practices are to be valued as popular majorities think best.

Whether a constitution can be meaningfully interpreted without a background knowledge of fundamental cultural and social practices, however, is contestable. On what basis, after all, can constitutional interpreters assume that the Constitution of the United States is written in English? The claim that popular majorities should determine whether marriage is a fundamental right seems rooted in a constitutional commitment to majoritarianism or democracy that is nowhere explicitly mentioned in the constitutional text. Common constitutional norms, such as the norm that the police officers must normally obtain a warrant in circumstances where people have "reasonable expectations of privacy," require constitutional decision-makers to refer to cultural practices concerning what our society regards as private when determining the constitutional status of official actions.

American political leaders have consistently maintained that Americans are a distinctive people with a distinctive political mission. The Declaration of Independence repeatedly insisted that Americans were "one people." John Jay in *The Federalist Papers* declared, "Providence has been pleased to give this one connected country to one united people—a people descended from the same ancestors, speaking the same language, professing the same religion, attached to the same principles of government, very similar in their manners and customs, and who, by their joint counsels, arms, and efforts, fighting side by side throughout a long and bloody war, have nobly established general liberty and independence."[22] Antebellum proponents of state rights countered that persons living in the United States were first and foremost Virginians or New Yorkers rather than distinctively American. Politicians who when seeking office during the Progressive Era referred to foreign-born citizens as "hyphenated Americans" promoted xenophobic conceptions of American national identity. Fiorello LaGuardia relied on more pluralist understandings of American national identity when speaking Yiddish and Italian during campaign stops in ethnic New York neighborhoods. Contemporary politicians make appeals to national identity when they claim that Americans are the sort of people who will never accept defeat in Iraq or are united by a faith in the future.

Efforts to characterize Americans for constitutional purposes are controversial and often divide as well as unite. Whether Americans could be described fairly as "one people" when Jefferson and Jay wrote or presently is contestable. The Civil War was arguably fought over whether the *United States* is a singular or plural noun. Professor Rogers Smith of the University of Pennsylvania has documented how political movements throughout history have claimed that true Americans are united by race or ethnicity.[23] Stephen Douglas during the first debate with Abraham Lincoln asserted, "I believe this government was made on the white basis....I believe it was made by white men, for the benefit of white men and their posterity for ever, and I am in favour of confining citizenship to white men."[24] Whether contemporary Americans can be characterized less offensively is unclear. Prominent constitutional thinkers propose various bases for constituting a common American constitutional identity. "Those who favor liberal democratic conceptions of citizenship," Smith urges, "must... define compelling senses of national identity that can build support for living in accordance with liberal democratic principles within specific political societies."[25] Professor Mark Tushnet of Harvard Law School suggests "the nation's commitment to the [principles set out in the Declaration of Independence] constitutes us as the people of the United States, and constituting a people is a morally worthy project."[26] The members of U.S. English, Inc., advance a different conception of American identity when they assert on their website their dedication "to preserving the unifying role of the English language in the United States." Perhaps, however, all that unites Americans is that they live in a common geographic space subjecting them to the jurisdiction of the Constitution. Nevertheless, political leaders will continue appealing to national identities and commitments. In light of this reality, the better strategy may be to consider what politically viable vision of Americanism best reflects our constitutional experience and aspirations.

Plato and Aristotle would be pleased that constitutional education has been an ongoing concern in the United States. A civic republican tradition that dates from at least the early nineteenth century has emphasized how good public schools make good public citizens. John Dewey pointed out that "a government resting upon popular suffrage cannot be successful unless those who elect and those who obey their governors are educated." Moreover, Dewey observed, democratic education produced a democratic citizen. Proper democratic education, he believed, was vital for "breaking down... those barriers of class, race, and national territory which kept men from perceiving the full import of their activity."[27] One survey found "40 state constitutions that mention the importance of civic literacy among citizens; 13 of these constitutions state that the central purpose of their educational system is to promote good citizenship, democracy, and free government."[28] Most school systems offer a mandatory civics class in which students learn about and are typically encouraged to revere basic constitutional practices and rights.

Commentators celebrate the purported educative value of various constitutional practices. The Supreme Court is frequently described as a "republican schoolmaster," charged with instructing citizens about their constitutional rights and responsibilities.[29] Participants in constitutional controversies debate how rival policies mold the character of the citizenry. Those who favor regulating racist invective insist that tolerating such speech fosters indifference to discrimination. "The failure of the legal system to redress the harms of racism and racist insults," Professor Richard Delgado of the University of Alabama School of Law declares, "conveys to all the lesson that egalitarianism is not a fundamental principle; the law, through inaction, implicitly teaches us that respect for individuals is of little importance."[30] Opponents think that permitting such speech fashions more tolerant citizens. President Lee Bollinger of Columbia University maintains, "Free speech involves a special act of carving out one area of social interaction for extraordinary self-restraint, the purpose of which is to develop and demonstrate a social capacity to control feelings evoked by a host of social encounters."[31]

The classical perspective provides a framework for thinking about and evaluating constitutional activities that do not fit under the rubric of constitutional law.[32] Constitutional systems are unlikely to function well when persons merely refrain from acting illegally. Citizens, elected officials, and justices must also behave in ways that are constitutionally appropriate and praiseworthy.[33] Consider the contemporary presidential press conference. A purely legal analysis of that event would be limited to noting that presidents have no constitutional duty to hold press conferences and that no constitutional limitations constrain media behavior. Nevertheless, a good case can be made that in well-ordered contemporary constitutional democracies presidents hold press conferences frequently, the media asks critical questions respectfully, and the public scrutinizes presidential answers carefully. The president had a different constitutional relationship with the American people before the twentieth century. Professor Jeffrey Tulis of the University of Texas details how President Andrew Johnson's attempt to rally public opinion against Reconstruction by directly appealing to the general public in a series of speeches was considered a constitutionally inappropriate means of curtailing legislative deliberation.[34]

The classical perspective emphasizes and the American constitutional experience demonstrates that constitutional practices cannot be hermetically (or hermeneutically) sealed off from other social practices. Change any significant institution in a society, and every other significant institution is likely to be transformed, often in a surprising manner. The rise of pragmatism in American philosophy at the turn of the twentieth century influenced both elementary education and constitutional doctrine during the New Deal. Proponents of the Thirteenth Amendment were aware that ending slavery would change southern politics and economics, but they may not have anticipated how emancipation altered domestic relations in the former Confederate states.[35] Only a clairvoyant could have predicted how the invention of safe, cheap, and effective birth control put in motion a chain of events that, through the medium of *Roe v. Wade* (1973), dramatically politicized the process by which Supreme Court justices are nominated and confirmed. Constitutional practices in the twenty-first century, the American past suggests, are likely to be as influenced by rapid changes in technology and the price of oil as by partisan competition and the text of Article III. The fate of the Internet and gas pump, in turn, are likely to be held hostage, in part, to dominant conceptions of the First Amendment and executive power.

2. Modern Constitutionalism

Modern constitutionalism is characterized by a hierarchy of legal authority, the rule of law, and limited government. Political thinkers at the time the
Constitution of the United States was ratified regarded constitutions as legal
texts. Cultural practices might influence legal texts, but the structure of family life and the economy were not considered to be constitutional phenomena.
Constitutions in the eighteenth century were thought to be valuable means
for constraining government and only secondarily, if at all, devices for fashion-
ing a virtuous citizenry. With important exceptions, the framers took human
nature as relatively fixed. They sought to establish institutions that secured the
best government they could achieve in light of what they perceived to be the
existing interests and capacities of the American people rather than governing
practices that might make the citizenry better or at least improve capacities for
self-government. All modern constitutions are committed to a hierarchy of legal
authority, the rule of law, and limited government, but important differences
exist over what each commitment entails and the relationships between these
constitutional values. Important constitutional disputes in the United States are
rooted in controversies over the nature of limited government and how fundamental law constrains governing officials.

Modern constitutions need not be embodied in a single written text. Colonial
Americans referred to the English Constitution and complained about being
deprived of their constitutional rights as Englishmen even though no such document as the Constitution of Great Britain is on display in Westminster Hall or in
any other place. The United Kingdom is nevertheless usually regarded as a constitutional democracy. The Constitution of Great Britain is sometimes thought
to consist of a series of enactments, the most important of which are the Magna
Carta (1215) and the English Bill of Rights (1689). Alternatively, the English
Constitution may consist of customary principles and understandings that constrain governing officials as effectively as written declarations in other constitutional regimes. "The essential principles to which Burke and Camden and Otis
appealed," Professor Charles McIlwain wrote in 1947, "were no less constitutional because they were 'unwritten.'" In his view, "limitations on arbitrary rule
have become so firmly fixed in the national tradition that no threats against them
have seemed serious enough to warrant the adoption of a formal code."[36]

2.1 Fundamental Law

Politics in modern constitutional regimes is constrained by higher or fundamental law. Constitutions establish legal authority for all other legal enactments and actions. "The constitution," McIlwain's influential study of modern

constitutionalism declares, "is 'antecedent' to the government,... defines the authority which the people commits to its government, and in doing so thereby limits it."[37] Constitutions provide the legal foundations for ordinary lawmaking by establishing the rules for determining who makes the law, setting out the processes by which those governing officials make laws, and limiting the laws those governing officials enact. Provisions in Article I of the Constitution of the United States lay out the rules for electing members of the national legislature, require majorities in both Houses of Congress for a bill to become a law, and forbid bills of attainder. In sharp contrast to certain strands of classical constitutionalism, constitutional principles and rules are regarded as legally binding. No person has any legal obligation to obey an official decree not sanctioned by the constitution. If the constitution declares that government may not establish a church, then governing officials have no legal authority to declare Reform Judaism the law of the land. If the constitution declares that a president must win a majority of the Electoral College votes, then the proclamations of a candidate who received only a majority of the popular votes have no legal standing. In constitutional government, McIlwain states, "Any exercise of authority beyond those limits by any government is an exercise of 'power without right.' "[38]

As higher law, constitutional provisions control when conflicts arise with other legal enactments. In the absence of constitutional authority, the principle "last in time, first in line" resolves legal inconsistencies. When determining which of two conflicting statutes establishes present legal standards, the correct choice is the one most recently enacted. If the California Drag Racing Law of 1980 declares that "no person under eighteen may compete in a professional automobile race" and the California Safe Driving Law of 1990 declares that "no person under twenty may drive a car," the 1990 law supersedes the 1980 law. "Last in time, first in line" does not resolve conflicts between constitutional and statutory provisions. If the California Constitution includes an amendment passed in 1970 that forbids legislative restrictions on drivers over seventeen years of age, then the California Licensing Law of 1990 is a legal nullity. Older teenagers must be allowed to compete in professional races because the earlier constitutional amendment is a higher legal authority than later legislation.

Constitutions derive their higher law status from three possible sources. Constitutionalists during the Middle Ages regarded fundamental law as rooted in divine law. Kings preserved the constitution and fundamental law by making sure that God's will was maintained on Earth. Constitutional law in seventeenth-century England was often thought rooted in customary practice. The unwritten constitution reflected political commitments whose origins were lost in antiquity but were manifested by enduring historical practice. By the late eighteenth century, constitutionalism had become an expression of popular sovereignty. Constitutions were consciously constructed by a distinctive people at a specific time. They were legally binding higher law because that particular people had consented to the fundamental rules by which they would be forever governed.

Social contract theory provided the philosophical glue for melding popular sovereignty and fundamental law when the Constitution of the United States was framed and ratified. John Locke and other English liberals maintained that legitimate government was derived from an agreement between citizens to establish the legal authority necessary to protect individual rights and secure other social interests. Locke's *Second Treatise on Civil Government* asserted that a hypothetical bargain provided sufficient foundations for government as long as fundamental rights were protected. Americans treated their constitutions as actual social contracts.[39] Alexander Hamilton stated that the Constitution of the United States was a "compact made between the society at large and each individual."[40] Constitutions had higher or fundamental law status, the framers believed, because they were the agreements made by the people as a whole that provided the necessary authorization for government actions. "All power in just free governments," James Madison wrote, "is derived from compact."[41]

Contract remains the most powerful metaphor of American constitutionalism. The plurality opinion in *Planned Parenthood v. Casey* (1992) described the Constitution as "a covenant running from the first generation of Americans to us." Professor Keith Whittington of Princeton University declares that the Constitution is "an actual contract, an agreement among diverse parties, with real or separate interests."[42] *Dred Scott and the Problem of Constitutional Evil* analogizes the Constitution to "a relational contract intended to form a political order that benefitted Americans from all sections."[43] Commentators who acknowledge the difference between constitutions and contracts nevertheless assert that constitutions should be interpreted as if they were contracts. Professor Randy Barnett of Georgetown Law Center does "not view the Constitution as a contract in a literal sense" but thinks "the constitution of the United States is a written document and it is writtenness that makes relevant contract law theory pertaining to those contracts that are also in writing."[44]

This popular contract metaphor suffers from several problems. Who originally agreed to the Constitution is controversial. Antebellum Americans fought and died over whether states or citizens were the proper parties to the constitutional contract. Constitutions do not meet the most important condition for a legally enforceable bargain. Many Americans in 1789 and hardly any Americans at present consented to the Constitution in ways that provide binding consent to a contract. Finally, the contract metaphor may not resolve constitutional controversies. No more agreement exists in contract law than in constitutional law over proper interpretive practices. Legal opinions and law review articles debate whether provisions in constitutions and whether provisions in contracts must mean what those provisions meant when ratified.

The process by which constitutions or constitutional contracts are ratified reflects their fundamental or higher law status. Americans after the Revolution rejected claims that the same elected officials who made ordinary law could help determine constitutional law. Voters in late eighteenth-century Massachusetts turned down a proposed state constitution in part because that text had been drafted by the state legislature. Constitutions, state citizens demanded, should be drafted and ratified only by special constitutional conventions that existed solely for that purpose and whose legal authority terminated the instant the ratification process concluded. The Massachusetts experience played a decisive role when Americans began considering a new national constitution. To confirm the Constitution's status as higher law, the framers had the Constitution of the United States drafted by a special constitutional convention and ratified by special constitutional conventions in every state.

The amendment process also reflects the higher or fundamental law status of constitutions. The Constitution of the United States can be amended only by several supermajoritarian votes. The most popular amendment process requires a two-thirds vote in both houses of Congress and ratification by three-fourths of the states. Alternatively, the states by a two-thirds vote may call a convention for proposing amendments. Any amendment so proposed must be ratified by three-quarters of all states. Most state constitutions do not regard supermajorities as necessary for amendment. Many state constitutions permit the people to ratify constitutional amendments by majority vote in a referendum. Nevertheless, no state permits the state constitution to be amended by the same processes sufficient to change ordinary law.

Whether fundamental or higher law must be judicially enforceable is controversial. Some constitutional theorists believe that constitutions limit government only when the constitutional rules that constrain lawmaking are enforced by some institution other than those responsible for making laws. Judicial review, in this view, is a necessary condition for constitutionalism. Allowing elected officials to determine the scope of their powers, John Marshall declared in *Marbury v. Madison* (1803), "would be giving to the legislature a practical and real omnipotence, with the same breath which professes to restrict their powers within narrow limits. It is prescribing limits, and declaring that those limits may be passed at pleasure."[45] Other commentators disagree. In their view, constitutionalism requires only a commitment on the part of government officials to following the constitutional rules. "As it is the duty of legislators as well as judges to consult" the Constitution, Chief Justice Waties of South Carolina wrote in 1812, "so it should be presumed that all their acts do conform to [the Constitution]."[46]

The fundamental or higher law of the Constitution is not exempt from ordinary politics. Partisan political struggles routinely take place over proposals for constitutional amendment. Political movements engage in the same tactics during disputes over the merits of constitutional bans on same-sex marriage as they do during controversies over ordinary laws banning same-sex marriage. Partisan politics also influences how fundamental and higher laws are interpreted. Democrats and Republicans, liberals and conservatives, libertarians and socialists dispute the limits on the executive power set out in Article II and the meaning of the due process clauses of the Fifth and Fourteenth Amendments. What constitutional clauses mean in practice is partly the consequence of decisions made over a 200-year period and partly the consequence of more recent political struggles to gain control over the institutions responsible for establishing official constitutional meanings. Americans for the foreseeable future are likely to retain a constitutional commitment to both federalism and free speech. Whether those commitments will entail increased limits on federal power to regulate ordinary crimes or campaign finance is likely to be influenced significantly by the results in the next series of national elections.

The politics of constitutional meaning highlights tensions between the American constitutional commitments to higher law and popular sovereignty. Americans believe that certain principles should be above politics but are also dedicated to majority rule, even on questions of constitutional practice. From Thomas Jefferson to Barack Obama, candidates for national office have sought the popular support necessary to implement particular constitutional visions ranging from a renewed emphasis on federalism to overturning judicial decisions finding a constitutional right to unlimited independent campaign expenditures. Significantly perhaps, these campaigns almost always assert a commitment to restoring or maintaining existing constitutional values rather than a desire to challenge accepted constitutional norms. President Obama criticized the judicial ruling in *Citizens United v. Federal Elections Commission* (2010) for misinterpreting the First Amendment. He did not criticize the persons responsible for the First Amendment for saddling Americans with a constitutional provision that gives corporations the right to support political candidates and causes. Indeed, no candidate for offices ranging from the presidency to dogcatcher is likely to gain many votes by claiming the Constitution is badly flawed. Popular sovereignty and constitutionalism may be partly reconciled in the United States because strong majorities believe the Constitution entrenches sound political values, however much the content of those values is disputed.

2.2 Rule by Law

The constitutional commitment to fundamental law entails a commitment to the rule of law. All government actions in a regime that respects the rule of law must be authorized or justified by reference to preexisting rules and norms. People may not be arrested because a police officer, most voters, or every distinguished moral philosopher believe that they have done something wrong. Government may punish, regulate, and reward only when a constitutionally empowered institution has previously passed a law mandating that the conduct in question be punished, regulated, or rewarded. People who habitually forget appointments may suffer severe social sanctions. They cannot be sanctioned legally in the absence of any law criminalizing such outrageous conduct.

The rule of law is almost universally regarded as "an unqualified human good."[47] That good is intrinsic to the benefits of being governed by rules rather than to the benefits of any particular rule. Professor Frederick Schauer of the University of Virginia Law School explains how officials who are following imperfect rules promote important social goods:

> Arguments for rule-based decision-making have traditionally focused on the ability of rules to foster the interrelated virtues of reliance, predictability, and certainty. According to such arguments, decision-makers who follow rules even when other results appear preferable enable those affected to predict in advance what the decisions are likely to be. Consequently, those affected by the decisions of others can plan their activities more successfully under a regime of rules than under more particularistic decision-making.[48]

Persons in regimes that respect the rule of law know the legal consequences of contemplated actions. All citizens are capable of learning in advance what conduct government permits, what conduct government sanctions, and how severely government sanctions that conduct. This legal regularity enables people to preserve their liberty by acting consistently with known laws. We know that we risk a ticket by driving considerably above the speed limit but are safe from legal sanction if we do not.

The rule of law is not costless. Government by preexisting law may prevent political actors from making the best decisions. "There is nothing essentially *just* about rule-based decision-making," Schauer observes:

> There is no reason to believe, and much reason to disbelieve, that rule-based decision-making is intrinsically more just than decision-making in which rules do not block a decision-maker,

especially a just decision-maker, from considering every factor that would assist her in reaching the best decision. Insofar as factors screened from consideration by a rule might in a particular case turn out to be those necessary to reach a just result, rules stand in the way of justice in those cases and impede optimal justice in the long term.[49]

Even though we know that considerable differences in driving ability exist, expert police officers guided by the rule of law do not judge for themselves whether a given motorist can safely drive considerably over the speed limit or cannot drive safely at the speed limit. If a police officer gives a newly minted driver a ticket for driving thirty-seven miles an hour in a twenty-five-mile-an-hour zone, the officer must give the same ticket to a professional NASCAR driver going at the same speed in the same place.

Professor Lon Fuller of Harvard Law School suggests that regimes that respect the rule of law are guided by the following eight standards:[50]

1. Government lays down rules of general application and does not attempt to decide individual cases on an ad hoc basis.
2. Laws are sufficiently public so that citizens are capable of learning the rules.
3. Laws are not retroactive, punishing actions that were legal when performed.
4. Laws are sufficiently clear so that they can be comprehended by those whose conduct is regulated.
5. Laws are consistent. The rules do not sanction both the performance of an action and the failure to perform that action.
6. Laws do not require the impossible.
7. Laws are sufficiently stable over time.
8. The laws as enacted by the legislature guide the law as implemented by the police and other executive officials.

These eight standards enable persons to be guided by law. When governments respect these and related standards,[51] citizens have the ability to learn the legal norms of their society and rely on those norms when deciding how to act.

The rule of law is intrinsically valuable even when laws are bad. Severe oppression may take place in a regime committed to the rule of law. Governing officials respect the rule of law when they punish jaywalking by death and ban all speech critical of the government, as long as they are constitutionally authorized to make those laws, follow the constitutionally mandated procedures for making those laws, publicize those laws, and do not discriminate when implementing those laws. Citizens living in these regimes are, nevertheless, arguably better off than their counterparts in societies whose governments randomly execute persons. At the very least, critics of the government and persons prone to jaywalking who live under the rule of law retain the freedom to decide whether to risk martyrdom for their cherished causes, a valuable freedom for many ordinary citizens.

The constitutional commitment to the rule of law is sometimes equated with the constitutional commitment to limited government. The rule of law does constrain government in the sense that all government actions must be sanctioned by the constitution. If the constitution declares that the president must be at least thirty-five years old, then any action by a younger person purporting to occupy that office has no legal status. If the constitution declares that government must permit free speech, then official bans on political dissent have no legal status. Fundamental laws may limit government discretion by mandating as well as by forbidding government action. If the constitution grants people the right to certain basic necessities, then governing officials violate the law of the land when they refrain from making policies that provide food for the hungry. Still, the rule of law for the most part imposes only procedural limits on government. Constitutions may empower governing officials to punish, regulate, or reward almost all human behaviors as long as the constitutionally prescribed procedures are followed and the rules are consistent with the eight standards previously listed. Elected officials respect the rule of law, no matter what their laws on religious freedom, as long as the laws are general, prospective, consistent, comprehensible, and do not demand the impossible.

One should, nevertheless, not underestimate how constitutional procedures often provide practical constraints on government action. If laws must be made in certain ways, some rules are unlikely to be made. The persons responsible for the Constitution of the United States thought that frequent elections better prevented legislative majorities from violating fundamental rights than textual guarantees. Constitutions in badly divided societies often provide crucial groups with the right to veto objectionable laws, a procedure that provides a more realistic means for protecting their interests than explicit provisions that might be ignored by electoral majorities.

American constitutionalism includes practices inconsistent with a strict commitment to the rule of law. Good faith debate exists over the meaning of "to regulate commerce...among the several States" in Article I and "unreasonable searches" in the Fourth Amendment. Even sophisticated computer programs do not predict a very high percentage of Supreme Court decisions correctly. Human beings tend to do much worse.[52] Law in the contemporary administrative state is rarely made by constitutionally prescribed procedures. Environmental standards are set by the Environmental Protection Agency under only the loosest guidelines established by federal law. Enforcement problems are endemic. Many laws on the books are not enforced. Others have historically been enforced in ways that discriminate against persons of color and other powerless minorities. Whether one can effectively exercise many legal rights in the United States often depends more on access to effective legal assistance than on constitutional language or judicial opinions.

These constitutional failures have three sources. The first is human imperfection. No one has the ability or foresight to write laws whose dictates are clear in every possible circumstance. The likelihood of ambiguity increases when multimembered drafting bodies must regulate complex subjects. The second is human venality. The law enforcement officials who assisted lynchings were making no effort to preserve the rule of law. Vagueness is often the preferred legislative technique for avoiding political responsibility. The third is that other values, some of which are constitutional, conflict with the rule of law. Liberty may be better protected by vesting constitutional decision-makers with some discretion over what constitutes an "unreasonable search" than by attempting to provide guidelines for all possible situations. The environment may be cleaner when elected officials permit administrative experts to make rules. The extent to which the United States respects the rule of law depends in large part on which of these three rationales best explains the limits of legality in American constitutionalism.

2.3 Limited Government

Modern constitutions limit government. The most common restrictions are enumerated powers and bills of rights. Article I, Section 8 enumerates the powers of the national government. Congress may not make any law, no matter how necessary or beneficent, unless exercising a constitutionally mandated power. President James Madison vetoed a law providing for national roads that he believed would help unify the nation because he did not believe the Constitution vested Congress with the power to fund internal improvements.[53] The Supreme Court in *Hammer v. Dagenhart* (1918) asserted that the authority to ban child labor was not within the enumerated powers of Congress. Article I, Sections 9 and 10, as well as many constitutional amendments, declare that government officials may not violate certain rights. Congress and the president must respect these liberties, even when exercising enumerated powers. The Supreme Court in *New York Times Co. v. United States* (1971) allowed newspapers to publish information that had some tendency to compromise national security because the judicial majority believed censoring the newspapers violated the First Amendment. Some actions may be outside the enumerated powers of Congress and may violate fundamental rights. The Kentucky and Virginia Resolutions of 1798 maintained that the Sedition Act was unconstitutional because Congress had no power to pass a law for the purpose of preventing criticism of the John Adams administration and because that measure violated constitutional protections for the freedom of speech.[54] Enumerated powers were the source of most constitutional limitations on government power in the nineteenth century. Individual rights are the source of most constitutional limitations at present.[55]

The Constitution of the United States provides two other limits on government power. Several provisions forbid government from interfering with values other than individual rights. Article I, Section 9 declares, "No Preference shall be given to any regulation of Commerce or revenue to the Ports of one State over those of another." Other constitutional procedures limit government by making certain kinds of regulations practically impossible to pass. State equality in the Senate provides a practical guarantee that such large states as New York and California will not be able to slough off their fair share of tax burdens on to such small states as Rhode Island and Delaware. Such constraints are valuable when people cannot predict in advance what rights, interests, or values will require protection. Consider whether one of our children would be better off under a family constitution that guaranteed spaghetti and meatballs every Tuesday or a family constitution that empowered her to choose the family dinner every Tuesday night.

Constitutional limitations take different forms. The simplest forbid government from ever taking a particular action. Article I, Section 9 states, "No Title of Nobility shall be granted by the United States." American heroes may be invited to the White House, but they can never be dubbed lords or ladies. Other constitutional provisions forbid government action unless certain circumstances exist. The Fourth Amendment prohibits "unreasonable searches and seizures." Police officers may search dorm rooms, but only when they have good reason to believe they will find contraband or evidence of criminal activity. Finally, constitutional provisions may limit official purposes. The federal government may not establish a religion, but under contemporary constitutional law governing officials may sometimes provide assistance to religious institutions when doing so serves such legitimate constitutional purposes as regulating interstate commerce or spending for the general welfare.

The more complex forms of constitutional restrictions on federal power raise practical questions about the constitutional commitment in the United States to limited government. The enumerated powers as written or interpreted may provide the federal government with practically unlimited power. "The clause which vests the power to pass all laws which are proper and necessary, to carry the powers given into execution," Anti-Federalists complained, "leaves the legislature at liberty, to do everything, which in their judgment is best."[56] These fears were partly realized when, from 1937 until 1995, the Supreme Court never declared national legislation outside the enumerated powers of Congress. Rights as written or interpreted may similarly fail to provide practical constraints on official powers. If, as many constitutional decision-makers at the turn of the twentieth century insisted, government may regulate any speech that has some tendency to cause any social ill, then only the most innocuous speech is likely to be protected.

Supreme Court justices in the 5-4 decision that sustained most provisions of the Affordable Care Act (*National Federation of Independent Business v. Sebelius* [2012]) debated the nature of constitutional limitations in the United States. Chief Justice Roberts and the four dissenters insisted that the government was limited because the Constitution restricted federal power. Chief Justice Roberts asserted:

> The Federal Government "is acknowledged by all to be one of enumer-ated powers." That is, rather than granting general authority to perform all the conceivable functions of government, the Constitution lists, or enumerates, the Federal Government's powers.... The enumeration of powers is also a limitation of powers, because "the enumeration presup-poses something not enumerated." The Constitution's express confer-ral of some powers makes clear that it does not grant others. And the Federal Government "can exercise only the powers granted to it."...If no enumerated power authorizes Congress to pass a certain law, that law may not be enacted, even if it would not violate any of the express prohibitions in the Bill of Rights or elsewhere in the Constitution.

Justice Ruth Bader Ginsburg and the three more liberal justices responded that the Constitution "armed" the national government "with a positive & compleat authority in all cases where uniform measures are necessary" and that ordinary pol-itics could be trusted to restrain governmental power. Her opinion described "the democratic process" as "a formidable check on congressional power." Ginsburg continued, "As the controversy surrounding the passage of the Affordable Care Act attests, purchase mandates are likely to engender political resistance. This prospect is borne out by the behavior of state legislators. Despite their possession of unques-tioned authority to impose mandates, state governments have rarely done so."

This debate between Roberts and Ginsburg hinges on the best interpretation of a particular event that took place when the Constitution was framed. Shortly before the Committee on Detail began polishing constitutional language, the Constitutional Convention voted to vest the national government with the power "to legislate in all Cases for the general Interests of the Union." Had this resolu-tion been incorporated into the Constitution verbatim, no constitutional con-straint would have existed on any congressional action plausibly in the national interest. No one protested when the Committee on Detail chose to enumerate specific powers rather than include a more general powers clause. Whether that alteration fundamentally changed the Constitution is controversial. Proponents of more limited federal authority think that constitutional principles were significantly influenced by the decision to enumerate.[57] Proponents of more expansive federal authority think that the enumerated powers combined with the power to "provide for...general Welfare of the United States" did not weaken the original constitutional commitment to a broad power to act for "the general Interests of Union."[58] The historical record is sparse. The correct position may depend in part on whether fundamental law or limited government is more central to contemporary American constitutionalism. The legitimacy of the New Deal, which rested on assertions of broad constitutional power to legislate in the national interest, may be at stake in this debate.

2.4 Liberal Constitutionalism

Many modern political thinkers identify constitutionalism with a system of "protected freedom for the individual." Giovanni Sartori, the leading proponent of this position, regards a constitution as "a fundamental law, or a fundamental set of principles, and a correlative institutional arrangement, which would restrict arbitrary power and ensure a 'limited government.'" Constitutionalism, so conceptualized, is more than a commitment to the rule of law. Prominent contemporary thinkers reject claims that "*any* plan of government amount(s) to a constitution." Constitutions by their nature establish textual and practical protections for certain liberties. Sartori claims, "A frame of government [must] provide for a bill of rights and the institutional devices that would secure its observance." Walter Murphy, James Fleming, Sotirios Barber, and Stephen Macedo agree that, where individual rights are concerned:

> The legitimacy of public policy depends,...not merely on the authenticity of the decision makers credentials but also on the substance of their work. There are some fundamental rights that government may not trample on, even with the active support of the overwhelming majority of the population. For a constitutionalist, a law enacted by a Congress chosen after open public debate and free elections and signed by a President similarly chosen would still be illegitimate if it violated a fundamental guarantee, such as the right to free exercise of religion.[59]

The liberal constitutional commitment to individual rights need not be embodied in a particular text or collection of legal writings. Sartori regards "the written, complete document [as] only a means....What really matters is the end, the *telos*."[60] Constitutional government is government whose institutions are designed to protect certain fundamental freedoms. These freedoms may or may not be specified in a constitutional text as long as governing institutions as a whole are designed to secure their protection. The Philadelphia Convention of

1787 drafted a liberal constitution, even though the resulting text mentioned few fundamental rights. The purpose of the governing arrangements set out in the text was to protect fundamental rights. What some scholars label *constitutional theocracies*[61] are not, in this view, constitutional governments to the extent their telos is the propagation of the one true religion and not the protection of fundamental rights.

This *guarantisme* conception of constitutionalism is closely associated with the political liberalism of the seventeenth and eighteenth centuries. Such political liberals as John Locke insisted that government existed to protect fundamental rights. Thomas Jefferson articulated the liberal creed when he declared, "We hold these truths to be self evident: that all men are created equal; that they are endowed by their Creator with CERTAIN inalienable rights; that among these are life, liberty, and the pursuit of happiness; that to secure these rights governments are instituted among men."[62] Liberal constitutions serve these liberal values. The crucial feature of a liberal constitution is the commitment to a set of (liberal) rights and to the institutional arrangements thought to protect these rights.

Liberal constitutions protect two kinds of rights. The first kind, fundamental or natural rights, exists apart from the constitution. Political liberalism, at least eighteenth-century political liberalism, is committed to some version of universal rights, the claim that persons have some rights simply by virtue of their being persons. These rights may be "endowed by the Creator," as Thomas Jefferson maintained, or inherent in some aspect of the human condition, as many philosophers believe. Liberal constitutions recognize and guarantee these fundamental rights but do not create them. Modern political liberals believe all persons have a fundamental right to the free exercise of religion no matter what the legal status of religion in a particular regime or the particular conditions of their polity. The second kind, sometimes known as positive rights,[63] is created by the constitution or laws passed under the constitution. The right to bring a lawsuit in a lower federal court is not a natural right that preexists the Constitution. The Constitution provides the legislative authority necessary to create lower federal courts, which do not exist in a state of nature. State constitutions and legislatures routinely establish such new positive rights as the right to swim in a public pool or the right to deduct charitable contributions when paying income taxes.[64] Constitutional government ceases, liberal constitutionalists believe, when fundamental or natural rights are no longer constitutionally guaranteed. No analogous constitutional crisis occurs when positive rights are repealed by statutory revision or constitutional amendment.

Constitutional protections for fundamental rights were in the process of an important transformation when the Constitution of the United States was framed and ratified. Liberal constitutions were originally understood as means for limiting royal power to oppress the people or, in the case of the Magna Carta, the nobility. Colonial and revolutionary Americans thought popular elections a sufficient guarantee for fundamental rights. Popular majorities, they recognized, were unlikely to elect and reelect persons who tyrannized the entire population. By the late 1780s, James Madison and others had become increasingly concerned with constitutional protections for minority rights. Elections were not an adequate safeguard for the unpopular. Popularly elected officials might well secure reelection by oppressing minorities, particularly when they redistributed the property holdings of the few rich to the many poor. Such constitutional practices as the separation of powers, federalism, the Bill of Rights, and judicial review are all means by which the Constitution of the United States seeks to protect the fundamental rights of both majorities and minorities.

Whether Sartori and others are correct when they equate liberal constitutionalism with constitutionalism is doubtful. Liberal political principles have historically played a crucial role in American and English constitutional development. The preamble to the Constitution of the United States declares a constitutional commitment to "secur[ing] the Blessings of Liberty." Nevertheless, good reasons exist for weakening the connection between constitutionalism and eighteenth-century political liberalism. Treating constitutionalism as identical to liberal constitutionalism inhibits the study of other national constitutions, many of which seem committed to decidedly nonliberal principles. Constitutional commitments to religious intolerance and racial supremacy may be illiberal and evil, but they do not seem less constitutional than constitutional commitments to religious pluralism and racial equality. Indeed, if constitutions by definition are committed to fundamental human rights, then, to the extent the antebellum political order in the United States was committed to slavery and white supremacy,[65] what we call "the Constitution of the United States" first became a constitution after the Civil War, with the passage of the Thirteenth and Fourteenth Amendments.[66] Whether the Constitution of the United States should be amended to provide basic necessities to all persons or more radically altered to provide foundations for a Christian commonwealth should be determined on the merits of those proposals, not on whether such proposals are consistent with the best definition of *constitution*.

3. Contemporary Constitutionalism

The late twentieth century witnessed a wave of constitution-writing as nations emerging from colonial rule sought to establish fundamental law. Virtually all democracies at present are constitutional democracies. Many nondemocratic societies have adopted constitutions that purport to empower and constrain government officials. Important aspects of contemporary constitutions resemble the modern constitutions of the late eighteenth century, but other features do not. The modifications raise questions about whether the new constitutionalism is merely a more detailed version of modern constitutionalism or a different constitutional species. Classification may have practical consequences. If modern and contemporary constitutions have different natures, they are likely to have different purposes and be subject to different principles of interpretation.

Most contemporary constitutions do not resemble modern constitutions in appearance or content. Professor Peter Quint of the University of Maryland Law School identified six important differences between such contemporary constitutions as the Constitution of Germany and the Constitution of South Africa and such modern constitutions as the Constitution of the United States.[67]

1. Contemporary constitutions are much longer than modern constitutions.
2. Modern constitutions protect rights by forbidding government from acting in certain ways. Contemporary constitutions protect rights by mandating that government provide citizens with certain basic necessities and services.
3. Contemporary constitutions have explicit provisions detailing the constitutional status of many institutions, such as political parties, that became politically important only during the nineteenth and twentieth centuries. Modern constitutions do not mention these institutions.
4. Contemporary constitutions contain provisions that authorize suspending the constitution during times of emergency. Modern constitutions lack these clauses.
5. Contemporary constitutions tend to include declaration of rights and the circumstances under which rights can be abridged. Modern constitutions tend to include only declarations of rights.
6. Contemporary constitutions have explicit provisions incorporating certain principles of international law. Modern constitutions do not.

Quint suggests that the world may now be witnessing a third generation of constitutions, which include "such diffuse and aspirational guarantees as a right to 'international peace and security'" or "guarantee to minority groups the preservation of their language and culture."[68]

Whether these contemporary constitutions are different in kind or different in degree from the Constitution of the United States is unclear. The constitutions of Germany and South Africa may merely set out explicitly constitutional commands that are implicit in the United States. Governing officials in both the United States and Germany have ruled that elected officials may constitutionally restrict speech under certain conditions. The difference is that the German constitution plainly sets out the principles under which expression can be limited while those principles in the United States are found in judicial opinions interpreting the First Amendment. On another view, the rule of law suffers when constitutions ratified in the eighteenth century are interpreted to encompass twentieth-century phenomenon with no obvious analog two hundred years ago. When framing and ratifying their constitution, Germans made a conscious decision to treat political parties as constitutional institutions, and they provided constitutional standards for regulation. American constitutionalists, in the absence of any clear constitutional text, might be making up constitutional rules for regulating political parties on the fly.

Debates over the constitutional status of welfare rights demonstrate that possible distinctions between modern and contemporary constitutions have important practical consequences. Many constitutional commentators in the United States insist that modern constitutions protect only negative liberties, freedoms from government action. They assert that fundamental laws made during the eighteenth century cannot legitimately be interpreted as creating governmental obligations to supply people with certain goods and necessities. Judge Richard Posner, a prominent libertarian, declares that "the men who wrote the Bill of Rights were not concerned that Government might do too little for the people but that it might do too much to them. The Fourteenth Amendment sought to protect Americans from oppression by state government, not to secure them basic government services."[69] Other constitutionalists insist that both modern and contemporary constitutions obligate government to take certain actions. In their view, constitutional birthdays do not influence the nature of constitutional rights. Professor Sotirios Barber of Notre Dame contends, "The Constitution is . . . a welfarist constitution," and "there is no successful way to deny a fully constitutional obligation . . . to facilitate the well-being of all responsible persons."[70] Posner and Barber agree that the Constitution of the United States limits government power, but they dispute why and how the Constitution imposes those restrictions. Posner thinks that constitutionalism as limited government is committed to preventing bad government actions. Constitutions limit official power for the purpose of protecting liberty. Barber thinks that constitutionalism as limited government is committed to compelling good government action. Constitutions foster human welfare by obligating government officials and citizens to secure the public good. These and other constitutional purposes are the subject of the next chapter.

3

Constitutional Purposes

Constitutions attempt to secure important social benefits by establishing fundamental laws, mandating the rule of law, entrenching political procedures, limiting government powers, and, in liberal orders, guaranteeing basic human rights. Entrenched constitutional provisions that are more difficult to alter than ordinary laws are particularly important to American constitutionalism. As Chapter 2 detailed, constitutional provisions in the United States may not be revised by ordinary legislation. Some entrenchments are absolute. Others are partial. The Constitution of the United States prohibits any amendment to the provision mandating equal state representation in the Senate but permits Americans by a supermajoritarian vote to abolish the Electoral College. Some entrenchments are time bound. Congress could not constitutionally prohibit the international slave trade until 1808. Entrenchment also exists when constitutional principles and practices are so deeply ingrained that repeal is unthinkable. *Brown v. Board of Education* (1954) is presently as practically immune to revision as the First Amendment.[1]

Constitutionalism is a means for achieving better political and social outcomes. Some advantages are intrinsic to all constitutions and the entrenchment process. Chapter 2 explains why the constitutional commitment to the rule of law, which enables persons to know in advance what conduct government will reward and punish, is sometimes considered "an unqualified human good."[2] Entrenched constitutional provisions promise additional benefits. Such clauses organize government, vest governing officials with necessary powers, structure politics, enable government to make credible commitments to investors and foreign powers, facilitate coordination between subnational governing units, prevent self-dealing by governing officials, promote deliberation on the public interest, offer some insurance against uncertain futures, articulate national aspirations, and foster compromises among persons who disagree on national aspirations. Other advantages of constitutional government are distinctive to American constitutionalism. The Constitution of the United States proposes to help Americans secure national union, social peace, commercial prosperity, and various liberal rights. The Preamble states these constitutional purposes when declaring, "We the People of the United States, in Order to form a more perfect Union, establish Justice, insure domestic Tranquility, provide for the common defence, promote the general Welfare, and secure the Blessings of Liberty to ourselves and our Posterity, do ordain and establish this Constitution for the United States of America." Readers prone to consider that passage little more than a collection of clichés might remember how many polities are committed to enriching particular families, ruling the world, or promoting the one true religion.

Some commentators posit a hierarchy of constitutional purposes, with establishing and maintaining certain fundamental values at the apex. "Constitutionalism," Professor Walter Murphy claims, "demand[s] adherence...to principles that center on respect for human dignity and the obligations that flow from those principles."[3] Such claims have intuitive appeal. Such constitutional goods as social peace and credible commitments are partly means for fostering individual liberty. War is evil because military force is usually inimical to human flourishing. People are freer to make economic choices when they know government will not expropriate their property. The hierarchy of constitutional purposes provides guidelines for resolving conflicts among constitutional ends. Violence is constitutionally justified when protecting fundamental human rights requires abandoning the social peace.[4]

Human dignity is nevertheless not the raison d'être of constitutionalism, constitutional democracy, or American constitutionalism. Constitutions often entrench provisions that do not promote basic rights. Many constitutions establish a religious theocracy.[5] The Constitution of 1789 provided protection for slavery. These constitutional evils suggest that whether a society is governed constitutionally depends on commitments to the rule of law and the extent of entrenchments, not on the merits of particular laws or entrenchments. Besides, commitments to human dignity may not distinguish constitutional from other political orders. Most, if not all, regimes rely on some conception of human flourishing when justifying basic institutions. Adolf Hitler claimed to be securing the dignity of the Aryan race, with the proviso that persons of color, Jews, and other non-Aryans were not fully human. Appealing to a general constitutional commitment to human dignity rarely resolves debates within and between regimes over what governing institutions and rights are most consistent with the best conceptions of the human condition. Proponents and opponents of legal abortion, same-sex marriage, affirmative action, obscenity, and progressive taxation trot out "human dignity" and similar phrases with great alacrity (and most could probably pass a lie detector test if questioned on their sincerity). Many constitutional practices are compromises between persons who dispute what constitutes human dignity rather than expressions of a shared commitment to that value.

Constitutional government is not necessarily good government. Regimes may be committed to such evil purposes as racial supremacy or world domination.

Basic social institutions may be structured to further those abhorrent ends. Constitutionalism as higher law may entrench practices that are or become stupid, inefficient, and venal. Consider the provision in Article V that constitutionally prohibited the national government from banning the international slave trade until 1808 or, more controversially, the provisions of Article II that allow presidents to remain in power for more than two years after their policies are decisively repudiated in a national midterm election. Entrenchment dulls the spirit of innovation that may be vital for well-functioning democratic orders.[6] Constitutionalism as limited government may prevent government from implementing policies vital to the national welfare. The cruel and unusual punishment clause of the Eighth Amendment may hinder intelligence agencies from using torture to learn about terrorist plots. The broad diffusion of authority mandated by federalism and the separation of powers may inhibit the coordinated actions necessary to alleviate an economic depression. Of course, constitutions often mandate intelligent, efficient, and just practices. The establishment clause of the First Amendment outlaws an American version of the Spanish Inquisition. The requirement that Congress must declare war may ensure the necessary broad social support for lengthy military excursions. Still, if general agreement exists on the merits of these rules, entrenchment is unnecessary. Citizens and elected officials might simply do whatever they believe is best and not consider themselves bound by relatively ancient constitutional texts. A fundamental question of constitutional government is why people should entrench practices they believe beneficial today when they are aware that they might change their minds in the future on what constitutes good government.[7]

1. Constitutionalism and Democracy: The Dead Hand Problem

This concern with entrenchment highlights a potential conflict between constitutionalism and democracy, often known as the dead hand problem. Constitutionalism entails some rule by previous majorities. This is not normally considered a virtue in a democratic regime. The rule of law presents a dead hand problem by requiring adherence to precepts laid down in the past rather than the best-considered judgments of the present. Constitutional provisions that cannot be revised by ordinary legislation place further dead hand limits on popular government. Americans are not constitutionally free to decide whether permitting teachers to lead voluntary prayer exercises in public schools, all things considered, promotes the public good. We must instead determine whether that policy is consistent with some words ratified more than two hundred years ago by men who owned slaves and wore hideous wigs. Simple majorities cannot repeal our presidential system or the Second Amendment. Americans who favor parliamentary rule must gain the supermajority mandated by Article V. Americans who think state equality in the Senate is responsible for inefficient and unjust allocations of federal funds are not even constitutionally free to secure alternative institutional arrangements. Article V forbids the use of the amendment process to change the composition of the Senate.

Common everyday experiences suggest some reasons why these precommitments are nevertheless beneficial and empowering. Consider BB and MJ, two stereotypical teenagers from the 1950s, deciding whether to go steady senior year. By doing so, each makes a commitment go on a date with the other on Saturday night, even should they conclude during a particular week that they might be better off playing the field, going out with a different person, or staying home (*dead hand problem*). Each might nevertheless conclude they will more likely enhance their prospects by making a yearlong commitment than by relying on their best all-things-considered judgment every week. Rethinking relationships after every date is time-consuming and anxiety provoking (*organizing political decisions and establishing priorities*). By promising to go steady, BB and MJ increase their probability of inducing a highly valued promise to go steady from the other (*credible commitments*). Their commitment to go steady may limit manipulative behavior. Neither BB nor MJ can use the threat of staying home to leverage a date at the sock hop because each has already committed to going out together to the movies on Saturday night (*preventing self-dealing*). Agreeing to go steady in October guarantees BB and MJ a prom date in May. Such assurances are particularly valuable if each is more fearful of not having a prom date than of not going to prom with the absolutely right person (*insurance*). The commitment to a long-term relationship facilitates planning, enabling BB and MJ to take steps that are in their long-term interest. They can buy matching prom clothes in December, when dresses and tuxedos are on sale, rather than in April, when such items are marked up (*improved coordination*). Their commitment to going steady helps each avoid such temptations as excess drinking, which might weaken the relationship (*aspirations*). Believing that long-term commitments are, all things being equal, better than playing the field, BB and MJ will be more inclined to help each other overcome problems and find ways to accommodate their different tastes in movies (*compromises*). For all these reasons, BB and MJ may conclude their future options will be better if they constrain their conduct in the present.

Constitutionalism and democracy may also be complementary rather than antagonistic, as this analogy with ancient 1950s mating rituals suggests. Constitutional provisions and going steady both impose legal or conventional limits on behavior. Congress may not constitutionally grant titles of nobility. BB may date only MJ. Citizens in a pure democracy could grant peerages to authors of particularly valued manuscripts. Teenagers not going steady may play the field. Nevertheless, both democracies and teenage relationships are always partly constitutionalized. Constitutive rules are necessary for structuring all governing practices and human relationships. Pure democracies require fundamental laws that define what constitutes an authoritative expression of the popular will. Teenage couples who do not go steady remain just friends, a status that entails different social conventions about appropriate behavior. Political and romantic decisions that do not place legal or conventional restrictions on future behavior also constrain future political and romantic options. A Supreme Court decision in 1954 declaring that states could segregate students on the basis of race would have adversely affected American foreign relations with Third World countries and have increased racial unrest.[8] Persons who refuse to go steady gain reputations as "playing hard to get" or "being unwilling to commit," which influence their subsequent dating opportunities.

Constitutionalism is often a democratic choice. Popular majorities (and teenagers) in the United States remain free to renounce previous commitments. Americans may choose to grant titles of nobility. What Congress cannot do is claim *constitutional authority* to grant titles of nobility. Whether citizens choose to grant titles of nobility or respect constitutional authority depends on which choice they presently believe is most likely to improve future prospects. As is the case with romantic relationships, the decision to retain inherited limits on behavior is more empowering than constraining when a people are able to achieve more of their desires and values over time by limiting their present options.

2. Basic Constitutional Purposes

2.1 Establishing Legal Authority

Constitutions give political actions legal meaning. By creating a framework for making, enforcing, interpreting, and revising laws, constitutions expand the range of human possibilities. Just as persons cannot compose music if no rules define the significance of various musical notations, so persons cannot ban abortion or run for Congress if no rules establish how one enacts statutes or runs for public office. In the absence of constitutive constitutional norms, no one has the legal power to do anything. Popular majorities in Congress may tax gasoline only because Article I, Section 8 permits Congress to tax for the general welfare, Article I, Section 3 identifies the processes for determining who are the members of Congress, and Article I, Section 4 determines the processes by which Congress may pass laws.

Professor Stephen Holmes details how, contrary to the dead hand problem, entrenched constitutional rules or precommitments empower citizens:

> Constitutions may be usefully compared to the rules of a game and even to the rules of grammar. While *regulative* rules (e.g., "no smoking") govern preexistent activities, *constitutive* rules (e.g., "bishops move diagonally") make a practice possible for the first time. Rules of the latter sort cannot be conceived simply as hindrances or chains. Grammatical principles, for example, do not merely restrain a speaker, repressing his unruly impulses while permitting orderly ones to filter through. Far from simply handcuffing people, linguistic rules allow them to do many things they would not otherwise have been able to do or even have thought of doing.[9]

Howard Schweber observes how constitutions create a common language for discussing vital political questions. We cannot meaningfully debate or vote on whether to prohibit flag burning or impeach federal justices, he maintains, unless we have a shared political vocabulary.[10] Try having a conversation about the powers of the Supreme Court without having any agreement on who is a Supreme Court justice or what counts as a Supreme Court decision.

Fundamental laws facilitate legality. Precommitments make ordinary politics possible by establishing the legal standards for making legally binding rules and staffing official positions. Holmes writes:

> A democratic constitution does not merely hobble majorities and officials. The American Constitution helped create the Union. It also assigns powers (gives structure to the government, guarantees popular participation and so forth), and regulates the way in which these powers are employed (in accord, for example, with principles such as due process and equal treatment). In general, constitutional rules are enabling, not disabling; and it is therefore unsatisfactory to identify constitutionalism exclusively with limitations on power.[11]

Constitutions provide a structure for making political choices. People cannot govern themselves effectively if every political question is open for debate at every moment. Preexisting rules are necessary for determining what can be voted on and how voting takes place. Holmes notes, "It is meaningless to speak about popular government apart from some sort of legal framework which enables the electorate to have a coherent will. . . ." Decisions are made on the basis of predecisions. When they enter the voting booth, for instance, voters decide who shall be the president but not how many presidents there shall be.[12]

Good constitutional rules may improve democratic debate by paradoxically placing some issues off limits. "If we can take for granted certain procedures and institutions fixed in the past," Holmes asserts, "we can achieve our present goals more effectively than we could if we were constantly being sidetracked by the recurrent need to establish a basic framework for political life."[13] Disabled by inherited commitments from pondering the merits of bicameralism, Americans are better able to focus on the merits of the agricultural policies being considered by the House of Representatives and the Senate.

Constitutions, these observations suggest, simultaneously empower and constrain government. Too crude versions of the dead hand problem overlook how fundamental laws that give actions legal meaning enable officials to perform some actions while disabling them from performing others. Constitutional limitations are often merely collateral consequences of constitutional empowerments. If the constitution of the University of Maryland Bird Club authorizes the treasurer to spend up to $100 for binoculars, then the treasurer may spend neither $200 for binoculars nor $100 for birdseed. Constitutional rules empowering the Senate to try impeachments forbid the House of Representatives from doing the same. The absence of a constitution would result not in granting the treasurer of the bird club or the Senate unlimited legal power but in an anarchic state where no one has any legal authority.

The virtues of *entrenched* constitutive constitutional rules may nevertheless be overstated. Political debate would be impossible if every law could be debated at once. We can vote to revise the tax code only by agreeing, at least temporarily, to not voting on or debating existing procedures for revising the tax code. Nevertheless, the constitutive function of constitutional law requires, at most, very weak and partial entrenchments. The rule of law is maintained when virtually all laws may be revised or repealed legally by ordinary political procedures as long as preexisting laws determine which policies and procedures are modified at any particular time. Popular majorities can choose whether they want to vote on the date of presidential elections or on who should be the next president, even if they cannot choose to do both at the same time.

Whether entrenching numerous constitutional procedures promotes better policies is open to question. Melissa Schwartzberg of New York University, after analyzing a range of legal entrenchments, from classical Greece to contemporary Germany, concluded that such constitutional strategies are "futile and best and pernicious at worst."[14] Persons who believe that constitutional norms in the United States are unduly biased against changing the status quo are unlikely to celebrate hard to amend procedures that force them to convince majorities in three separate governing institutions to reverse political course. Most important, proof that all legal orders require some entrenchment certainly does not justify American constitutional practice. The Constitution of the United States includes far more precommitments than are necessary to organize government, empower officials, and structure politics. Americans could do without substantial chunks of Articles I, II and III, repeal all of Article IV, modify Article V to make the amendment process easier, and scrap every constitutional amendment but the Twelfth and still achieve most of the virtues of precommitment. These precommitments must be justified, if they are justifiable, by other constitutional virtues.

2.2 Rule of Law, Coordination, and Credible Commitments

The constitutional commitment to the rule of law serves many desirable social ends. As noted in Chapter 2, legality facilitates planning. People are aware of the legal consequences of their actions before they act. Persons in the United States attend the religious service of their choice without worrying whether government officials approve of their behavior. Businesses are aware that local government may regulate the hours their employees work and insist on safety standards, but they do not fear that their property will be expropriated without compensation. Nothing in life is absolutely certain. We cannot guarantee that the president will obey a subpoena from Congress or predict whether the Supreme Court will continue protecting abortion rights in the future. Nevertheless, constitutional rules substantially increase legal certainty and stability.

Constitutional provisions that increase legal stability facilitate material prosperity, beneficial international relations, and peaceful cooperation. Nations have long-term interests in gaining a reputation as reliable bargaining partners. Investors will more freely loan money to a government when they are assured of repayment. Foreign countries are more prone to form alliances with regimes they believe unlikely to abrogate treaties. Minorities are less likely to secede or riot when they are assured their interests will be protected. Constitutional provisions and practices make those promises to guarantee property rights, honor treaties, and respect all citizens more credible. Investors, allies, and minorities who are confident that constitutional and other bargains will be kept have greater incentives to partner with domestic government officials in efforts to improve the overall welfare.

Entrenching constitutional commitments is often vital to their credibility. Promises are cheap when enforcement mechanisms are weak. History demonstrates that political actors often have short-term interests that motivate them to renege on domestic and foreign agreements. Desperate for money and unwilling to raise taxes, legislatures repudiate past debts. Chief executives renounce treaties to avoid what have become unpopular international obligations. Majorities oppress minorities throughout the world. While such actions have immediate payoffs, they severely constrain official actions in the future. Governments that repudiate past debts are likely to be required to pay much higher interest rates when they next seek to borrow money. Properly designed constitutions provide greater assurances to vital domestic and foreign actors by reducing government capacity to stray from established commitments.

Much literature on political economy highlights how constitutions provide the reasonable guarantees to private investors believed necessary for them to make the investments that promote material prosperity. Douglas North and Barry Weingast insist, "For economic growth to occur the sovereign or government must not merely establish the relevant set of rights, but must make a credible commitment to them."[15] Economic actors need assurances before they invest that government will not expropriate their assets. Entrepreneurs build factories that provide jobs in impoverished regions only when they think the government is unlikely to confiscate their assets should their enterprise be profitable. Potential investors who believe that government officials will renege on public obligations and refrain from enforcing private obligations either demand more onerous terms up front or take their money elsewhere. Constitutions provide these entrepreneurs with two forms of assurance. First, the constitution may provide textual guarantees that private and public obligations will be enforced. The contracts clause of Article I promotes investment by forbidding states from canceling contractual debts. Second, constitutions may establish a set of institutions that make enforcement more probable. The affluent are more likely to loan money to the government when disputes over repayment are resolved by independent courts likely to be staffed by justices sympathetic to members of the investment class.

Constitutions facilitate the credible commitments necessary for a successful foreign policy. The Continental Congress declared independence from England and called on states to adopt new constitutions in part to assure France and Spain that Americans were committed to rendering their ties with England permanently. By adopting and maintaining constitutions, new nations may establish the stability necessary for convincing established powers that they are worthy allies and treaty partners. The Supremacy Clause promotes foreign agreements by declaring treaties the law of the land. That provision, combined with the constitutional jurisdiction of federal courts laid out in Article III, permits foreign nationals to assert their treaty rights in federal courts, whose judges are thought more likely than state judges to protect the legitimate interests of foreigners. Although the constitutional requirement that treaties be approved by two-thirds of the Senate makes ratification more difficult, that procedure may also demonstrate the broad consensus necessary to convince foreign ministers that the United States is unlikely to repudiate the treaty immediately after the party in power loses an election.

One person's credible commitment is another's unjust enrichment. While hardly anyone disputes that political actors should prefer enduring to transient national interests, what constitutes enduring and transient interests is contestable.

Proponents of debt repudiation contend that repayment will result in economic ruin. Perhaps, however, existing government debt holders gained particularly favorable terms through undue influence. Repudiation in that case may promote economic fairness. Charles Beard suggested that pro-constitutional elites during the 1780s took advantage of desperate Revolutionary War veterans whose need for money led them to sell their government bonds at far less than their face value.[16] The Constitution they framed and ratified protected investments that from an Anti-Federalist perspective were ill-gotten gains. Constitutional designers and ordinary citizens may still determine that honoring all debts is likely to be better policy in the long run. Nevertheless, the decision to favor creditors is as much a political choice as the decision to prefer the debtor. By increasing the capacity of a nation to make certain credible commitments, constitutional designers privilege some values and persons at the expense of others. No entrenched constitutional provision ensures only what all agree are policies that reflect enduring rather than transient national interests.

2.3 Preventing Self-Dealing

Many constitutional rules and practices prevent self-dealing by governing officials. Present electoral majorities may understand contemporary interests and values better than past electoral majorities, but the officials they elect often have incentives for acting contrary to the general will. Robert Michels's famous iron law of oligarchy postulated that all political leaders have interests different from that of their constituents.[17] Student government leaders may pull some punches in fights against tuition increases because, unlike ordinary undergraduates, they have the opportunity to obtain a glowing letter of recommendation for law school from the university president. Popular majorities have an interest in selecting the representative that will best advance their interests and values. Most elected officials have a distinctive interest in remaining in public office. On most matters, this concern with reelection promotes official behavior that advances majoritarian concerns. Representatives who make policies that expand the economy promote both the public good and their political careers. Nevertheless, important conflicts exist. Incumbents often seek to restrict the campaign contributions necessary for challengers to gain name recognition. Executive officials seek to keep documents detailing their misdeeds confidential. Well-designed constitutions help guarantee that these conflicts between the interests of political leaders and those of ordinary citizens are resolved consistently with the public good.

The dead hand of the past may empower the voice of the people in the present by entrenching fundamental laws that inhibit incumbents from unfairly restructuring electoral arrangements. Fixed rules prevent elected officials from repeatedly gerrymandering legislative districts, alternating electoral practices in ways that maximize their chances of retaining office. Constitutional procedures for electing officials that have severe democratic inadequacies may nevertheless be preferable to a system that gives legislative majorities control over the conditions of contest for the next election. Consider the incumbency advantage that would result if, three months before a national election, the sitting president could determine whether to retain the Electoral College, have the election decided by majority vote, or adopt any other scheme for electing an executive found in at least one democratic constitution across the world.

Fixed rules established in the past may be the preferred means for regulating how ordinary citizens engage in political activity. Elected officials may not be the best judges of whether speech criticizing their performance should be prohibited. The First Amendment, from this perspective, empowers citizens by limiting the capacity of elected officials to structure political debate. Fixed constitutional rules for rewarding governing officials may better promote democratic goals than letting such issues be resolved by governing officials themselves. One might not trust members of the legislature to determine their salary. The Twenty-Seventh Amendment to the Constitution facilitates popular control over legislative compensation by providing that no salary increase shall go into effect until an intervening election. Elected officials enjoy pay raises only when their constituents approve.[18]

Some constitutional rules and practices limit self-dealing by powerful popular movements. Fixed electoral rules and free speech rights prevent both partisan and legislative majorities from entrenching power. A majority coalition that believes their partisan fortunes will fare better in the long run by electing the president by popular vote is constitutionally constrained from abolishing the Electoral College. Constitutional guarantees of equality require that popular and legislative majorities govern by general rules. Majorities determine whether abortion should be banned or whether troops shall be sent into combat. They may not prohibit only Baptists from terminating pregnancies or draft only poorer persons to fight a war. This commitment to equal protection may provide substantial protection for fundamental rights. "There is no more effective practical guarantee against arbitrary and unreasonable government," Justice Robert Jackson declared, "than to require that the principles of law which government impose upon a minority must be imposed generally."[19] The separation of powers may make legislating for purely private benefits more difficult. "Increasing the number of veto players," North and Weingast believe, enables the "larger set of constituencies [to] protect themselves against political assault, thus markedly reducing the circumstances under which opportunistic behavior by the government c[an] take place."[20] Crassly put, the more officials a corrupt businessperson must bribe, the less likely that bribery will take place.

Some constitutional provisions prevent self-dealing by subnational units. Elected officials in each state have clear incentives to adopt policies that benefit local constituents, even when their measures are not in the national interest. Elected officials in Wisconsin might secure reelection by banning out-of-state apples. Elected judges in New York might improve their popular standing by permitting their neighbors to renege on debts owed to France. Constitutions prevent such destructive local behaviors by forbidding some state actions and giving the national government the power to ban others. Article I, Section 10 prohibits states from making private treaties without the consent of Congress. Article III, Section 2 permits Congress to vest federal courts with the power to adjudicate legal controversies between citizens of different states. Transferring cases to the federal judiciary limits the "home-court advantage" and eliminates potential conflicts between states over the proper legal forum. Under present federal law, if you are sued for more than $75,000 in damages allegedly caused during your out-of-state spring vacation, you will at least be able to prevent the case from being heard by a local judge elected by local constituents, including no doubt the person who is suing you.

As was the case for credible commitments, one person's self-dealing is another's democratic practice. Americans dispute whether campaign finance reform provides additional protection for political incumbents or levels the campaign playing field for all citizens. The line beyond which free speech becomes incitement is contested. Constitutional provisions limiting state capacity to interfere with national policies have been interpreted as requiring local officials to accept trash and contaminated waste generated in other jurisdictions and return without trial persons of color claimed as fugitive slaves.[21] These controversies demonstrate that constitutional rules and practices can never be fine-tuned to prevent only the sort of self-dealing by elected officials and legislative majorities that is obvious to all neutral observers. Controversial constitutional rules for regulating political self-dealing inevitably privilege the election of some candidates, the formation of some majorities, and the interest of some states at the expense of other candidates, other putative majorities, and other states.

2.4 Promoting the Public Interest

Constitutions entrench a political process that "encourage[s] the kind of lawmaking that gives concrete meaning to a substantive conception of the public interest."[22] Governing institutions must be carefully designed because many constitutional purposes cannot be directly secured by constitutional law, fiat, or exhortation. Capable military commanders are necessary for protecting the country from foreign attack. A constitutional provision declaring that "the president shall appoint only competent generals" is worthless unless the president has the ability and incentive to distinguish better from worse military leaders. Aware that constitutional law could not effectively command wise practices, the framers chose constitutional rules for selecting the president that they believed would guarantee as far as humanly possible that the persons elected as commander-in-chief had the ability to select intelligent officers. Article I, Section 8 gives Congress the power to regulate interstate commerce. The constitutional system for electing representatives is designed to ensure that Congress is composed of people capable of making economic regulations that facilitate material prosperity. Constitutional exhortations "to provide for the common defense" in the absence of constitutional provisions promoting political leaders who understand military strategy (or have advisors who understand military strategy) are likely to be no more effective than the frequent exhortation "we really need a hit" in my adult league softball experience was in the absence of any particular batting skills on my part.[23]

Entrenching certain practices for selected governing officials was the first constitutional means by which the framers fostered political deliberation and intelligent public policy. "The aim of every political constitution," James Madison wrote, is "first to obtain for rulers men who possess most wisdom to discern, and most virtue to pursue, the common good of the society."[24] Properly constructed representation would "refine and enlarge the public views by passing them through the medium of a chosen body of citizens, whose wisdom may best discern the true interest of their country."[25] Federalist 10 insists that constitutional provisions expanding the size of the electorate increase the number of worthy candidates and force voters to transcend parochial concerns when casting ballots. Madison thought relatively long terms of office promoted the public interest. The framers would not have representatives govern indefinitely in the face of public opinion. Still, they believed that a public official should have a lengthy enough term to guarantee "that there would be time enough before [the next election] to make the community sensible of the propriety of the measures he might incline to pursue."[26]

The separation of powers was the second constitutional means for promoting legislation in the public interest. If two, three, and four heads are better than one, then requiring legislation to be approved by the Senate, House of Representatives, president, and Supreme Court is likely to yield particularly intelligent laws. Multiple institutions with overlapping jurisdictions may foster deliberation and expand the number of interests that governing officials must consider before passing laws. Professor Stephen Elkin writes:

> The Madisonian constitutional design provides incentives to draw lawmakers away from being the servant of narrow interests or pursuing the small but comfortable legislative life. The separation of powers, which

is meant not only to prevent faction but also to promote public delib-eration, is crucial here. Each branch not only has controls over the oth-ers so that it may protect its independence, but the separation of powers also sets up an institutional structure in which national lawmaking must revolve around the efforts of the branches to convince one another of the merits of its views. Each branch has the constitutional means to resist the blandishments of other branches: their cooperation thus can most easily be secured through persuasion. And given that a significant portion of this persuasion will take place publicly, arguments showing how the legislation at issue serves the public interest will be common. Such arguments will be attractive to the citizenry at large whose appro-bation is needed if the cooperation of other branches is to be gained. Moreover, since officials of each branch reach office by different means, the efforts of each branch to convince the others will bring into play a larger range of opinions and interests than if the officials of the branches were selected in the same way.[27]

Complex government arrangements protect against rash behavior by a particular governing official or institution. "The necessity of a Senate," *Federalist* 62 states, "is not less indicated by the propensity of all single and numerous assemblies to yield to the impulse of sudden and violent passions, and to be seduced by fac-tious leaders into intemperate and pernicious resolutions."[28] Americans may not experience tyranny, this analysis suggests, as long as virtue reigns in at least one branch of the national government.

Federalism is a third constitutional means for promoting intelligent decision-making. By dividing power between the federal government and the states, the Constitution of the United States creates a division of labor that facili-tates policymaking by legislators most familiar with the issues. National issues are resolved by national officials who have developed expertise in national prob-lems. The *Federalist Papers* championed biennial rather than annual elections for the House of Representations to enable national legislators to become "masters of the public business."[29] Local issues are resolved by local officials who have developed expertise in local problems. "All the more domestic and personal interests of the people will be regulated and provided for," Madison wrote, by officials chosen by state citizens who will be "familiarly and minutely conver-sant" with conditions in their neighborhoods.[30] Federalism allows for policy experimentation and diversity, as local officials respond to local conditions, pressures, and sentiment. The policy experiences of one state may inform and improve policy judgments in others. Sharp constitutional distinctions between national and local powers may increase government capacity by improving accountability. Citizens who know what governing institutions made particular decisions are better able to reelect incumbents responsible for wise policies and to unseat officials responsible for stupid or unjust measures.

Whether American constitutional practices actually promote deliberation and the public interest is a subject of ongoing debate. Large election districts may favor the affluent rather than the meritorious. The separation of powers may promote paralysis as well as intelligence. Corruption in one governing institution may be sufficient to preserve a status quo that has become unjust. Federalism may replace national tyranny with local tyranny. Significantly perhaps, few contemporary constitutional regimes have adopted American-style elections, separation of powers, or federalism.

The constitutional attempt to promote intelligent government by institutional design collapses strong distinctions between ordinary and constitutional politics. Constitutional law in the United States may not directly determine what policies will best create "good jobs at good wages." Nevertheless, blaming individual politicians or the general public for economic programs that fail to combat unemployment may be constitutionally myopic. Perhaps the Constitution contains a design flaw that inhibits national capacity to make commercial policy in the public interest. If members of the House of Representatives were elected in an at-large general election, they might have more incentive to pursue national ends than to bring home the bacon for a narrow constituency. Large election districts in media-saturated campaigns may better facilitate entertainment than policy. At the very least, attention to constitutions as means for facilitating the public interest is another reminder of how crucial aspects of constitutionalism cannot be reduced to constitutional law.

2.5 Insurance

Constitutions provide insurance against an uncertain future. Influential political thinkers during the Enlightenment believed all republics had an inherent tendency to degenerate over time. Intelligent framers could slow and possibly halt this corruption process by designing constitutional rules and governing institutions that preserved their virtuous spirit. "Youth is the seed time of good habits as well in nations as in individuals," Thomas Paine wrote when urging Americans to break from England and frame a national constitution.[31] Paine and others believed that by entrenching sound institutions and values early, constitutions could fashion the sort of citizenry most likely to maintain good constitutions in the future. Justice Antonin Scalia is a leading proponent of this constitutional commitment to preserving inherited political virtues. The "whole purpose" of a constitution, he declares, "is to prevent change—to embed certain rights in such a manner that future generations cannot readily take them away."[32] The Constitution of 1789 entrenched the anti-aristocratic values of the framers by permanently banning titles of nobility. The Thirteenth Amendment entrenched the political values of the victorious Union army by permanently prohibiting slavery in the United States.

Many contemporary constitutions freeze, at least partially, existing political arrangements. Professor Tom Ginsburg of the University of Chicago Law School describes constitution making in much of Asia as grand bargains between numerous political factions, each fearful of being left out of future governing coalitions. Apprehensive politicians anticipate that judicially enforceable constitutions will guarantee that a certain balance of power will be preserved over time. Politicians who "foresee themselves losing in postconstitutional elections," Ginsburg details, "may seek to entrench judicial review as a form of political insurance."[33] Professor Ran Hirschl of the University of Toronto notes how constitutions are often means for maintaining the political power of weakened elite coalitions. His hegemonic preservation thesis declares, "When their policy preferences have been, or are likely to be, increasingly challenged in majoritarian decision-making arenas, elites that possess disproportionate access to, and influence over, the legal arena may initiate a constitutional entrenchment of rights and judicial review in order to transfer power to supreme courts."[34]

Many historians believe American constitutionalism was influenced by elite desires to forestall political change. The most influential work of constitutional history in the early twentieth century, Charles Beard's *An Economic Interpretation of the Constitution of the United States,* charged that the constitutional framers sought to establish governing institutions and practices that would secure the value of their government bonds and Western land holdings.[35] While few contemporary scholars subscribe to the Beard thesis, more sophisticated versions abound. Professor Gordon Wood of Brown University regards the Constitution as the means by which national elites sought to hold off a more popular politics. In his view, "the Constitution was intrinsically an aristocratic document designed to check the democratic tendencies of the period."[36]

Constitutional insurance is valuable only for societies or social movements that have more reason to fear than to anticipate the future. If all regimes have a powerful tendency to become more corrupt over time or good reason exists for thinking cherished political interests and values are likely to weaken politically, then entrenching present practices and balances of political power is desirable. More hopeful societies, political movements, and persons have less reason to lock in the practices and values of the past. Constitutional provisions that reflect the values or balance of power at a particular time become outdated. Many contemporary Americans believe state equality in the Senate, an important concession to smaller northern states in 1787, no longer serves any legitimate purpose. Constitutional insurance policies may also generate perverse results when framers poorly construct social institutions or fail to predict the future. The

Constitution of the United States, designed to prevent the rise of mass political parties, actually facilitated their development. By mandating large election districts and diffusing power among numerous governing institutions, framers who abhorred two-party politics unwittingly created a governing structure that provides fertile ground for this type of partisan competition.[37] Madison hated the mass politics of the Jacksonian era that the constitutional institutions he helped design made possible.

2.6 National Aspirations

Constitutions embody national aspirations. Members of a national community may aspire to protect fundamental rights, have a vigorous economy, or rule the world. As is the case with all commitments, people do not always act consistently with their notions of the best life or a good regime. Students aspiring to go to law school have been known to miss class when tempted by a movie, ball game, or various romantic liaisons. Nations have been known to adopt policies that do not seem consistent with their notions of justice. Franklin Roosevelt's decision to intern Japanese American citizens during World War Two is now universally regarded as a gross violation of American constitutional norms and human rights. Entrenched constitutional commitments are means for reducing such deviations from our personal or national ambitions.

Several elements of constitutionalism weaken the allure of unconstitutional temptations. The constitutional text constantly reminds political leaders and citizens of national aspirations. The First Amendment informs political dissenters that they have a right to criticize the government. Political leaders who propose to silence their critics must explain why their actions do not violate that cherished liberty. This constitutional obligation to justify policy as consistent with certain fundamental norms may in the long run foster actions consistent with those commitments. Through a combination of socialization and reflection on constitutional values, Americans may develop a greater appreciation for the freedom of religion and speech. Madison thought that textual declarations of rights would help "establish the public opinion in their favor, and rouse the attention of the whole community."[38] Constitutions provide mechanisms for correcting temporary deviations from national aspirations. Unelected Supreme Court justices may be immune from short-term pressures to silence political dissent. Life tenure, in this view, facilitates decisions based on what is best about American constitutionalism rather than on transient passions.

Abraham Lincoln in 1857 emphasized the aspirational function of constitutive texts when articulating the foundations for the constitutional commitment to the abolition of slavery. The assertion that "all men are created equal," he stated:

> was of no practical use in effecting our separation from Great Britain; and it was placed in the Declaration, nor for that, but for future use. Its authors meant it to be, thank God, it is now proving itself, a stumbling block to those who in after times might seek to turn a free people back into the hateful paths of despotism. They knew the proneness of prosperity to breed tyrants, and they meant when such should re-appear in this fair land and commence their vocation they should find left for them at least one hard nut to crack.[39]

In Lincoln's view, Thomas Jefferson and other framers recognized that slavery was wrong. While unwilling or unable to free their slaves in the present, they placed powerful antislavery rhetoric at the heart of American identity. At the very least, political activists who repeated the catechism "all men were created equal" would solidly ground antislavery advocacy in the American constitutional tradition. More optimistically, the founding commitment to the eventual abolition of slavery would fashion a citizenry increasingly committed to finding the means for eradicating that hateful institution.

Entrenched constitutional aspirations are means for promoting progress as opposed to insurance schemes that limit backsliding. Lincoln insisted that the Constitution committed Americans to freeing all slaves and did not merely forbid enslaving those persons of color who were free in 1789. The constitutional aspiration to "form a more perfect Union and establish Justice" suggests a national aspiration for improving public life. Professor Jack Balkin of Yale Law School declares that constitutional faith is rooted in the belief that "despite constitutional evil, adequate resources for constitutional redemption exist: in the text of the Constitution, in the multiple layers of the constitutional tradition, and in the moral aspirations and commitments of the people who live under the Constitution and carry the project of self-government forward through time."[40] This difference between constitutional insurance and constitutional aspirations has interpretive consequences. As noted in the previous section, Justice Scalia and others who regard entrenchment as a way of preserving existing virtues insist that constitutional provisions should not normally be read as compelling government officials to abandon inherited practices. Proponents of aspirational theories of constitutional interpretation believe that Americans are obligated to abandon inherited practices that they realize are inconsistent with more fundamental constitutional values. "The Constitution's coherence," one prominent aspirational thinker writes, "depends partly on its capacity to be reinterpreted, if need be, in light of better conceptions of justice."[41]

Not all plausible constitutional aspirations are admirable. While Lincoln perceived a constitutional commitment to emancipation, many antebellum Southerners detected more proslavery aspirations. Human bondage, Justice Peter Daniel asserted in *Dred Scott*, is "the only private property which the Constitution has *specifically recognized,* and has imposed it as a direct obligation both on the States and the Federal Government to protect and *enforce*."[42] Many Americans have asserted a constitutional commitment to white supremacy. "Through most of U.S. history," Rogers Smith details, "lawmakers pervasively and unapologetically structured U.S. citizenship in terms of illiberal and undemocratic racial, ethnic, and gender hierarchies."[43] Other (sometimes the same) Americans have asserted constitutional commitments to nativism, to manifest destiny, and to other -isms now deemed evil by most citizens. If the Declaration of Independence helped fashion antislavery citizens, the disturbing possibility exists that such constitutional protections for human bondage as the fugitive slave clause in Article IV may have fashioned citizens who thought slavery a positive good or at least a policy that good Northern citizens ought not find very objectionable.

2.7 Constitutions as Compromises

Constitutions are compromises between persons and political movements representing very different interests and national aspirations. Entrenched rules or principles in such regimes guarantee that government officials sufficiently accommodate those crucial political actors whose support is necessary for maintaining political order. The Constitution of the United States must not seem unduly oppressive to most corporate managers or union members. The Constitution of Iraq must satisfy most Shiites and Sunnis. Accommodations may be substantive or procedural. The fugitive slave clause forbade states from declaring free a slave who escaped from a state whose law permitted slavery. The Electoral College guaranteed that citizens of the slave states would have special influence on presidential elections.[44] Constitutional framers may also encourage compromise and consensus building in the operation of the governments that they set in motion. American politics has largely operated on the principle that constitutional government should accommodate all major political interests. Policy proposals must run a difficult obstacle course before becoming settled law. Many opportunities exist for interests to influence, slow, or defeat legislation that might too adversely affect them. Divided government, Senate filibusters, presidential veto threats, and judicial review moderate policy swings, encouraging negotiation and consensus building. Policies that are vetted by the House of Representatives, the Senate, the president, and the Supreme Court are unlikely to be inconsistent with the fundamental values or the interests of any substantial social group, particularly if those policies require some implementation by state officials.

Constitutional compromises promote consensus as opposed to majoritarian democracy. Consensus democrats think the best governing processes maximize the number of persons who influence public policy rather than the number of persons who think the best policy was chosen. Constitutional institutions in consensus democracy are structured to make policy that large majorities find tolerable rather than those 51% of the populace may think highly desirable. Professor Arend Lijphart of the University of California, San Diego declares that "instead of being satisfied with narrow decision-making majorities" popular government should "aim at broad participation in government and broad agreement on the policies government should pursue."[45] Consensus democracy promises a more egalitarian policymaking process and may preserve public order better than majoritarian democracy. "In plural societies" where people are divided "into virtually separate subsocieties with their own political parties, interest groups, and media of communication," Lijphart asserts, "majority rule is not only undemocratic but also dangerous because minorities that are continually denied access to power will feel excluded and discriminated against and may lose their allegiance to the regime."[46] Factions that lose every vital vote are likely to seek ways of exiting a social club, a union, or a political order.

The Constitution of the United States was as much a compromise as an expression of shared values. Benjamin Franklin described the drafting process as resembling a game of dice with many players, "their ideas so different, their prejudices so strong and so various, and their particular interests, independent of the general, seeming so opposite, that not a move can be made that is not contested."[47] Federalists reminded their contemporaries that "a faultless plan was not to be expected."[48] *Federalist* 37 emphasized how the diversity of interests present at the Philadelphia convention guaranteed that the Constitution would not resemble "that artificial structure and regular symmetry which an abstract view of the subject might lead an ingenious theorist to bestow on a Constitution planned in his closet or in his imagination."[49] Madison gave up trying to find any coherent justification for treating slaves as three-fifths of a person. He simply pronounced the relevant constitutional provision one of many "compromising expedient[s] of the Constitution."[50] Three-fifths was the rule, rather than zero, one, four-sevenths, or two-thirds, because that was the compromise agreed upon.

The compromising function of many constitutions is the inverse of the aspirational function. Constitutional aspirations reach above our disagreements and appeal to the "better angels of our nature." Constitutional compromises reflect the ways we live with our disagreements. They introduce discordant notes into the harmony of the constitutional system. The price of national unity or peaceful coexistence in a society with diverse interests and values may be a less coherent constitution. Those who consider themselves more virtuous may have to make concessions to those whom they regard as vicious. Imperfections, expediencies, and ambiguities may have to be tolerated to build support for a constitution that will be broadly acceptable. Article IV, Section 2 required free-state citizens to return fugitive slaves to their southern owners. The Tenth Amendment's declaration that "the powers not delegated to the United States by the Constitution…are reserved to the States respectively" provided some assurance to Anti-Federalists that national powers were limited. By not repeating in the Tenth Amendment the "expressly delegated" language of the Articles of Confederation, the First Congress also assured Federalists that national powers were less limited than was previously the case.

Constitutional compromises may be necessary for preserving order in plural societies, but their implementation is always problematic. The line between necessary accommodations and undue tolerance for evil is thin, particularly when, as was the case in the antebellum United States, the victims of the evil have no say in the bargaining.[51] Just as constitutional aspirations may fashion a citizenry committed to political virtues, constitutional compromises may fashion a citizenry indifferent to political wrongs. Northern Democrats before the Civil War, eager to preserve the Union and please their coalition partners from the South, publicly declared that they "did not care whether slavery was voted up or down" in the territories.[52] Constitutional compromises are also likely to outlive their usefulness, particularly when crucial elements of the compromise are provisions that make the Constitution hard to amend. Idaho and Wyoming are presently the primary beneficiaries of state equality in the Senate, even though neither was even a territory of the United States when the Constitution was framed and ratified.

3. American Constitutional Purposes

3.1 The Original Constitutional Purposes

The framers regarded the Constitution of the United States as a means for securing liberal political purposes (as *liberal* was understood in the late eighteenth century), including preserving social peace, promoting material prosperity, and maintaining popular sovereignty.[53] Federalists sought constitutional institutions that would prevent conflicts with foreign nations and between the states, would promote a national market within the United States, and would prevent a traditional aristocracy from forming in any state. The Constitution was also a means for upholding the liberal commitment to the rule of law. Madison urged constitutional improvements that would simplify, stabilize, and provide better means for enforcing national law. As classical liberals, most Federalists were not concerned with military glory[54] or saving souls, at least when they drafted the national constitution.

The persons responsible for the Constitution of the United States were particularly concerned with solving coordination problems. The public interest required amicable relationships with foreign countries and between states. Under the Articles of Confederation, states had incentives to pursue local benefits at the expense of the general good. Connecticut could protect state farmers by taxing wheat imported from New York. No enforceable guarantee before 1787 existed to ensure that forbearance on Connecticut's part when regulating wheat imported from New York would induce similar forbearance on New York's part when regulating corn imported from Connecticut. A stronger national government, the framers hoped, could overcome these tendencies to seek local benefits by entrenching and enforcing prohibitions on state policies that enriched local citizens at the expense of the nation. Article I, Section 10, for example, prevents local trade wars by declaring, "No State shall, without the Consent of Congress, lay any Imposts or Duties on Imports or Exports."

The Constitution ratified between 1787 and 1789 was committed to promoting justice. Madison complained about "trespasses of the States on the rights of each others" and the "injustices of the laws of States."[55] The precise content of these rights and injustices is the subject of a two-hundred-year debate. Read broadly as an aspiration, Madison might have been asserting a constitutional commitment to developing and acting upon ever improving conceptions of individual right. Read narrowly as insurance, Madison might have been insisting on little more than a constitutional commitment to guaranteeing that all debts were fully paid. A middle position might treat the Constitution as committed to some unspecified liberal conception of fundamental liberties. Not surprisingly, while Americans have historically endorsed a constitutional commitment to justice, no consensus has ever existed on the content of that constitutional end.

3.2 American Constitutional Purposes over Time

Constitutional amendments changed the appearance of the constitutional text and the focus of American constitutionalism. With rare exception, the constitutional provisions ratified between 1787 and 1789 delineate the structure and powers of governing institutions. The persons responsible for the original Constitution sought to entrench political practices that they thought would best secure such consensual constitutional purposes as national security and individual liberty. With rare exception, the most important constitutional amendments ratified after 1789 delineate fundamental rights. The persons responsible for the Bill of Rights and post–Civil War constitutional amendments sought to clarify the individual liberties that previously entrenched political practices were expected to secure. The typical two-semester constitutional law course in the United States reflects this division of constitutional labor. Constitutional materials on the structure of government focus almost exclusively on the Constitution of 1787. Constitutional materials on civil liberties focus almost exclusively on the Bill of Rights and post–Civil War amendments.

Controversy exists over whether this change in the subject matter of constitutional provisions reflects an adjustment in American constitutional purposes. Lincoln claimed that the original Constitution was committed to placing slavery "on a course of ultimate extinction"[56] and was "dedicated to the proposition that all men are created equal."[57] The Thirteenth, Fourteenth, and Fifteenth Amendments, from this perspective, were means for better realizing inherited constitutional commitments. Other constitutionalists insist that the Reconstruction amendments represent a sharp break from the American constitutional past. Various works claim that radical Republicans during the 1860s entrenched a fundamental constitutional commitment to equality,[58] individual rights as opposed to majority rule,[59] or majority rule as opposed to a sectional balance of power.[60] Professor Christopher Eisgruber of Princeton University contends that Americans altered the very "core" of the constitutional order when ratifying the post–Civil War amendments. "The Fourteenth Amendment," he states, "changed the Constitution from an ambiguously contractual law into a kind of law best described by the representative concept of constitutionalism," law that "enable[s] Americans to think constructively about the values and relationships that characterize them as a people."[61]

Answers to such questions as the constitutional status of affirmative action, the relationship between the states and the federal government, and the proper methods for interpreting the Constitution rely, in part, on contested conceptions of the constitutional purposes underlying the Reconstruction amendments. Consider the debate between the justices on the Supreme Court in the *Slaughter-House Cases* (1873). The narrow issue before the court was whether the Thirteenth and Fourteenth Amendments prohibited states from giving some butchers a monopoly on the right to slaughter animals. Justice Samuel Miller rejected claims that the constitutional rights of the aggrieved butchers had been violated. He believed the newly entrenched provisions prohibiting slavery and mandating equal protection were means for ensuring the equal citizenship of newly freed slaves. White butchers gained no new rights after 1865 because the Civil War was not fought to secure their liberties. The "pervading purpose" of the three new constitutional amendments, Miller wrote, "was the freedom of the slave race, the security and firm establishment of that freedom, and the protection of the newly-made freeman and citizen from the oppressions of those who had formerly exercised unlimited dominion over him."[62] Justice Stephen Field's dissent insisted that constitutional rights had been violated. The Fourteenth

Amendment committed Americans to protecting fundamental rights of all citizens from state infringement. Field's Civil War was fought to preserve the natural liberties of all persons. New constitutional provisions were designed to guarantee "the privileges and immunities...which of right belong to the citizens of all free governments," among which was "the right to pursue a lawful employment in a lawful manner, without other restraint than such as equally affects all persons."[63]

Later constitutional amendments may have further modified distinctive American constitutional purposes. The Fifteenth, Seventeenth, Nineteenth, Twenty-Third, Twenty-Fourth, and Twenty-Sixth Amendments, all of which expand voting rights, might have transforming the United States from a republic to a democracy.[64] John W. Burgess, a prominent political scientist during the Progressive Era, vociferously complained that the constitutional amendments providing for the progressive income tax and the popular elections of senators undermined the original constitutional commitment to limited government.[65] Several contemporary scholars insist that fundamental constitutional commitments may be transformed by important political events as well as by constitutional amendments ratified consistently with the procedures set out in Article V. Bruce Ackerman, whose work is considered in Chapter 6, maintains that the New Deal established a constitutional commitment to the welfare state and that the Civil Rights Act of 1964 and related measures modified the constitutional understanding of equality.[66]

4. The Virtues (and Vices) of Constitutionalism

The global explosion of constitutional government suggests that an increasing number of citizens in diverse countries appreciate the virtues of constitutionalism. The twentieth-century legacy of fascism and communism left political activists with a renewed appreciation of the rule of law and constitutional practices that prevent self-dealing by those in power. Many new nations are attracted by the ways fixed constitutional rules may encourage investment in their developing nations, assert national aspirations, and provide grounds for compromises between previously warring fashions. Political elites are attracted to constitutional insurance, should they fall from power.

Americans heartily encourage constitutional celebrations. An overwhelming consensus exists that the Constitution of the United States has enabled Americans to achieve many laudatory goals. Citizens commonly praise the framers for successfully organizing the national government; establishing the rule of law; making credible commitments to foreign countries and government bondholders; preventing self-dealing by politicians, popular majorities, and states; fostering government in the public interest; preserving the best liberal values of the eighteenth century; articulating national aspirations to a more just future; and setting out reasonable compromises between rival political factions. Everything good that happens in the United States, from winning the Civil War to curing polio to the stunning ice hockey victory over the Soviet Union during the 1980 Winter Olympic Games, is credited at least partly to the Constitution. The evils of American life are almost always thought to have nonconstitutional foundations. Gridlock results from too many interest groups making too many demands or from politicians who just do not get along. Few point out that the constitutional system for making laws fosters stasis by giving numerous factions a veto on public policy. Almost every citizen finds some flaw in the national response to the tragedy of September 11, 2001, but few blame the framers for failing to include constitutional provisions explicitly allocating powers during a national emergency. Americans do commonly accuse each other of misinterpreting the Constitution. Libertarians blame the welfare state on constitutional authorities who they claim have abandoned the original constitutional commitment to limited government. Law reviews issue daily bulletins from liberal law professors constitutionally condemning decisions handed down by Republican judicial appointees. Rarely do these commentators ponder whether constitutional arrangements might be partly to blame for empowering constitutionally incompetent interpreters. Perhaps if the framers had laid down better rules for selecting constitutional decision-makers, governing officials in the United States would be making better constitutional decisions.

Constitutional purposes and constitutional interpretation are closely yoked. Constitutional purposes often depend on constitutional interpretation. The framing effort to prevent domestic trade wars will fail if local taxes on out-of-state goods are not interpreted as the "Imposts or Duties on Imports" prohibited by Article I, Section 10. Constitutional interpretation depends on constitutional purposes. The equal protection clause protects women only if the Fourteenth Amendment entrenched a constitutional commitment to realizing the best notion of human equality and not to preventing backsliding from dominant understandings of equality in 1868. Whether the Constitution of the United States provides credible commitments that debts will be repaid or empowers elected officials to promote the welfare of their constituents influences whether state laws enabling students to repay college loans back over a longer period than originally bargained for are consistent with the contracts clause.

4

Constitutional Interpretation

The persons responsible for the Constitution of the United States thought they had designed a constitutional order that could be maintained by persons who acted primarily on the basis of self-interest. Their "incentive-compatible constitution" relied heavily on "self-reinforcing institutional arrangements" to preserve the constitutional order.[1] Constitutional institutions were designed in ways the framers thought would tie "the interest of the man" to "the constitutional rights of the place."[2] Senators motivated solely by the desire to maximize their power had self-interested reasons to reject judicial nominees who they believed would make decisions that unduly augmented executive authority. James Madison claimed that a large republic prevented the formation of the interest-based majority factions that were most likely to violate constitutional rights.[3] The national government would protect religious freedom because no religious group could gain the political power necessary to oppress other religious groups, and, if they could not oppress others, all religious groups had self-interested reasons for promoting religious freedom for all believers as a second-best policy.

History belies the power of these structural incentives and guarantees. Political structures have substantial influence on political outcomes. Just ask the four losing presidential candidates who gained more popular votes than the Electoral College winner. Constitutional institutions do not, however, function to preserve the faction-free constitutional order envisioned by Madison and other framers.[4] Contemporary senators more often vote as members of a political party than as representatives of the upper house of Congress.[5] Republicans and Democrats support those judicial nominees who share their constitutional vision, not those they believe most likely to uphold the constitutional powers of their home institution. Nationally organized groups, many concerned solely with the interests of members, play a major role in American politics. Madison and his associates no more anticipated the Chamber of Commerce and the National Rifle Association than they did the Democratic Party. Officials and citizens in this political context cannot expect the Constitution to be "a machine that would go by itself."[6] They must often consciously and accurately determine what the Constitution means if the constitutional order is to be maintained.

The processes by which constitutional meanings are determined raise normative and empirical questions. The normative questions are about the best methods for ascertaining the meaning of constitutional provisions. Much controversy exists over the legitimate forms of constitutional reasoning, the application of those forms, and whether all forms of constitutional exegesis can be described as constitutional interpretation. Justices, elected officials, and citizens dispute whether constitutional provisions should be interpreted consistently with the meaning of the text at the time the text was ratified, how one determines the meaning of the text at the time of ratification, and what the meaning of particular constitutional texts was at the time of ratification. The empirical questions are about whether persons when determining constitutional meanings actually rely on legitimate methods of constitutional interpretation or construction. Very prominent political scientists insist that constitutional decision-makers are interested only in making good policy. Constitutional arguments, in this view, mask conclusions reached on other grounds.

The stakes in these debates are the influence of constitutionalism on politics. At one extreme is the common view that legal and policy arguments are theoretically distinct, that notions of good policy should play no role in constitutional analysis. At the other extreme is the equally common view that no practical difference exists between legal and policy arguments, that persons using common methods of constitutional interpretation support whatever policies they believe best. The actual relationship between law and politics is more complex than these simplistic legal and attitudinal models suggest. The methods for determining constitutional meanings are best understood as practices that constrain and structure value voting, not as devices that assure a complete separation of law and politics. Whether constitutionalism is a distinctive form of politics depends on whether persons making constitutional arguments frequently reach different conclusions than persons making purely policy arguments, not on whether policy commitments play some role in constitutional decision-making.

Questions about constitutional meaning are related but not identical to questions about constitutional authority. Whether Congress has the power to prohibit cigarette companies from advertising is a question about the meaning of the commerce clause and the First Amendment. Whether elected officials should consider themselves bound by past judicial decisions on commercial speech is a question about constitutional authority. This chapter discusses how constitutional meanings are determined. Chapter 5 discusses how controversies over constitutional meanings are settled.

1. The Living Constitution and Its Discontents

1.1 Strict Construction and the Living Constitution

Debates between strict constructionists and living constitutionalists structured controversies over constitutional meaning throughout much of the twentieth century. Strict constructionists in the twentieth century[7] maintained that governing authorities had no business injecting personal values when making constitutional decisions. When campaigning for the presidency in 1968, Richard Nixon promised to appoint to the Supreme Court "strict constructionists" who would "see themselves as caretakers of the Constitution and servants of the people, not superlegislators with a free hand to impose their social and political viewpoints on the American people."[8] Judges considering whether capital punishment was constitutional consulted the constitutional text, history, and precedent but not public opinion polls or philosophical treatises on the death penalty. Proponents of the living Constitution insisted that constitutional provisions should be interpreted in light of changing social and political values. Chief Justice Earl Warren declared, "The words of the [Eighth] Amendment are not precise, and…their scope is not static. The Amendment must draw its meaning from the evolving standards of decency that mark the progress of a maturing society."[9] These evolving standards of decency justified judicial decisions declaring capital punishment unconstitutional, even though that sanction was not thought cruel and unusual when the Bill of Rights was ratified or for most of American history. Strict constructionists scored points in these debates by highlighting that constitutional decision-makers relying on evolving standards of decency were likely to do little more than consult personal beliefs about right and wrong. More often than not, evolving standards of decency reflected the mores of the chattering classes than either those of the framers or what Richard Nixon referred to as "the silent majority." Living constitutionalists, particularly after 1964, scored points by emphasizing that constitutional decision-makers who insisted that constitutional meanings and applications were static and saw "their duty as interpreting law and not making law"[10] could not justify *Brown v. Board of Education* (1954). Given the widespread practice of racial segregation in the North at the time the equal protection clause was ratified and such judicial precedents as *Plessy v. Ferguson* (1896), which explicitly pointed to the accepted constitutionality of segregated schools when sustaining a Louisiana law segregating passengers on railroad cars, only a living Constitution seemed to provide adequate grounds for striking down Jim Crow education.

During the last decades of the twentieth century, practitioners modified both strict construction and living constitutionalism to meet these objections. Constitutional commentators of all persuasions presently place more emphasis

than do their immediate ancestors on the constitutional text. Strict construction evolved into originalism. Originalists increasingly distinguished between
the original meaning of a constitutional provision and the practice at the time
the provision was ratified. These adjustments enabled critics of most liberal
Warren Court decisions to provide constitutional foundations for *Brown*. Raoul
Berger caused a stir in 1977 when he both defended originalism and asserted
that the statements prominent Republicans made during the debates over the
Fourteenth Amendment opposing desegregated public schools demonstrated
that *Brown* was wrongly decided.[11] Robert Bork, writing as an originalist a decade
later, claimed that *Brown* was "compelled by...the original understanding of the
fourteenth amendment's equal protection clause." Rather than focus on practices in 1868, Bork emphasized the language of the equal protection clause, noting "it had been apparent for some time that segregation rarely if ever produced
equality."[12] At the same time strict constructionism was being transformed into
originalism, most living constitutionalists abandoned talk of the *unwritten constitution* or *noninterpretativism*. Thomas Grey in 1975 boldly defended what he
declared was a noninterpretivist approach to constitutional decision-making:

> The most fundamental question we can ask about our fundamental
> law is whether when reviewing laws for constitutionality, should our
> judges confine themselves to determining whether those laws conflict
> with norms derived from the written Constitution...or may they also
> enforce principles of liberty and Justice when the normative content of
> those principles is not to be found within the four corners of our found-
> ing document?[13]

Grey now believes that "it is better to treat all approaches to constitutional adjudication as constrained to the interpretation of the sources of constitutional law,
and then to argue about what those sources are and how much relative weight
they should have."[14] Other prominent defenders of liberal judicial activism sing a
similar tune. In a series of influential articles, Ronald Dworkin maintains that the
correct constitutional question at issue in *Roe v. Wade* is whether the due process
clause, properly interpreted, protects abortion rights, not whether women have
an unenumerated constitutional right to terminate their pregnancies.[15] One consequence of these modifications is that formerly sharp differences between strict
constructionists or originalists and living constitutionalists have been blurred.
Different practitioners place more or less weight on framing practice, but most
agree on the primacy of the constitutional text and that framing practice is not
always dispositive when determining constitutional meaning.

Contemporary constitutional politics has further obscured the line between
strict construction or originalism and the living Constitution. Political liberals

were far more enthusiastic than political conservatives about evolving standards of decency during the New Deal and Great Society era in part because constitutional law in those years evolved only in liberal directions. Living constitutionalism meant fewer restrictions on sexually explicit speech and greater protection for criminal defendants, not more rights for property holders and increased solicitude for gun owners. As the national government and federal judiciary moved rightward during the Reagan era, a new generation of liberal and conservative constitutional thinkers began adjusting inherited dogmas. Originalism is being refined in ways that often justify conservative judicial decisions declaring unconstitutional such liberal practices as affirmative action.[16] Prominent political liberals exhibit a new appreciation for precedent, particularly when a Republican president nominates a justice who might overrule *Roe*. Established ways of thinking about constitutional interpretation still retain some power. Liberals insist that the Fourteenth Amendment forbids state governments from violating the freedom of speech, even though federal courts are at least as likely to shield major corporations as socialists from local restrictions. Most, not all, conservatives who call on the justices to overrule *Roe* do not demand that the Supreme Court rule that legal abortion violates the due process rights of the unborn. Still, while the media continues to use *strict construction* and *living Constitution* to describe constitutional positions, theoretical and political developments have rendered these labels less, if at all, useful for describing the contending positions in most contemporary constitutional debates.

1.2 Interpretation, Construction, and Hard Cases

Some version of living constitutionalism is unavoidable when constitutional disputes arise that were not contemplated or resolved by the framers. The persons responsible for the Constitution of the United States recognized that ratification did not settle every possible controversy over the meaning of constitutional provisions. "All new laws," Madison wrote in *Federalist* 37, "are considered as more or less obscure and equivocal, until their meaning be liquidated and ascertained by a series of particular discussions and adjudications."[17] Constitutional silences and ambiguities bedeviled Americans from the birth of the republic. The ink was hardly dry on the constitutional text when members of the First Congress realized that no provisions specified whether Senate consent was necessary for the president to remove an executive branch official. "Perhaps this is an omitted case," Madison confessed to the House of Representatives.[18] Strict construction was meaningless in the absence of a clear constitutional text, precedents, or an implicit framing understanding. Unanticipated events, new technologies, and new precedents have created additional constitutional ambiguities. How free speech principles apply to the Internet cannot be ascertained solely by reference to words ratified in 1791 or precedents that are based on the distinctive qualities of other means for communication. Constitutional decisions that resolve some disputes often create or add fuel to other constitutional controversies. *Lawrence v. Texas* (2003) temporarily settled as a matter of constitutional law that states may not prosecute consenting adults for homosexual conduct while temporarily unsettled the constitutional status of gay marriage.

Apparent constitutional silences and ambiguities raise hard constitutional questions that many scholars believe cannot be resolved by conventional forms of constitutional interpretation. Keith Whittington maintains that constitutional disputes not contemplated or resolved by the framers have no determinate answers:

> Traditional tools of interpretive analysis can be exhausted without providing a constitutional meaning that is sufficiently clear to guide government action. The text may specify a principle that is itself identifiable but is nonetheless indeterminate in its application to a particular situation. Either the principle itself may break down in a specific context or the facts at issue may be deeply controversial. Alternatively, the principle established by the text may be unclear: the text may contain contradictory requirements with little or no indication of how to weigh the particular values at stake or how much force to give to particular, atypical requirements; there may not be sufficient information for an interpreter to arbitrate among contested meanings; or the text may be simply silent on issues that are nonetheless substantively constitutional.[19]

Whittington and others maintain that arguments about constitutional meanings when the text is indeterminate are better characterized as constructions than as interpretations. "Something external to the text—whether political principle, social interest, or partisan consideration," Whittington states, "must be alloyed with it in order for the text to have a determinate and controlling meaning within a given governing context."[20]

Other constitutional analysts challenge the interpretation–construction divide. Dworkin insists that hard constitutional questions are in principle resolved by the same interpretive strategies as easy constitutional questions. In his opinion, disagreements over the best constitutional answer should not be confused with claims that no right constitutional answer exists.[21] "Controversial constitutional issues," Dworkin says, "call for interpretation, not amendment. Courts and legislatures, officials and citizens confront these issues under the regulative assumption that ordinary one interpretation–one view of free speech or equal protection or due process actually requires–provides a better justification of standing constitutional practice than any other: that is one interpretation is a better answer … of law."[22]

Dworkin and others agree that interpreters must often have recourse to political principle when resolving hard cases, but they insist that the relevant political principles are internal to the constitutional text and not something brought in from the outside. Theories of free speech, in this view, are not external to the Constitution but are crucial for interpreting the First Amendment.

Both the interpretation–construction distinction and the no-right-answer thesis may be too sophisticated for their own good. If, as many literary theorists believe, no text is fully self-contained, then readers always bring something external to the process of determining the meaning of any text, including constitutional texts. This suggests that all forms of constitutional exegesis are construction, not interpretation. Knowing that a question has a right answer may not help one identify that answer. The question, "Do you have specific ancestors who lived three thousand years ago?" has a right answer, but most of us have no means for determining who those ancestors were and where they lived. As important, both the interpretation–construction distinction and the no-right-answer thesis risk making important constitutional questions turn on controversies in literary theory (what constitutes interpretation?) and ontology (do objective right answers exist?). Constitutional theory must often borrow and borrow heavily from these and other disciplines. Nevertheless, we should rely on a definition of interpretation that suits the purposes of the constitutional enterprise and not one designed to facilitate reading Proust or religious scripture.

2. Constitutional Arguments

The constitutional text plainly resolves some matters while leaving others open for debate and investigation. The young college football player who most recently won the Heisman Trophy is not constitutionally eligible to be president of the United States, even though some twenty-somethings are almost certainly as capable of wielding executive power as the leading candidates for the presidency. The president, Article II plainly states, must be at least thirty-five years old. The constitutional status of federal laws imposing capital punishment cannot be discerned as easily. The Eighth Amendment forbids "cruel and unusual punishments" without elaborating what specific punishments are cruel and unusual or listing any elements of a cruel and unusual punishment. Constitutional decision-makers use various approaches when determining the meaning of less clear constitutional provisions.[23]

Constitutional arguments differ from policy, moral, or other forms of political argument by focusing on the proper interpretation of a distinctive

constitutional text, a distinctive constitutional history, and distinctive constitutional values. Constitutional arguments are about the meaning of particular constitutional provisions, not about the best all-things-considered policy.
Clear constitutional language, such as Article I's mandate that senators serve
six-year terms, cannot be overcome by demonstrating that better policy would
be made by representatives who served for longer periods. Americans determine whether law-abiding persons have a right to carry concealed weapons by
analyzing the language of the Second Amendment. They may contemplate the
rights of man or compare murder rates in jurisdictions with different handgun
policies only to the extent such analysis provides insight into the meaning of
"the right to bear arms." When constitutional language is not clear, Americans
are limited to considering policies that are consistent with the particular meaning of constitutional provisions when they were ratified, the particular history
of those constitutional provisions, or the particular values embodied by those
constitutional provisions. Those who would outlaw revolvers must demonstrate that the Second Amendment was originally understood as permitting
that ban, that the Second Amendment has been interpreted throughout history
as permitting that ban, or that the best principle that justifies the right to bear
arms permits that ban. Constitutional claims that are consistent with original
meanings, historical practice, and constitutional values are stronger than claims
that are inconsistent with one of these three sources for determining the meaning of constitutional provisions.

The methods for determining constitutional meanings are not as distinct in
practice as they might appear in the following classification scheme. The border
between textualism and originalism is thin, as in the line between some structural and aspirational arguments. Constitutional decisions made during the
first George Washington administration might be treated as evidence of original meaning or as an early precedent. Governing officials and citizens further
muddy textbook classifications by relying on multiple methods when making
claims about the meaning of constitutional provisions. Justice Felix Frankfurter
made at least five distinctive kinds of constitutional arguments in one sentence
when asserting that the Fourteenth Amendment did not require state courts to
respect Fifth Amendment rights:

> Those reading the English language with the meaning which it ordinar-
> ily conveys, those conversant with the political and legal history of the
> concept of due process, those sensitive to the relations of the States to
> the central government as well as the relation of some of the provisions
> of the Bill of Rights to the process of justice, would hardly recognize the
> Fourteenth Amendment as a cover for the various explicit provisions of
> the first eight Amendments.[24]

The passage interprets a constitutional provision by examining the plain meaning of the constitutional text (textualism), the meaning of due process when the Fourteenth Amendment was ratified (originalism), the subsequent history of due process (doctrinalism), the significance of federalism (structuralism), and the constitutional commitment to justice (aspirationalism). Not satisfied with a five-spot, Frankfurter concluded the previous quote with a prudential argument about the consequences of "uproot[ing] ... established methods for prosecuting crime."[25]

The following methods for interpreting or constructing the Constitution are described as *legitimate* only in the broadest sense. Most constitutional decision-makers use all these forms of argument at some point during their career. Most professors acknowledge that students employing one of these logics are making constitutional arguments, although this is only a generalization and not a guarantee. Constitutional commentators who reject aspirationalism as a proper means of constitutional interpretation recognize that aspirationalists are nevertheless doing constitutional analysis in ways that those who determine constitutional meaning by consulting the Oracle at Delphi are not. Significant disagreements exist, however, on both the proper use of these methods and the weight each should be given. Different versions of originalism, textualism, and aspirationalism exist. Many prominent commentators maintain that persons determining what constitutional provisions mean should rely primarily on text, history, and perhaps precedent. Structural, prudential, and aspirational arguments, in this view, should be used only as tiebreakers when more basic methods are clearly inconclusive. Other prominent constitutionalists employ structural, prudential, and aspirational arguments whenever any ambiguity exists in the constitutional text, history, or precedent.

Constitutional interpretation channels moral and policy considerations rather than eliminating them entirely. All approaches to determining constitutional meaning regard value judgments as legally appropriate to some degree and in some instances but as not legally appropriate to a greater degree or in other instances. Many originalists permit elected officials, but not judges, to determine the meaning of constitutional provisions in light of contested moral and political theories. Prominent aspirationalists maintain that persons interpreting the meaning of such phrases as *equal protection* are constitutionally obligated to make value judgments. An official who ruled that bans on gay marriage violate the Fourteenth Amendment without contemplating what practices best promote equality, in this view, illegally ignores the constitutional aspiration to become a more egalitarian society.

The different uses constitutional interpreters make of value and policy judgments confound *value-neutral* efforts to make sharp distinctions between value or policy voting and constitutional decision-making solely on the basis of law.

Constitutional decision-makers and commentators vigorously dispute when the law permits or requires constitutional interpreters to consider moral philosophy or policy outcomes. When Justice Ruth Bader Ginsburg in *National Federation of Independent Business v. Sebelius* (2012) claimed that states could not by themselves solve the problems created by persons without health insurance, she thought she was simultaneously making a policy argument (federal regulation of health care is best) and a constitutional argument (the commerce clause permits the federal government to regulate whenever state regulation is likely to be ineffective). The justices who disagreed saw only a policy argument because, on their interpretation of the commerce clause, federal power over interstate commerce did not extend to all matters on which state regulation might be ineffective. This example and many others highlight how common claims in both the law reviews and the political science literature, which state that governing officials have made decisions solely on the basis of policy to the complete exclusion of constitutional law, always rest on contested theories of constitutional interpretation.[26] We can say that Justice Ginsburg in *Sebelius* voted solely on the basis of her policy preferences only if we make the non-value-neutral claim that the commerce clause, best interpreted, does not permit the federal government to regulate whenever state regulation is likely to be ineffective. Similarly, justices who make moral arguments about equality in opinions declaring a right to same-sex marriage can be said to vote solely on the basis of value judgments only if the Fourteenth Amendment does not permit constitutional decision-makers from considering general theories of equality or human dignity when resolving constitutional controversies.

2.1 Textualism

Textualist arguments emphasize the specific language of the Constitution, the relationships between the terms used, and the common meaning of those terms. Textualists claim that persons considering whether Congress has the right to prohibit child labor or whether New York may restrict pornography should rely on the *plain meaning* of the relevant constitutional words and clauses. Justice Joseph Story called on interpreters to look only at "what is written" and not to "scattered documents" and "probable guesses" about what those who adopted the text meant. "It is obvious," he wrote, "that there can be no security to the people in any constitution of government, if they are not to judge of it by the fair meaning of the words of the text."[27] Some textualists place constitutional language within the specific context of the drafting period, sometimes employing eighteenth-century dictionaries.[28] Other textualists focus on the language without regard to any particular historical context, making ready use of modern sources. A leading contemporary textualist "believes it is inappropriate for judges to strike down statutes on the basis of anything other than a principle fairly inferable from the constitutional text (although such principle need not have been present in the conscious minds of the framers)."[29]

Professor Akhil Amar of Yale Law School champions what he describes as *intratextualism*. Persons determining constitutional meanings, he believes, should "read a contested word or phrase that appears in the Constitution in light of another passage in the Constitution featuring the same (or a very similar) word or phrase."[30] *Necessary* in the necessary and proper clause should be presumed to have the same meaning as *needful* in Article IV, Section 1's decree that "Congress shall have Power to dispose of and make all needful Rules and Regulations respecting the Territory or other Property belonging to the United States." Amar determines the meaning of the right of citizens to vote in the Twenty-Fourth Amendment by examining the meaning of the right of citizens to vote in the Fifteenth Amendment. If the Fifteenth Amendment was understood as entailing a right to vote on juries as well as for political candidates, then the same language in the Twenty-Fourth Amendment should be given the same meaning.[31]

The most famous textual argument in American constitutional history is Justice Hugo Black's claim that the First Amendment prohibited all speech regulations, no matter how dangerous the speech, because the text states that "Congress shall make no law... abridging the freedom of speech." In a public interview, he declared:

> The beginning of the First Amendment is that "congress shall make no law." I understand that it is rather old-fashioned and shows a slight naiveté to say that "no law" means no law.... But what it *says* is "Congress shall make no law respecting an establishment of religion."...
>
> .... Then I move on to the words "abridging the freedom of speech or of the press." It *says* Congress shall make no law doing that.... When I get down to the really basic reason why I believe that "no law" means no law, I presume it could come to this, that I took an obligation to support and defend the Constitution as I understand it. And being a rather backward country fellow, I understand it to mean what the words say.[32]

Justice Black did not do extensive historical research on free speech practices in 1791 or on the general principle the framers might have constitutionalized. That the text said *no law* was good enough for him.

Textualism is the master principle of American constitutional interpretation. When the text (and context) is clear, commentators do not employ other methods for determining the meaning of constitutional provisions. The Seventh

Amendment gives parties to common law suits in federal court a right to a trial when "the value in controversy shall exceed twenty dollars," not when the value in controversy is at least the equivalent of what twenty dollars would buy in 1791. Birth by Cesarean section does not disqualify anyone from the presidency. The context plainly demonstrates that the reference to "a natural born Citizen" in Article II is to persons born in the United States.

Constitutional arguments rooted in constitutional language have limits. The plain meaning of the First Amendment did not enable Justice Black to avoid making what appear to be subjective judgments. In *Cohen v. California* (1971), the majority of justices on the Supreme Court ruled that the First Amendment protected a person who wore a jacket with the words "FUCK THE DRAFT" emblazoned on the back. Justice John Harlan's opinion maintained, "It is...often true that one man's vulgarity is another's lyric."[33] Justice Black joined Justice Harry Blackmun's dissent, which asserted that "Cohen's absurd and immature antic...was mainly conduct and little speech."[34] While the justices almost certainly agreed on the meaning of *no law*, textualism did not resolve debates over what constituted *speech*.

2.2 Originalism

Originalist arguments maintain that constitutional provisions mean what they meant when they were ratified. Whether the Constitution permits states to regulate abortion or to adopt affirmative action programs depends on how ordinary persons in 1868 understood the phrases *due process of law* or *equal protection*. "On every question of construction, carry ourselves back to the time when the Constitution was adopted," Thomas Jefferson advised Supreme Court Justice William Johnson, "recollect the spirit manifested in the debates and, instead of trying what meaning may be squeezed out of the text or invented against it, conform to the probable one in which it was passed."[35] There is a long tradition of originalist argumentation in American constitutionalism, but originalism as a method of constitutional interpretation became increasingly visible and controversial during the Reagan Era. Building on the example of some earlier judges and scholars, President Ronald Reagan and his attorney general, Edwin Meese, made originalist arguments a centerpiece of their conservative constitutional philosophy. Judge Robert Bork, Justice Antonin Scalia, and Justice Clarence Thomas have been prominent proponents of originalism. Justice Thomas is particularly distinctive in the emphasis he places on originalist arguments and in his willingness to overrule many crucial precedents underlying the New Deal constitutional order in light of his historical research. While commonly associated with constitutional conservatism, originalist arguments have recently become of interest to scholars across the political spectrum.

Proponents of originalism sometimes refer to the original "intentions" underlying constitutional provisions, but most emphasize original "meanings." As Professor Randy Barnett describes original meaning, "each word must be interpreted the way a normal speaker of English would have read it when it was enacted."[36] What matters is the public meaning of the constitutional text at the time the provision was ratified, not private understandings between particular framers, specific goals or expectations at the time the text was ratified, or what that constitutional language might mean at the present. That most framers thought Washington would become the first president of the United States had no constitutional significance in the absence of a provision declaring this to be so. The framing expectation that presidential electors would exercise independent judgment has no constitutional significance because that prediction was not incorporated into the constitutional text.

Originalists dispute how to interpret such relatively abstract clauses as "Congress shall make no law...abridging the freedom of speech." Some look primarily to practices at the time the First and Fourteenth Amendments were ratified. Justice Thomas is a leading proponent of this view. When considering whether a high school student could be disciplined for advocating drug use during a school event, he wrote:

> The history of public education suggests that the First Amendment, as originally understood, does not protect student speech in public schools. Although colonial schools were exclusively private, public education proliferated in the early 1800s. By the time the States ratified the Fourteenth Amendment, public schools had become relatively common.... If students in public schools were originally understood as having free-speech rights, one would have expected 19th-century public schools to have respected those rights and courts to have enforced them. They did not.[37]

Others believe that relatively abstract clauses demonstrate a constitutional commitment to a particular value but not to any specific application of that value. Professor Jack Balkin of Yale Law School is a leading advocate of this approach:

> I reject the assumption that fidelity to the text means fidelity to original expected application. I maintain instead that constitutional interpretation requires fidelity to the original meaning of the Constitution and to the principles that underlie the text. The task of interpretation is to look to original meaning and underlying principle and decide how best to apply them in current circumstances.[38]

Constitutional meaning is determined by the framing commitment to the free-dom of speech, not to the legal protections for free speech in place when the First Amendment was ratified. Balkin believes that maintaining fidelity to origi-nal principles, but not original applications, promotes "a basic law whose reach and application evolve over time, a basic law that leaves to each generation the task of how to make sense of the Constitution's words and principles."[39] His crit-ics charge that, by defining framing principles at too abstract a level, proponents of this originalism substitute modern values for those of the framers. In their view, an originalism focused on what people thought constitutional provisions entailed when they were ratified better preserves the stability of constitutional meanings and the rule of law.[40] What the framers meant by equal protection of the law, more traditional originalists contend, were the practices then thought to guarantee equality, not a commitment to some generalized notion of equality that might justify or condemn almost any official policy.[41]

2.3 Doctrinalism

Doctrinal arguments resolve contemporary constitutional controversies by interpreting past precedents. Rather than emphasize constitutional language or practices at the time of ratification, doctrinal arguments focus on what govern-ment officials have said about the Constitution over time. Persons employing doctrinal argument rely on analogies to previous constitutional decisions. They claim that the principle underlying a past decision, known as the holding of the case, provides the standard for interpreting the Constitution in future cases. If constitutional decision-makers have declared that the Constitution protects the right to burn the flag of the United States, then the same principle should com-pel constitutional decision-makers to declare that the Constitution protects the right to burn a map of the United States or the state flag of Texas.

This emphasis on interpreting precedent and extending principles articulated in one case to analogous cases is characteristic of the common law method of reasoning that Americans inherited from England. Such early twentieth-century jurists as Justice Oliver Wendell Holmes emphasized how precedential reason-ing allowed the law to develop and grow over time as judges applied, extended, and adjusted legal principles when new cases arose. In his view, "when we are dealing with words that also are a constituent act, like the Constitution of the United States, we must realize that they have called into life a being the develop-ment of which could not have been foreseen completely by the most gifted of its begetters."[42] Constitutional precedents may be established by judges, presidents, or legislators. Most judicial decisions concentrate on elaborating previous judi-cial precedents, but constitutional decision-makers on and off the bench also cite previous legislative and executive actions when justifying their rulings. The justices in *Youngstown Sheet & Tube Company v. Sawyer* (1952) disputed whether past executive practice was consistent with President Harry Truman's decision to seize steel plants without congressional authorization.[43] When vetoing legislation rechartering the national bank, President Andrew Jackson stated that previous federal and state legislative decisions supported his conclusion that Congress had no constitutional authority to pass that bill.[44]

Persons making doctrinal arguments frequently dispute the proper application of a past precedent. The meaning of *Brown v. Board of Education* (1954) is particularly controversial. Justices who oppose efforts to use race when integrating public schools not previously segregated by law cite *Brown* as holding that the Constitution is "color-blind" and racial classifications are constitutionally odious. "When it comes to using race to assign children to schools," Chief Justice Roberts wrote in *Parents Involved in Community Schools v. Seattle School Dist. No. 1* (2007):

> History will be heard. In *Brown v. Board of Education . . .*, we held that segregation deprived black children of equal educational opportunities regardless of whether school facilities and other tangible factors were equal, because government classification and separation on grounds of race themselves denoted inferiority. . . . It was not the inequality of the facilities but the fact of legally separating children on the basis of race on which the Court relied to find a constitutional violation in 1954.[45]

Justice Thomas went further. "Disfavoring a color-blind interpretation of the Constitution," he declared, proponents of race-conscious school admissions policies "would give school boards a free hand to make decisions on the basis of race—an approach reminiscent of that advocated by the segregationists in *Brown v. Board of Education*."[46] The dissenting justices in *Parents Involved* insisted that *Brown* sanctioned race-conscious policies whenever doing so promoted integration or reduced the historic subordination of persons of color in the United States. Justice Breyer stated:

> These cases consider the longstanding efforts of two local school boards to integrate their public schools. The school board plans before us resemble many others adopted in the last 50 years by primary and secondary schools throughout the Nation. All of those plans represent local efforts to bring about the kind of racially integrated education that *Brown v. Board of Education . . .* long ago promised—efforts that this Court has repeatedly required, permitted, and encouraged local authorities to undertake.[47]

Justice John Paul Stevens relied on the antisubordination interpretation of *Brown* when asserting that "there is a cruel irony in the Chief Justice's reliance on our decision in *Brown v. Board of Education,*" given that "only black schoolchildren" were prohibited from attending the schools of their choice. "The history books," he pointed out, "do not tell stories of white children struggling to attend black schools."[48]

Precedents do not have the same binding force as constitutional text. Constitutional decision-makers may not disregard constitutional provisions they believe stupid or venal. They may overrule precedents they believe clearly erroneous. Supreme Court justices repeatedly declare:

> Stare decisis is not an inexorable command; rather, it "is a principle of policy and not a mechanical formula of adherence to the latest decision"...This is particularly true in constitutional cases, because in such cases "correction through legislative action is practically impossible."[49]

Justices overrule past cases when persuaded that a particular precedent wrongly interpreted the Constitution. The justices in *Lawrence v. Texas* (2003) overruled *Bowers v. Hardwick* (1986). Justice Anthony Kennedy's majority opinion held that the former decision sustaining a state ban on sodomy was constitutionally wrong when handed down and had been undermined by subsequent judicial and legislative precedents. In theory, the constitutional error must be significant for a case to be overruled. Whether that describes actual practice is contested.

Justices more often "distinguish" a dubious precedent from the case at hand. They claim that the previous decision and the present case are not analogous. The past case remains good law, at least in theory, but is determined not to cover the matter before the court. Consider Justice Samuel Alito's opinion distinguishing *Hein v. Freedom from Religion Foundation, Inc.* (2007) from *Flast v. Cohen* (1968). Alito stated that in *Flast* the justices granted standing to a taxpayer who claimed the right to challenge congressional legislation providing benefits to religious organizations. The principled basis for that decision, Alito maintained, did not justify a similar decision in *Hein,* when a taxpayer claimed the right to challenge an *executive* order providing benefits to religious organizations. *Flast* remained the law of the land when Congress provided benefits to religious organizations. That precedent was nevertheless limited to cases involving legislation.

What precedents stand for and whether they can be distinguished persuasively is controversial. Justice Scalia found Justice Alito's distinctions unconvincing. "Either *Flast*...should be applied to... *all* challenges to the governmental expenditure of general tax revenues in a manner alleged to violate a constitutional provision specifically limiting the taxing and spending power," his concurrence insisted, "or *Flast* should be repudiated."[50] *Hein* may be an example of the common tendency for justices to distinguish precedents they believe are wrongly decided. Some prochoice advocates fear the Roberts Court will render *Roe v. Wade* meaningless by consistently sustaining all regulations on abortion rights without actually overruling the decision.

2.4 Structuralism

Structural arguments deduce constitutional powers and limitations from the general arrangements of the constitutional order and the relationships between governing institutions. *Separation of powers, federalism,* and *democracy* are core American constitutional commitments, even though none are stated explicitly in the constitutional text. Structuralists ascertain the implications of such constitutional language as "the powers not delegated to the United States by the Constitution, nor prohibited by it to the States, are reserved to the States respectively, or to the people" in light of these values. Charles Black, the scholar most responsible for developing structural arguments, maintained that this method for determining constitutional meanings provides an "inference from the structures and relationships created by the constitution in all its parts or in some principal part," rather than an "exegesis of [a] particular textual passage."[51] Some structural arguments are historical. The Rehnquist Court majority in *Alden v. Maine* (1999) concluded that a background principle of state sovereign immunity from lawsuits was built into the federal system. Other structural arguments are more pragmatic. From the premise "the power to tax involves the power to destroy," Chief Justice John Marshall deduced that national governmental entities must be free from the state taxing power to preserve federal authority.[52]

Quite frequently, all parties to a constitutional controversy appeal to the separation of powers, federalism, or other consensual structural commitments of American constitutionalism. Consider common debates over the nature and scope of executive privilege. The George W. Bush administration, when claiming a right to keep executive branch deliberations secret, asserted that the separation of powers entails a constitutional commitment to a unified executive branch that operated free from intrusive legislative fishing expeditions.[53] Critics of executive secrecy insisted that the constitutional commitment to checks and balances requires that Congress be given access to such materials to ensure that legislative programs are properly implemented.[54]

Federalism provides fertile grounds for structural arguments. Justice Scalia's majority opinion in *Printz v. United States* (1997), which declared unconstitutional a federal law requiring local officials to implement federal gun control regulations, provides a good example of this interpretive strategy.

After acknowledging that "there is no constitutional text speaking to this precise question," Scalia "turn[ed]...to consideration of the structure of the Constitution." In his view, the Constitution "contemplates that a State's government will represent and remain accountable to its own citizens." Scalia then observed that elected officials remain practically accountable to local citizens only when they are not called on to enforce both federal and state law. The campus police at state universities may not have the time to enforce local parking restrictions if they are overwhelmed by federal mandates requiring them to repeatedly test all students for drugs. Preventing the federal government from "impress[ing] into its service—at no cost to itself"—the police officers to whom local citizens have assigned other tasks, the *Printz* opinion concluded, was essential to maintaining a "healthy balance of power between the States and the Federal Government." Persons opposed to judicial protections for federalism make a different structural argument. They claim that judicial supervision of the federal–state relationship is unnecessary and inefficient. The national political process is organized in ways they believe provide adequate securities for local concerns.[55] Justice Blackmun, when calling on his brethren to abandon rigorous scrutiny of laws that allegedly limited state sovereignty, declared:

> The principal means chosen by the Framers to ensure the role of the States in the federal system lies in the structure of the Federal Government itself. It is no novelty to observe that the composition of the Federal Government was designed in large part to protect the States from overreaching by Congress. The Framers thus gave the States a role in the selection both of the Executive and the Legislative Branches of the Federal Government. The States were vested with indirect influence over the House of Representatives and the Presidency by their control of electoral qualifications and their role in Presidential elections.... They were given more direct influence in the Senate, where each State received equal representation and each Senator was to be selected by the legislature of his State.[56]

Proponents of judicial solicitude for federalism reject this sanguine depiction of federal power. Justice Lewis Powell asserted that the "variety of structural and political changes occurring in this century," most notably the nationalization of elections for all members of the national legislature, "ha[s] combined to make Congress particularly insensitive to state and local values."[57] The important point, for present purposes, is that all parties to the debate look to the structure of the national government and constitutional institutions when determining whether federalism should be a matter of constitutional law made by the judiciary or political expedience determined by Congress.

2.5 Prudentialism

Prudential arguments determine constitutional meanings by examining the costs and benefits of different policies. Justice Robert Jackson's famous aphorism in *Terminiello v. City of Chicago* (1949) emphasized the harmful consequences of interpreting the First Amendment as protecting speakers who direct abusive language at their audience. "If the Court does not temper its doctrinaire logic with a little practical wisdom," his dissent warned, "it will convert the constitutional Bill of Rights into a suicide pact."[58] Justice Powell advanced a different prudential argument in *McCleskey v. Kemp* (1987). His majority opinion sustained the procedures Georgia used to impose capital punishment, even though statistics demonstrated that racial bias had skewed the sentencing process. Powell acknowledged the probability that race influenced some decisions to execute persons convicted of murder. Nevertheless, he was concerned that judicial decisions striking down state practices on the basis of statistics demonstrating generalized racism would ultimately prevent states from implementing the criminal law. Powell's majority opinion declared:

> McCleskey's claim, taken to its logical conclusion, throws into serious question the principles that underlie our entire criminal justice system. The Eighth Amendment is not limited in application to capital punishment, but applies to all penalties.... Thus, if we accepted McCleskey's claim that racial bias has impermissibly tainted the capital sentencing decision, we could soon be faced with similar claims as to other types of penalty. Moreover, the claim that his sentence rests on the irrelevant factor of race easily could be extended to apply to claims based on unexplained discrepancies that correlate to membership in other minority groups, and even to gender. Similarly, since McCleskey's claim relates to the race of his victim, other claims could apply with equally logical force to statistical disparities that correlate with the race or sex of other actors in the criminal justice system, such as defense attorneys or judges.[59]

Just as the Lord Chancellor in Gilbert and Sullivan's *Iolanthe* would not interpret the fairy law in ways he believed would legally compel executing every fairy, so Justice Powell would not interpret the equal protection clause in ways he believed would require declaring almost all criminal sentences unconstitutional. "I can't slaughter the entire company" is a rule of interpretation in both comic opera and constitutionalism.

Appeals to dire consequences are common when important constitutional issues are debated. Justice Blackmun predicted that if the Supreme Court over-ruled *Roe v. Wade* and permitted states to ban abortion:

> Every year hundreds of thousands of women, in desperation, would defy the law, and place their health and safety in the unclean and unsympathetic hands of back-alley abortionists, or they would attempt to perform abortions upon themselves, with disastrous results. Every year, many women, especially poor and minority women, would die or suffer debilitating physical trauma, all in the name of enforced morality or religious dictates or lack of compassion, as it may be.[60]

Justice Scalia predicted that a judicial decision granting habeas corpus to alleged terrorists detained at Guantanamo Bay would "almost certainly cause more Americans to be killed."[61] Whether these claims are rhetorical flourishes or seri-ous aids to ascertaining constitutional meanings is sometimes difficult to discern. They are perhaps best interpreted as adding weight to conclusions reached by other methods of interpreting the constitution. Scalia, for example, treated the potentially disastrous consequences of the court's decision in *Boumediene v. Bush* (2008) as another justification for not "abandon[ing]" what he claimed were "set-tled precedents" entitling the president to detain prisoners of war indefinitely.[62]

Justices often employ prudential arguments when determining whether litigants have a constitutional right to have federal courts adjudicate their legal claims. Article III declares that "the judicial power shall extend to... Cases" and "Controversies." Professor Alexander Bickel, a leading proponent of constitu-tional prudentialism, urged justices to interpret these words narrowly to avoid resolving hot-button constitutional issues that might damage judicial prestige.[63] The Supreme Court in *Commonwealth of Massachusetts v. Mellon* (1923) antici-pated Bickel's advice when ruling that federal courts could not ordinarily hear cases brought by taxpayers complaining about unconstitutional government expenditures. The "attendant inconveniences," which included a flood of litiga-tion after every citizen who paid taxes was permitted to challenge any govern-ment action that might be thought unconstitutional, Justice George Sutherland believed, provided grounds for interpreting constitutional provisions on stand-ing to sue in federal court as requiring potential litigants to demonstrate they suffered a particularized injury as a result of the unlawful action.[64]

Constitutional decision-makers often act prudently even when they do not use prudential arguments for discerning the meaning of constitutional provi-sions. Justice Jackson in *Korematsu v. United States* (1944) urged his brethren not to decide whether the executive decision detaining Japanese Americans during World War Two was constitutional. "If we cannot confine military expedients by the Constitution," he wrote, "neither would I distort the Constitution to approve all that the military may deem expedient."[65] Jackson sought to avoid a constitutional decision that might later sanction what he thought were racist policies. Prudence, in his view, counseled against making any effort to determine the constitutional meaning of *equal protection*, less the justices establish a precedent that would have damaging repercussions in peacetime. The judicial decision in *Brown v. Board of Education II* (1955) to forgo immediate desegregation may be another instance of prudential decision-making in the face of probable popular resistance.

2.6 Aspirationalism

Aspirational arguments are based on the particular conception of justice underlying the Constitution. Such efforts to determine what *equal protection* or *due process* mean first discern the general principles and values that best explain and justify the constitutional order. Constitutional provisions are then interpreted and applied in light of these broader constitutional commitments. Justice Kennedy's opinion in *Lawrence v. Texas* is a good example of aspirationalism. Kennedy began with a statement of what he believed were fundamental constitutional principles: "Liberty protects the person from unwarranted government intrusions into a dwelling or other private places. In our tradition the State is not omnipresent in the home. And there are other spheres of our lives and existence, outside the home, where the State should not be a dominant presence."[66] From these principles, he deduced that government could not constitutionally prohibit consenting adults from engaging in homosexual activities.

Constitutional decision-makers of all persuasions make aspirational arguments. Justice William Brennan, the leading legal liberal on the Supreme Court from the Dwight Eisenhower to the George H. W. Bush administrations, was a vocal advocate of this method for determining constitutional meanings. His Constitution was "a sublime oration on the dignity of man, a bold commitment by the people to the ideal of libertarian dignity protected through law."[67] Relying on these constitutional aspirations, Brennan determined that executions were cruel and unusual punishments and that bans on abortion were inconsistent with due process. Justice Thomas, a far more conservative justice, invokes constitutional commitments to different principles when condemning racial classifications as inconsistent with "the principle of equality embodied in the Declaration of Independence and the Equal Protection Clause." He interprets the Fourteenth Amendment in light of Justice John Harlan's famous assertion that "our Constitution is color-blind, and neither knows nor tolerates classes among citizens."[68]

Professor Dworkin is the leading academic proponent of aspirationalism. His writings insist that constitutional decision-makers must make the constitution "the best it can be."[69] They do so by determining what moral principles best justify and explain American constitutional practices. The fit between constitutional norms and historical practices need not be perfect, just sufficient to connect the norm to important strands of American constitutional practice. "No theory can count as an adequate justification of institutional history unless it provides a good fit with that history," Dworkin declares, "but if two or more theories each provide an adequate fit, on that test, then the theory among these that is morally the strongest provides the best justification, even though it exposes more decisions as mistakes than another."[70] Contemporary Americans may constitutionally reject racial segregation and *Plessy v. Ferguson* (1896) in the name of racial equality and *Brown v. Board of Education*. They cannot constitutionally abandon federalism as hopelessly inefficient or religious freedom as sacrilegious in light of powerful historic commitments to both values.

Some critics insist that aspirationalism is always an illegitimate method for interpreting the Constitution. They claim that constitutional provisions protect specific manifestations of more general values, not the general values themselves. Free speech may be a necessary condition for autonomous human life. Nevertheless, the First Amendment protects only free speech, not whatever liberties might be entailed by the *ideal of libertarian dignity*. "I like my privacy as well as the next one," Justice Black declared when dissenting from a Supreme Court ruling granting married people the right to use birth control, "but I am nevertheless compelled to admit that government has a right to invade it unless prohibited by some specific constitutional provision."[71]

Other critics complain about the actual balance between morality and fit in too many aspirational arguments. Justice Scalia acknowledges that moral principles inevitably and appropriately influence how constitutional provisions are interpreted. It may not be "a bad characteristic for a[n] [originalist] constitutional theory," he states, that "the inevitable tendency of justices to think the law is what they would like it to be will...cause most errors in judicial historiography to be made in the direction of projecting upon the age of 1789 current, modern values."[72] Still, constitutional decision-makers who emphasize the original meaning of the constitutional text appropriately cabin value voting to the relatively rare instances when more basic sources of constitutional meaning do not provide clear guidance. Scalia contends that aspirationalism unduly licenses decisions based on personal preferences. He observes, "It is very difficult for a person to discern a difference between those political values that he personally thinks most important, and those political values that are 'fundamental to our society.'"[73] Noting that Dworkin consistently reaches politically liberal conclusions when making constitutional arguments, Professor Rogers Smith similarly concludes that aspirational arguments in practice make the interpreter's "view of a decision's overall political and moral rightness and goodness far more definitive of constitutionality than fit is."[74]

3. Constitutional Interpretation and Constitutional Purposes

The methods for interpreting constitutional provisions are means for realizing the constitutional purposes detailed in Chapter 3. When employed correctly, these forms of constitutional argument will guarantee legal stability, inhibit undue straying from past commitments, constructively channel future change, facilitate the public interest, and prevent disastrous political choices. Constitutional decision-makers choose their preferred forms of constitutional argument on the basis of the various weights they give to such constitutional purposes as promoting the rule of law, making credible commitments, preventing self-dealing, facilitating policy in the public interest, insuring against risky futures, realizing national aspirations, and maintaining the social peace between different social groups. Textualism and doctrinalism facilitate legal stability. Originalism as practiced by Justice Thomas corrects deviations from inherited practices. Aspirationalism as practiced by Justice Brennan constructively channels political change. Structuralism fosters deliberation on the public interest. Prudentialism avoids disastrous policies.

How well a particular constitutional logic promotes a particular constitutional end is often controversial. Consider the debates between formalists and functionalists over the separation of powers. Formalists believe a strict textualism will best facilitate government in the public interest. "We have not yet found a better way to preserve freedom than by making the exercise of power subject to the carefully crafted restraints spelled out in the Constitution,"[75] Chief Justice Warren Burger wrote when striking down federal laws that permitted the Congress to "veto" decisions made by executive branch officials and administrative agencies. Functionalists believe prudentialism is the wiser approach for resolving conflicts over the powers of national institutions. Justice Byron White would have the court sustain "legislative vetoes" as "an important if not indispensable political invention that allows the President and Congress to resolve major constitutional and policy differences, assures the accountability of independent regulatory agencies, and preserves Congress' control over lawmaking."[76]

Disputes over what methods of constitutional interpretation promote the most essential constitutional purposes frequently arise when constitutional decision-makers are considering how broadly to construe a constitutional text, precedent, or tradition. Justice Scalia insists that constitutional interpreters should narrowly construe constitutional norms. Justices, he claims, must "refer to the most specific level at which a relevant tradition protecting, or denying protection to, the asserted right can be identified." Doing so fosters legal stability, prevents self-dealing by judicial elites, and prevents tampering with valued inherited practices. Scalia insists:

Because such general traditions provide such imprecise guidance, they permit judges to dictate rather than discern the society's
views.... Although assuredly having the virtue (if it be that) of leaving
judges free to decide as they think best when the unanticipated occurs,
a rule of law that binds neither by text nor by any particular, identifiable
tradition is no rule of law at all.[77]

Justice Brennan sharply condemned this view, insisting on a far broader construction of American constitutional values. "In construing the Fourteenth
Amendment to offer shelter only to those interests specifically protected by historical practice," he charged, "Justice Scalia ignores the kind of society in which
our Constitution exists." Brennan continued:

The document that the plurality construes today is unfamiliar to me. It
is not the living charter that I have taken to be our Constitution; it is
instead a stagnant, archaic, hidebound document steeped in the prejudices and superstitions of a time long past. This Constitution does not
recognize that times change, does not see that sometimes a practice or
rule outlives its foundations. I cannot accept an interpretive method that
does such violence to the charter that I am bound by oath to uphold.[78]

This understanding of tradition constructively channels social change, prevents
self-dealing by bigoted majorities, and maintains credible commitments to
minority rights.

4. The Politics of Constitutional Argument

The extent to which constitutional arguments actually constrain constitutional
practice is the subject of much debate. Particular methods for determining
constitutional meanings or the methods as a whole may be so capacious as to
generate arguments for any policy position Americans might wish to defend.
Two prominent law professors declare, "The range of permissible constitutional
arguments now extends so far that a few workable ones are always available in
a pinch."[79] Structural arguments may be employed by persons who oppose any
judicial protection for federalism and by persons who think the Supreme Court
must vigilantly guard state sovereignty. During the 1850s, both the Southerners
who favored human bondage in American territories and their antislavery rivals
plausibly invoked text, history, practice, structure, prudence, and national aspirations when making constitutional arguments on behalf of their cherished policies.[80] Proponents and opponents of gay marriage at present make reasonable

use of almost every accepted method for determining the constitutional meaning of equal protection.

Even if legitimate methods of constitutional decision-making constrain in theory, political actors may not make good faith efforts to interpret the Constitution when doing so is inimical to their policy preferences. Prominent representatives of political movements might either rely on some illegitimate method of constitutional decision-making or misapply a legitimate method. Such accusations are commonly made. Conservatives charge liberal prochoice advocates with failing to respect the original meaning of constitutional provisions when manufacturing out of thin jurisprudential air a due process right to abortion. Liberals charge conservatives with grossly distorting precedent to hand George W. Bush the 2000 presidential election. The capacious quality of constitutional arguments combined with insincere constitutional decision-making threatens to wreak havoc on American constitutionalism. Officials acting in good or bad faith will be able to justify constitutionally whatever actions they wish to take if legitimate constitutional arguments may be made on behalf of almost any political position.

These problems are not as destructive to American constitutionalism as first appearances indicate. Policy preferences influence how Americans employ various methods for determining constitutional meanings and the conclusions they reach. Nevertheless, constitutionalism in the United States also generates a good deal of agreement on matters that would otherwise be controversial. Consider a trivial example, the issue of equal state representation in the Senate. As a constitutional matter, everyone agrees that both California and Wyoming are entitled to be represented by two senators. As a policy matter, we expect most Californians think this arrangement unfair. A distinctive constitutional text in this instance generates a consensus among persons who would disagree if they employed other forms of political argument. In other instances, constitutional decisions integrate law and policy. Consider again Justice Ginsburg's assertion in *Sebelius* that the commerce clause permitted Congress to pass the Affordable Care Act because states by themselves could not effectively solve the problems raised by persons without health insurance. Values mattered, but only because they could be translated into constitutional norms supported by constitutional text, history, and precedent. Ginsburg did not insist her favorite health care policy was constitutionally mandated because no constitutionally plausible arguments justified that constitutional conclusion.

4.1 Policy and Constitutional Decision-Making: The Attitudinal and Strategic Models

Many prominent political scientists think the evidence convincingly establishes that constitutional arguments do not constrain constitutional interpreters.

Decisions advertised as legal rulings are, in fact, based almost entirely on policy preferences. Harold Spaeth and Jeffrey Segal, the two leading proponents of the attitudinal model of judicial decision-making, maintain that Supreme Court justices exercise "virtually untrammeled policy-making authority" and "make decisions by considering the facts of the case in light of their ideological attitudes and values...."[81] "Most justices, in most cases," the leading work on the strategic model of judicial decision-making agrees, "pursue policy; that is, they want to move the substantive content of law as close as possible to their preferred position." Similar assertions litter the political science literature.[82]

Common observations and rigorous empirical studies routinely find that judicial disagreements are rooted in different policy commitments rather than in different conceptions of the legitimate methods for determining constitutional meaning. Justices who served in the Franklin D. Roosevelt administration before being appointed to the bench always sustained New Deal measures. Justices who had previously served in or advised the William McKinley, William Howard Taft, and Warren Harding administrations often wrote and joined opinions declaring New Deal measures unconstitutional. Judicial disagreements extend beyond particular issues. The justices routinely form durable ideological voting blocs that hold together across a range of issues and apparently different legal contexts. Whether the issue is federalism, religion, or the rights of criminal defendants, judicial divisions are consistently between the same bloc of liberals and the same bloc of conservatives. Contemporary liberals on the Supreme Court tend to support abortion rights but insist local governments can regulate property in the public interest. Contemporary conservatives tend to support property rights but insist that elected majorities are free to regulate abortion. No faction on the court is more committed to precedent than any other.[83] Each tends to cite historians whose conclusions are congenial to their preferred policy commitments when disputes arise over the original meaning of constitutional provisions. Justice Scalia in District of Columbia v. Heller (2008) confidently relied on historical research done by scholars who concluded that the Second Amendment protected an individual right to self-defense. Justice Stevens's dissent in that case as confidently relied on historical research done by scholars who concluded that Second Amendment rights were limited to participation in the state militia. No justice thought valuable historical research that was inconsistent with his or her general conservative or liberal predisposition.

Proponents of the attitudinal and strategic models of decision-making dispute how policy preferences influence judicial decisions. Attitudinalists maintain that Supreme Court justices engage in sincere voting. Justices, in their view, vote for the policy they think best. Justices who believe capital punishment is morally wrong always reverse death sentences. Justice William Rehnquist, during his years as the most conservative member of the Burger Court, earned the nickname the Lone Ranger for writing more solo dissenting opinions than any other member of that tribunal. Rehnquist voted and wrote as he thought best, making little effort to form alliances with the slightly less conservative justices on the court to form majorities. Scholars who champion the strategic model maintain that justices engage in sophisticated voting. Justices, in their view, champion the legal position closest to their ideal that will attain the support from other justices and governing officials necessary to maximize their policy commitments in practice. Strategic justices who believe capital punishment morally wrong will sustain a death sentence if they expect the public backlash from a contrary decision to set in motion a series of political events that might result in more persons being executed in the future. Justice Brennan exhibited this pattern on the Burger and Rehnquist Courts, consistently compromising on doctrine with more moderate justices to maintain some protection for what he believed were fundamental rights.

Professor Lawrence Baum of Ohio State University provides an intriguing variation on these themes. He maintains that Supreme Court behavior is often motivated by desires for popularity rather than concern for policy.[84] The crucial swing justices on the Rehnquist Court, some evidence suggests, took positions they hoped would impress the national media. This tendency has been labeled "the Greenhouse effect," after Linda Greenhouse, the long-time Supreme Court correspondent for the *New York Times*.[85] The crucial point is that when persons who claim "the death penalty is unconstitutional" are motivated by moral opposition to the death penalty or the desire to curry favor with a liberal professor, they are basing decisions on concerns external to the law rather than on their best understanding of legal rules.

The strategic and attitudinal models seek to explain judicial behavior, but no good reason exists for thinking that elected officials and interest groups are more often motivated by desires to make good law than are legal practitioners. If persons with legal training and expertise exhibit no tendency to be constrained by legitimate methods for determining constitutional meaning, then, barring evidence to the contrary, we may safely conclude that distinctively legal considerations probably do not constrain any prominent constitutional decision-maker.[86] Public opinion surveys and political practice support this intuition. Ideology explains public attitudes toward most judicial decisions. Political liberals believe *Roe v. Wade* correctly decided and abhor *Bush v. Gore*. Political conservatives support the result in *Bush v. Gore* and condemn *Roe v. Wade*.[87] Presidents almost always nominate members of their political party for positions on the federal judiciary. Ideology and partisanship explain most Senate votes during the confirmation process.[88] Constitutional rhetoric, inside and outside courts, seems little more than a mask for independent values and preferences.

We need not assume overt bad faith on the part of the justices, elected officials, and citizens who consistently reach the happy conclusion that constitutional commands coincide with their policy preferences. Human beings have
a marvelous capacity to rationalize their wants as rooted in eternal principles
of right and wrong. Segal and Spaeth note that "the ability to convince oneself
of the propriety of what one prefers to believe psychologically approximates
the human reflex."[89] Rabid sports fans persuade themselves that the home team
really deserves to win. Prominent members of political movements persuade
themselves that the death penalty or New Deal state really is unconstitutional.
The bottom line remains that, whatever the psychological processes by which
people determine constitutional meanings, "ideology...drives their conclusions."[90] Such, at least, is the credo of contemporary judicial behavioralism.

4.2 Law and Constitutional Decision-Making: The
Legal and Historical Institutionalist Perspective

Proponents of the legal model believe such factors as text, precedent, and history
have a strong and independent influence on constitutional decision-making.
Many judges and some law professors insist that judicial values and policy preferences play little or no role when such issues as abortion and federal power
to regulate health care are before courts. Judicial nominees, under oath, consistently tell the Senate that personal values will never influence their behavior
if confirmed to the Supreme Court. Chief Justice Roberts has analogized justices to umpires, who call balls and strikes without showing any partisan favor
to either team in the game. Repeated studies documenting powerful ideological
influence on Supreme Court voting, from this perspective, either demonstrate
how statistics can be deceiving or highlight one of those unexplained mysteries
of the universe.

Historical institutionalists offer a more nuanced perspective on the influence of law and policy on constitutional decision-making. Constitutional
decision-makers are neither automatons who leave all personal considerations
out of their rulings or single-minded policy entrepreneurs. Rather, most constitutional decisions are products of complex interactions among constitutional
texts, precedents, values, and policy preferences. In some instances, judges and
others try to make the best decision from a value or policy perspective that is permitted by legal texts, history, and precedents. In other instances, law influences
the policy preferences and values that motivate constitutional decision-makers.

Attitudinal, strategic, and legal factors often cannot be neatly isolated. The
judicial majority on the Chase Court (1864–1873) avoided making decisions that would directly challenge Civil War and Reconstruction policies by
taking advantage of precedents holding that courts should exercise appellate

jurisdiction only when Congress had explicitly granted appellate jurisdiction. *Ex parte McCardle* (1869), which held that Congress could repeal federal jurisdiction at any time before a judicial decision was announced was, thus, both strategic (the justices did not want to antagonize Congress) and legal (the justices had previously made a decision to deny jurisdiction in a similar circumstance in a case of no political consequence). As noted already, Dworkin and others believe that justices have a constitutional obligation to act on their best understanding of abstract principles. Thurgood Marshall's insistence that the death penalty was cruel and unusual punishment was simultaneously legal (the law required him to act on his best understanding of *cruel*) and attitudinal (he believed capital punishment was unjust).

Constitutional history provides one avenue by which law influences constitutional decision-making. Consider why contemporary liberals are more inclined to support a constitutional right to legal abortion than to basic necessities. As a matter of policy, most liberals support both. During the 1960s, more prominent liberals wrote law review articles defending a constitutional right to basic necessities than penned constitutional justifications of legal abortion. History took a different path. Such constitutional decisions as *Roe v. Wade* and *Planned Parenthood v. Casey* (1992) provide very strong precedential support for a constitutional right to legal abortion. By comparison, in a series of cases beginning with *Dandridge v. Williams* (1970), the Supreme Court consistently rejected constitutional welfare rights. These legal precedents help explain why most liberals in the early twenty-first century think legal abortion is both a constitutional right and a just policy, while many progressives treat access to basic necessities is an example of a very desirable policy that is not constitutionally mandated.

Institutional positions similarly influence constitutional decision-making. People with legal experience develop different values and preferences from persons who have legislative experience, spend large chunks of their lives as doctors in emergency rooms, or drive trucks. Lawyers, unsurprisingly, are more committed to the constitutional powers of federal courts than are legislators or members of the executive branch. Lawyers by socialization and experience also tend to be more concerned with the due process rights of criminal suspects than members of the public without legal experience. The unanimous judicial decision in *United States v. Jones* (2012), holding that police needed a warrant to attach a global positioning system (GPS) device to a private car, was simultaneously attitudinal (the justices were more sympathetic to the rights of the criminal suspect than members of the executive branch) and legal (legal socialization and experiences help explain why the justices were more sympathetic than police officers to the rights of the criminal suspect).

History provides numerous instances in which elected officials, justices, and prominent political actors who reasoned constitutionally reached different conclusions than they did when they relied on other normative or political logics. Abraham Lincoln believed that slavery was an atrocious evil but that the Constitution forbade federal interference with human bondage in the states and that free states had a constitutional obligation to surrender fugitive slaves.[91] Felix Frankfurter fought for the rights of political dissenters before joining the bench. Once on the Supreme Court, he led the judicial bloc that interpreted the First Amendment narrowly, voting to sustain many repressive policies he opposed politically.[92] Many instances exist when voting alignments in institutions whose members are charged with making political and policy decisions differ from voting alignments in institutions that are limited to making legal decisions. Republicans and Democrats in the elected branches of the national government fought tooth and nail over every incident associated with the investigation and failed impeachment of President Bill Clinton. Republicans and Democrats on the Supreme Court during the same time period unanimously concluded that Article II did not vest Clinton with absolute immunity from all civil lawsuits while in office.[93]

Constitutional controversies are structured differently than related normative, political, or policy controversies. The range of constitutional disagreement on a particular issue is often far narrower than the range of policy disagreements. Prochoice and prolife activists dispute the morality and policy consequences of both legal abortion and bans on reproductive choice. Their constitutional dispute is limited to whether laws prohibiting reproductive choice violate the due process clauses of the Fifth and Fourteenth Amendments. Almost all proponents and opponents of *Roe v. Wade* agree that states may constitutionally permit and fund abortion.[94] Social conservatives and social liberals engage in policy debates over funding for federal family planning programs but agree that Congress is constitutionally authorized to choose the proper dollar amount. Constitutional disagreements highlight different features of the issue being disputed than policy disagreements. Attitudes toward tort reform in the elected branches of government are related to beliefs about major corporations and trial lawyers. Conservative Republicans in the White House and Congress aggressively champion legislation that caps punitive damages as a means for promoting business enterprise. Attitudes toward punitive damages on the Supreme Court are more closely related to beliefs about whether the due process clauses of the Fifth and Fourteenth Amendment protect any substantive liberty. Justices Scalia and Thomas, the two leading opponents of using the due process clause to protect abortion rights, are also the two leading opponents of using the due process clause to limit excessive jury verdicts.[95] No governing official using standard policy or political logics makes any connection between tort reform and abortion.

Whether the accepted methods for determining the meaning of constitutional provisions adequately constrain constitutional decision-makers is an open question. Persons who have some sympathy for strict construction think distinctive constitutional norms play too little a role in contemporary constitutional practice. Living constitutionalists worry that distinctive constitutional norms often have undue influence when contemporary constitutional decisions are made. The evidence demonstrates only that distinctive forms of constitutional reasoning play a greater role in constitutional decision-making than they do in many political science models, not that Americans at the turn of the twenty-first century always employ constitutional arguments in ways that maximize the achievement of basic constitutional purposes. In particular, law functions to generate agreement on some constitutional issues where disagreement exists in politics and structures the way participants in constitutional debates disagree.

4.3 Generating Agreement

Constitutional practices often facilitate legal consensus on issues characterized by normative, political, and policy disagreements. Some examples are obvious. Students in comparative politics classes debate whether parliamentary systems are better than presidential systems and whether justices on constitutional courts should be limited to a fixed ten-year term. No plausible constitutional argument can be made that the United States has a parliamentary system of government or that justices on the Supreme Court must leave the bench a decade after they are appointed. On many matters, agreement exists that the Constitution permits elected officials to make a wide range of controversial policy choices. Elected officials debate at great length every element of the Defense Department budget, but no one thinks the number, kind, and price of various weapon systems raise constitutional questions.

The "thou shalt not" structure of many constitutional commands highlights a subtler distinction between constitutional and policy disputes. The Constitution of the United States more often prohibits than compels official action. The Eighth Amendment forbids cruel and unusual punishments, but no constitutional provision bans unusually lenient criminal sentences. For this reason, while opponents of capital punishment object on moral, policy, and constitutional grounds to legislation punishing murder by death, proponents of capital punishment raise only moral and policy arguments to legislative decisions not to punish murder by death. More generally, almost all policy disputes have a constitutional safe harbor, a politically controversial decision that all agree that government officials are constitutionally empowered to make. No constitutional controversy arises when elected officials repeal laws banning the possession of concealed weapons or when the president, rejecting the political wishes of close advisors, seeks approval from Congress before sending troops into foreign combat.

The agreement function of constitutional norms explains why most political controversies in the United States do not raise legal or constitutional issues suitable for judicial resolution. Frederick Schauer's comparison of judicial and political agendas at the turn of the twenty-first century refutes common impressions "that the Constitution, constitutional law, and the Supreme Court not only occupy a major role in American policymaking, but also in fact made a great deal of American policy."[96] The issues that elected officials resolve using ordinary policy and political logics, he details, are far more important to the general public than the issues justices resolve using legal and constitutional logics. The Rehnquist Court did not make policy on such controversial matters as "fuel prices, the minimum wage, income taxes, the estate tax, Social Security, inflation, interest rates, avian flu, or the nuclear capabilities of Iran and North Korea." Judicial decisions "related to healthcare, employment, and education," Schauer adds, "could not seriously be described as in any way connected with current or past policy debates on these topics."[97] The ratio of policy to constitutional disputes has been this large throughout American history. Another study found that, with the exception of slavery, hardly any national political question that arose in the Jacksonian era was resolved into a judicial question resolved by the Supreme Court of the United States.[98] More recently, federal courts have failed to resolve disputes that "encompassed almost all of World War Two, European postwar recovery, the occupation of Japan, the Berlin Airlift, the Cold War, the Korean War, nuclear disarmament, Cuba, farm policy and agricultural subsidies, recession, the creation of the interstate highway system, the establishment of Medicare, the war in Vietnam, double-digit inflation, severe gas shortages, and military operations in the Dominican Republic, Panama, Somalia, Lebanon, Kosovo, and Iraq, among others."[99]

As Chapter 5 will outline, constitutional issues that are not adjudicated by courts often arise. Still, barring the unlikely possibility that the justices unanimously agreed with federal policy on all the aforementioned matters, the best explanation for judicial restraint in most circumstances is the general understanding that policy disputes over the budget deficit, the best deployment of troops abroad, and the merits of federal farm aid do not present substantial constitutional questions.

4.4 Structuring Disagreement

Constitutional controversies often have a different structure from the underlying policy or partisan controversy because the methods for determining what constitutional provisions mean focus attention on different aspects of a general dispute than political or partisan logics. Consider the political and constitutional debates over whether states should intentionally create congressional districts that have a majority of African American voters. The political debate is over which party benefits from majority–minority districts. Conventional wisdom presently suggests that, by creating a few supermajoritarian Democratic districts, racial districting increases the total number of congressional districts with a slight Republican bias.[100] Eager to exploit opportunities for political advantage or concerned with preventing such exploitation, many Republicans support and many Democrats oppose legislative apportionments that maximize the congressional districts with African American majorities.[101] Justices employing constitutional logic seem immune to this partisan imperative. From a constitutional perspective, black majority districts raise questions about whether the Fourteenth Amendment permits elected officials to divide voters on the basis of race. Committed to reasoning constitutionally, liberal justices vote to sustain and conservative justices vote to strike down majority–minority congressional districts.[102] Attitudes toward affirmative action predict votes on the constitutionality of using race when drawing electoral boundary lines, not partisan identification.

Howard Gillman's *The Constitution Besieged: The Rise and Demise of Lochner Era Police Powers Jurisprudence* provides another illustration of how distinctive constitutional logics shape constitutional controversies. His work details the two separate debates that took place during the late nineteenth and early twentieth century over government supervision of the relationship between employers and employees. The political debate was over the merits of laissez-faire, over whether government should regulate economic life. The legal debate was over the application of the consensual constitutional animus to class legislation, legislation that provided benefits to one class of citizens at the expense of another class. *The Constitution Besieged* demonstrates that the political and legal debates had a different structure, that justices consistently applied legal logics when determining the constitutional status of minimum wage and maximum hours laws, and that these legal logics explain why conservative justices made legal distinctions when there was no analogous policy distinction. Gillman concludes:

> That the justices were by and large motivated by a principled commitment to the application of a constitutional ideology of state neutrality, as manifested in the requirement that legislation advance a discernible public purpose . . . explains a good deal more of the dependent variable (judicial behavior) than do hypotheses that suggest the justices were basing decisions on a blind adherence to laissez-faire or on a desire to see members of their class win specific lawsuits or on an interest in imposing their idiosyncratic policy preferences on the country.[103]

Policy commitments influenced how different justices applied the constitutional commitment to state neutrality. Justices who were more sympathetic to state regulation were more likely to find a discernible public purpose than those who did not. Focusing only on judicial disagreements, however, overlooks how constitutional battles over class legislation did not mirror policy struggles over national regulation of commercial life. Constitutional decision-makers sustained hundreds of laws that political conservatives insisted were economically unwise. No policymaker in the legislature voted on policy questions as any justice did on the underlying constitutional questions. Persons who based decisions on the "constitutional ideology of state neutrality" behaved differently than those who based decisions on the merits of the night watchman state.

The constitutional decisions made by the late Burger and Rehnquist Courts also cannot be mapped onto conventional policy or partisan preferences. Professor Tom Keck of Syracuse University compared the judicial coalitions that declared fifty-three federal laws unconstitutional between 1980 and 2004 with the legislative and executive coalitions that passed those measures. Judicial voting patterns proved distinctive. Justices did not vote as liberals or conservatives did in the national legislature, nor did they identify clearly as Republicans or Democrats. On a tribunal that "never included more than two Democratic appointees," Keck observes:

> More than 70% of its judicial review decisions were issued by bipartisan coalitions and more than 80% invalidated statutes that had been enacted with substantial Republican legislative support. Similarly, more than 60% of the decisions are inconsistent with a model of policy-motivated judging, either because they were joined by both liberal and conservative justices or because they reached results that are difficult to place in ideological space.[104]

Bipartisan coalitions in Congress frequently voted to restrict commercial advertising. Bipartisan coalitions on the Supreme Court voted to declare many of those laws unconstitutional.[105] Sometimes the justices disagreed on whether the commercial speech before the court was protected by the First Amendment.[106] As political science models predict, the more conservative justices were far more willing to strike down bans on cigarette advertising than the more liberal justices. Nevertheless, when elected officials and justices are compared, the justices most willing to sustain restrictions on advertising still offered more protection for commercial speech than most members of Congress. Judicial divisions over commercial speech took place on a different terrain than political debates over the same subject.

Commercial speech regulations and cases may illustrate a subtler way constitutions influence politics. The difference between the ways elected officials and justices analyze laws regulating advertising may better reflect institutional affiliation than commitments to constitutional reasoning. Congressional majorities may have concluded that persons proposing business transactions are not engaged in constitutionally protected speech. This conclusion is not unreasonable. The Supreme Court did not protect commercial speech until the 1970s.[107] Still, Keck has made the important observation that institutional identities influence how governing officials interpret or construe the Constitution. Justices, whether liberal or conservative, are particularly prone to see free speech issues when determining whether an advertisement may be regulated. Elected officials, whether liberal or conservative, are more likely to be concerned with the public welfare. Constitutions may successfully entrench particular values, this analysis indicates, by entrusting authority to settle constitutional disputes in the institutions whose members are mostly to take those values into account. This is the subject to which we turn in Chapter 5.

‖ 5 ‖

Constitutional Authority

Everybody interprets the Constitution, but not everyone may resolve disputes over what constitutional provisions mean. Constitutional interpretation is open-ended. Justices, elected officials, civil servants, political activists, and ordinary citizens all participate in constitutional dialogues with each other. Any person who has access to the Internet and knows a computer savvy twelve-year-old has the capacity to set up a blog that will broadcast his or her constitutional opinions to the world. Constitutional authority is not as open-ended. Some constitutional proclamations have official consequences. Others do not. Judicial opinions on the death penalty affect who may be constitutionally executed. *New York Times* editorials on capital punishment have only persuasive value.

The precise allocation of constitutional authority among governing institutions is as contested as the meaning of particular constitutional provisions. Presidents from Thomas Jefferson to Barack Obama have insisted on a right to make constitutional decisions inconsistent with the most recent Supreme Court rulings. Internal quarrels take place between federal justices over the degree to which they should defer to elected officials when deciding free speech cases. Sectional tensions before the Civil War were exacerbated by disagreements over whether individual states had the power to determine the constitutionality of federal laws. Andrew Johnson and the Reconstruction Congress disputed whether presidents could refrain from enforcing laws they believed unconstitutional.

Every governing institution in the United States and most American citizens make some decisions that, at least temporarily and with respect to a particular manifestation of a constitutional issue, determine legal rights and governmental powers. Presidents veto legislation they believe violates the Fifth Amendment. Members of Congress, who believe that law constitutional, vote to override the veto. Some traffic court judges void citations for moving violations when they conclude the local speed trap does not provide the notice to motorists required by the due process clause of the Fourteenth Amendment (don't count on this!). Private citizens make legally binding constitutional decisions when they waive potentially valid constitutional claims. Your decision to settle a dispute with a state agency over whether you were unconstitutionally discriminated against when you applied for a job settles that particular constitutional controversy.

Difficult problems arise when conflicts take place between participants in the constitutional decision-making process. The president and Congress may dispute whether a ban on late-term abortions is constitutional. The Supreme Court of the United States and the Supreme Court of Utah may dispute whether unfunded federal mandates violate the Tenth Amendment. Sometimes, a consensual hierarchal relationship exists between different constitutional decision-makers, with members of the inferior institution recognizing their obligation to respect mandates from the superior institution. General agreement exists that, within the federal judiciary, the lower federal courts must follow the most recent decisions made by the Supreme Court. Other governing institutions share constitutional authority. The House of Representatives and Senate must agree on constitutional standards for restricting online pornography to pass legislation regulating the Internet.

Contemporary commentaries on constitutional authority focus on judicial power. Americans debate whether the Supreme Court of the United States should have the power to declare laws unconstitutional, how the Supreme Court should exercise that power, and the extent to which judicial decisions in constitutional cases should bind other governing officials. Most American judges, elected officials, and citizens have concluded that courts have the power both to interpret the Constitution when adjudicating specific cases and to provide authoritative constitutional guidelines for other governing officials. These two powers are distinct, even though they are often conflated in popular accounts. Judicial review is the power to ignore unconstitutional acts when resolving cases. Judicial supremacy is the power to establish principles that bind all other political actors.

Much commentary on constitutional decision-making verges on judicial exclusivity. Ronald Dworkin implies that courts are the only institution in the United States that engages in serious constitutional reasoning when he declares, "We have an institution that calls some issues from the battleground of power politics to the forum of principle."[1] Alexis de Tocqueville celebrated judicial authority when he famously asserted, "Scarcely any political question arises in the United States that is not resolved, sooner or later, into a judicial question."[2] These frequently repeated and paraphrased quotations treat all-important questions about constitutional decision-making in the United States as questions about what courts have done and should do in constitutional cases. The standard high school civics course, undergraduate constitutional law class, law school curriculum, and evening news analysis, all of which typically limit constitutional analysis to discussions of judicial opinions, do little to dispel this impression.

This constitutional obsession with the federal judiciary unduly minimizes constitutional decision-making by elected officials and grossly exaggerates the independent role of the Supreme Court as a constitutional authority. All governing institutions in the United States routinely make authoritative constitutional decisions. Elected officials when revising the penal code decide whether executing murderers is cruel and unusual punishment. Presidents often pardon persons they believe were unconstitutionally convicted of criminal offenses. Many constitutional questions are debated and settled without judicial intervention. The Supreme Court did not determine whether the Louisiana Purchase was constitutional or whether President Bill Clinton committed an impeachable offense when he lied under oath about a sexual liaison, even though both raised serious constitutional issues. Ordinary citizens frequently make constitutional decisions and exercise constitutional authority.[3] Many state elections include referenda on state constitutional amendments that may limit affirmative action or restrict marriage to a man and a woman. Jurors have historically freed political dissidents when they have thought the speech in question should be constitutionally protected.

Elected officials influence the decisions federal justices make and the impact of judicial decisions. Legislatures remove barriers to constitutional adjudication by financing legal services. They create additional obstructions to constitutional adjudication by limiting the jurisdiction of federal courts. Presidents nominate justices to the federal bench who share their constitutional vision. Both Franklin Roosevelt and Richard Nixon, given sufficient appointments, changed the direction of Supreme Court decision-making.[4] Supreme Court rulings affect public policy only to the extent they are implemented by other governing officials. President Dwight Eisenhower ordered federal troops to enforce Supreme Court decisions desegregating public schools in Little Rock, Arkansas. President Andrew Jackson, by comparison, allegedly declared that seventy-five-year-old Chief Justice John Marshall was responsible for enforcing the mandate in *Worcester v. Georgia* (1832) that Georgia release several missionaries from prison. While never renouncing judicial supremacy, most justices most of the time have found means for avoiding direct confrontations with powerful political forces bent on defying federal courts.

Both the judicial power to make constitutional decisions and the judicial authority to settle constitutional controversies have been contested throughout American history. Prominent Jeffersonian political leaders condemned judicial review. "The Legislature have the exclusive right to interpret the Constitution, in what regards the law-making power," Senator John Breckinridge of Virginia informed his peers in 1801, "and the judges are bound to execute the laws they make."[5] Abraham Lincoln challenged judicial supremacy. While conceding that judicial decisions in constitutional cases "must be binding... upon the parties to a suit," the sixteenth president asserted, "if the policy of the government... is to be irrevocably fixed by decisions of the Supreme Court..., the people will have ceased, to be their own rulers."[6]

American constitutionalism confounds efforts to draw neat lines of constitutional authority. Constitutional authority is more often shared by participants in constitutional dialogues than hoarded by political actors eager to have the sole or last word on the fundamental law of the land. The constitutional rights of gays and lesbians in the United States has been influenced by such Supreme Court decisions as *Lawrence v. Texas* (2003) (holding that states cannot ban homosexual sodomy between consenting adults); state court decisions finding a state constitutional right to same-sex marriage; the litigation strategies of gay rights activists, which help determined how issues were framed before courts; state referenda approving amendments limiting marriage to a man and a woman; and the Obama administration's decision to urge courts to find certain provisions in the Defense of Marriage Act unconstitutional. Constitutional decisions in one governing institution influence constitutional decisions in another, even if the participants in "constitutional dialogues" are not in the same room having a conversation.

Members of one institution often empower members of other institutions to make constitutional decisions. The Supreme Court has adopted various rules and practices that vest elected officials with absolute authority over some and temporary authority over many other constitutional issues. The political questions doctrine, the requirement that litigants making constitutional claims demonstrate a concrete injury, and the expense of bringing constitutional lawsuits all facilitate constitutional authority outside the federal judiciary. Elected officials, when given opportunities to make constitutional choices, often choose instead to empower courts by deliberately enacting vague statutes or by eliminating various procedural barriers to judicial intervention. Federalism is both a high political principle and an excuse national officials make when foisting difficult constitutional questions on to local authorities. Judicial authority in the United States is as much politically constructed by elected officials interested in buttressing their constitutional visions or managing their political coalitions as judicially constructed by legal opinions proclaiming judicial authority over all constitutional matters.

The pattern of constitutional authority that has resulted from these complex interactions among elected officials, political activists, and unelected justices more resembles the chaos of the local garage band than the precision of a Mozart symphony. Some version of judicial supremacy has historically been the dominant theory but less often the actual practice. Supreme Court decisions will influence whether college students serve prison time after police find illegal downloads of Miley Cyrus albums during a warrantless search of their dorm room, but so will the attitudes of the local prosecutor, the skill of their defense lawyers, the willingness of the trial judge to believe police testimony that the recordings were in plain view, the sympathies of the local jury, the interest local civil rights organizations take in financing an appeal, and whether the most recent appointments to the federal bench were made by a president determined to appear tough on crime. The fate of these pure unfortunate souls will turn in part on who won the most recent election but also on constitutional under-standings about whose decisions are authoritative. This end result is hardly the pristine vision found in most civics books but *may* (and only may) reflect the rough balance between fundamental law and popular sovereignty that underlies a functioning constitutional democracy.

1. The Countermajoritarian Difficulty, Judicial Activism, and Judicial Restraint

The countermajoritarian difficulty has shaped debates over constitutional authority for the past fifty years. American commitments to judicial review and supremacy, several generations of commentators have worried, appar-ently empower a small, elite body of unaccountable justices to strike down laws passed by those elected officials who are normally responsible for making policy in a democracy. Worse, justices often insist their animating mission is to resist democratic majorities and their policy preferences. This judicial power aggra-vates the dead hand problem discussed in Chapter 3. Constitutionalism not only authorizes the dead to rule over the living but also seemingly entrusts the least representative branch of the national government with the power to interpret their ancient commands.

Alexander Bickel in 1962 offered the most famous account of the potential conflict between democracy and judicial power:

> The root difficulty is that judicial review is a counter-majoritarian force in our system.... When the Supreme Court declares unconstitutional a legislative act or the action of an elected executive, it thwarts the will of representatives of the actual people of the here and now; it exercises control, not in behalf of the prevailing majority, but against it.

Bickel concluded from these observations that judicial review is "a deviant insti-tution in our democracy."[7] The challenge he laid down for justices and their academic supporters is whether they can devise a satisfactory justification for judicial authority in a regime committed to popular sovereignty.

The countermajoritarian problem was formulated during mid-twentieth century debates over the merits of judicial restraint and judicial activism. Proponents of judicial restraint agreed with Bickel's assertion that judicial power was suspect in a democratic society. Justice Felix Frankfurter, the most prominent champion of judicial modesty on the New Deal and early Great Society Court, repeatedly declared that unelected justices should rarely question legislative choices. "Courts are not representative bodies," Frankfurter asserted when voting to sustain congressional restrictions on Communist activities. His opinion continued:

> They are not designed to be a good reflex of a democratic society. Their judgment is best informed, and therefore most dependable, within narrow limits.... History teaches that the independence of the judiciary is jeopardized when courts become embroiled in the passions of the day and assume primary responsibility in choosing between competing political, economic and social pressures.
>
> Primary responsibility for adjusting the interests which compete in the situation before us of necessity belongs to the Congress.... We are to set aside the judgment of those whose duty it is to legislate only if there is no reasonable basis for it.[8]

Proponents of judicial activism insisted that courts played as vital a role in a constitutional democracy as elected officials. They rejected a judicial obligation to defer to legislatures when fundamental rights were at stake. "The very purpose of a Bill of Rights," Justice Robert Jackson declared in an opinion striking down laws mandating flag salutes in public schools, "was to withdraw certain subjects from the vicissitudes of political controversy, to place them beyond the reach of majorities and officials and to establish them as legal principles to be applied by the courts."[9] Justice Hugo Black agreed: "Under our constitutional system courts stand against any winds that blow as havens of refuge for those who might otherwise suffer because they are helpless, weak, outnumbered, or because they are non-conforming victims of prejudice and public excitement."[10] Frankfurter and his allies charged proponents of judicial activism with repeating the mistakes made by the Supreme Court justices who during the 1930s declared New Deal measures unconstitutional. Chief Justice Earl Warren and his allies charged proponents of judicial restraint with insensitivity to the rights of political dissenters and African Americans.

Modest justices during the New Deal and Great Society years often championed legal practices and techniques that enabled justices to avoid making any constitutional decision on hotly contested questions. "Courts ought not enter this political thicket," Frankfurter declared in 1946 when concluding that the federal judiciary should not determine whether legislative apportionments violated the Guarantee Clause of the Constitution because such constitutional issues were "political questions" best resolved by other governing institutions.[11] Proponents of judicial restraint urged justices to decide cases on fairly narrow grounds, particularly when they believed the government had acted unconstitutionally. Professor Robert McCloskey of the Harvard Government Department claimed that the "Court's greatest successes have been achieved when it has operated near the margins rather than in the center of political controversy, when it has nudged and gently tugged the nation, instead of trying to rule it." He approved judicial decisions requiring states to use careful procedures before determining whether speech was obscene. Such rulings promised to improve legislative deliberation without curtailing legislative power. When the justices went further and handed down edicts prohibiting bans on sexually explicit expression, McCloskey sharply disapproved.[12]

Judicial activists believed that justices were well suited to settle the most important constitutional disputes of their era. "Judicial standards under the Equal Protection Clause are well developed and familiar,"[13] Justice William Brennan asserted in 1962 when ruling that the Supreme Court could determine whether legislative apportionments violated the Fourteenth Amendment. Warren, Brennan, and other activist justices favored judicial decisions that announced broad constitutional principles. While Frankfurter would determine on a case-by-case basis what state procedures abridged rights guaranteed by the due process clause of the Fourteenth Amendment, Justice Hugo Black insisted that persons accused of local crimes were entitled to every security for their freedom set out in the first eight amendments to the Constitution. Black scorned claims that justices should defer to local judgments about the criminal procedures that best promoted the dual goals of truth-seeking and procedural fairness. "I have never believed," he declared, "that under the guise of federalism the States should be able to experiment with the protections afforded our citizens through the Bill of Rights."[14]

The grand constitutional theory that became academically fashionable after 1970 is largely devoted to reconciling judicial review and democracy. Prominent originalists insist that Americans reap the benefits of both popular sovereignty and fundamental law only when Supreme Court decisions declaring laws unconstitutional are based on what constitutional provisions meant when ratified. Judicial review by originalist justices does not raise countermajoritarian problems, Robert Bork asserts, because the public has "consent[ed] to be ruled undemocratically within defined areas by certain enduring principles believed to be stated in, and placed beyond the reach of majorities by, the Constitution."[15] John McGinnis and Michael Rappaport think originalist courts act democratically when they uphold constitutional norms ratified by supermajorities in the past.[16] Other commentators maintain that judicial review, properly exercised, improves democratic deliberation. Christopher Eisgruber contends that "Supreme Court justices" have "a special ability to represent the American people with respect to issues of moral and political principle."[17] Michael Seidman and Terri Peretti claim that judicial review fosters democratic participation by unsettling constitutional decisions made by elected officials and providing another forum for public debate over fundamental values.[18] Bruce Ackerman's argument that justices should maintain constitutional settlements reached during times of unusually high political mobilization offers another democratic justification for judicial review.[19]

The most popular contemporary attempts to reconcile judicial power and majority rule justify judicial review when justices declare unconstitutional laws that restrict democratic processes or discriminate against persons who belong to groups that cannot take full advantage of democratic processes. The basic idea is that judicial review is justified when and only when some democratic flaw exists in the legislation under constitutional attack or the process by which that legislation was enacted. This "representation-reinforcing" understanding of judicial review was central to the influential footnote four in *United States v. Carolene Products Co.* (1938), a footnote generally credited with altering the focus of judicial activism from a conservative concern with property rights to a liberal concern with free speech and racial equality. When rejecting judicial supervision of economic legislation, Chief Justice Harlan Fiske Stone noted that "legislation which restricts those political processes which can ordinarily be expected to bring about repeal of undesirable legislation" might "be subjected to more exacting judicial scrutiny under the general prohibitions of the Fourteenth Amendment than are most other types of legislation." He added that more exacting scrutiny might also be warranted when "prejudice against discrete and insular minorities . . . curtail[s] the operation of those political processes ordinarily to be relied upon to protect minorities."[20] Professor John Hart Ely elaborated on these insights at some length in his influential *Democracy and Distrust*. He defended judicial power when the justices protected free speech and vitiate Jim Crow but maintained that courts have no authority to second-guess legislative decisions banning abortion or regulating wages.[21] Ely insisted that representation-reinforcing judicial review supported Warren Court activism but not the Burger Court's decision in *Roe v. Wade* (1973) to find a constitutional right to terminate pregnancies.

Critics identify possible flaws with each of these efforts to solve or dissolve the countermajoritarian problem. The alleged democratic difficulty with originalism is that democracy usually entails rule by present majorities. That majorities, even supermajorities, in 1789 may have believed government should not abridge the obligation of contract does not provide a democratic reason for restricting the power of contemporary legislatures over commercial activity.

Professors who celebrate judicial review for promoting democratic deliberation never explain why Supreme Court justices must enjoy life tenure. We might
simultaneously promote democratic deliberation and reduce the countermajoritarian difficulty by establishing an appointed (or even elected) term-limited
judiciary whose members are ineligible for reelection (or election to any other
public office). The representation-reinforcing approach to the judicial function
may take vital decisions about democratic processes out of the hands of the voting public. In a democracy, one argument contends, popular majorities ought to
determine whether campaign finance regulations promote fair elections as well
as whether abortion should be restricted. Almost any exercise of judicial power
can be justified as protecting the rights of a discrete and insular majority. While
Ely thought *Roe* violated the basic tenets of representative reinforcement, other
scholars insist that democratic theory justifies judicial decision protecting reproductive choice because women are underrepresented in elected positions and
because abortion rights are necessary for women to participate as democratic
equals.[22] Justice Clarence Thomas cited the *Carolene Products* footnote when
he unsuccessfully urged the justices to declare unconstitutional a New London
law giving condemned private property to a private company. Such uses of eminent domain, Thomas claimed, disproportionately harmed the poor and racial
minorities.[23]

The grand constitutional theories developed in the last part of the twentieth century complicated what had previously been a relatively clear distinction
between judicial activism and judicial restraint. During the 1960s, everyone
agreed that the Warren Court was an activist tribunal because the justices
regularly intervened in heated constitutional controversies. Debate was over
whether the Supreme Court should have as prominent a role in American
constitutional politics. By the end of the twentieth century, judicial restraint
and activism seemed partly redefined. Many writings on the Supreme Court
defined activism and restraint in terms of author's conception of the judicial
function and theory of constitutional interpretation. Whether the Warren
Court was activist, from this perspective, depended on whether the justices
were acting consistently with a particular theory of constitutional authority
and not on how many laws or how many important laws the justices declared
unconstitutional. Many commentaries further confused matters by conflating
theories of the judicial function with theories of constitutional interpretation.
Neither Bork nor Ely, for example, specified whether originalism or representative reinforcement was a theory of the judicial function or a theory of constitutional interpretation. Their works did not explore whether an elected official
interpreting the Constitution might legitimately use methods other than originalism or democratic theory for ascertaining the meaning of constitutional
provisions. As a result, the work of Bork, Ely, and others tended to describe

as activist any decision that used what they considered the wrong theory of constitutional interpretation.

A Supreme Court reconstituted by justices appointed by presidents Ronald Reagan, George H. W. Bush, and George W. Bush further confounded distinctions between judicial restraint and activism. The Warren Court was divided between a liberal judicial majority that favored using judicial power to advance liberal constitutional causes and a liberal judicial minority that believed liberal causes were best advanced by elected officials. The Rehnquist Court was divided between a liberal wing that sought to extend the legacy of the Warren Court, a conservative wing that often exercised judicial power to advance conservative constitutional causes, and two swing justices, Sandra Day O'Connor and Anthony Kennedy, who were sympathetic to some liberal and some conservative causes. The end result was "the most activist Court in history" when measured by the frequency with which federal laws were declared unconstitutional.[24] "We have a Supreme Court that engages in unparalleled activism—from the left and the right simultaneously!" Michael Klarman observed.

> When Justices O'Connor and Kennedy are in their conservative mode, affirmative action, minority voting districts, hate speech regulations, and environmental land use restrictions are all constitutionally suspect, notwithstanding the absence of convincing originalist arguments against them. When these pivotal Justices are in their liberal mode, abortion restrictions, school prayer, restrictions on gay rights, exclusion of women from VMI, and limitations on the right to die fall victim to the Court's constitutional axe.[25]

Some commentators responded to this bipartisan activism by calling on justices to exercise greater restraint when making both liberal and conservative constitutional decisions.[26] At least as often, constitutional commentary distinguished judicial activism from judicial restraint by determining whose ox is gored. Liberal constitutionalists condemn judicial activism when the justices limit congressional power to enforce the Fourteenth Amendment while insisting that the justices are just doing their job when striking down bans on abortion.[27] Conservative constitutionalists rail against judicial activism when the justices protect reproductive choice but claim that the justices promote democracy when using the Tenth Amendment to limit federal power and merely enforce preexisting constitutional limitations when declaring unconstitutional provisions of the Affordable Care Act of 2010.[28]

Contemporary debates over judicial activism and restraint conflate too many distinctive questions to provide a useful structure for thinking about constitutional decision-making. When evaluating a military decision, we might ask whether General Jones was ultimately responsible for determining whether to attack the left flank, whether when making that decision General Jones ought to have deferred in whole or in part to Major Smith who was in the actual combat zone, and whether the decision to attack the left flank was tactically correct. The same questions should be distinguished when analyzing judicial power. Some questions about constitutional decision-making seek to identify the institution, if any, that bears the ultimate responsibility for determining the official meaning of the First Amendment or commerce clause. Others are about the extent to which persons authorized to make constitutional decisions should share that power in various ways with other governing officials. Still other questions are about whether particular decisions correctly interpret the Constitution. Chapter 4 examined the last question. The next two sections discuss the first two matters.

2. Allocating Constitutional Authority

Americans have proposed four different schemes for allocating constitutional authority. Judicial supremacists maintain that the Supreme Court of the United States is the ultimate authority for resolving all constitutional disputes. Should the justices declare that capital punishment violates the Eighth and Fourteenth Amendments, then neither federal nor state authorities may subsequently seek to punish murder by death. Departmentalists maintain that each department of the national government must make independent decisions when constitutional disputes arise. Judges may on constitutional grounds refuse to impose or sustain death sentences, but Congress may subsequently insist that death is the appropriate punishment for murder and federal prosecutors may continue to seek the death penalty when warranted by federal statute. Compact theorists maintain that each state has an independent right to determine the meaning of constitutional provisions. State authorities may execute murderers should they conclude that Supreme Court decisions to the contrary erroneously interpret the Constitution. Opponents of judicial review contend that the Supreme Court has no authority to declare any law unconstitutional. Both federal and state authorities may execute murderers, in this view, even when federal courts have ruled that capital punishment is unconstitutional. Different combinations of these positions are possible. One can be a judicial supremacist with respect to constitutional authority in the federal system while endorsing compact theory with respect to constitutional authority in the states. Compact theorists may reject judicial review altogether or may treat federal judicial decisions as binding only federal elected officials.

Judicial supremacy is the most widely shared understanding of constitutional authority, particularly since the Civil War. Supreme Court justices insist that the Supreme Court has the power to settle constitutional controversies. Most elected officials most of the time support this judicial power. A strong departmentalist tradition also exists in the United States. Thomas Jefferson, Andrew Jackson, Abraham Lincoln, Franklin Roosevelt, and Ronald Reagan all challenged judicial authority when in office. Compact theory had powerful adherents before the Civil War but not afterward. Some Americans question judicial review, but challenges to judicial authority are usually aimed at the judicial power to settle constitutional disputes, not the judicial power to make constitutional decisions whose impact is limited to the case before the justices.

2.1 Judicial Supremacy

Supreme Court justices for at least the past half-century have asserted that their decisions provide authoritative constitutional guidelines for all governing officials. When state officials in Arkansas declared they were unwilling and unable to comply with the judicial decision in *Brown v. Board of Education*, Chief Justice Earl Warren responded with a stern lecture on judicial supremacy. Elected officials, he and every other sitting justice agreed, had no constitutional business challenging judicial decisions interpreting the Constitution. "The federal judiciary is supreme in the exposition of the law of the Constitution," *Cooper v. Aaron* (1958) asserted, "and that principle has ... been respected by this Court and the Country as a permanent and indispensable feature of our constitutional system."[29] A unanimous Supreme Court has often delivered the same lecture to Congress. The judicial majority in *Oregon v. Smith* (1990) held that states could constitutionally burden religious practices as long as laws did not discriminate against religious believers. The Religious Freedom Restoration Act (RFRA) of 1993 sought to reverse that decision. That measure prohibited states from passing laws that significantly burdened religious practices, unless those laws served a compelling state interest. The justices in *City of Boerne v. Flores* (1997) declared that RFRA exceeded congressional power under Section 5 of the Fourteenth Amendment, repeating their claim in *Cooper* that the Supreme Court was the governing institution responsible for determining the proper interpretation of constitutional rights and powers. Justice Kennedy spoke for all nine justices when he asserted, "Our national experience teaches that the Constitution is preserved best when each part of the government respects both the Constitution and the proper actions and determinations of the other branches." He continued, "When the Court has interpreted the Constitution, it has acted within the province of the Judicial Branch, which embraces the duty to say what the law is."[30] Congress, in this view, must act within the constitutional parameters established by the Supreme Court and not make independent legal judgments concerning constitutional powers and rights.

Some judicial supremacists ground judicial authority in the intentions of the persons who framed and ratified the Constitution, the constitutional text, and historical practice. Some members of the Philadelphia drafting convention asserted that the Supreme Court would have the power to settle constitutional disputes. When rejecting a proposal to include Supreme Court justices on a Council of Revision empowered to veto legislation, several framers indicated that the constitutionality of all federal and state actions would come before the justices in the normal course of their business. Article III, which vests the Supreme Court with the power to adjudicate "all cases...arising under this Constitution," may be interpreted as establishing judicial authority to fix the meaning of constitutional provisions. Legal precedent provides additional support for judicial authority. The *Cooper* and *Boerne* opinions insisted that judicial supremacy had been the law of the land since *Marbury v. Madison* (1803), the Supreme Court decision conventionally understood as establishing the judicial power to make constitutional decisions. "Democracy does not insist on judges having the last word," Dworkin agrees, but "practice has now settled that courts do have a responsibility to declare and act on their best understanding of what the Constitution forbids."[31]

Proponents assert that judicial supremacy is a necessary ingredient of constitutionalism. If the Constitution is fundamental law, then the primary responsibility for interpreting the Constitution should be vested in the judiciary, the institution responsible for interpreting the law. As Chief Justice Marshall declared in 1803, "It is emphatically the province and duty of the judicial department to say what the law is."[32] If the Constitution is committed to limited government, then the officials who make the laws should not be given the authority to determine the constitutional limits on their powers. Justice Kennedy relied heavily on this principle in *Boerne* when he declared:

> If Congress could define its own powers by altering the Fourteenth Amendment's meaning, no longer would the Constitution be "superior paramount law, unchangeable by ordinary means." It would be "on a level with ordinary legislative acts, and, like other acts,...alterable when the legislature shall please to alter it." *Marbury* v. *Madison* (1803).... Under this approach, it is difficult to conceive of a principle that would limit congressional power.... Shifting legislative majorities could change the Constitution and effectively circumvent the difficult and detailed amendment process contained in Article V.[33]

Adherents proclaim that judicial supremacy exhibits three practical virtues. That judicial power enables constitutional debates to be settled authoritatively. Larry Alexander and Frederick Schauer insist that "settlement of contested issues is a crucial component of constitutionalism, that this goal can be achieved only by having an authoritative interpreter whose interpretations bind all others, and that the Supreme Court can best serve this role."[34] Regimes committed to judicial supremacy may guarantee that constitutional issues are decided on the basis of legal norms, not political expediency. "Ordinary politics," Dworkin writes, "generally aims at a political compromise that gives all powerful groups enough of what they want to prevent their disaffection, and reasoned argument elaborating underlying moral principles is rarely part or even congenial to such compromises."[35] Courts resolve constitutional issues differently. Dworkin declares:

> We have an institution that calls some issues from the battleground of power politics to the forum of principle. It holds out the promise that the deepest, most fundamental conflicts between individual and society will once, someplace, finally, become questions of justice. I do not call that religion or prophecy. I call it law.[36]

Henry Hart agreed that the Supreme Court "is predestined in the long run not only by the thrilling tradition of Anglo-American law but also by the hard facts of its position in the structure of American institutions to be a voice of reason, charged with the creative function of discerning afresh and of articulating and developing impersonal and durable principles of constitutional law."[37] Many judicial supremacists are convinced that judicial review is a vital means for protecting powerless minorities. "Under our constitutional system," Justice Hugo Black affirmed in *Chambers v. Florida*, "courts stand against any winds that blow as havens of refuge for those who might otherwise suffer because they are helpless, weak, outnumbered, or because they are non-conforming victims of prejudice and public excitement." These proponents of judicial supremacy believe justices have special capacities to "listen for voices from the margins."[38] Elected officials have many virtues, proponents of judicial supremacy admit, but they are too fickle to provide constitutional stability, too prone to compromise to promote constitutional justice, and too eager to seek reelection to protect the constitutional rights of minorities.

2.2 Departmentalism

Opponents of judicial supremacy trot out Abraham Lincoln and *Dred Scott* whenever proponents too vigorously celebrate *Brown* and the Warren Court. Lincoln refused to treat as authoritative the judicial declaration that Congress could not ban slavery in American territories. He declared when debating Stephen Douglas:

> We oppose the *Dred Scott* decision in a certain way. We do not propose that when Dred Scott has been decided to be a slave by the court, we, as a mob, will decide him to be free. We do not propose that, when any other one, or one thousand, shall be decided by that court to be slaves, we will in any violent way disturb the rights of property thus settled; but we nevertheless do oppose that decision as a political rule which shall be binding on the voter, to vote for nobody who thinks it wrong, which shall be binding on the members of Congress or the President to favor no measure that does not actually concur with the principles of that decision. We do not propose to be bound by it as a political rule in that way, because we think it lays the foundation not merely of enlarging and spreading out what we consider an evil, but it lays the foundation for spreading that evil into the States themselves. We propose so resisting it as to have it reversed if we can, and a new judicial rule established upon this subject.[39]

This challenge to judiciary supremacy is not a unique event in American history.[40] Thomas Jefferson and Andrew Jackson previously asserted independent presidential authority to interpret the Constitution. Similar claims would subsequently be made by Franklin Roosevelt and Ronald Reagan. "A constitutional decision is not the same as the Constitution itself," Reagan's attorney general Edwin Meese declared. "If it is not binding in the same way that the Constitution is," he continued, "we as citizens may respond to a decision with which we disagree." Meese's assertion that "constitutional decisions need not be seen as the last words in constitutional construction"[41] generated a political firestorm. Significantly, some political liberals, worried about the capacity of elitist courts to obstruct a more populist constitutionalism, endorsed the Reagan administration's critique of judicial power.[42]

Departmentalists believe that the Supreme Court may make constitutional decisions when adjudicating cases but that these rulings do not fix the meaning of the Constitution. Lincoln thought elected officials were bound by the legal verdict in the court case between Dred Scott and John Sanford. The government could not forcibly free Scott if the courts held that he was legally enslaved. Nevertheless, the government did not have to accept the broader "political rule" giving slaveholders those rights in American territories that the Supreme Court laid down. When in power, Republicans banned slavery in the federal territories and in the District of Columbia despite *Dred Scott*. President Thomas Jefferson justified this division of constitutional labor when explaining why he

pardoned all persons convicted of violating the Sedition Act of 1798. He wrote
to Abigail Adams:

> You seem to think it devolved on the judges to decide on the validity of
> the sedition law. But nothing in the Constitution has given them a right
> to decide for the Executive, more than to the Executive to decide for
> them. Both magistrates are equally independent in the sphere of action
> assigned to them. The judges, believing the law constitutional, had a
> right to pass a sentence of fine and imprisonment; because that power
> was placed in their hands by the Constitution. But the Executive, believ-
> ing the law to be unconstitutional, was bound to remit the execution of
> it; because that power had been confided to him by the Constitution.
> That instrument meant that its coordinate branches should be checks
> on each other. But the opinion which gives to the judges the right to
> decide what laws are constitutional, and what not, not only for them-
> selves in their own sphere of action, but for the Legislature & Executive
> also, in their spheres, would make the judiciary a despotic branch.[43]

Departmentalists point out that judicial supremacy is neither explicitly
provided for by the Constitution nor clearly implied by the constitutional
text or constitutional history. Article VI states that the Constitution shall be
the supreme law and bind all governing officials. No constitutional provision
plainly states that elected officials are also bound by Supreme Court decisions
on constitutional questions. Judicial power was not well established when the
Constitution was framed and ratified. Very few state justices had declared state
laws unconstitutional. Those who did in the late eighteenth century were often
severely reprimanded by the state legislature. While good evidence exists that
the framers believed states could not disobey judicial decrees, the expected division of constitutional authority within the federal government is unclear. Very
few statements on judicial power were made during the framing and ratification process. Hardly any endorsed judicial supremacy. Whether the congressional architects of the Thirteenth, Fourteenth, and Fifteenth Amendments
intended to empower a Supreme Court that had recently decided *Dred Scott* is
certainly open to debate. Precedent is not as one-sided as proponents of judicial supremacy sometimes maintain. Scholars debate whether John Marshall in
Marbury v. Madison intended to justify judicial review or judicial supremacy. The
political precedents are conflicting. Although some presidents have championed
courts as constitutional authorities, others, as noted already, have challenged the
claimed judicial monopoly on constitutional interpretation.

Judicial supremacy may be antithetical to both constitutionalism and
democracy. Judicial supremacy invites politicians to ignore their constitutional

responsibilities and allows unchecked judges to warp constitutional principles through abuse or misinterpretation. James Madison explained, "As the legislative, executive, and judicial departments are co-ordinate, and each equally bound to support the Constitution, it follows that each must, in the exercise of its functions, be guided by the text of the Constitution according to its own interpretation of it."[44] The several branches should and will often reach agreement on the proper interpretation of the Constitution, but the supremacy of judicial interpretations should not be automatically assumed. Arguments that derive judicial supremacy from the liberal constitutional commitment to limited government fail to explain what institution prevents the Supreme Court from ignoring the constitutional restrictions on judicial power. As Jefferson noted in his letter to Abigail Adams, any institution vested with the final authority over constitutional disputes exercises "despotic" power. This principle may extend constitutional authority to the people as well as to elected officials. Contemporary departmentalists, often writing as *popular constitutionalists,* point out that popular sovereignty and judicial supremacy do not easily mix. Larry Kramer explains, "The role of the people" in a constitutional democracy "is not confined to occasional acts of constitution making, but includes active and ongoing control over the interpretation and enforcement of constitutional law." All governing institutions, he insists, must be checked by "the people themselves."[45]

Departmentalists maintain that the practical benefits of judicial supremacy are overrated. The Supreme Court over time has demonstrated only a limited capacity to settle constitutional disputes. The *Dred Scott* decision hardly resolved the constitutional debate over the status of slavery in the territories. Judicial decisions on abortion have done more to heighten than diminish partisan tensions. Elected officials, by comparison, have settled many constitutional disputes, including politically disruptive controversies over whether Senate consent is needed for removing cabinet officials and the conditions under which the United States may acquire new territories. Judicial supremacists maintain that constitutional settlements require clear statements of legal rules, but few constitutional commentators reading contemporary Supreme Court decisions on such matters as affirmative action and federalism can predict with any certainty how the next case will be resolved. Whether settlement is always valuable is contested. Particular manifestations of conflicts must often be resolved. A final decision must be made on whether a condemned prisoner may be constitutionally executed this evening or whether the Constitution permits the president to bomb a foreign country without notifying Congress. No pressing need justifies resolving the constitutional status of capital punishment and the war power for all time. Keith Whittington notes, "It is sometimes better for constitutional rules to be relatively unsettled because it can foster socially beneficial experimentation and allow political diversity."[46]

Debate rages over whether the Supreme Court is a distinctive forum of constitutional principle in American life. Chapter 4 notes the evidence of partisan and ideological influence on Supreme Court decision-making as well as numerous instances when elected officials demonstrate fidelity to fundamental law. Participants in constitutional debates outside the courts often seem as constrained as justices by legitimate methods of constitutional interpretation. Lincoln's analysis of *Dred Scott*, the congressional speeches defending the constitutionality of the Civil Rights Act of 1964, and Jackson's messages vetoing internal improvement bills demonstrate as skillful constitutional crafting as many inspiring Supreme Court opinions. Elected officials have made more than their fair share of incompetent constitutional claims, but the same is true of the justices on the Supreme Court.

The historical record casts further doubt on the alleged judicial capacity to adhere more frequently to constitutional norms than elected officials. *Boiling v. Sharpe* (1954), which struck down federal laws mandating school segregation in the nation's capital, is the first instance in American history where a consensus presently exists that the Supreme Court when striking down a federal law interpreted the Constitution better than national elected officials. By comparison, most contemporary commentators of all political persuasions agree that the justices in numerous cases decided before 1954 wrongly declared federal laws unconstitutional. These include judicial decisions striking down federal bans on slavery in the territories (*Dred Scott*), federal laws forbidding discrimination in places of public accommodation (*Civil Rights Cases* [1883]), the federal income tax (*Pollock v. Farmer's Loan and Trust Co.* [1895]), federal protections for union members (*Adair v. United States* [1908]), and many New Deal measures. The justices have a better record when declaring state actions unconstitutional. Still, although different commentators would choose different cases, most persons familiar with constitutional history could cite dozens of cases in which they believe local officials interpreted constitutional powers and rights better than the federal judiciary. The record of state court decisions declaring state laws unconstitutional is no more inspiring.

Whether the Supreme Court has distinctive capacities to protect vulnerable minorities is controversial. *Dred Scott* is hardly an instance when the justices prevented majority tyranny, unless slaveholders are considered a vulnerable minority (as slaveholders regarded themselves). When national officials have suppressed vulnerable minorities, Supreme Court justices have tended to support their actions. Judicial majorities sustained the free speech restrictions enacted during World War One and the Japanese internment during World War Two. Judicial supremacists ignore or discount the frequent instances when elected officials have passed legislation protecting more vulnerable members of society. Examples include the Civil Rights Act of 1875, which forbade discrimination in places of public accommodation, and the Americans with Disabilities

Act of 1990, which required private employers and government actors to provide certain accommodations for handicapped persons. The Supreme Court
declared parts of both measures unconstitutional.[47]

2.3 Compact Theory

Compact theorists insist that each state retains the sovereign power to determine the meaning of constitutional provisions. The Constitution, in this view,
is analogous to a treaty. Unless otherwise explicitly specified by the signatories
to international agreements, each sovereign power reserves the right to interpret for itself its bargained-for responsibilities. States as sovereign entities after
the American Revolution, compact theory contends, retained this authority to decide what constitutional rights and powers were agreed on when the
Constitution was ratified.

The Virginia and Kentucky Resolutions of 1798, which asserted state
power to determine the constitutionality of the Alien and Sedition Acts, are
generally considered the canonical expressions of compact theory. "The government created by this compact was not made the exclusive or final judge
of the extent of the powers delegated to itself," Jefferson wrote, "but that, as
in all other cases of compact among powers having no common judge, each
party has an equal right to judge for itself, as well of infractions as of the mode
and measure of redress."[48] Many slave-state representatives championed compact theory before the Civil War. John C. Calhoun, defending state authority
to nullify federal laws, referred to the "fatal project of giving to the General
Government the sole and final right of interpreting the Constitution."[49] That
project, he believed, gave national majorities the power to run roughshod
over the rights of sectional minorities. State sovereignty soon crossed the
Mason-Dixon line. Some abolitionists insisted that the free states had a right
to decide for themselves whether the Fugitive Slave Acts of 1793 and 1850
were constitutional.

Compact theory enjoys little contemporary support. State authority to determine the meaning of constitutional provisions is in part unattractive because of
the historical association of state sovereignty with slavery and with southern
efforts to nullify *Brown v. Board of Education*. General, although not universal,
agreement presently exists that constitutional interpretation should not vary by
locality. Opponents of compact theory fear the consequences should such measures as the federal income tax or the draft be held to be constitutional in some
states but not in others. Justice Joseph Story, when justifying judicial power
to review state court decisions, noted the "jarring and discordant judgments"
as well as the "public mischiefs" that would result if each state independently
determined the meaning of the federal constitution, federal laws, and federal

treaties. "I do not think the United States would come to an end if we lost our power to declare an Act of Congress void," former Union officer Oliver Wendell Holmes Jr., claimed, but "I do think the Union would be imperiled if we could not make that declaration as to the laws of the several States."[50]

2.4 Executive/Legislative Supremacy

Some constitutional commentators reject any judicial power to declare laws unconstitutional. On the floor of Congress in 1802, Representative John Randolph of Virginia stated the basic case against granting unelected justices any authority to strike down laws. "The decision of a Constitutional question must rest somewhere," he asserted, and in a democratic republic that authority was best "confided to men immediately responsible to the people" rather than "those who are irresponsible."[51] Legislative or executive supremacy has never enjoyed strong popular support in the United States. Nevertheless, some prominent justices and professors throughout history have insisted that the democratic commitment to majority rule encompasses both constitutional and policy questions. Jeremy Waldron argues:

> When citizens or their representatives disagree about what rights we have or what those rights entail, it seems something of an insult to say that this is not something they are to be permitted to sort out by majoritarian processes, but that the issue is to be assigned instead for final determination to a small group of judges. It is particularly insulting when they discover that the judges disagree among themselves along exactly the same lines as the citizens and representatives do, and that the judges make their decisions, too, in the courtroom by majority-voting. The citizens may well feel that if disagreements on these matters are to be settled by counting heads, then it is their heads or those of their accountable representatives that should be counted.[52]

Mark Tushnet suggests that abolishing judicial review "may contribute to serious thinking about the Constitution outside the courts" and foster a "populist constitutional law," which "seeks to distribute constitutional responsibility throughout the population."[53]

Practice in other countries indicates that constitutionalism entails neither judicial supremacy nor judicial review. The United Kingdom is considered a constitutional democracy, even though courts in that regime do not void parliamentary enactments. William Blackstone, the most eminent Anglo-American legalist of the late eighteenth century, described the allocation of constitutional authority in England:

> But if the parliament will positively enact a thing to be done which is unreasonable, I know of no power that can control it: and the examples usually alleged in support of this sense of the rule do none of them prove, that where the main object of a statute is unreasonable the judges are at liberty to reject it; for that were to set the judicial power above that of the legislature, which would be subversive of all government.[54]

Blackstone thought that legislation inconsistent with divine law was not binding in conscience,[55] but he did not conclude from these premises that judges had the constitutional authority to determine whether parliamentary enactments met that standard. Judicial review only recently became popular throughout the world. Controversy exists over whether justices in other regimes with the power to declare laws unconstitutional protect unpopular majorities or affluent elites and whether judicial power realizes any other goal commonly attributed to that practice.[56]

The president and Congress have historically engaged in contentious debates over the allocation of constitutional authority between the elected branches of the national government. Daniel Webster insisted that the president could not veto on constitutional grounds legislation incorporating a national bank that Webster believed was firmly grounded in constitutional precedent. The House of Representatives impeached President Andrew Johnson for refusing to abide by the Tenure of Office Act, a measure Johnson thought unconstitutional. Presidential signing statements at present are provoking a similar controversy. The American Bar Association (ABA) "opposes, as contrary to the rule of law and our constitutional system of separation of powers, a President's issuance of signing statements to claim the authority or state the intention to disregard or decline to enforce all or part of a law he has signed." The ABA task force maintains that presidents have only one option when they conclude that Congress has passed legislation violating constitutional limitations. "Because the 'take care' obligation of the President requires him to faithfully execute all laws, his obligation is to veto bills he believes are unconstitutional," their report states. "He may not sign them into law and then emulate King James II by refusing to enforce them."[57] Other constitutional scholars insist that the president should ignore unconstitutional laws. Saikrishna Prakash insists, "The Constitution actually *requires* the President to disregard unconstitutional statutes." "This duty," he writes, reflects framing understandings that "such laws were seen as null and void"; is a consequence of the president's "unique constitutionally prescribed oath" to " 'preserve, protect, and defend' the Constitution"; and is part of the president's obligation under "the Faithful Execution Clause . . . to faithfully execute the laws."[58]

3. Sharing Constitutional Authority

Separated institutions share power in the United States[59] in ways not always fully accounted for in conventional debates over constitutional authority. Numerous tomes are devoted to Chief Justice Marshall's claim in *Marbury v. Madison* that federal courts have the right to declare laws unconstitutional. Commentaries on Lincoln's challenge to the Supreme Court fill the law reviews. Less attention is paid to the many instances when members of one branch of the national government insist that members of another branch have some authority to settle constitutional disputes. The Supreme Court has historically empowered elected officials by deferring to legislative fact-finding on constitutional issues and holding that Congress and the president are responsible for determining the meaning of Article IV's command that the "United States shall guarantee to every State . . . a Republican Form of Government." Elected officials have historically empowered federal courts by expanding federal jurisdiction and facilitating constitutional litigation. We cannot understand how constitutional authority is actually allocated until we consider the numerous ways governing institutions voluntarily share power (and sometimes eagerly disavow constitutional authority).

3.1 Judicial Sharing

The Supreme Court does not have a roving commission to intervene whenever a dispute breaks out over the meaning of some constitutional provision. Constitutional adjudication takes place only when certain jurisdictional requirements are met. These requirements legally prevent courts from resolving some constitutional controversies, practically prevent courts from resolving other constitutional controversies, and significantly delay adjudication of otherwise justiciable constitutional disputes. When making constitutional decisions, the justices often defer to elected officials or refrain from employing every legitimate method for determining constitutional meanings. Many rulings announce constitutional standards that, while resolving the case before the court, intentionally do not provide clear guidelines for related fact situations. Cases decided on narrow grounds empower elected officials to participate in constitutional dialogues with the justices on the proper interpretation of constitutional rights and powers.

3.2 Judicial Sharing When Deciding to Decide

Justices share constitutional authority when deciding what cases raising constitutional questions they will adjudicate. Federal statutory law at present permits the Supreme Court to determine in almost every instance whether the justices will hear an appeal from a constitutional decision made by a state court or a lower federal court. The justices have not used that authority to take a year's vacation (with pay), but in recent years they have reduced by half the number of constitutional decisions made on the merits. A Supreme Court decision not to hear an appeal effectively ends the case, leaving a previous constitutional judgment in place. The fewer constitutional pronouncements issued from the highest bench, the more responsibility lower courts and state courts have for settling constitutional controversies.

The case-or-controversy requirement of Article III provides constitutional restrictions on judicial power to make constitutional decisions. Persons seeking a judicial ruling must normally[60] claim an unconstitutional government action caused them to suffer a particularized concrete injury. Convicted murderers have standing to challenge the constitutionality of capital punishment because their life depends on the correct resolution of the constitutional issue. Citizens who are merely upset by the possibility that some killers may not be executed lack standing because their injury is not sufficiently concrete. Such persons must make their constitutional case to elected officials. Petitioners who meet standing requirements will not have their constitutional claims adjudicated if their case raises so-called political questions. The Constitution, the justices have ruled, entrusts the president or Congress with the power to settle some controversies over constitutional rights and powers. These matters include many issues of foreign policy, whether the United States is constitutionally at war, the constitutional rules for passing constitutional amendments, the constitutional procedures for impeaching federal officials, federal policy toward Native Americans, and the proper interpretation of the Guaranty Clause.

Procedural requirements provide additional barriers to constitutional adjudication. Constitutionally dubious laws often remain on the books until some person is brave enough to risk a criminal sanction by violating that measure. The Supreme Court will not normally determine whether a twenty-three-year-old graduate student has a constitutionally protected right to drink beer until the graduate student has been convicted by a trial court and that conviction is affirmed by the highest state court in that jurisdiction. The justices will hear appeals from the state court only when authorized to do so by a federal statute. When Congress fails to pass laws vesting federal courts with jurisdiction to resolve a constitutional dispute, the justices refuse to hear the case even when the case otherwise meets the constitutional requirements for federal adjudication. As early as 1796, the justices maintained, "If Congress has provided no rule to regulate our proceedings, we cannot exercise an appellate jurisdiction."[61] The justices also tend to honor state rules regulating the time for raising constitutional issues. Should the graduate student's defense lawyer fail at trial to object to evidence that may have been unconstitutionally obtained by police officers, the Supreme Court will normally consider the constitutional issue waived by the defendant and leave the state court decision standing. Whether federal courts adjudicate last-minute appeals from death-sentenced petitioners often depends on whether the justices believe the allegedly new constitutional claim could have been raised during the original trial.

These restrictions on judicial review frequently prevent Supreme Court justices from resolving important constitutional disputes. Some barriers are strictly legal. Standing requirements immunize from federal judicial review virtually all instances when elected officials or state courts provide greater constitutional protections for individual freedoms than those mandated by previous Supreme Court rulings. The Supreme Court will not strike down state laws sanctioning same-sex marriages even when the judicial majority concludes that elected officials acted on a mistaken interpretation of the equal protection clause because such measures do not cause constitutionally cognizable injuries. That state legislators erroneously believe they are constitutionally required to permit same-sex marriages is not a sufficient basis for litigation. Someone must assert that they were harmed by that decision (and that harm cannot simply consist of mere disagreement with the law). Constitutional adjudication also does not take place on political questions. The Supreme Court in *Nixon v. United States* (1993) employed the political questions doctrine when ruling that the Senate is constitutionally authorized to determine what procedures are used during impeachment trials.

Other legal restrictions on constitutional adjudication make judicial review practically impossible. No one is likely to suffer the particularized concrete injury necessary to bring a lawsuit challenging a congressional decision, in violation of Article I, Section 5, not to "keep a Journal of its Proceedings." No one may be able to meet the standing requirements necessary to adjudicate the constitutionality of presidential decisions giving property to religious groups after *Hein v. Freedom from Religion Fdn.* (2007) rejected claims that taxpayers could legally challenge that practice. The very requirement that courts make constitutional decisions only when adjudicating a case severely limits judicial power. Litigants with legal standing to bring a lawsuit often have practical reasons for forbearance. Bringing a case to the Supreme Court is very expensive and time-consuming. Settlement is very tempting when the prospect of victory is distant and cost of defeat is high. The Supreme Court heard few civil liberties cases during the nineteenth century when political dissenters and racial minorities rarely had the resources necessary to litigate their constitutional claims. Finances and risk aversion are not the only barriers to constitutional litigation. Klan and related violence explain why hardly any legal challenges were issued to Jim Crow policies in the Deep South before the 1960s. Imagine that your friends violate a university ban on keeping handguns in their dorm because they are confident that the Supreme Court will declare that the prohibition abridges the Second Amendment rights announced in *Heller v. District of Columbia* (2008). Even if they are guaranteed free legal representation by a local gun rights group, they may have second thoughts after they realize that they will have to litigate numerous appeals through state and federal courts, risking expulsion from college and a prison sentence should their predictions be wrong. Perhaps they are better off taking a plea bargain that requires only five days of public service (and expunges the convictions).

Other restrictions on constitutional adjudication delay Supreme Court decisions, leaving other governing institutions with temporary authority to determine constitutional rights and powers. The time lag between the onset of a constitutional controversy and Supreme Court adjudication often has a substantial impact on constitutional practice. The Supreme Court in 1944 and 1961 ruled that doctors lacked standing to challenge Connecticut's ban on birth control because state officials were not prosecuting physicians who prescribed contraception for their private patients. The majority opinions failed to note that every public birth control clinic in that state closed after the Supreme Court of Connecticut in 1940 sustained the state ban on contraception for married persons. Thus, until 1965, when the Supreme Court declared the contraceptive ban unconstitutional in *Griswold v. Connecticut,* federal constitutional rights were determined by state judges. The Supreme Court declared Abraham Lincoln's imposition of martial law unconstitutional only after the Civil War ended. That delay permitted the government during the hostilities to imprison without trial persons perceived to threaten the Union effort. The Supreme Court's requirement that persons bring federal habeas corpus claims first exhaust all possible avenues for relief in the state courts lengthens the stay on death row for persons whose constitutional claims will eventually be vindicated by a federal court. Until the federal court acts, such persons are treated as if the state court decision governs their status.

3.3 Judicial Sharing on the Merits

Justices have many means for sharing constitutional authority when deciding cases. Some commentators urge deference to legislative understandings of constitutional law. James Bradley Thayer famously insisted that justices were not authorized to strike down legislation after "conclud[ing] that upon a just and true construction the law is unconstitutional." Judicial action was appropriate only "when those who have the right to make laws have not merely made a mistake, but have made a very clear one—so clear that it is not open to rational question."[62] Justices who believe they should strike down only laws that no reasonable person might think constitutional might, in previous lives as federal legislators, vote in Congress against a gun control bill they conclude violates the

Second Amendment and then, after being appointed to the federal bench, vote to sustain the measure as not clearly unconstitutional. Other commentators propose limiting the methods justices employ when determining the meaning of constitutional provisions. Aspirational arguments (see Chapter 4) may be legitimate methods for legislative efforts to construct the Constitution but not for justices engaged in constitutional interpretation.[63] A judicial decision sustaining capital punishment as consistent with the original meaning of *cruel and unusual punishment* leaves elected officials free to decide whether capital punishment is consistent with the best constitutional understanding of justice.

Possible distinctions between the judicially enforceable constitution and the legal constitution provide related limitations on Supreme Court decision-making. Justices, Lawrence Sager contends, must "underenforce" such constitutional norms as equal protection because they lack the capacity to determine and enforce all the policies necessary for Americans to become fully equal citizens.[64] Courts in other countries often mandate that citizens have access to certain basic resources but leave to elected officials the choice about the means that best achieve that constitutional end.[65] Some state courts have mandated that all children in the state must have an equal education, but left state officials to determine what command means in practice.[66] Judicial deference of a different sort takes place when cases are decided on fairly narrow constitutional grounds, a practice that empowers other governing officials to retain at least temporary authority over other manifestations of some constitutional controversy. Cass Sunstein would have judicial opinions "say no more than necessary to justify an outcome, . . . leaving as much as possible undecided."[67] Justices deciding whether the affirmative action program at State U. is constitutional, in this view, should base their decision on the particular features of that program and not issue broad pronouncements that cover affirmative action programs at all institutions. This leaves other state institutions free to act on their best interpretation of the Constitution until the court decides whether their distinctive affirmative action admissions program is constitutional.

Judicial deference to elected officials on matters of constitutional law varies by judge and period. Justices before the Civil War often stressed that they would declare laws unconstitutional only in a clear case. "To authorize this court to pronounce any law void," Justice William Paterson stated in 1800, "it must be a clear and unequivocal breach of the constitution, not a doubtful and argumentative application."[68] Thayer's conception of the judicial function in constitutional cases influenced many proponents of judicial restraint during the first two-thirds of the twentieth century. "I think the word liberty in the 14th Amendment is perverted," Justice Oliver Wendell Holmes wrote when dissenting in *Lochner v. New York* (1905), "unless a rational and fair man necessarily would admit that the statute proposed would infringe on fundamental principles as they have been understood by the traditions of our people and our law." Some justices before the Civil War may have respected the distinction between interpretation and construction,[69] although this is more controversial historically. Present practice is far less deferential on matters of constitutional law. No justice on the Burger, Rehnquist, and Roberts has demonstrated much restraint when declaring laws unconstitutional. The more liberal and the more conservative justices in *Boerne* unanimously agreed that justices should not defer to congressional judgments about the meaning of the First and Fourteenth Amendments.

Judicial minimalism has had a greater influence on contemporary constitutional jurisprudence. The crucial swing justices on the Burger and Rehnquist Courts frequently insisted on narrow justifications for decisions striking down government actions. Justice O'Connor was particularly averse to making bold constitutional pronouncements. She tended to write either majority opinions that restricted rulings largely to the particular details of the case before the Supreme Court or concurring opinions that sharply limited the import of the majority's constitutional analysis. Her majority opinion in *Adarand Constructors, Inc. v. Pena* (1995), when reversing a lower federal court decision sustaining a federal minority set-aside program, indicated that well designed affirmative action measures might withstand constitutional scrutiny. Her majority opinion in *Grutter v. Bollinger* (2003) sustained an affirmative action program by focusing on the particular features of the University of Michigan Law School policy under constitutional attack. The University of Michigan had a different affirmative action program for undergraduates, and Justice O'Connor voted to declare that program unconstitutional in *Gratz v. Bollinger* (2003), the companion case to *Grutter*.

Justices sometimes defer to legislative fact-findings that influence constitutional decisions. Supreme Court justices consistently claim that their primary responsibility is to apply the law to the relevant facts as determined by a legislature or trial court. Justice Harlan Fiske Stone insisted that the Supreme Court should not declare economic measures unconstitutional "unless in the light of facts made known or generally assumed" the law was "of such a character as to preclude the assumption that it rests upon some rational basis within the knowledge or experience of legislatures." The Supreme Court in *Lassiter v. Northampton County Elections Board* (1959) rejected claims that literacy tests were unconstitutional per se. Seven years later, the justices in *South Carolina v. Katzenbach* (1966) sustained a congressional ban on literacy tests through most of the South, deferring to the factual conclusions Congress reached after an investigation revealed that such tests were means for preventing voting by persons of color.

Fact deference often enables elected officials and trial courts to exercise substantial influence over constitutional practice. Knowing the legal standards the Supreme Court uses when adjudicating cases, legislative committees and state judges may strategically make the fact-findings that best ensure their policies withstand constitutional scrutiny. Consider several rules that Alan Dershowitz believes structure the criminal process in the United States:

Rule IV: Almost all police lie about whether they violated the Constitution in order to convict guilty defendants.
Rule V: All prosecutors, judges, and defense attorneys are aware of Rule IV.
Rule VIII: Most trial judges pretend to believe police officers who they know are lying.[70]

If the Supreme Court generally defers to findings of fact made at trial and trial judges generally defer to police officers, then "imaginative" police officers have far more power in practice than official law suggests to determine the rights of criminal suspects. Police officers who believe they have no constitutional obligation to read Miranda rights may falsely claim on the stand that Miranda rights were read. If the trial judge, with a wink, accepts as true such perjured testimony and the Supreme Court as a matter of principle defers to the trial judge's fact-findings, the police officer's understanding of the Fifth and Fourteenth Amendments is what actually determines the rights of persons suspected of crime. Whether many affirmative action plans pass constitutional muster may depend on whether justices accept at face value the official justifications and explanations that university administrators give for those policies or engage in independent fact-finding.

3.4 Presidential and Congressional Sharing

Elected officials share constitutional authority with justices. Elections, legislation, and appointments are as responsible for establishing and maintaining judicial authority as judicial decisions. The Judiciary Act of 1789 made judicial review possible. In sharp contrast to the Confederate Congress, which never agreed on the legislation necessary to create the constitutionally mandated national judicial system, the First Congress immediately provided for the appointment of federal justices and specified when federal courts would meet. Section 25 of the Judiciary Act vested the Supreme Court with the power to adjudicate appeals from certain state court decisions interpreting the Constitution of the United States and authorized the justices to declare federal and state laws unconstitutional when deciding those cases. Congress during the 1820s and 1830s first refused to repeal Section 25 and then, in response to nullification, expanded the jurisdiction of federal courts. Elected officials after the Civil War passed a series of laws that presently enable justices on the Supreme Court, at their discretion, to adjudicate appeals from almost every case raising constitutional questions.[71]

Congress and the president have the power to remove or weaken the various barriers to constitutional adjudication discussed in the last section. Within certain limits, legislation may grant parties standing to challenge official actions. The Supreme Court in *Massachusetts v. EPA* (2007) held that Congress could vest states with the power to sue administrative agencies without having to demonstrate that the alleged illegal or unconstitutional action caused a particularized injury. Elected officials may assist private litigants who challenge federal and state statutes. Justice Department officials write amicus briefs urging courts to void laws inconsistent with shared constitutional visions. Congress passes legislation assisting litigants who make constitutional attacks on disfavored federal and state measures. The liberal judicial activism of the 1960s was facilitated by various executive and congressional decisions promoting litigation for liberal causes.[72] Solicitor general Archibald Cox in 1962 successfully urged the Supreme Court to declare unconstitutional malapportioned state election districts (which had conservative biases). Supreme Court activism on behalf of the poor increased sharply after Congress established and generously funded the Legal Services Program. As funding was reduced, judicial solicitude for the rights of the poor ebbed.[73]

The justices have historically been eager to exercise legislatively granted authority partly because presidents have consistently nominated and senators have consistently confirmed jurists to the federal bench who endorse the central principles of *Marbury v. Madison*. The prominent commentators in every era who have called for the abolition of judicial power have not been favored with appointments to the highest tribunal in the land. Contemporary critics of judicial power concede that candidates for the presidency would commit political suicide by promising to appoint federal justices who would never declare laws unconstitutional.[74] When populists and progressives at the turn of the twentieth century campaigned against the judicial power to declare laws unconstitutional, they were soundly defeated in national elections.[75]

Congressional power to determine federal jurisdiction plays a crucial, underappreciated role when constitutional authority is allocated. Article III, Section 1 declares, "The judicial Power of the United States, shall be vested in one supreme Court, and in such inferior Courts as the Congress may from time to time ordain and establish." Section 2 vests the Supreme Court with original jurisdiction over a few matters and appellate jurisdiction over most, "with such Exceptions...as the Congress shall make." The meaning of these clauses is controversial. Some commentators, most notably Justice Joseph Story, interpret these provisions as mandating that Congress must grant the Supreme Court (or perhaps some federal court) either appellate or original jurisdiction over every federal question mentioned in Article III.[76] Others assert that Congress may strip the Supreme Court and the federal court system of the power to adjudicate all or almost all constitutional disputes.[77] A third view contends that Congress must give the federal courts the power to monitor constitutional compliance effectively, but that power need not encompass the right or obligation to resolve all constitutional disputes.[78] General agreement exists, however, that the judiciary may not enforce a congressional obligation to empower federal courts, if such obligation exists. As noted already, case law dating from 1796 holds that the Supreme Court has no power to settle constitutional controversies when Congress fails to vest the justices with the necessary appellate jurisdiction. The justices in *Ex Parte McCardle* (1869) refrained from determining the constitutionality of crucial Reconstruction measures when Congress quickly repealed the law vesting jurisdiction after oral argument in that case had taken place. As long as *McCardle* and related cases are good law, Congress may immunize constitutional questions from judicial review by failing to pass or repealing the relevant jurisdictional statutes. Federal judicial authority to interpret the Constitution presently exists almost entirely by legislative grace.

The legislative foundations for judicial power undermine the conventional account of judicial power as countermajoritarian. Popular and legislative majorities throughout American history have consistently endorsed and facilitated the judicial power to declare laws unconstitutional. More often than not, elected officials favor judiciary supremacy as well as judicial review. "Political leaders, and most importantly presidents, have generally been willing to lend their support" when justices assert that their constitutional decisions bind all governing officials.[79] Elected officials may be judicial supremacists in part because they are convinced by the previously discussed arguments for judicial power. Popular support for judicial authority also has political foundations. Many governing officials at many times believe they will best secure their distinctive constitutional visions and other political goals by empowering courts.

4. The Politics of Shared Constitutional Authority

Constitutional politics further complicates the processes by which constitutional decisions are actually made and implemented. Some contests for constitutional authority pit judges against elected officials. When the Supreme Court declared the Religious Freedom Restoration Act unconstitutional, liberal and conservative justices on the court united against the liberals and conservatives in the elected branches of government who supported that legislation. More often, and often simultaneously, partisan coalitions and political movements battle each other for the control over all governing institutions necessary to make their constitutional vision the law of the land. Prochoice and prolife activists debate in courtrooms, in legislative chambers, and on campaign trails across the country. The Supreme Court is hardly above the partisan fray. When President Lyndon Johnson nominated Thurgood Marshall to the bench, he was seeking to empower an ally in his effort to eradicate Jim Crow and was not providing the country with a neutral arbiter for constitutional disputes about race. President Johnson's attempt to fashion a friendly judiciary is hardly anomalous. Elected officials throughout American history have developed numerous strategies for controlling and then empowering courts.

Contests for constitutional authority in American history are structured by the changing dynamics of partisan competition. When new coalitions first gain control of the elected branches of the national government, the presidency in particular, they must typically contend with members of the electorally deposed regime ensconced in the federal judiciary. Constitutional conflicts during this time are often between elected officials and unelected justices. Franklin Roosevelt threatened to pack a Supreme Court that, during his first term in office, declared many New Deal measures unconstitutional. Lincoln refused to obey a writ of habeas corpus issued by Chief Justice Roger Taney, a veteran Jacksonian jurist. As politics stabilize and justices more sympathetic to the new political order populate the federal bench, powerful elected officials often see the Supreme Court as a potential ally in their struggles against various political rivals. Conservative Republicans in the first third of the twentieth century limited the influence of more progressive Republicans in Congress by agreeing on vague statutory protections for labor unions that were interpreted, usually very narrowly, by conservative justices.[80] Racial liberals in the national government during the New Deal and Great Society encouraged racial liberals in the federal judiciary to strike down Jim Crow policies favored by local majorities in the South. Judicial supremacy is frequently championed by leaders of decaying political coalitions who must rely on the federal judiciary to buttress policies that no longer command powerful electoral support.[81] As their control over the elected branches waned during the 1970s and 1980s, Great Society liberals increasingly insisted that the federal judiciary best resolved constitutional controversies. Conservatives who when Ronald Reagan took office regarded originalism primarily as a means for slowing the tide of liberal judicial activism now frequently employ originalism when seeking to persuade the Republican majority on the Supreme Court to strike down such liberal policies on gun control and health care.[82]

The judicial nomination and confirmation process facilitates alliances between elected officials and unelected justices. Presidents select individuals for the bench whose constitutional philosophies are congruent with their own. Senators sometimes reject judicial nominees whose constitutional views they perceive as too extreme, *extreme* being defined as too distant from their views. When liberals control the White House and Senate, as they did in the 1930s and

1960s, they appoint liberals to the Supreme Court. When conservatives hold greater sway, as they did in the 1920s and 1980s, they appoint conservatives to the court. Although "mistakes" are made, the political scientist Robert Dahl correctly summarized the history when he observed, "It would appear... somewhat unrealistic to suppose that a Court whose members are recruited in the fashion of Supreme Court Justices would long hold to norms of Right or Justice substantially at odds with the rest of the political elite."[83]

The politics of judicial appointment practically guarantees that, with some lag, the center of the court will sit in the political mainstream. The Supreme Court had a Jacksonian majority by the time Andrew Jackson left the presidency. At the end of Franklin Roosevelt's second term, the Supreme Court was controlled by New Dealers committed to reversing any previous judicial decision that limited federal power to regulate the national economy. Life-tenured justices are likely to deviate over time from the preferences of any political coalition. Still, sitting members of the federal bench usually adapt to public sentiment and the broader trends of the political culture, sharing the common prejudices and values of their time. As Justice Benjamin Cardozo observed, the "great tides and currents which engulf the rest of men do not turn aside in their course and pass the judges by."[84]

Members of dominant national coalitions often make strenuous efforts to have ideologically sympathetic Supreme Court justices declare particular federal and state laws unconstitutional. Congress quite frequently passes vague or ambiguous legislation that encourages justices to make public policy in the guise of statutory or constitutional interpretation. The Compromise of 1850 and the Kansas-Nebraska Act of 1854 contained provisions eliminating procedural barriers to federal judicial review of cases raising questions about the constitutional status of slavery in the territories. One senator suggested that Congress had enacted lawsuits rather than laws.[85] Sometimes, elected officials bluntly issue invitations for judicial intervention. James K. Polk, Franklin Pierce, James Buchanan, Stephen Douglas, Jefferson Davis, and Henry Clay were among the numerous antebellum political leaders who urged Congress "to leave the question of slavery or no slavery to be declared by the only competent authority that can definitely settle it forever, the authority of the Supreme Court."[86] In other instances, governing officials passively acquiesce when federal courts end legislative stalemates by assuming responsibility for resolving constitutional controversies. After the Supreme Court in *Roe v. Wade* prohibited statutory bans on abortion, John Hart Ely noted "the sighs of relief as this particular albatross was cut from the legislative and executive necks."[87]

Judicial decisions declaring laws unconstitutional help presidents and legislators achieve various political goals. Many judicial decisions striking down state laws help federal government officials keep local political majorities in line. Warren Court rulings on constitutional criminal procedure made state police forces conform to national standards.[88] Presidents often regard the judiciary as a potential ally in political and constitutional struggles against institutions controlled by members of rival coalitions. Roosevelt and Harry Truman nominated racial liberals to the federal bench as a means for circumventing a Congress stalemated on civil rights legislation by Southern Democrats.[89] Political moderates often want to avoid difficult decisions that divide their political supporters. United by their opposition to the national bank and internal improvements, antebellum Jacksonian Democrats promoted the Supreme Court as the institution responsible for settling sectionally diverse slavery issues. Party leaders with a tenuous hold on elected office may want the insurance that courts will protect some of their interests when they are out of power. Lame duck Republicans in the late nineteenth century employed a version of this "partisan entrenchment"[90] strategy by expanding the jurisdiction of the Republican-controlled federal judiciary immediately after losing control of Congress in a national election.[91]

With the exception of the judicial decisions declaring New Deal legislation unconstitutional, virtually every other major exercise of judicial power in American history has enjoyed support from some members of the coalition in control of at least one of the elected branches of the national government. Marshall Court decisions striking down state laws after the War of 1812 promoted the commercial policies favored by national Republicans in the Congress and White House. Supreme Court rulings during the late nineteenth century sharply limiting antitrust prosecutions (*United States v. E. C. Knight Co.* [1895]), striking down the federal income tax (*Pollock v. Farmers' Loan and Trust Co.* [1895]), issuing injunctions against labor unions (*In re Debs* [1894]), and banning state regulation of interstate railroads (*Wabash, St. Louis & Pacific Railway Co. v. Illinois* [1886]) "are best viewed as 'politically inspired,'" as "part of the Republican Party's effort to restructure national institutions better to facilitate national economic development."[92] Lucas Powe details how the Warren Court was "a functioning part of the Kennedy-Johnson liberalism of the mid and late 1960s."[93] Prominent members of the Reagan, G. H. W. Bush, and G. W. Bush administrations supported Rehnquist Court decisions reinvigorating the Tenth Amendment and providing other constitutional limits on federal power.[94] *Roe v. Wade* presently remains good constitutional law because prochoice Democrats for the past generation have retained just enough political power to prevent the appointment of five Supreme Court justices on record as opposing judicial protection for abortion rights.

Constitutional politics do not end when the judiciary speaks. Justices do not enforce their decrees. Other governing officials bear that responsibility. As Alexander Hamilton recognized in *Federalist 78*:

> The judiciary...has no influence over either the sword or the purse; no direction either of the strength or of the wealth of the society; and

can take no active resolution whatever. It may truly be said to have neither FORCE nor WILL, but merely judgment; and must ultimately
depend upon the aid of the executive arm even for the efficacy of its
judgments.[95]

Quite frequently, the same elected officials who adopted a particular policy
must implement judicial decisions declaring their actions unconstitutional.
Not surprisingly, executive cooperation has varied by time, place, and issue.
The Eisenhower administration immediately announced that public schools
in the District of Columbia would be desegregated after the Supreme Court
declared in *Bolling v. Sharpe* (1954) that the Constitution permitted neither
the federal government nor the states to separate children by race. The Georgia
legislature responded very differently to the Supreme Court's decision in
Chisholm v. Georgia (1793), which allowed out-of-state citizens to sue that
state in federal court. Georgia officials immediately passed legislation imposing the death penalty for anyone found guilty of attempting to implement that
judicial decree.

Elected officials frequently do not comply with constitutional orders in cases
they believe wrongly decided. "Where there is local hostility to change," Gerald
Rosenberg's study of judicial power concludes, "court orders will be ignored." He
finds that "community pressure, violence or threats of violence, and lack of market response all serve to curtail actions to implement court decisions."[96] Many
famous judicial decisions declaring laws unconstitutional had almost no immediate consequence. Ten years after *Brown v. Board of Education* was decided, less
than 2% of African American children in the Deep South were attending integrated schools.[97] Judicial decisions prohibiting state-organized prayer in public schools had little effect on that religious practice in homerooms across the
United States.[98]

Judicial skeptics observe that Supreme Court decisions often have perverse effects, unanticipated by either the successful litigants or the judicial
majority. Political backlash is one possibility. Rosenberg found that "one
result of litigation to produce significant social reform is to strengthen the
opponents of such change."[99] Commentators blame *Roe v. Wade* for the rise of
conservative Christian political activism and suspect that socially conservative voters mobilized by litigation campaigns for same-sex marriage played a
crucial role in delivering the presidency to Republicans in the 2004 national
election.[100] Liberal judicial victories have harmed liberal political causes by
preventing necessary compromises between liberal coalition partners. The
federal court decisions that helped desegregate unions aggravated the tensions between the labor movement and the civil rights movement that contributed to the decline of the Democratic Party in the late 1960s.[101] Most

observers expected that judicial decisions mandating one person, one vote would increase the political strength of urban areas. In practice, those rulings empowered suburbs and facilitated gerrymandering. Judicial decisions that achieve their desired constitutional end often do so through surprising paths. Michael Klarman maintains that Southern voters responded to *Brown* by electing racial extremists. The resulting massive resistance to any desegregation and extreme racial violence caused a second backlash outside the South that eventually inspired the Civil Rights Act of 1964.[102] Setting in motion the events that led Bull Connor to have police dogs attack African American children while television cameras were transmitting these events to disgusted Northern voters was not exactly how the National Association for the Advancement of Colored People (NAACP) conceived that their litigation campaign would produce a more integrated society.

Many studies on compliance and the impact of judicial decision find that judicial decrees matter more and have fewer perverse effects than the skeptics suggest. State Supreme Court decisions declaring unconstitutional local bans on abortion dramatically increased the number of legal abortions in the affected state.[103] Other constitutional decisions have had far greater impact than might be predicted from their narrow legal holdings. Many localities on tight budgets responded to judicial decisions providing only slightly more protection for certain property rights by settling out of court numerous disputes over environmental regulations rather than incurring the legal costs necessary to maintain land use policies elected officials sincerely believed would pass constitutional muster.[104] Robert Post and Reva Siegel contend that critics of constitutional litigation "overestimate the costs of backlash and...underestimate" how political struggles over contested Supreme Court rulings "invigorate the democratic legitimacy of constitutional interpretation."[105] Gay rights activists insist that their litigation campaigns have mobilized more socially progressive voters than Christian conservatives.[106] Tom Keck's study of litigation over abortion, gay rights, gun control, and affirmative action found numerous instances in which public policy shifted in response to judicial decisions.[107] Political movements need not even triumph in court to benefit from constitutional adjudication. Unsuccessful litigation campaigns may increase the membership of and contributions to advocacy organizations.[108]

Political struggles over constitutional meaning occur even when most elected officials support judicial rulings. Political movements hardly ever fold their tents after litigation campaigns fail to secure desired constitutional policies. The Republican Party after *Dred Scott* remained committed to prohibiting slavery in the territories. Contemporary prolife forces remain committed to reversing Supreme Court decisions prohibiting bans on abortion. Contemporary prochoice forces remain committed to reversing Supreme Court decisions sustaining regulations on abortion. Constitutional conflicts are settled politically, not legally. Constitutional politics come to an end only when the political forces backing the losing issue concede defeat, lose political interest in the issue, or, as was the case in the 1860s, are slaughtered on the battlefield.

Justices respond to the politics of constitutional authority. Legislative and presidential encouragement often inspires broad judicial decisions. The Supreme Court determined that Congress could not ban slavery in American territories only after repeatedly being invited by elected officials to settle sectional controversies. One member of the *Dred Scott* majority declared, "The Court would not fulfill public expectations or discharge its duties by maintaining silence upon [the] questio[n]."[109] After the Truman administration submitted an amicus brief urging the justices to overrule *Plessey v. Ferguson* (1896), the Supreme Court abandoned case-by-case adjudication and declared segregated public education inherently unconstitutional. Justices pull punches when the political environment is less hospitable. Supreme Court majorities during the Civil War offered various jurisdictional excuses for not determining the constitutionality of Lincoln's unilateral decision to declare martial law in some free-state counties. Shortly after Robert E. Lee's surrender, that policy was unanimously declared unconstitutional in *Ex parte Milligan* (1865). "One bombshell at a time is enough," Frankfurter declared in 1956 when explaining why shortly after deciding *Brown* the Supreme Court would not consider whether bans on interracial marriage were constitutional.[110] A decade later, in a far friendlier environment, the Warren Court in *Loving v. Virginia* (1967) unanimously ruled that miscegenation laws violated the equal protection clause of the Fourteenth Amendment.

Justices participate in the politics of constitutional authority. Many lobbied presidents and Congress to appoint specific persons when vacancies opened on the Supreme Court. Others have advised presidents (Abe Fortas), drafted legislation (Story), ran political campaigns (John Catron), and sought the presidency while on the bench (John McLean, Salmon Chase, Charles Evans Hughes). Members of the Hughes Court worked with sympathetic members of Congress to defeat Roosevelt's proposed court-packing plan. Justices on occasion have helped choose allied elected officials. The five conservative justices on the Rehnquist Court in *Bush v. Gore* (2000) doomed Al Gore's chances for the presidency by declaring the methods for recounting ballots in Florida unconstitutional. Supreme Court decisions in reapportionment cases have had a substantial impact on who is elected to public office, although not necessarily the impact Warren Court majorities envisioned when first declaring the one person, one vote principle.

The Supreme Court and federal judiciary remain distinctive institutions, even though their staffing and decision-making process are influenced significantly by other branches of the national government. Institutional affiliation matters.

Proponents of the New Deal in Congress disputed the merits of President Roosevelt's proposal to pack the Supreme Court. Every proponent of the New Deal on the Supreme Court opposed that plan. The appointments process matters. Every justice on the Warren Court was a racial liberal because they were either appointed by a racially liberal president (Truman) or vetted by a Justice Department largely controlled by racial liberals (Eisenhower, Roosevelt).[111] Their eventual unanimous opposition to Jim Crow mirrored neither attitudes in the country at large nor the commitments of any political party during the 1950s. Finally, certain constitutional considerations have historically played a greater and more consistent role than partisan concerns when justices make constitutional decisions. Contemporary justices appointed by Republican presidents have been less willing as a group than contemporary justices appointed by Democratic presidents to question the constitutionality of detention policies during the war on terror. Nevertheless, both Republican and Democratic judicial appointees on the federal bench have more frequently voted against detention policies than their partisan counterparts in Congress. We cannot determine whether these votes demonstrate that Supreme Court justices take constitutional considerations more seriously than elected officials or merely that Supreme Court justices take different constitutional considerations more seriously than elected officials. Legislators may be more attuned to presidential power under Article II than justices, while justices are more concerned with preserving habeas corpus. What the voting patterns scrutinized in this paragraph and in Chapter 4 indicate is the clear influence of institutional affiliation on constitutional decision-making. Justices do not behave as do elected officials, even when both are influenced by both constitutional norms and policy considerations.

5. Shared Constitutional Authority as Politics, Law, and Constitutionalism

The politics of constitutional authority is distinctively constitutional, even though ordinary political concerns significantly influence how constitutional controversies are settled in the United States. Constitutional rules determine the participants in constitutional dialogues. Presidents typically nominate justices who share their constitutional vision, but Article III permits them to make nominations only after a sitting justice leaves the bench or Congress passes legislation increasing the number of federal justices. Informal constitutional norms foster judicial independence and a professional judiciary. Prominent members of Congress have frequently, but not always, refused to impeach federal justices, to place severe limits on federal jurisdiction, or to expand the number of seats on the Supreme Court, even after judicial majorities have struck down policies that national legislative majorities believe easily pass constitutional muster. Contemporary presidents are expected to appoint well-respected lawyers to the federal bench. When they do not, as was the case with Homer Thornberry (1968), Harold Carswell (1971), and, arguably, Harriet Miers (2006), some of their partisan allies in the Senate do not support confirmation.

Judicial decisions allocating constitutional authority reflect the same complex interaction between political interests and legal norms as judicial decisions determining the meaning of the commerce clause or First Amendment. Ideology often matters when justices are considering whether a constitutional issue is properly before the court. The justices who most narrowly interpret Fourth Amendment rights (as incorporated by the Fourteenth Amendment) are the justices most inclined to find that Fourth Amendment claims cannot be adjudicated because the claim was not properly raised in a state court proceeding. Many other judicial disputes over whether to adjudicate claims of constitutional wrong are more rooted in different beliefs about the appropriate functions of judicial power than partisan gain. The debate over whether reapportionment was justiciable pitted liberal proponents of judicial activism against liberal proponents of judicial restraint. The liberal justices on the contemporary Supreme Court are far more likely than the conservative justices to consider whether gerrymandered legislative districts violate equal protection, even though Democrats gerrymander districts as often as Republicans.

The contemporary Supreme Court occupies a privileged position among diverse constitutional authorities. Presidents, legislators, state officials, and political activists all influence American constitutional development, but the federal judiciary at the turn of the twenty-first century on most constitutional issues most of the time has a little more influence than other institutions. This privileged position is partly rooted in a general sense among the public and elected officials that, while justices are not perfect, an institution whose members are chosen for their legal expertise may better interpret the Constitution than institutions whose members are selected mostly for other reasons. Rightly or wrongly, many people fear elected officials may one day run amok and believe that the Supreme Court provides some insurance against potentially severe violations of individual liberties. Most important perhaps, most of the time on most issues, elected officials have had more reason to support than oppose judicial review and supremacy. This tendency explains why far more political and legal precedents presently exist for judicial power than against.[112]

Supreme Court justices may find their privileged position threatened in the near future. Political coalitions most often challenge judicial authority when they first gain power and confront federal justices who insist on maintaining the constitutional vision that inspired the deposed regime. Recent elections may auger a more durable shift in partisan control of Congress and the White House. Should an emerging Democratic majority in the elected branches of government or in the White House find crucial constitutional goals stymied by conservative justices on the Roberts Court, a significant constitutional clash is quite possible. President Obama may have signaled the beginnings of a renewed struggle for control over constitutional development when his 2011 State of the Union address attacked judicial decisions striking down campaign finance legislation. So far the battlefields are quiet, but such a contest for constitutional authority would hardly be an unprecedented event in American constitutional history.

The actual politics of shared constitutional authority raise complicated questions about the relationship between fundamental law and popular sovereignty in a constitutional democracy. Many constitutional theorists still worry about the countermajoritarian difficulties that arise when unelected justices "thwart the will" of elected officials. Perhaps citizens should be as concerned with elected officials who "run from daylight," obscuring their policy goals and constitutional commitments by sponsoring judicial review and other practices that "attract less attention" than legislation.[113] "Legislators" who "covertly shift responsibility for divisive choices to less accountable actors," political scientists point out, "raise substantial concerns about the transparency and responsiveness of legislative processes."[114] Whether more restrained justices might cure this democratic deficiency is difficult to determine. Optimists think that elected officials will be forced to take public responsibility for more issues once courts refrain from taking those matters off their hands. Pessimists think legislators who cannot use ambiguous language and other techniques to foist political responsibility on to judges will simply use ambiguous language and other techniques to foist political responsibility on to administrative agencies or some other governing institution.

How well a system of separated institutions sharing constitutional authority in which the judiciary enjoys a privileged position promotes the values underlying American constitutionalism is controversial. Judicial supremacists and departmentalists dispute which governing institutions or combination of governing institutions are most likely to interpret constitutional provisions correctly. The complex sharing of constitutional authority discussed in this chapter may foster popular participation by providing numerous opportunities for citizens and political movements to influence how fundamental laws are construed in the United States. That complexity may also weaken accountability, preventing citizens from determining which governing officials are most responsible for a particular constitutional decision. Having all governing institutions share constitutional responsibility promises to improve the quality of constitutional decision-making by ensuring that multiple perspectives are considered before constitutional controversies are temporarily or permanently settled. Contemporary practice is also a recipe for incoherence when, as was the case with race policy during the Great Society and campaign finance at present, different institutions resolving different manifestations of a constitutional controversy employ conflicting principles, leaving the final policy a morass that no intelligent person would ever had independently selected.[115]

All systems for making political decisions have biases. A constitutional system in which justices have a privileged position is no exception to this generalization. American history suggests that judicial review in practice has some tendency to privilege nationalism, executive power, educated elites, and libertarian values. Judicial decisions exhibit these biases because justices are chosen by national officials, because the president has historically had greater input than the Senate into the judicial selection process, because most justices selected during the past century attended elite universities, and because judicial decisions ordering government officials to refrain from acting are more often implemented than judicial decisions requiring government officials to act in certain ways. These biases are likely to be influenced only at the margins by academic arguments providing better foundations for originalism, more doctrinal support for *Roe v. Wade*, or a sounder justification for congressional control over the appellate jurisdiction of the Supreme Court. When constitutional authority is broadly shared, political movements can change significantly the general trend of constitutional decision-making only if they change significantly the occupants of most government offices. Those who conclude that the politics of constitutional authority in the United States has historically been insufficiently legal, democratic, or coherent should probably pay greater attention to the structure of basic constitutional institutions than to the tendencies of the particular nine persons who happen to sit on the Supreme Court at a particular time.

|| 6 ||

Constitutional Change

Long-standing democratic constitutions rest on broad consensual foundations. Most citizens and most social movements must believe that the constitution supports, or at least does not thwart, their most cherished values and interests. Constitutional stability is not necessarily threatened when ordinary politics is partly about the meaning of particular constitutional provisions or minor constitutional revisions. Debates over whether the due process clause of the Fourteenth Amendment protects abortion rights, whether Article II gives the president the right to detain suspected terrorists without trial, or whether a balanced budget amendment should be ratified have not undermined American constitutionalism. Such disputes, as Chapter 5 details, comprise ordinary constitutional politics. Constitutional politics becomes extraordinary when prominent political factions contend that the constitution either obstructs their vital concerns or is likely to be interpreted for the foreseeable future in ways that obstruct their vital concerns. Should such a faction gain control of national institutions, officials may ignore constitutional restraints and processes, refuse to honor existing rules for constitutional reform, and perhaps propose a new constitution with a distinctive ratification process. When such factions lose elections and are geographically concentrated, secession and civil war are likely.

Framers and their descendants must somehow devise and operate constitutional processes that prevent inevitable political, social, cultural, and technological changes from fostering substantial discontent with the constitutional order. This task is likely to become increasingly difficult over time. Constitutional processes may immediately fail to function as anticipated or slowly lose their capacity to generate desirable outcomes. Confounding the framers, members of the Electoral College never exercised independent judgment when casting presidential ballots. Constitutional politics in the Jacksonian era dashed original expectations that presidents and senators would be above the partisan fray. Future citizens may use different standards than the framing generation when evaluating constitutional processes and rules. Far more Americans at present than two hundred years ago expect the national government to devise a health-care program and to manage economic cycles. A constitution designed to mediate controversies over slavery must now mediate controversies over abortion and gay marriage. Enduring constitutions must directly incorporate these extralegal developments or be updated by formal amendment. Both constitutional processes must be managed to maintain the necessary consensual foundations for democratic constitutionalism.

The Constitution of the United States has several features designed to establish and preserve broad popular support. Chapter 4 outlines how constitutional language and the legitimate methods for determining the meaning of constitutional provisions are sufficiently capacious to encompass many technological and social developments. Throughout American history, the vast majority of prominent political movements have claimed that the Constitution supports their platform, whether those platforms are dedicated to slavery, national expansion, laissez-faire, the administrative state, or multiculturalism. Chapter 5 discusses how separated institutions sharing constitutional power tend to generate tolerable temporary and permanent settlements to constitutional controversies, the constitutional controversies over slavery immediately before the Civil War being the obvious exception. Citizens may not like the most recent constitutional decision on abortion or presidential power, but such rulings usually inspire greater recourse to the constitutional processes for obtaining better rulings than actions that pose serious threats to the legitimacy of the constitutional order. The constitutional rules for ratification and amendment further guarantee that constitutional principles will rest on broad consensual foundations. Both Article V and Article VII mandate that most Americans from all sections of the United States approve all textual changes to the fundamental constitutional law of the land.

Problems of constitutional ratification and amendment seem simpler than problems of constitutional interpretation and authority. The relevant constitutional rules are set out in the constitutional text. They appear fairly unambiguous. "The Ratification of the Conventions of Nine States," Article VII plainly declares, "shall be sufficient for the Establishment of this Constitution." Article V establishes clear rules for constitutional amendments. When two-thirds of both houses propose a constitutional amendment, that amendment must be ratified by three-fourths of all state legislatures or by conventions in three-fourths of all states, with Congress choosing the mode of state ratification. Two-thirds of the states may call a convention for proposing amendments that, again, must be ratified by three-quarters of all states. Both processes require a strong national consensus before constitutional change takes place.

History reveals some minor problems with these schemes. The constitutional status of North Carolina and Rhode Island, neither of which had ratified the Constitution, was unclear when George Washington was inaugurated. No one really knew whether North Carolina and Rhode Island in April 1789 were independent states or still bound by the Articles of Confederation. Fortunately for the United States, but unfortunately for persons fond of constitutional puzzles, both states soon officially signed up. By making ratification unanimous, North Carolina and Rhode Island resolved as a practical matter all theoretical questions concerning the interpretation of Article VII. Article V in practice has presented more difficult interpretive questions. Americans debate whether states may rescind a vote approving a constitutional amendment before that amendment is ratified, whether Congress may set a time limit for ratification, and whether Congress must set a time limit.[1] The Supreme Court has refrained from setting any legal standard, ruling that the proper interpretation of Article V raises nonjusticiable political questions.[2] Still, with the very important exceptions of the Fourteenth and Twenty-Seventh Amendments, little substantial dispute has taken place over whether proposed Amendments have been ratified consistently with Article V.

The plain words of Articles V and VII do not, however, cover important issues of constitutional change in the United States. No constitutional provision discusses secession, a matter of some significance during the nineteenth century, or the conditions under which the Constitution might no longer be the fundamental law of the land. Contrary to Article VII, following the constitutional rules laid out in the text is not a sufficient condition for formal constitutional change. Constitutions do not become authoritative sources of fundamental law merely because their internal conditions for ratification are satisfied. Otherwise, you could write a new Constitution of the United States and condition legitimacy on approval by your five best friends. Whether all amendments ratified by the procedures set out in Article V are binding constitutional law is controversial. Some constitutional commentators in the United States and some constitutional courts in other countries insist that an amendment ratified consistently with the constitutional procedures for constitutional change might nevertheless be unconstitutional if that amendment is inconsistent with fundamental constitutional principles. Following the constitutional rules laid out in Article V may also not be a necessary condition for formal constitutional change. Some scholars maintain that a combination of vigorously contested elections, high-profile judicial decisions, and "super statutes" should be treated as valid constitutional amendments, having the same constitutional status as textual provisions ratified consistently with constitutional text.

Americans experience semiformal as well as formal constitutional change. Federal justices, presidents, and congressional leaders often reject or modify the constitutional understandings that guided their predecessors. Instead of providing new or repealing old texts, constitutional decision-makers reinterpret existing constitutional provisions. Presidents in the Jacksonian Era were the first to claim the veto power could be constitutionally used as an ordinary policy tool as well as a means for preventing unconstitutional legislation. The Supreme Court changes the constitutional standards that determine when state governments may constitutionally regulate interstate commerce every thirty years or so. Many constitutional decisions, controversial when made, have as much or more influence than the constitutional text on subsequent constitutional decisions. Supreme Court justices debate the original meaning of *Brown v. Board of Education* (1954) rather than the original meaning of the Fourteenth Amendment when deciding whether school boards may use race when assigning children to public schools. The understanding that federal judges should not engage in partisan politics and cannot be removed for partisan reasons dates from the failed impeachment of Justice Samuel Chase in 1805, not the drafting of Article III of the Constitution in 1787.

Some vital constitutional developments take place entirely off the books.[3] These informal constitutional changes are memorialized neither by constitutional text nor by constitutional decisions but occur when important political or social practices are reorganized in ways that have constitutional significance. The development of the party system in the early Republic dramatically changed expected relationships between the elected branches of the national government and may have been partly responsible for the increased influence of the federal judiciary. Industrialization undermined the prohibition on class legislation at the heart of the Fourteenth Amendment[4] and threatened inherited constitutional distinctions between intrastate and interstate commerce. These informal constitutional changes are often legally uncontroversial, even if sometimes thought constitutionally inappropriate. No constitutional rule prohibited the rise of candidate-centered elections for the Senate during the 1960s. Nevertheless, such extralegal developments often undermine the political and social foundations for ongoing constitutional practices. Scholars detail how senators less beholden to party leaders explain the increased politicization of the judicial selection process during the late twentieth century. The increased politicization, in turn, significantly influenced important constitutional decisions.[5]

Both law and politics structure all forms of constitutional development. Elections and ordinary political tactics determine whether formal and semiformal constitution changes take place. Informal constitutional developments determine how the crucial ballots are cast. Suffragettes appealed to American constitutional aspirations and racist sentiments during the national and statewide political campaigns that gained the constitutionally mandated supermajorities necessary to ratify the Nineteenth Amendment. The constitutional status of reproductive rights in the United States will depend on whether prochoice or prolife forces make better use of the Internet during their struggles for the political control over the institutions constitutionally authorized to influence or determine whether legal abortion remains the constitutional law of the land. Politics shapes decisions to seek constitutional amendments and the subsequent impact of the resulting formal constitutional changes. The Fourteenth Amendment was a consequence of the political struggle between Andrew Johnson and the Republican Congress for control over Reconstruction. The text ratified in 1868 had less influence on the lives of most former slaves than many framers expected because, during the Gilded and Progressive Ages, proponents of racial equality lost the political power necessary to enforce constitutional mandates imposed on the former Confederate states. The Civil Rights Act of 1964, arguably at least a semiformal change in the constitutional law of racial equality, was made possible by liberal victories during the 1962 and 1964 national elections and the increasing prominence of television news, which regularly provided Northern voters with footage of Southern police officers using brutal tactics to suppress protests by persons of color.

1. Formal Constitutional Change

Formal constitutional changes consciously alter constitutional powers, constitutional rights, or the structure of constitutional institutions. Persons ratifying a constitution intend to create a distinctive political order. Secessionists claim that inherited constitutional rules are no longer legally binding. Proponents of various amendments propose to modify or clarify constitutional rules. Some amendments establish entirely new constitutional powers, limitations, rights, duties, or processes. The Thirteenth Amendment abolished slavery throughout the United States. Others resolve interpretive disputes over the meaning of existing constitutional provisions. During the late nineteenth century, a constitutional controversy broke out over whether Article I permitted the national government to tax ordinary incomes. The Supreme Court in *Pollock v. Farmer's Loan and Trust Co.* (1895) declared such measures unconstitutional. The national legislature then proposed and the states soon ratified the Sixteenth Amendment, which declared, "Congress shall have power to lay and collect taxes on incomes, from whatever source derived, without apportionment among the several States, and without regard to any census or enumeration." That provision settled the constitutional status of the income tax.

Formal constitutional changes are efficacious only when supported by informal constitutional practices. The Constitution of the United States could be legally ratified by any nine of the thirteen states. Union would nevertheless have been politically impossible had New York, Virginia, Massachusetts, and Pennsylvania been the four dissenters. Prohibitionists in the early twentieth century enjoyed the political support necessary to ratify the Eighteenth Amendment and pass federal statutes banning the consumption of alcoholic beverages. They lacked the social resources and commitments necessary to make these legal bans on drinking a practical reality.

1.1 Ratification

Suppose you wrote a new constitution for the United States, one that guaranteed all students the right to a free college education and unlimited downloads from the Internet. Akhil Amar claims that your constitution would become the law of the land if a bare majority of American voters signed a petition for a national constitutional convention, a majority of the delegates at that convention endorsed your constitution, and that constitution was subsequently approved by a national electoral majority.[6] You might cite as strong precedent for your decision to ignore the rules for constitutional change laid down by Article V (and Article VII) the framing decision in 1789 to ignore the rules for constitutional change laid down by the Articles of Confederation. Americans throughout history have recognized that new constitutions need not be ratified consistently with the conditions for amendment specified by the old constitution. This freedom from inherited constitutional norms does not entail a freedom to decide on any conditions for ratification. You cannot create a legitimate constitution by specifying your standards of legitimacy and then meeting those standards. Otherwise, I could write a constitution that required all citizens to buy this text and condition ratification on approval by the marketing division of Oxford University Press and my mother.

Prominent framers recognized that persons proposing new constitutional regimes do not need to do so within the confines of the existing constitutional order. Members of the drafting convention cheerfully admitted that their decision to abandon the Articles of Confederation was not sanctioned by the Continental Congress and that ratification by nine states was quite different from the unanimous state approval for constitutional change set out by the Articles. Political leaders in the late 1780s nevertheless insisted that any collection of notables could propose a new constitution without obtaining the necessary permissions from established institutions. James Madison maintained that the persons who framed the Constitution of the United States "must have reflected, that in all great changes of established governments, ... since it is impossible for the people spontaneously and universally to move in concert towards their object; ... it is therefore essential that such changes be instituted by some *informal and unauthorized propositions,* made by some patriotic and respectable citizen or number of citizens." How constitutions are drafted is of no legal significance. Madison asserted that republican constitutions become fundamental law, no matter what their origins, when ratified by the general public. A legitimate ratification procedure expunged any illegitimacy in the drafting process. In Madison's view, "as the plan to be framed and proposed was to be submitted *to the people themselves,* the disapprobation of this supreme authority would destroy it forever; its approbation blot out antecedent errors and irregularities."[7]

Ratification by the people themselves combines formal and informal constitutional processes. A broad societal consensus must exist that the constitution is fundamental law. Meeting the conditions for legitimacy specified by the constitution is usually a necessary, but not a sufficient, condition for obtaining this crucial constitutional foundation. Americans were not prepared to treat the Constitution as fundamental law if only six states ratified. Nevertheless, constitutions that barely meet internal conditions for ratification are unlikely to generate stable political orders. Most persons who oppose ratification must nevertheless regard the internal rules for ratification as legitimate or have other grounds for adhering to the new constitutional order.[8] The acquiescence of the Anti-Federalists was as important to the establishment of the Constitution as Federalist support. Constitutional politics in the United States would have been quite different had Anti-Federalists insisted that the Constitution was illegitimate and refused en masse to obey the George Washington administration.[9]

Anti-Federalists had two reasons for treating the new constitution as fundamental law. First, broad support existed for the principle that state conventions could ratify constitutions. Most Anti-Federalists believed their state's decision was legally binding. Anti-Federalists in Virginia and other states abandoned opposition after their jurisdiction voted to join the Union. Second, acquiescence proved relatively painless. Anti-Federalists soon learned that they could pursue their cherished values and interests under the Constitution. Many soon concluded that, given the difficulties inherent in creating and revising any constitution, they were better off working within the Constitution of 1789 than wasting political capital securing more favorable constitutional language.

Constitutions require continuous informal ratification. As was the case in 1789, this continuous ratification combines legal and practical understandings. Contemporary Americans treat the Constitution as fundamental law in part because most think the Constitution was fairly ratified and never formally abandoned. They may also regard the Constitution as authoritative because the Constitution in practice enables them to at least partly secure cherished interests and values. As was the case with the Anti-Federalists in 1789, most Americans who would favor different constitutional arrangements are nevertheless convinced that, given the difficulties inherent in creating and revising constitutions, they are better off working within the Constitution than wasting political capital securing more favorable constitutional language.

Whether stable democratic constitutional orders can rest on bare majoritarian consent is doubtful. Proposed referendums to ratify a new and very different Constitution of the United States will succeed in practice only if either both proponents and many opponents of the new constitution agree that popular majorities may ratify constitutions or if many members of the "Old Constitutionalist" minority conclude that they are better off working within the new constitution than acting as if Americans are still governed by rules largely laid down in the eighteenth century. How likely such behavior is cannot be determined at this moment in time, given that no majoritarian referendum is imminent or even remotely likely. The crucial point is that satisfying formal conditions for ratification is only one of several hurdles nation builders must clear. Constitutional legitimacy is an ongoing political process that is not merely a matter of specifying some contested rule for ratification, drafting a constitution that includes that rule, and satisfying that rule during an initial ratification process.

1.2 Amendments

The formal procedures for ratifying constitutional amendments also rest on informal constitutional foundations. Following the rules laid down in Article V no more guarantees actual compliance with new constitutional norms than followings the rules laid down in Article VII guaranteed that Anti-Federalists would respect the new constitutional order. Amendments that do not rest on a broad consensus are often flouted or ignored after ratification. The former slave states citizens who were practically compelled to ratify the post–Civil War amendments soon found means for instituting a new version of white supremacy. As Northern support for racial equality faded, states became practically free to disenfranchise persons of color and reduce them to second-class citizens, despite the words of the Fourteenth and Fifteenth Amendments.

Article V raises several other, less familiar interpretive problems. Some scholars claim that constitutionally valid amendments may adjust, but not dramatically revise, constitutional principles. Americans, they argue, are constitutionally free to change the date when presidents first take office. Such an amendment merely improves constitutional means for realizing preexisting constitutional ends. No supermajoritarian process, however, could repeal the constitutional guarantee of free speech or the Thirteenth Amendment's prohibition on slavery. These revisions would transform, not modify, the constitutional order. Other commentators maintain that Article V does not provide the exclusive procedures for ratifying a constitutional amendment. Constitutional commitments to popular sovereignty may justify other paths to formal constitutional change when popular majorities clearly express their desire to adjust constitutional powers, limitations, rights, duties, or processes.

Both unconstitutional constitutional amendments and constitutional amendments outside of Article V raise questions about the essential elements

of American constitutionalism. Constitutional theorists who insist that procedurally valid constitutional amendments may nevertheless be unconstitutional
contend that American constitutionalism is committed to certain substantive
values, such as the promotion of human dignity. A constitution that sanctioned
torturing the innocent could not be the Constitution of the United States. Those
who insist that constitutional amendments may be ratified outside of Article V
maintain that popular sovereignty is the core commitment of American constitutionalism. They think Americans have the right to decide whether torturing the innocent is constitutional, as long as that constitutional commitment is
rooted in a clear expression of the popular will.

1.3 Unconstitutional Constitutional Amendments?

Most citizens assume that any proposal that meets the conditions set out in Article
V becomes part of the fundamental law of the land. Constitutions cannot specify
the conditions for their ratification, but surely framers can specify the conditions for constitutional amendments. Americans in 1789 approved the rules
for constitutional change laid down in Article V by ratifying the Constitution.
Interesting theoretical problems are raised by the possibility of a constitutional
amendment repealing the provision in Article V forbidding amendments that
affect the equal state representation in the Senate mandated by Article I. All
other possible amendments seem fair constitutional game. If Congress proposes
an amendment declaring that the United States shall be governed by a communist dictatorship and that amendment is passed by three-fourths of the states,
then constitutional law mandates a communist dictatorship.

The Supreme Court in 1943 recognized the broad scope of Article V when
considering the statutory requirements for citizenship. The precise issue in
Schneiderman v. United States was whether an acknowledged communist committed perjury when he swore he was "attached to the principles of the Constitution
of the United States." Justice Frank Murphy's opinion for the court concluded
that Marxists could be sincerely committed to the American Constitution as
fundamental law. His analysis placed particular emphasis on the Constitution's
seemingly open-ended provision for formal change:

> Article V contains procedural provisions for constitutional change by
> amendment without any present limitation whatsoever except that no
> State may be deprived of equal representation in the Senate without
> its consent.... This provision and the many important and far-reaching
> changes made in the Constitution since 1787 refute the idea that
> attachment to any particular provision or provisions is essential, or that
> one who advocates radical changes is necessarily not attached to the

Constitution....As Justice Holmes said, "Surely it cannot show lack of attachment to the principles of the Constitution that...[one] thinks it can be improved."[10]

Justice Murphy treated no provision in Articles I, II, and III as sacred. A valid Article V amendment, in his view, could also abolish all constitutional protections for private property. Communists, jihadists, monarchists, anarchists, secessionists, racists, and goths are good constitutional citizens, according to *Schneiderman,* as long as they are committed to pursuing constitutional amendments and, perhaps, are unwilling to challenge state equality in the Senate.

Some leading constitutional commentators disagree. They interpret the text of Article V as acknowledging the possibility of an unconstitutional constitutional amendment. Walter Murphy points out that *amendment* means something different from *replacement*: "The word *amend* comes from the Latin *emendere*, to correct. Thus an 'amendment' corrects or modifies a system without fundamentally changing its nature—that is, an amendment operates within the boundaries of the existing constitutional order." So interpreted, Article V permits only constitutional changes consistent with basic constitutional principles. "Abolishing constitutional democracy and substituting a different system would not be an amendment at all," Murphy writes, "but a re-creation, a re-forming, not simply of political structures but also of the people themselves."[11] Common usage provides some support for this reading. We describe cobblers as "mending" when they fix a hole in the sole. We use a different verb to describe what people do when they bronze their baby's first shoes.

Several constitutional democracies allow constitutional challenges to amendments ratified consistently with procedural requirements. The German Constitutional Court in 1951 stated that both constitutional amendments and constitutional provisions may be unconstitutional. "That a constitutional provision itself may be null and void is not conceptually impossible," the justices declared. "There are constitutional provisions that are so fundamental...that they also bind the framer of the constitution, and other constitutional provisions that do not rank so high may be null and void because they contravene these principles."[12] The South African Constitutional Court and the Supreme Court of India have struck down constitutional amendments ratified consistently with the procedures set out in the national constitution on the ground that amendments are limited to constitutional adjustments, not provisions dramatically altering the nature of the constitutional order. The Supreme Court of India in *S. R. Bommai v. Union of India* (1994) declared:

There are certain *basic features* of the Constitution of India, which cannot be altered in exercise of the power to amend it, under Article 368

[India's version of Article V of the American Constitution]. If, therefore, a Constitutional Amendment Act seeks to alter the basic structure of framework of the Constitution, the Court would be entitled
to annul it on the ground of *ultra vires,* because the word 'amend', in
Article 368, means only changes other than altering the very structure of the Constitution, which would be tantamount to making a new
Constitution.

On these grounds, that tribunal declared unconstitutional two constitutional
amendments and parts of three others.[13]

The Supreme Court of the United States in *Leser v. Garnett* (1922) heard a
claim that Americans had passed an unconstitutional constitutional amendment. Opponents of the Nineteenth Amendment insisted that the principles
underlying constitutional federalism prohibited using Article V processes
to change a state electorate without the permission of every state. Thomas
F. Cadwalader and William L. Marbury, when contending that states retained
the right to restrict the franchise to men, asserted that "no [constitutional]
power was conferred upon any of the agencies of government" to "destroy any of
the States, by taking away in whole or in part any one of the 'functions essential
to their separate and independent existence' as States." They continued: "When
an amendment is adopted...which changes the electorate, the original State is
destroyed and a new State created." This constitutional principle explained why
they thought a majority of the states could not compel any state to give the ballot
to women. As Cadwalader and Marbury stated, "Article V must be so construed
as not to defeat the main purpose of the Constitution itself."[14]

A unanimous Supreme Court rebuffed this argument. Justice Brandeis
declared:

> The first contention is that the power of amendment conferred by
> the Federal Constitution and sought to be exercised does not extend
> to this Amendment, because of its character. The argument is that so
> great an addition to the electorate, if made without the State's consent,
> destroys its autonomy as a political body. This Amendment is in char-
> acter and phraseology precisely similar to the Fifteenth. For each the
> same method of adoption was pursued. One cannot be valid and the
> other invalid.[15]

Leser at present is the uncontested law of Article V. Questions about unconstitutional constitutional amendments do not trouble most contemporary constitutional decision-makers in the United States, although they continue to be
debated in American academic circles.

1.4 Amending the Constitution outside of Article V

Some law professors claim that the Constitution may be amended by procedures other than those specified by Article V. The constitutional text, they note, nowhere states explicitly that Article V provides the sole means for formal constitutional change. Other interpretations, rooted in constitutional norms or history, are possible. Akhil Amar believes that the constitutional commitment to majority rule entails the right of an absolute majority of voters to ratify whatever amendments they think best. Bruce Ackerman argues that Americans in practice recognize that the Constitution may be formally revised during certain *constitutional moments*. On these occasions, political movements gain the popular support necessary to speak for the people and make their constitutional vision the law of the land. Amar's claim is presently limited to theory. He acknowledges that no majoritarian amendment has actually occurred in American history. Ackerman maintains that numerous major and minor constitutional moments have formally amended the Constitution. Such important historical events as the Jeffersonian victory in 1800, the success of the New Deal in 1930s, and the victory of the civil rights movement in the 1960s are examples of constitutional moments. Ackerman further insists that Reconstruction is best characterized as a constitutional moment, given the substantial procedural irregularities that took place when the post–Civil War amendments were ratified.[16] The policies adopted during such periods of heightened popular mobilization, he claims, alter fundamental constitutional norms, and do not merely reinterpret preexisting constitutional provisions. Constitutional decision-makers who recognize constitutional moments interpret the constitutional visions articulated by successful political entrepreneurs as if they were written into the constitutional text.

Ackerman asserts that a four-step process is necessary for a constitutional amendment to be formally ratified outside of Article V. The first step is a "signaling phase," when a political "movement earns the constitutional authority to claim that…its reform agenda should be placed at the center of sustained public scrutiny." A proposal phase follows in which the "movement" develops "more or less operational proposals for constitutional reform." The third phase is "mobilized political deliberation," in which a series of elections test whether strong popular majorities support the proposals for constitutional reform. If the movement is electorally triumphant, then a ratification and codification process begins. Political institutions that previously resisted the popular movement abandon their opposition. Constitutional moments end when all branches of the national government regard the movement's constitutional vision as the fundamental law of the land.[17] The New Deal exemplifies this process of constitutional change. Liberal Democrats by their landslide victories in the 1932 and 1934 elections signaled that they were prepared to expand dramatically congressional power under Article I over commercial life. President Franklin Roosevelt and his political allies then proposed the extraordinary uses of federal power they believed necessary for the general welfare. After the Supreme Court declared these measures unconstitutional, New Deal Democrats engaged in the extensive political mobilization that was responsible for Roosevelt winning the most lopsided presidential election in American history. The Republican Party and Supreme Court responded to the election of 1936 by abandoning constitutional opposition to the administrative state. By 1940, every governing institution and both major political parties in the United States treated the constitutional claims of the New Deal as the law of the land. Ackerman contends that these events and not decisions made in 1789 explain why Congress in 2013 may constitutionally regulate every facet of commercial life in the United States.

Most law professors question whether the Constitution may be legitimately amended outside of Article V. They interpret Article V as setting out the exclusive processes for constitutional change. The constitutional provisions for amendment, one critic comments, are "an example of yet another text the meaning of which is essentially clear." He adds that permitting committed popular majorities to amend the Constitution without going through the demanding Article V process weakens the constitutional commitment to liberty: "If the Constitution is to continue to be the ultimate source that protects individual rights against encroachment by government power and political majorities, then the affirmative words in Article V must be understood to negative other conceivable modes of amendment."[18] Another criticism questions whether Ackerman's theory of constitutional moments better describes constitutional practice than Article V exclusivity. Americans think *Brown* is the law of the land because they believe that decision is the best interpretation of the Fourteenth Amendment, not because they think a procedurally irregular constitutional amendment during the 1950s and 1960s reversed what had been the constitutionally legitimate reign of Jim Crow and *Plessy v. Ferguson* (1896). The details of particular constitutional moments are controversial. Given the complex amalgam of issues and alliances in most elections, proving that the American public as a whole at any particular time voted for certain policies is difficult. Barry Cushman's survey of opinion polls suggests that although Roosevelt during the 1930s was personally very popular, most Democratic voters did not mean to endorse the constitutional vision underlying the New Deal.[19] Ackerman's analysis may be biased toward liberal constitutional reform. Every constitutional moment he has detected during the past 150 years constitutionalizes the visions of the political left. While Ackerman recognizes that conservatives have enjoyed much political success recently, he adamantly refuses to describe such events as the Reagan presidency or the election of 1994 as conservative constitutional moments.[20]

Ackerman's theory of constitutional moments may better describe semiformal constitutional politics than formal constitutional law. Throughout American history, whenever partisan coalitions have acquired relatively durable control over all national institutions, their constitutional vision has become the law of the land. Governing officials in the United States after 1937 sanctioned all New Deal measures because New Dealers or persons who accepted the New Deal dominated the Congress, presidency, and Supreme Court. Whether New Dealers believed they were restoring original constitutional understandings, adopting constitutional forms to changing circumstances, or creating a new constitutional order is not entirely certain. What we know is that the official constitutional law of the land became constitutional law as espoused by the Roosevelt administration and would remain constitutional law as espoused by the Roosevelt administration until critics during the 1980s and 1990s gained the partial control of national governing institutions necessary to modify some elements of the New Deal constitutional order. Constitutional moments change the course of politics, American history confirms, whatever their correct characterization and legitimacy. Should a political movement committed to the principle that the Second Amendment requires all citizens to own weapons gain total control of the national government during the next series of elections, you should strongly consider buying a gun, emigrating, or learning to like prison food because justices appointed by leaders of that political movement are likely to believe the Constitution permits states to criminalize the failure to be adequately armed.

1.5 Failure

The Constitution of the United States does not have an expiration date. No provision details the rules for making a new constitution or the conditions under which the Constitution is no longer fundamental law. John Marshall spoke for almost every person in the framing generation when he asserted that the Constitution was "intended to endure for ages to come, and consequently, to be adapted to the various crises of human affairs."[21] No provision details conditions for secession or the circumstances under which parts of the United States might be expelled from the Union. When explaining why Texas was not legally independent during the Civil War, Chief Justice Salmon Chase declared that the "Constitution, in all its provisions, looks to an indestructible Union, composed of indestructible States."[22]

Thomas Jefferson was the only prominent member of the framing generation who disputed this claim of enduring constitutional authority. He insisted that constitutional revision was a political obligation given the necessarily limited life span of any written constitution. Committed to the proposition that "one generation has [no] right to bind another," Jefferson concluded that constitutions did not outlive their framers. He wrote in 1789:

It may be proved that no society can make a perpetual constitution, or even a perpetual law. The earth belongs always to the living generation: they may manage it, then, and what proceeds from it, as they please, during their usufruct.... The constitution and the laws of their predecessors are extinguished then, in their natural course, with those whose will gave them being.... Every constitution, then, and every law, naturally expires at the end of thirty-four years. If it be enforced longer, it is an act of force, and not of right.[23]

Perhaps out of old age or courtesy to President James Monroe, Jefferson decided not to press the point that, by his logic, the Constitution of the United States lacked official status after 1823 (nor did Jefferson resign in 1808, despite informing Madison in 1789 that constitutions automatically expired after 19 years). The Constitution will remain fundamental law, most critics have since contended, until formally abandoned.

Prominent slave-state citizens asserted a constitutional right to secession grounded in the compact theory reviewed in Chapter 5. Treating the Constitution as analogous to a treaty, they contended that states as signatories retained the right to abrogate that agreement as well as the power to interpret the meaning of constitutional provisions. South Carolinians in 1860 "maintain[ed] that in every compact between two or more parties, the obligation is mutual; that the failure of one of the contracting parties to perform a material part of the agreement, entirely releases the obligation of the other." Their Secession Ordinance contended, "Where no arbiter is provided, each party is remitted to his own judgment to determine the fact of failure, with all its consequences."[24] Jefferson Davis claimed that the Tenth Amendment implicitly recognized that states were constitutionally authorized to leave the Union and that subunits of the national government had a fundamental political right to secede. "Secession," he stated, "was the assertion of the inalienable right of a people to change their government, whenever it ceased to fulfill the purposes for which it was ordained and established."[25]

Abraham Lincoln rejected these justifications for secession immediately upon taking office. His first inaugural address declared that neither the Constitution nor more enduring principles of constitutionalism permitted states to adjure the Union.[26] "I hold, that in contemplation of universal law, and of the Constitution, the Union of these States is perpetual. Perpetuity is implied, if not expressed, in the fundamental law of all national governments. It is safe to assert that no government proper ever had a provision in its organic law for its own termination." Compact theory, Lincoln asserted, was committed to the mistaken view that states had sovereign powers that predated ratification. Secessionists failed to acknowledge that the "Union is older than any of the States; and, in fact, it created them as States." As states were not parties to the constitutional contract, they lacked the power to abrogate that agreement. Moreover, Lincoln continued, the logic of secession could not be confined to states. "If a minority in such case will secede rather than acquiesce," he stated, "they make a precedent which in turn will divide and ruin them, for a minority of their own will secede from them whenever a majority refuses to be controlled by such minority." This process would undermine popular government. As Lincoln informed his fellow citizens, "the central idea of secession is the essence of anarchy." He and Davis agreed that a revolutionary, as opposed to a constitutional, right of secession existed in theory. The first inaugural maintained, "If by the mere force of numbers a majority should deprive a minority of any clearly written constitutional right, it might in a moral point of view justify revolution." Nevertheless, Lincoln strongly disputed claims that the Republican Party's willingness to ban slavery in the territories constituted a grievance that might justify a natural right to rebel, particularly in light of Republican commitments to protecting slavery in the slave states and enforcing the fugitive slave clause. With the Union victory in the Civil War, this defense of perpetual union became constitutional gospel.

Prominent critics in every generation have called for substantial constitutional reform. Several contemporary works complain that the Constitution aggravates the countermajoritarian tendencies of contemporary American politics. Article I undemocratically skews public policy by mandating equal state representation in the upper chamber of the national legislature. Article II vests too much power in an insufficiently accountable executive. Article III allows politically unaccountable octogenarians on the federal bench, even if senile, to make vital constitutional decisions. "It is increasingly difficult to construct a theory of democratic constitutionalism," one survey of alleged constitutional failings claims, "that vindicates the Constitution under which we are governed."[27]

Most Americans bluntly reject calls to repudiate the Constitution. Some think critics underestimate the value of existing constitutional practices. The presidential veto makes legislation hard to pass but also promotes democratic majoritarianism by ensuring that the only national official elected by the entire country vets all federal laws. Constitutional critics may underestimate the value of entrenched constitutional provisions. Better a slightly countermajoritarian electoral college than constitutional practices that permit the politicians who presently hold political power to establish the rules for the next series of elections. If such constitutional compromises as the Senate are abandoned, Americans may find making credible constitutional commitments more difficult in the future.

Constitutions fail even when not explicitly replaced or repudiated. Text must correspond to practice. "Constitutionalism," scholars note, entails that "both citizens and institutional actors...fashion their behaviors in accordance with constitutional standards."[28] In a healthy constitutional regime, political actors consistently give good faith constitutional justifications for their actions. At the very least, the constitutional rules must provide a reasonable guide to the allocation of power. Many alleged constitutional polities do not even meet this minimum standard. "Facade constitutions" give "no reliable information about the real government process" in a polity.[29] Textual provisions in such regimes proclaim parliamentary sovereignty and guarantee free speech rights while, in fact, a military general establishes legal standards and murders those citizens who criticize the substance of those decrees or even their tendency to be written in the passive voice. Where the United States falls on this spectrum is controversial. Chapter 4 suggests that many commentators underestimate the extent to which constitutional rules and the methods for determining constitutional meanings structure American politics. Still, we frequently hear (and make) comments that conservatives on the federal bench or liberals in the Justice Department are making nominally constitutional decisions that have no plausible constitutional foundations. Whether such common complaints are ordinary political bombast or acute diagnosis of constitutional failures is for the reader to decide.

1.6 Difficulty

The persons responsible for the Constitution believed that solidly entrenched constitutional provisions best promoted the fundamental constitutional purposes examined in Chapter 3. Formal constitutional change, in their view, should be difficult. Revisions should take place only when a broad societal consensus existed on the constitutional flaws to be repaired and the constitutional patches to be installed. Article V's requirement that amendments be ratified by supermajorities in both houses of Congress and three-fourths of the states was designed to prevent geographically concentrated majority factions from altering constitutional arrangements. Most members of the founding generation hoped to avoid future constitutional conventions in which fundamental constitutional arrangements might be abandoned or substantially modified.

Madison dreaded that the very threat of constitutional change would weaken the constitutional order. He acknowledged that "a constitutional road to the decision of the people ought to be marked out and kept open, for certain great and extraordinary occasions." Nevertheless, Madison raised "insuperable objections" to repeated constitutional conventions and frequent use of the amendment process. Ongoing constitutional revisions undermined public confidence in constitutional institutions and practices. Madison wrote:

It may be considered as an objection inherent in the principle that as every appeal to the people would carry an implication of some defect in the government, frequent appeals would, in great measure deprive the government of that veneration which time bestows on everything, and without which perhaps the wisest and freest governments would not possess the requisite stability.

Mere majoritarian processes for constitutional amendment fostered partisan control over crucial constitutional powers and rights. "The danger of disturbing the public tranquility by interesting too strongly the public passions," Madison thought, is a "more serious objection against a frequent reference of constitutional questions to the decision of the whole society." The Philadelphia convention was a rare circumstance in which "no spirit of party" influenced constitutional proposals, but such "experiments are of too ticklish a nature to be unnecessarily multiplied."[30]

Thomas Jefferson rejected this fear of formal constitutional change. Frequent constitutional revisions, in his view, were vital for a progressive republic. He would have Americans establish institutions that enabled national and state constitutions to keep up with the times. Jefferson wrote in 1816:

> Some men look at constitutions with sanctimonious reverence and deem them like the arc of the covenant, too sacred to be touched. They ascribe to the men of the preceding age a wisdom more than human, and suppose what they did to be beyond amendment. I knew that age well; I belonged to it, and labored with it. It deserved well of its country. It was very like the present, but without the experience of the present; and forty years of experience in government is worth a century of book-reading.... Laws and institutions must go hand in hand with the progress of the human mind. As that becomes more developed, more enlightened, as new discoveries are made, new truths disclosed, and manners and opinions change with the change of circumstances, institutions must advance also, and keep pace with the times. We might as well require a man to wear still the coat which fitted him when a boy, as civilized society to remain ever under the regimen of their barbarous ancestors.... Let us ... avail ourselves of our reason and experience, to correct the crude essays of our first and unexperienced, although wise, virtuous, and well-meaning councils. And lastly, let us provide in our constitution for its revision at stated periods.

In sharp contrast to his friend James Madison, who hoped the Constitution would be venerated, Jefferson worried that American constitutionalism might degenerate into ancestor worship. "The dead have no rights," he wrote. His democratic constitutionalism trusted the living with the power to determine the proper ends of government and the proper means to achieve those ends. Jefferson concluded that the "majority...has a right to depute representatives to a convention, and to make the constitution what they think will be the best for themselves."[31]

The dispute between Madison and Jefferson over the ease and merits of formal constitutional changes rages on at present. Contemporary Madisonians insist that experience demonstrates why the Constitution of the United States should be difficult to amend. Kathleen Sullivan writes:

> It is a bad idea to politicize the Constitution. The very idea of a constitution turns on the separation of the legal and political realms. The Constitution sets up the framework of government. It also sets forth a few fundamental political ideas (equality, representation, individual liberties) that place limits on how far any temporary majority may go. This is our higher law. All the rest is left to politics. Losers in the short run yield to the winners out of respect for the constitutional framework set up for the long run. This makes the peaceful conduct of ordinary politics possible. Without such respect for the constitutional framework, politics would degenerate into fractious war. But the more a constitution is politicized, the less it operates as a fundamental charter of government. The more a constitution is amended, the more it seems like ordinary legislation.[32]

Contemporary Jeffersonians believe that the same experience demonstrates the need for a far more majoritarian amendment process. Article V may prevent majority factions from changing the constitutional text, but those provisions also enable minority factions to sabotage vital constitutional reforms. Levinson condemns "the ability of thirteen houses in as many states to block constitutional amendments desired by the overwhelming majority of Americans as well as, possibly, eight-six out of the ninety-nine legislative houses in the American states." He contends that "Article V constitutes what may be the most important bars of our constitutional iron cage precisely because it works to make practically impossible needed changes in our polity."[33]

State constitutionalism provides a potential laboratory for testing the vices and virtues of frequent constitutional alterations. Most states have had multiple constitutions. Louisiana leads the pack, having ratified eleven separate charters. Virtually all state constitutions may be amended by a popular referendum initiated by the state legislature, a separate initiative, a special convention, or a commission. These more majoritarian processes have generated far more constitutional amendments than the Constitution of the United States, even if *constitutional moments* count as official constitutional changes. On average, each extant state constitution has been amended more than one hundred times. The Constitution of Alabama has had 726 amendments.[34] Whether these frequent constitutional changes unduly politicize state constitutions, as Sullivan fears, or responsibly update fundamental laws and political practices, as Levinson hopes, is the subject of increased investigation.[35]

The stakes in the debate over how difficult amending the Constitution should be are not as stark as participants sometimes suggest. One survey of the United States, American states, and foreign countries found that regimes with different official rules for constitutional amendments nevertheless experience similar rates of constitutional change. Constitutional decision-makers find ways of making necessary adjustments in response to changing circumstances. "A low amendment rate," Donald Lutz details, "strongly implies the use of some alternative means of revision to supplement the formal amendment process." This informal amendment process typically relies on methods for determining constitutional meanings that allow crucial constitutional norms to be reinterpreted in light of political and social developments. Lutz concludes that the more rigid the practice of formal constitutional amendment, the less rigid are likely to be the dominant practices of judicial construction; "the more important the role of the judiciary in constitutional revision, the less likely the judiciary is to use the theories of 'strict construction.' "[36]

The relationship between amendments and interpretations is nevertheless more complicated than a simple equilibrium in which semiformal processes compensate automatically for overly demanding formal rules for constitutional change. Most constitutional provisions detailing the structure and staffing of constitutional institutions are not interpretively adaptable. Californians cannot plausibly assert they are constitutionally entitled to more representation in the Senate than Rhode Islanders. No serious constitutional argument concludes that Paris Hilton in 2013 or the latest teen idol today is eligible to become president. State equality in the Senate, age restrictions on constitutional office holding, and related constitutional requirements may be altered only by formal constitutional processes. Constitutional provisions detailing powers and rights are more flexible. The Constitution does not explicitly define the *freedom of speech* or the power to spend for the *general welfare*. Constitutional changes on these matters do take place semiformally, as constitutional decision-makers modify and adjust previous constitutional understandings. Americans cannot easily revise the Fourteenth Amendment formally, but they have employed methods for interpretation that permit new political movements to couch their seemingly novel demands in the inherited language of *due process* and *equal protection of the laws*.

2. Semiformal Constitutional Change

Semiformal constitutional change takes place when constitutional authorities reinterpret the Constitution. The Emancipation Proclamation stated that, contrary to the previous understanding that the federal government could not constitutionally interfere with human bondage in the states, the president could constitutionally free all slaves in areas under the control of the Confederate Government. The Supreme Court in *Knox v. Lee* (1871) overruled *Hepburn v. Griswold* (1870), ruling that Congress could constitutionally require creditors to accept paper money for all debts. Such developments do not constitute formal constitutional changes. Official decision-makers insist that they are clarifying constitutional meanings, correcting mistaken interpretations, restoring original meanings, applying preexisting constitutional principles in new circumstances, or interpreting a living Constitution but not creating new or repealing old constitutional powers, limitations, rights, duties, and processes. Lincoln claimed that constitutional restrictions on federal laws emancipating slaves did not limit presidential power during an actual rebellion. Justice Miller declared that previous Supreme Court decisions striking down legal tender acts were based on an erroneous understanding of Article I and the Fifth Amendment. Semiformal constitutional changes are legally significant. Persons of color who left their home plantation in 1863 were no longer subject to the Fugitive Slave Clause. After *Knox* was decided, debtors could satisfy their obligations by supplying their lenders with the appropriate amount of federally printed greenbacks.

American constitutional development is littered with semiformal constitutional changes. Barry Friedman and Steven Smith observe that "the United States Constitution is not the Constitution of 1787" but has "been layered over constantly with popular understandings...found...in the decisions of the Supreme Court, in statutory law, in the actions of our governmental bodies, in the works of our forebearers, and the common practices of our people."[37] Crucial constitutional understandings that structure politics at a particular time are often quite different from the constitutional understandings that had previously structured politics. Most "right-thinking" men during the late nineteenth century thought states could constitutionally prohibit women from practicing law. Hardly any right-thinking man or woman presently thinks that form of gender discrimination constitutional. Historical interpretations of what took place during the Reconstruction Era change dramatically, and those changes influence how proponents of all methods of constitutional decision-making interpret the post–Civil War Constitution.[38] Law professors who during the 1970s taught their students that no judicial enforceable limits existed on the commerce power are rewriting their lectures in light of such cases as *Lopez v. United States* (1995) and *National Federation of Independent Business v. Sibelius* (2012). Constitutionalists in the near future may treat as unquestioned constitutional law the right to marry a person of any gender or sharp prohibitions on state power to condemn private property.

Decisions reinterpreting constitutional provisions are a form of constitutional change. Governing officials act on their best, not the best, understanding of constitutional powers and rights. When these understandings or officials change, the course of constitutional decision-making also changes. American constitutional law presently treats constitutional decisions made by the appropriate constitutional authorities[39] as having legal consequences that endure even after those rulings are recognized as mistaken. Semiformal constitutional developments help settle questions left open when constitutions or constitutional amendments are ratified. These decisions, in turn, become legal precedents for subsequent constitutional rulings. Several semiformal constitutional changes are as or more difficult to reverse in practice as formal constitutional amendments.

2.1 Semiformal Change as Constitutional Change

Formal constitutional processes explain few of the numerous changes that have occurred throughout American history in the dominant understandings of constitutional powers, limitations, rights, duties, and processes. Most constitutional developments are consequences of evolving constitutional interpretations. These transformations affect how government functions in practice and what individual freedoms persons legally enjoy. Presidents in the Jacksonian era vetoed internal improvement bills, claiming that the national government had no constitutional power to build or fund roads in the states. Contemporary presidents without much constitutional controversy allocate billions of dollars for the interstate highway system. For most of American history, almost all constitutional authorities believed the First and Fourteenth Amendments placed few if any constraints on officials who censored sex scenes in popular entertainment. After a series of Supreme Court decisions during the 1960s and 1970s, most erotic material is considered constitutionally protected. Copies of *Playboy* and *Cosmopolitan* that might have been confiscated during the 1930s are now sold openly at convenience stores. The constitutional requirements for a fair criminal trial vary by the decade, even as each generation of constitutional decision-makers insists that its standards best reflect unchanging constitutional commitments. These and numerous other analogous constitutional developments are consequences of judicial decisions, federal laws, presidential proclamations, and underlying political movements, not constitutional amendments, however constitutional amendments are defined.

Official decisions shape the *working constitution*, the understandings of constitutional powers, limitations, rights, duties, and processes that structure the political order during particular eras. Congressional power over agriculture in 1935 and the scope of legitimate political dissent during World War One depended on the constitutional rulings handed down at those times, not on the one true meaning of the commerce clause or First Amendment. Henry David Thoreau may have been philosophically correct when he asserted that a person "more right than his neighbors constitutes a majority of one."[40] Nevertheless, although most contemporary constitutionalists think Eugene Debs in 1919 was more right than the Woodrow Wilson administration or the Supreme Court when he insisted the Constitution protected sharp criticisms of the draft, Debs languished in prison after the justices unanimously sustained his conviction for violating the Espionage Act.[41]

Constitutional law treats constitutional mistakes as having some official status, even after errors are corrected by the appropriate constitutional authority. Unconstitutional laws or rulings, in theory, are legal nullities. An unconstitutional action, the Supreme Court stated in 1886, "confers no rights; it imposes no duties; it affords no protection; it creates no office; it is, in legal contemplation, as inoperative as though it had never been passed."[42] Nevertheless, most political actors regard unconstitutional decisions as legally binding, at least temporarily. They are "considered as an existing juridical fact until overruled."[43] Abraham Lincoln respected the Supreme Court's decision that Dred Scott was legally enslaved, even though he believed that ruling based on a misinterpretation of federal power in the territories. The Supreme Court in 1871 ruled that a person who bought slaves on the installment plan had to pay the reminder of the purchase price, even after the Thirteenth Amendment declared slavery illegal throughout the United States, because the contract was legal when made.[44] Mapp v. Ohio (1961) decided that prosecutors could not use unconstitutionally obtained evidence in criminal trials. The Supreme Court then ruled that no prisoner whose state court conviction became final before Mapp was handed down could constitutionally obtain a new trial, even if their conviction was based on unconstitutionally obtained evidence.[45] We suspect you would have difficulty persuading a person whose life sentence became final in 1960 that the Supreme Court's decision in that case did not change the meaning of the Fourth Amendment.

The framers acknowledged that subsequent decisions could constitutionally settle legal matters left unclear or undecided in 1789. James Madison in the Federalist Papers provided some insight into the actual process of constitutional evolution when, as noted previously, he explained, "all new laws, though penned with the greatest technical skill, and passed on the fullest and most mature deliberation, are considered as more or less obscure and equivocal, until their meaning be liquidated and ascertained by a series of particular discussions and adjudications."[46] Madison in 1815 asserted that legitimate constitutional development had taken place when he recanted his assertion in 1791 that Congress could not constitutionally incorporate a national bank. Constitutional decisions to the contrary for almost twenty-five years provided sufficient precedential grounds for decisively resolving what had been a contentious constitutional issue. Questions about "the constitutional authority of the Legislature to establish an incorporated bank," Madison stated, were "precluded ... by repeated recognitions under varied circumstances of the validity of such an institution in acts of the legislative, executive, and judicial branches of the Government, accompanied by indications, in different modes, of a concurrence of the general will of the nation."[47]

Important constitutional decisions purport to resolve constitutional ambiguities or make law where the Constitution is silent. Sometimes, constitutional authorities claim that the persons responsible for the Constitution overlooked a potential problem. Article II, Section 2 provides rules for appointing executive branch officials, but no constitutional provision specifies how they are to be removed from office. "Perhaps this is an omitted case," Madison declared when urging Congress to allow presidential removals.[48] Other opinions assert that constitutional language and history are too vague to provide authoritative grounds for any constitutional decision. "Just what our forefathers did envision," Justice Robert Jackson wrote when rejecting presidential power to seize steel mines during the Korean War, "must be divined from materials almost as enigmatic as the dreams Joseph was called on to interpret for Pharaoh."[49] Chief Justice Earl Warren in *Brown* concluded that what "Congress and the state legislatures had in mind" when ratifying the equal protection clause "cannot be determined with any degree of certainty."[50] Some constitutional ambiguities may be intentional. Thomas Paine informed Jefferson that no established constitutional rules determined whether the United States could purchase Louisiana from France. Members of the constitutional convention, he wrote, thought "it was prudent to say nothing about" westward expansion.[51]

The original decisions that clarify constitutional silences and ambiguities become precedents that shape subsequent constitutional decisions and commitments. The debates over whether the president could remove cabinet members without Senate consent in the First Congress provided the primary sources for constitutional arguments when removal issues were reconsidered during the Jacksonian era, Reconstruction, and the New Deal. Justice Jackson's opinion in *Youngstown* served as a framework for later judicial opinions determining whether the president could freeze Iranian assets during the 1980 hostage crisis or use military commissions to try suspect terrorists after September 11. Expansionists and anti-expansionists insisted that Jefferson's decision to purchase Louisiana provided constitutional support for their different positions on the annexation of Texas. The parties to contemporary debates over affirmative action contest the original meaning of *Brown*. Some ordinary political decisions develop constitutional significance through repetition over time. One example is the tradition, begun by George Washington, that presidents serve no more than two terms of office. When Franklin Roosevelt violated what by the twentieth century had become a semiformal constitutional understanding, Congress proposed and states quickly ratified the Twenty-Second Amendment.

Official decisions change constitutional law by creating as well as by resolving ambiguities. The Supreme Court's decision in *Brown* established that Jim Crow public schooling violated the equal protection clause while casting doubt on whether long-standing bans on interracial marriage would remain good law. All constitutional opinions, whether issued by justices or other governing officials, become precedents that make some constitutional arguments more plausible while subverting the legal foundations for other constitutional claims. The Supreme Court's decision in *Griswold v. Connecticut* (1965) that married people had a right to use birth control provided constitutional support for emerging legal attacks on state laws banning abortion. Frequent presidential assertions that the Supreme Court is constitutionally authorized to settle constitutional disputes have weakened the force of less frequent presidential challenges to judicial authority.

Litigation campaigns illustrate how constitutional decisions settle some questions while unsettling others. Legal activists often recognize their cherished constitutional claims seem implausible to most citizens and constitutional authorities. Rather than accept certain defeat or meekly acquiesce to the status quo, they may litigate a narrower point that has stronger constitutional foundations. Persons who believe the Constitution should protect the right to marry more than one person might first assert that the right to intimate relationships announced in *Lawrence v. Texas* (2003) encompasses a constitutional right to have intimate relations with more than one consenting adult over a period of time. If successful in establishing legal foundations for le ménage a trois, that precedent could then be used to challenge the constitutionality of laws criminalizing consensual adultery. Each legal victory in this campaign further entrenches past gains while providing increased doctrinal support for formerly implausible constitutional arguments. By the time courts rule that married couples have a constitutional right to make contracts with third parties covering traditional domestic subjects, many former skeptics may think existing precedents justify, even compel, decisions protecting the constitutional right to polygamy and polyandry.

The constitutional status of Jim Crow provides a good example for thinking about how semiformal constitutional changes should be understood, how they should occur, and under what circumstances they are legitimate. In 1900, most well-trained lawyers thought that state-mandated racial segregation was an acceptable practice under the equal protection clause of the Fourteenth Amendment. After *Brown v. Board of Education* (1954), government-sponsored racial segregation was hardly ever considered constitutionally valid. Effective constitutional requirements had radically changed, even though no new constitutional text was adopted. Some argue that "the Constitution" had not changed but that judges, government officials, and lawyers had previously misinterpreted the equal protection clause. Others think the underlying constitutional principles stayed the same, but the application of those constitutional principles changed in response to new circumstances or new thinking. Constitutional commands remained constant, but doctrines applying those edicts were adjusted in light of political developments. On another view, the court, in cooperation with other government officials, modified previous constitutional rules. Perhaps the constitutional status of segregation was a matter to be "liquidated and ascertained" over time and potentially reversed in such decisions as *Brown*. Perhaps segregation was acceptable under the original Fourteenth Amendment, and *Brown* was part of the process that altered the meaning of that constitutional provision.

These different characterizations of American constitutional development have important future implications. If the rule of *Brown* is and was always constitutionally correct, then constitutional decision-makers must be guided by that rule unless a formal constitutional amendment is ratified. If the rule of *Brown* is correct only in light of the distinctive political and cultural developments that took place during the twentieth century, then a different rule might better reflect basic constitutional principles in light of the political and cultural developments taking place during the twenty-first century. If the rule of *Brown* is and has always been constitutionally wrong, then perhaps the decision ought to be abandoned as soon as constitutionally possible.

Controversies over semiformal constitutional changes often reflect underlying controversies over the proper methods for determining constitutional meanings discussed in Chapter 4. Constitutional decision-makers must make law when the Constitution is silent, ambiguous, or perhaps extremely difficult to interpret correctly. Whether the Constitution is actually silent, ambiguous, or extremely difficult to interpret correctly on a particular matter is as contested as the correct meaning of a constitutional provision. The same contested methods for determining the meaning of constitutional provisions determine whether a constitutional decision has applied clear constitutional rules to a novel fact pattern, clarified constitutional ambiguities, or illegitimately attempted to replace established constitutional norms without formal amendment. Constitutional logics that generate different answers to questions about what rights are protected by the First Amendment also generate different answers to questions about what free speech rights are difficult or impossible to determine objectively. A textualist might conclude that lying under oath about a sexual indiscretion is clearly a "high crime or misde-meanor" under Article II, Section 4, is clearly not an impeachment offense, or has a constitutionally ambiguous status for impeachment purposes. Most constitutional opinions muddy the waters by insisting that their conclusions are straightforward applications of accepted methods of constitutional inter-pretation and that opinions to the contrary are little more than disguised efforts at constitutional amendment. The majority, concurring, and dissenting opinions in *Roe v. Wade* all insisted their conclusions on the constitutional status of abortion were jurisprudentially uncontroversial derivations from the constitutional text and precedent. Characterizing constitutional decisions as based on law, politics, or some combination of both, this and other examples suggest, is as much an inherently controversial interpretive exercise as deter-mining constitutional meanings.

2.2 Superprecedents?

Not all constitutional precedents are created equal. Some past decisions on constitutional issues have a higher legal authority than others. These "superprecedents," conventional wisdom maintains, have a constitutional status in between an amendment and a normal precedent. They may be overturned, but not merely for reasons that might justify reversing an ordinary constitutional decision. Consider Mark Tushnet's analysis of the status of Social Security in American law. "Repealing the basic Social Security Act," he comments, "would almost certainly be more difficult than amending the Constitution. Put another way, the Social Security Act is as deeply embedded in our political order as anything in the written Constitution. For that reason, and because of its social importance, the Act should be regarded as 'constitutional.' "[52] Certainly Aristotle, employing the classical constitutional understandings explained in Chapter 2, would think Social Security constitutional.

Superprecedents rest on several foundations. Some constitutional decisions are practically impossible to overrule because a general consensus exists that they are right as a matter of justice. *Brown* is the obvious example of such a prec-edent. Other superprecedents reflect very long-standing constitutional practice. Presidential authority to fire cabinet officers without Senate approval is an exam-ple of a constitutional practice dating from the early republic that has become uncontested over time. Statutes that settle hotly contested constitutional issues have been considered candidates for superprecedent status. Lincoln described the Missouri Compromise as a "contract made between North and South" that both parties were honor bound to maintain.[53] The Compromise of 1832, which promised to abolish protective tariffs over a ten-year period, was regarded as a constitutional precedent that bound future Whigs and Jacksonians.[54] Some constitutional decisions have consequences that make reversal politically impossible. Texas may have been unconstitutionally annexed in 1845, but only a few fringe movements think declaring that state an independent republic is a viable constitutional option at present.

Whether judicial decisions that purport to settle bitterly contested constitutional issues acquire superprecedent status is controversial. The plurality opinion in *Planned Parenthood of Southeastern Pennsylvania v. Casey* (1992) insisted that *Roe* ended the constitutional controversy over abortion. Justices Sandra Day O'Connor, Anthony Kennedy, and David Souter stated:

> Where, in the performance of its judicial duties the Court decides a case in such a way as to resolve the sort of intensely divisive controversy reflected in *Roe* and those rare, comparable cases, its decision has a dimension that the resolution of the normal case does not carry. It is the dimension present whenever the Court's interpretation of the Constitution calls the contending sides of a national controversy to end their national division by accepting a common mandate rooted in the Constitution.
>
> ....Whatever the premises of opposition may be, only the most convincing justification under accepted standards of precedent could suffice to demonstrate that a later decision overruling the first was anything but a surrender to political pressure, and an unjustified repudiation of the principle on which the Court staked its authority in the first instance. So to overrule under fire in the absence of the most compelling reason to reexamine a watershed decision would subvert the Court's legitimacy beyond any serious question.[55]

Legislative proponents of legal abortion advanced a similar claim during the confirmation hearings of Justices John Roberts and Samuel Alito when they asked those jurists to affirm that *Roe* and other liberal decisions were superprecedents that should not lightly be overruled by the federal judiciary. Opponents of *Roe* dispute claims that controversial judicial decisions are more sacred than normal precedents. Justice Antonin Scalia responded to the plurality opinion in *Casey* by declaring:

> Not only did *Roe* not, as the Court suggests, resolve the deeply divisive issue of abortion; it did more than anything else to nourish it, by elevating it to the national level where it is infinitely more difficult to resolve....Profound disagreement existed among our citizens over the issue,...but that disagreement was being worked out at the state level. As with many other issues, the division of sentiment within each

State was not as closely balanced as it was among the population of the Nation as a whole, meaning not only that more people would be satisfied with the results of state-by-state resolution, but also that those results would be more stable....

...I cannot agree with, indeed I am appalled by, the Court's suggestion that the decision whether to stand by an erroneous constitutional decision must be strongly influenced—*against* overruling, no less—by the substantial and continuing public opposition the decision has generated.[56]

Superprecedents often reflect the distinctive constitutional understanding of a particular constitutional regime. The Missouri Compromise expressed the Jeffersonian–Jacksonian commitment to the balance of sectional power. The Supreme Court decisions that sustained Roosevelt's economic policies articulated the New Deal commitment to providing national legislative solutions for all perceived national problems. These decisions were considered of higher constitutional status than ordinary precedents because their principles were accepted by all major political coalitions. Jacksonians and Whigs during the 1830s and 1840s respected both the Missouri Compromise line and the underlying principle that the free and slave states would in some manner share the territories. Roosevelt and Dwight Eisenhower's judicial appointees regarded such decisions as *National Labor Relations Board v. Jones & Laughlin Steel Corporation* (1937) and *Wickard v. Filburn* (1942) as settling the scope of federal power under the commerce clause. *Roe*, lacking strong bipartisan support, does not meet this possible qualification for superprecedential status.

Superprecedents are more vulnerable to constitutional politics than formal constitutional amendments. Slavery and the Black Codes, abolished by formal constitutional changes, did not reemerge in the late nineteenth century, even as constitutional decision-makers less committed than Reconstruction Republicans to racial equality sanctioned many racist practices. The semiformal constitutional commitments of particular eras, by comparison, have had a more varied fate after constitutional regime changes. Some superprecedents survive the fall of their original political sponsors, becoming almost as entrenched as the constitutional provisions they interpret. No prominent constitutional decision-maker during the New Deal, Great Society, or Reagan era questioned the Supreme Court's decision in *Gitlow v. New York* (1925) that the due process clause of the Fourteenth Amendment protects free speech rights against state infringement. Other superprecedents are retained in modified form by adherents of the new constitutional order. The Rehnquist Court accepted the New Deal understanding that the national government may constitutionally regulate local commercial activity while insisting that the relevant constitutional decisions did not authorize Congress to regulate local non-economic activities. New constitutional regimes sometimes abandon what were previously thought superprecedents. Jacksonian compromises on sectional issues did not survive secession. The Lincoln administration first obtained laws banning slavery in all territories, then declared all slaves free who resided in areas under Confederate control, and finally secured the passage of a constitutional amendment banning human bondage.

3. Informal Constitutional Change

Informal constitutional change takes place when constitutionally significant assumptions, behaviors, or practices are undermined, modified, or abandoned. These extralegal elements of a constitutional order provide crucial political foundations for more legal processes, rules, and interpretations. The structure of political competition in well-designed constitutional orders helps generate the constitutionally desirable outcomes discussed in Chapter 3. National parties that during the Jacksonian era competed for votes in both the free and slave states promoted the constitutional compromises on sectional issues that the framers recognized were vital for preserving the union. Demography and popular culture make various constitutional constructions seem natural. During the early nineteenth century, when virtually all political elites were Protestant, congressional decisions sending Christian missionaries to convert Native Americans seemed constitutionally uncontroversial. When the structure of political competition and demography changed, new constitutional practices and understandings developed. Lincoln was unwilling to compromise on the status of slavery in the territories partly because the Republican Party did not seek Southern votes. Increased religious diversity helps explain why mainstream constitutional decision-makers no longer consider funding missionaries or refer to the United States as a "Christian nation."

Constitutional provisions and interpretations assume, seek to bring forth, or are grounded in a particular political world. As this political world fades or fails to materialize as expected, new constitutional demands arise, constitutional practices evolve, and constitutional politics must adjust to new or unexpected conditions. Some changes affect the functioning of political institutions. The communications revolution enables national majorities to form and coordinate their actions in ways Madison could not imagine when in *Federalist* 10 he insisted that the large republic would prevent interest groups from significantly influencing constitutional life. Other developments alter the constitutional balance of power counted on to ensure political moderation. Unanticipated population growth in the Northwest destroyed the fragile equilibrium between free and slave states established by the framers and reinforced by the Missouri Compromise. Political developments undermine assumptions underlying particular provisions. Some scholars claim that the Second Amendment, which asserts that "[a] well regulated Militia, being necessary to the security of a free State, the right of the people to keep and bear Arms, shall not be infringed," has no meaning in light of the practical disappearance of state militias.[57] Cultural shifts empower citizens and political movements with little commitment to many inherited constitutional practices or understandings. Standards for constitutionally offensive speech reflect changing social norms. Students at many public universities presently risk expulsion for making comments about race or gender that might have seemed mildly liberal fifty years ago and unacceptably radical in 1789. Characters on cable television shows presently blurt expletives that would have resulted in the station's license being pulled during the 1950s.

Conventional constitutional processes easily integrate some constitutionally significant political developments. The persons responsible for the Constitution may have feared the rise of the two-party system and designed institutions that they thought would prevent the formation of a two-party system. Nevertheless, the rules laid down in 1789 proved capable of managing partisan competition throughout American history. Then as now, presidential aspirants must gain a majority of Electoral College votes, seats in the House of Representatives are allocated by population, and newspapers may call on the First Amendment as a shield against government censorship. Constitutional rules yield very different results than initially anticipated, but the rules themselves remain recognizable. If the rules are unsatisfactory, then we might consider amending or abolishing the Constitution.

Much constitutional language enables various social developments to be incorporated into the constitutional order without much interpretive difficulty. The framers could barely imagine airplanes and did not conceive of the Internet, but no one questions that Congress under the interstate commerce clause may regulate online sales of tickets for flights between Boston and Los Angeles. Time affects the application of some constitutional principles but not the principles themselves. Punishments become "unusual" without changing the meaning of the "cruel and unusual punishment" clause. New technologies raise more complicated interpretive problems. Supreme Court justices in *Olmstead v. United States* (1928) debated whether wiretapping was an unconstitutional invasion of privacy or a constitutional form of investigation that did not involve a physical trespass. Nevertheless, that dispute over what constituted a reasonable "search and seizure" was arguably no different jurisprudentially from similar debates over investigatory activities well-known to the framers.

Other informal constitutional changes pose greater constitutional challenges. Some difficulties are interpretive. Modern economic life played havoc with such

preindustrial constitutional understandings as the prohibition on class legislation and principle that the commerce power was "restricted to that commerce
which concerns more states than one."[58] What modern weapons are encompassed by the right to bear arms remains a mystery, even to many experts on the
Second Amendment. Other hard problems arise after extralegal developments
transform constitutional processes. Many people believe that the contemporary
politicized judicial selection process increases the probability that federal courts
will be staffed by constitutional ideologues or relatively obscure lawyers. Neither
is likely to make sound decisions, unless other means are found that compensate
for this constitutional failure. Informal constitutional changes may have precipi-
tated the Civil War. After the Northwest Territories were settled and achieved
statehood more rapidly than the framers anticipated, the free states were soon
able to destroy the original constitutional balance of power between the sections. When Lincoln was elected president by only free-state votes, Southerners
were convinced that controversies over the constitutional status of slavery would
forevermore be decided as Northern majorities thought best. Secession quickly
followed.

The informal constitutional changes may buttress as well as weaken a constitutional order. Political parties in the United States ensure a modicum of coordination between what otherwise might be too separated governing institutions.
The politicized judicial selection process facilitates popular participation in the
staffing of an important constitutional institution. Entrenched constitutional
processes may even have some tendency to generate supportive social institutions. Given the difficulty of formal constitutional amendment, political actors
may decide they will best achieve valued ends by establishing practices that, by
their lights, improve the performance of existing constitutional institutions.
Rather than seek a constitutional amendment that would eliminate judicial
review, Republicans furious with the Southern tilt of the Taney Court passed
the Judiciary Act of 1862. That measure reorganized the federal judiciary so that
most justices on the Supreme Court for the foreseeable future would hail from
the free states.

The informal constitutional practices and developments briefly discussed
in this section shape American constitutionalism as much as, if not more than,
the legal decisions that are too often the sole object of constitutional study.
Functioning constitutional orders are structured by a set of political commitments, a set of governing processes thought to promote those commitments,
and a people who both share those commitments and are capable of operating
the governing processes.[59] Some of these elements are legal. Others are not. All
are subject to change over time. Constitutions may specify the qualifications
of a president or a Supreme Court justice, but law cannot guarantee that the
president will understand modern warfare or that Supreme Court justices will

take the constitutional text seriously. The best framers can achieve are governing processes that, given correct assumptions about political institutions and the
citizenry, privilege the election and selection of constitutional decision-makers
with the right combination of abilities, values, and interests. When these vital
constitutional expectations are frustrated, major constitutional transformations
of some sort will occur. Presidents who were expected to be neutral umpires,
after the rise of the party system, became party leaders who often dangerously
polarized politics when pursuing partisan ends. When a constitutional people
develop new interests or abandon old values, the Constitution will probably be
interpreted in light of these emerging concerns and governing processes restruc-
tured to better satisfy new constitutional demands. Constitutional provisions
designed to protect persons of color, after the rise of industrialization, were more
often invoked to structure the relationship between employers and employees
than safeguard the rights of former slaves. Constitutions that fail to prevent
or respond to changes in the nature of political competition or the underlying
political culture do not have long shelf lives. Constitutional systems, like cars, do
not function well when their constituent parts are out of alignment.

4. The Law and Politics of Constitutional Change

Constitutional change is inevitable. Framers, by intention or inadvertence, fail to
settle all possible constitutional questions. Constitutional decisions that clarify
some constitutional ambiguities often simultaneously unsettle what had been
more stable constitutional understandings. A constitutional regime in which
most citizens receive political information online is different from one in which
the town green is the main source of information, no matter what the constitutional rules for regulating the Internet. To the extent that values legitimately
influence constitutional decision-making, constitutional developments will be
structured by evolving conceptions of justice as well as by the successes and failures of political movements committed to particular constitutional visions. Few
governing officials were troubled in 1873 when the Supreme Court ruled that
states could prohibit women from practicing law. Most Americans of all political persuasions presently think the Constitution significantly limits government
power to make this and other gender discriminations, even though the Equal
Rights Amendment was not ratified.

Constitutional change during the next generation will continue to be structured by constitutional norms and political exigencies. Whether future reformers
prefer formal to semiformal constitutional change will depend on constitutional
language, prevailing methods for determining constitutional meanings, and
estimations about the likelihood of success of different strategies for pursuing

particular constitutional visions. Many gay and lesbian political activists initially championed adjudication as their preferred means for achieving a constitutional right to same-sex marriage. Their motivations were partly legal. The language of the equal protection clauses in the national and many state constitutions, as well as precedents finding a constitutional right to interracial marriage and a constitutional right for consenting adults to engage in homosexual sodomy, provided plausible legal foundations for a constitutional right to gay marriage. Litigation at the turn of the twenty-first century offered the best practical chance of achieving their constitutional vision. More justices than elected officials were initially willing to support gay marriage. Opponents of gay marriage preferred legislation and promoted state constitutional amendments limiting marriage to one man and one woman. Politics partly explain this strategy. As of 2008, no state legislature had legalized same-sex marriage, and many state electorates had ratified "defense of marriage" amendments. Law also matters. Militant supporters of gay marriage on the federal and state benches are unlikely to protect the right to marry a person of the same gender when the relevant constitutional text explicitly limits marriage to one man and one woman. Informal constitutional changes are altering this landscape. As the public becomes more supportive of same-sex marriage, constitutional movements are adjusting strategies. Gay rights activists are persuading legislatures in "blue" states to pass laws legalizing same-sex marriage. Proponents of traditional marriage are going to court, insisting that religious believers have constitutional rights not to participate or recognize such relationships. Social and cultural developments are likely to dictate the ultimate outcome of this struggle. Should evangelical political movements gain strength, the next generation of constitutional decision-makers will be less sympathetic to a constitutional right to gay marriage. Alternatively, Americans will become more supportive of gay rights as they become more familiar with openly gay couples in their neighborhoods and civic groups. The only predictions that can be made with some confidence are that the constitutional status of gays and lesbians at the turn of the twenty-second century will be different from the present and that those differences will reflect a combination of formal, semiformal, and informal constitutional changes.

‖ 7 ‖

American Constitutionalism in Global Perspective

American constitutionalism exists in a global environment. The Constitution shapes and is shaped by foreign affairs as well as by domestic politics. The United States as a world power is expected to enforce and act consistently with international law. The resulting engagements with other political regimes provide occasions for exporting American constitutional norms as well as opportunities for learning about alternative constitutional arrangements that may cast light on or inform constitutional practices at home.

This global environment presents different challenges for American constitutionalism. Much theory and some practice suggest that the United States has two distinctive constitutions, one for external affairs and the other for internal matters. This claimed distinction has generated numerous constitutional disputes throughout American history, from the governance of various American territories during the nineteenth century to presidential power during the present struggle against terrorism. Unlike the debates discussed in Chapter 4 over what constitutional provisions mean, these struggles are often over whether the president, Congress, or executive branch officials when forming alliances or conducting drug raids abroad must conform to the Fourth Amendment or exercise only the enumerated powers laid out in Article I. No consensus exists on the proper relationship between international law and constitutional law. Whether American government officials are constitutionally obligated to adhere to international law and the nature of those responsibilities is controversial. Prominent international lawyers insist that the law of nations is the highest form of law and binds the United States, even when contrary actions are constitutionally permissible. The increased popularity of constitutionalism throughout the world provides greater comparative perspectives on American constitutionalism. Some constitutional purposes, methods of ascertaining the meaning of constitutional provisions, allocations of constitutional authority, and modes of constitutional change seem near universal. Others vary considerably, even among constitutional democracies. A contentious debate is taking place between Supreme

Court justices, legal commentators, and members of Congress over the extent to which Americans should be constitutional borrowers as well as lenders.

The American constitutional experience with foreign affairs, the law of nations, and comparative constitutional law is shaped by the tension between the particular and the universal elements of the Constitution. This difficult balance is as much rooted in the different understandings of constitutionalism discussed in Chapter 2 as in the unique features of constitutional politics in the United States. Aristotle emphasized the constitutional effort to discern the distinctive rules that would best promote the distinctive values and interests of a distinctive people. Justice Stephen Field pointed to the provincial ambitions of American constitutionalism when he reminded fellow citizens that "by the constitution a government is ordained and established 'for the United States of America,' and not for countries outside of their limits."[1] The liberal constitutionalists of the eighteenth century emphasized the constitutional effort to promote fundamental human freedoms by limiting government. Justice Field pointed to this facet of American constitutionalism when he insisted that the phrase "privileges and immunities" in the Fourteenth Amendment "refers to the natural and inalienable rights which belong to all citizens."[2] Field's assertions, as well as similar claims made by many prominent constitutional actors, are not necessarily inconsistent. The Constitution could protect the natural rights of all Americans while authorizing Americans to violate the natural rights of other persons when doing so is perceived to be in the national interest. Nevertheless, if not logically inconsistent, the liberal constitutional commitments to fundamental rights and limited government do not always rest comfortably with constitutional commitments to promote the welfare of a particular people. The resulting tensions between particular and universal constitutional ambitions have historically been particularly acute when Americans debate the constitutional limits on official actions abroad or relationships with foreign countries, determine the extent to which the Constitution commits government officials to act consistently with international law, and consider whether American constitutional practices are so distinctively American that they can be interpreted only by reference to distinctively American sources.

1. Foreign Policy: Two Constitutions?

The constitutional rules for shaping foreign policy differ from the constitutional rules for shaping domestic policy. Some distinctions are relatively straightforward and present no unusual constitutional problems. The Constitution explicitly prescribes different processes for building roads and building alliances. The national legislature initiates and the national executive responds on most internal matters. On many external matters, the president initiates and one or both houses of Congress respond. Congress may no more constitutionally compel the president to sign a treaty with the prime minister of England than the president may constitutionally compel Congress to allocate more money for constructing parking spaces at major universities. When constitutional controversies over foreign policy arise, participants often make use of the same methods for determining the meaning of constitutional provisions as they do when debating constitutional restrictions on domestic policymaking. Proponents and opponents of the Vietnam War argued over the original meaning of the Congressional power "To declare War" and the extent to which past precedents supported presidential power to escalate the military conflict in Southeast Asia. Many prominent Americans, however, perceive more fundamental constitutional distinctions between internal and external affairs. They claim many restrictions on national authority and constitutional principles such as the separation of powers either function differently or do not function at all when the United States acts abroad. On one view of this thesis, "the powers of the United States to conduct relations with other nations do not derive from the Constitution" but from the mere fact that the United States is a sovereign nation.[3] On another, related view, "the conduct and control of foreign policy [is] inherently 'executive' in nature" and, as such, is not subject to the same controls as the domestic powers shared among all three branches of the national government.[4]

George Sutherland, a senator, secretary of state, and Supreme Court justice during the early twentieth century, advanced one influential conception of this constitutional dichotomy when he maintained that national power over internal and external affairs had fundamentally different foundations.[5] Sutherland insisted that sovereignty was sharply bifurcated after Americans declared independence in 1776. Each state gained sovereignty over domestic affairs, while the Continental Congress retained sovereignty over international matters. "As a result of the separation from Great Britain by the colonies, acting as a unit," he wrote, "the powers of external sovereignty passed from the Crown not to the colonies severally, but to the colonies in their collective and corporate capacity as the United States of America." The national government acquired additional domestic powers when the Constitution was ratified in 1789, but ratification did not add to or subtract from the previously possessed national authority over foreign affairs. Power over external affairs was vested in the national government because the United States was an independent nation, not because of some constitutional edict. Sutherland contended:

> The investment of the federal government with the powers of external sovereignty did not depend upon the affirmative grants of the Constitution. The powers to declare and wage war, to conclude peace,

to make treaties, to maintain diplomatic relations with other sovereignties, if they had never been mentioned in the Constitution, would
have vested in the federal government as necessary concomitants of
nationality.

The dual sources of federal power entail different conceptions of federal authority
over internal and external affairs. Sutherland and those who accept his premises
believe that constitutional restrictions derived from the notion of enumerated
powers and perhaps from the Bill of Rights Sutherland and those who accept
his premises believe, limit only federal power over domestic affairs. In their view,
Congress may appropriate funds for the relief of famine-stricken countries even
if that action cannot be derived from the powers listed in Article I. The power
to assist other countries is an example of a "necessary concomitant of nationality" that does not need explicit constitutional sanction. The Tenth Amendment's
reference to the "powers not delegated to the United States by the Constitution"
similarly has no bearing on foreign affairs. States never had the power to declare
war or make treaties.

Many proponents of the "two-constitutions" thesis contend that presidential
power over foreign affairs is not subject to the same constitutional limitations
as presidential power over domestic affairs. Sutherland declared, "In this vast
external realm, with its important, complicated, delicate and manifold problems,
the President alone has the power to speak or listen as a representative of the
nation." Contemporary proponents of executive power point to the constitutional text as well as to history when justifying aggressive, unilateral presidential uses of American power abroad to advance national interests. Noting that
Article II, Section 1 declares, "*The executive power shall* be vested in a President
of the United States," while Article I, Section 1 states, "*All legislative Powers herein
granted shall* be vested in a Congress of the United States," John Yoo concludes
that the president has "unenumerated foreign affairs powers not given elsewhere
to the other branches."[6]

Critics raise several objections to these claims about "unenumerated foreign
affairs powers." Some challenge the history. In their view, the framers did not recognize any sharp distinction between domestic and foreign policy. "The system
of war powers the Framers appear to have favored," one critique asserts, "com-
ports quite well with their well-established embrace of checks and balances,
a belief that was itself rooted in their practical experience with the dangers of
unconstrained executive authority, particularly in war."[7] Others fear unenumerated presidential power in foreign affairs will invariably threaten enumerated
restrictions on national power at home. "Artificially splitting the Constitution
into a document of broad foreign policy powers assigned to the national government (Sutherland) or the President (Yoo)," Gordon Silverstein writes, "actually

exposes us to a far more dangerous threat to liberty—it is the danger that these extraordinary, extra-constitutional powers in foreign policy can, will, come home to undermine civil liberties." In his view, "the Constitution is a delicate machine, designed to work as an integrated whole."[8] Too much presidential independence, paradoxically, may weaken the presidency. Silverstein maintains that presidents tempted to govern without active congressional cooperation risk losing the vital public support necessary for the practical achievement of their foreign policy goals.[9]

Whether the national executive or the national legislature when acting outside the states is bound by the same or at least some constitutional restraints on domestic policymaking is a subject of ongoing controversy.[10] Daniel Webster contended that Congress was not limited by constitutional prohibitions on federal power when governing American territories. If "the very first principle" of the Constitution was that "all within its influence and comprehension shall be represented in the Legislature," he argued, then "extend[ing] the Constitution of the United States to the Territories" which were not represented in Congress was "utterly impossible."[11] The Supreme Court in 1891 declared that "the Constitution can have no operation in another country" when ruling that a sailor found guilty of murder after a trial presided over by the American consul in Japan had no due process rights. Constitutional guarantees "against accusation of capital or infamous crimes, except by indictment or presentment by a grand jury, and for an impartial trial by a jury when thus accused," the justices stated, "apply only to citizens and others within the United States . . . and not to residents or temporary sojourners abroad."[12]

While contemporary constitutional law rejects these positions, no constitutional consensus has ever developed that constitutional limitations operate in full force throughout the world. The application and the force of such restrictions as the prohibition on unreasonable searches in the Fourth Amendment presently depends on where the federal action takes place and the identity of the persons claiming the rights violations. In a series of cases decided at the turn of the twentieth century, a closely divided Supreme Court ruled that Congress was constrained by the Bill of Rights and other prohibitions only when governing the states or territories being prepared for statehood. Federal grand juries were required for indicting persons who stole horses in the Arizona territory but not in the Philippines.[13] These decisions remain good law today. Whether the Constitution restricts national officials in foreign countries is a function of whether an American citizen is claiming a rights violation, where the claimed rights violation took place, and the practicality of recognizing the right.[14] Judicial majorities balancing these factors have extended habeas corpus rights to suspected terrorists detained in Guantanamo Bay,[15] ruled that Americans living on military bases have rights to a jury trial,[16] but determined that German nationals in custody of the

Army after World War Two could be tried by a military commission.[17] More conservative constitutional authorities insist that noncitizens do not have any constitutional rights against American action abroad. Chief Justice William Rehnquist maintained that "there is no indication that the Fourth Amendment was understood by contemporaries of the Framers to apply to activities of the United States directed against aliens in foreign territory or in international waters."[18] More liberal constitutional authorities contend that constitutional restrictions on government officials limit national power no matter where that power is exercised and no matter who claims a rights violation. "The focus of the Fourth Amendment is on *what* the Government can and cannot do, and *how* it may act," Justice William Brennan stated, "not on *against whom* these actions may be taken."[19]

The treaty power has historically provided an alternative source for overcoming constitutional limits on domestic policymaking. Present constitutional law permits the national legislature to pass laws not sanctioned by Article I when implementing international agreements. In *Missouri v. Holland* (1920), the Supreme Court declared that Congress could enact a statute implementing a treaty with Canada that called on both nations to pass legislation protecting migratory birds. Justice Oliver Wendell Holmes conceded that the federal law under constitutional attack might not be within any enumerated power. Nevertheless, he rejected claims that "what an act of Congress could not do unaided...a treaty cannot do." Holmes stated, "There may be matters of the sharpest exigency for the national well-being that an act of Congress could not deal with but that a treaty followed by such an act could."[20]

What constitutional limitations exist on the treaty power is presently unclear. Some prominent Americans insist that no constitutional restrictions limit agreements with foreign countries. The authority to make treaties may be a sovereign power that need not be vested by constitutional edict. Holmes in *Missouri v. Holland* suggested such a broad scope for international agreements when he noted that "acts of Congress are the supreme law of the land when made in pursuance of the Constitution, while treaties are declared to be so when made under the authority of the United States."[21] If the United States can buy Alaska from Russia, then perhaps under this notion of the treaty power Americans could sell Florida to heat-starved Iceland. Others insist that treaties must constitutionally encompass legitimate questions of foreign policy. Charles Evans Hughes maintained that the United States could not sign or ratify a treaty that had "no relation to international concerns."[22] What constitutes an international concern, of course, is contestable. Consider whether a hypothetical treaty outlawing capital punishment should be regarded as a presidential attempt to avoid domestic limits on executive power or as a humanitarian effort to promote international human rights. On yet another view, the treaty power is restricted by explicit limits on federal power. Justice Field declared that the "treaty power...is in terms unlimited except by those restraints which are found in [the Constitution] against the action of the government or of its departments."[23] This emphasis on textual prohibitions suggests that a treaty may not be inconsistent with the First Amendment, which explicitly declares that Congress shall not take certain actions but does not necessarily have to be within the enumerated powers of Congress. Many commentators reject any use of the treaty power to expand federal authority. They insist that *Missouri v. Holland* should be overruled, that a treaty is constitutional only if, in the absence of a treaty, Congress could constitutionally pass the rules in question. More expansive understandings of the treaty power, this school of thought claims, "conflict with the limited and enumerated powers structure of the Constitution."[24]

The president and Senate need not involve the House of Representatives when using the treaty power as a foundation for exercising otherwise impermissible (or permissible) constitutional powers. The United States, unlike most constitutional democracies, treats most international agreements as sufficient for creating both international and domestic obligations. In the majority of European countries, domestic law does not change until the national legislature passes laws implementing the treaty. Should the chief executives of Sweden and Norway sign a treaty agreeing to keep ski slopes in both countries open all year, resort owners outside Oslo and Stockholm will have new legal duties only when and if the legislatures of their home countries revise the civil code. Under American constitutional law, treaties may create binding domestic law without the need for subsequent legislation. Subject to a contingency noted in the following paragraph, resort owners in Aspen have new judicially enforceable obligations the instant a similar treaty is ratified by the Senate. Chief Justice Marshall stated almost two hundred years ago, "Our constitution declares a treaty to be the law of the land. It is, consequently, to be regarded in courts of justice as equivalent to act of the legislature, whenever it operates of itself without the aid of any legislative process."[25]

The last qualification, "whenever it operates of itself," is crucial. So-called self-executing treaties become binding law when ratified by the Senate. An international agreement to keep ski resorts in national parks open all year is an example of a self-executing treaty. A non-self-executing treaty is not binding law when ratified by the Senate, because either the text or subject matter plainly requires Congress to enact additional legislation. Should the president in a treaty merely promise to seek legislation compelling private ski resorts to stay open all year, that treaty is not self-executing. Controversies rage over whether particular treaties are self-executing. In *Medellin v. Texas* (2008), a divided Supreme Court ruled that a treaty giving citizens of other countries a right to contact their consulate after being detained by the police was not self-executing. The justices in *Medellin* also held that federal courts are empowered to determine whether enabling legislation is necessary to implement a treaty, rejecting George W. Bush administration claims that presidents have the power to decide whether international agreements are self-executing.

Controversies over the extraterritorial status of the Constitution and the scope of the treaty power are often rooted in disputes over what is American about American constitutionalism. On one view, American constitutionalism is primarily concerned with how Americans govern. All government actions, unless otherwise explicitly specified, must meet the same constitutional standards. Americans, in this view, are committed to protecting such fundamental rights as free speech no matter where government action takes place and whose expression is affected. On another view, American constitutionalism is primarily concerned with how Americans govern other Americans. The Constitution does not require governing officials to adhere to the same standards when negotiating with France as they must when negotiating with Vermont. Proponents of this constitutional understanding maintain that excessive solicitude for protecting rights abroad may often not be in the national interest and threaten liberty at home. The first position might be described as idealistic or naive. The second might be realistic or cynical. All four adjectives are probably appropriate.

2. Comparative Constitutionalism: Universal or Particular

The past fifty years have witnessed a dramatic increase across the globe in the constitutionalization of politics. Countries as diverse as Nepal, South Africa, Hungary, and Israel have ratified new constitutions or constitution-like laws. Existing constitutional democracies have reallocated authority for making constitutional decisions. Americans have officially and unofficially contributed to these developments. The United States often provides economic, military, and technical assistance to new constitutional regimes. Professors of American constitutional law help draft constitutions for countries making the transition from authoritarianism to democracy. Some American constitutional practices are quite popular abroad, even as they are modified at the edges. Most emerging constitutional democracies adopt a Bill of Rights that guarantees many familiar liberties. New constitutions usually empower the national judiciary to declare laws unconstitutional. Other features of American constitutionalism are not as popular. Few national constitutions diffuse power among as many different institutions as the Constitution of the United States. Most justices on constitutional courts serve for a fixed term of years. Divergences between the Constitution of the United States and the constitutions of other regimes seem to be increasing. David Law and Mila Versteeg observe, "The U.S. Constitution has become an increasingly unpopular model for constitutional framers elsewhere. Possible explanations include the sheer brevity of the Constitution, its imperviousness to formal amendment, its omission of some of the world's generic constitutional rights, and its inclusion of certain rights that are increasingly rare by global standards."[26] These developments abroad are interesting in their own right and for the perspectives they offer on American constitutionalism.[27] Comparative constitutional analysis often exposes the parochialism of common assertions that a particular American constitutional practice is inherent in constitutionalism or necessary for preserving justice and liberty. A brief survey of free speech policies in various constitutional democracies suggests that regimes do not degenerate into tyranny when constitutional decision makers provide less protection for hate speech and campaign finance reform than does the Supreme Court of the United States. American practice may be better (or worse) than practice abroad, or at least better for Americans. Nevertheless, American constitutionalists exaggerate significantly when they declare that "neither liberty nor justice would exist" if the distinctive protections courts in the United States provide for criminal defendants and women seeking abortions "were sacrificed."[28] Better awareness of American particularism, in turn, may promote better explanations and evaluations of American practice. Rather than treat judicial supremacy as a natural consequence of constitutionalism, constitutional commentators in the United States who are aware that constitutional authority is allocated differently in other constitutional regimes might consider why Americans vest so much power in the Supreme Court and whether that power best promotes constitutional democracy. For two centuries, Americans have interpreted their Constitution in light of differences between the United States and other regimes. Some constitutional commentators and governing officials believe, given the increased worldwide commitment to constitutional democracy, that the Constitution should now be interpreted in light of the similarities between the United States and other regimes.

2.1 Comparing American Constitutionalism

Constitutional democracies across the globe have many common features. All constitutional regimes entrench fundamental laws and respect the rule of law. Liberal constitutional regimes guarantee such fundamental rights as the freedom of speech and private property. Constitutional arguments throughout most of the world have a similar structure, relying on combinations of original meanings, more general principles, and prudence to generate answers to various constitutional questions. Formal, semiformal, and informal constitutional changes occur constantly in all constitutional polities. Some constitutional practices appear to have universal tendencies. Comparative constitutional analysis suggests that written constitutions tend to empower national judiciaries and generate common interpretive practices.

Constitutional democracies nevertheless vary across every dimension of constitutional practice. Constitutional regimes have different purposes, interpretative practices, allocations of constitutional authority, and means for constitutional change. Constitutional powers, limitations, rights, duties, and processes are different in different countries. Some differences are grounded in different constitutional texts. The Constitution of the United States and the Constitution of Germany have different rules for amendment. These different rules for formal constitutional change, in turn, influence the rates of semiformal constitutional changes in different countries.[29] Other differences stem from different constitutional commitments or interpretive practices. One study found that constitutional protections in the United States, Canada, Germany, and Japan for hate speech and libel reflect the distinctive histories and cultures of these regimes.[30]

2.2 Comparative Constitutional Purposes

Constitutional democracies share a set of core commitments rooted in the liberal and republican political thought of the eighteenth century, including popular sovereignty, preserving the peace, promoting commercial prosperity, and respecting the rights that classical liberal and republican thinkers thought were essential for preserving human dignity.[31] Article I of the French Constitution proclaims, "France shall be an indivisible, secular, democratic and social Republic. It shall ensure the equality of all citizens before the law, without distinction of origin, race or religion. It shall respect all beliefs. It shall be organised on a decentralised basis." The Preamble to the Constitution of Germany states, "Conscious of their responsibility before God and Men, Animated by the resolve to serve world peace as an equal partner in a united Europe, the German people have adopted, by virtue of their constituent power, this Basic Law."

Considerable variation exists within liberal–republican constitutional practice. Some constitutional democracies assert a commitment to both a particular religion and the right to free exercise of religion. The Basic Law of Israel declares a national aspiration to "protect human dignity and liberty" and a commitment to establish "the values of the State of Israel as a Jewish and democratic state." Many constitutional democracies place greater weight on republican or communal purposes than the United States, whose constitutional commitments have historically reflected strands of liberal thought that emphasize the value of personal autonomy. Crucial sections of the Canadian Constitution and Canadian constitutional practice offer more protection for group rights than do their neighbors to the immediate south. Chapter 2 points out that many new constitutions declare a national commitment to providing all citizens with a minimum standard of living. The Constitution of South Africa declares:

1. Everyone has the right to have access to

    1. health care services, including reproductive health care;
    2. sufficient food and water; and
    3. social security, including, if they are unable to support themselves and their dependants, appropriate social assistance.

2. The state must take reasonable legislative and other measures, within its available resources, to achieve the progressive realisation of each of these rights.
3. No one may be refused emergency medical treatment.[32]

Some American commentators interpret the due process clause of the Fourteenth Amendment as guaranteeing similar rights, but contemporary American constitutional practice, at least with respect to the Constitution of the United States, presently rejects any governmental obligation to provide citizens with basic necessities.[33]

Constitutional regimes do not need to be liberal or republican democracies, at least if constitutionalism is understood as requiring commitments only to legality and fundamental law. Many constitutional texts announce illiberal constitutional purposes. Constitutional theocracies mandate that all laws shall be consistent with specific religious traditions. Article 2 of the Constitution of Egypt states, "Islam is the religion of the State, Arabic is its official language, and the principles of Islamic Shari'a are the principal source of legislation."[34] The Republic of Singapore demonstrates how regimes can abide by their constitutional rules, maintaining the property and contract rights necessary to establish the credible commitments that create a healthy climate for foreign investment while employing those same formal constitutional procedures when restricting democratic freedoms.[35] Jacksonians, who during the years before the Civil War insisted the Constitution of the United States was made for white people, were hardly the only political actors in history who perceived a constitutional commitment to racial or ethnic supremacy.[36]

2.3 Comparative Constitutional Interpretation

A global interpretive community is developing. Constitutional authorities and commentators throughout the world increasingly cite materials from other countries when discussing particular issues such as the constitutionality of limits on campaign finance[37] and legitimate methods for interpreting national constitutions.[38] Given the newness of many constitutions and the paucity of work on comparative constitutional interpretation, generalizations are necessarily tentative. Still, some preliminary evidence indicates interesting similarities and differences between American practice and constitutional interpretation in other regimes.

Basic elements for discerning the meaning of constitutional provisions do not vary by constitutional democracy. Constitutional arguments from India to Canada tend to rely on the materials and logics discussed in Chapter 4: "the words of the constitutional text, understood in the context of related provisions; other evidence of the intentions, understandings or purposes of the founders; presumptions favoring broad, and purposive, interpretations; precedent and doctrine developed from it; so-called 'structural' principles regarded as underlying particular provisions or groups of provisions; and considerations of justice, practicality and public policy."[39] Constitutional commentators in Germany might disagree with claims that restrictions on abortion are inconsistent with the original meaning of the Constitution of South Korea or that the South African constitutional commitment to human dignity entails a constitutional right to state-supplied experts at criminal trials, but they would recognize these claims as legitimate, if mistaken, constitutional arguments.

Persons in different countries when making constitutional arguments do place more or less emphasis on different sources. Jeffrey Goldsworthy, a leading Australian constitutional thinker, observes:

> Precedents naturally play a much larger role in the interpretation of older constitutions, because there are more of them; academic opinion has far more influence in Germany than elsewhere; original intentions or understandings are relied on more in Australia, Germany, and the United States than in Canada and India; 'structural' principles play a more pervasive role in Canada, Germany, India and South Africa than in Australia or the United States; justice and public policy seem more influential in India than elsewhere; and comparative law is given much less attention in the United States than in other countries.

Goldsworthy is particularly impressed by "substantial differences in the general philosophies of interpretation currently favoured by courts." His survey found that "Australian and German judges tend to be much more strongly attracted to legalist philosophies than Canadian and Indian judges, with South African judges arguably sitting somewhere in between, and American judges being more divided over these issues."[40] These differences may be rooted in different legal cultures, whether judicial appointments tend to come from a narrow stratum of professional judges or whether citizens in particular regimes have historically trusted elected officials.[41]

Constitutional authorities in many countries often employ a practice becoming known as proportional review (or simply proportionality) when determining the meaning and application of constitutional rights provisions. Government officials are free to limit the exercise of all rights, practitioners agree, as long as the justification for the restriction is reasonably related to the justification for curtailing the right. As one commentator describes the interpretive process, "The state, having established a sufficiently important objective, rationally pursued with minimal impairment of the right, must demonstrate that the desired and actual benefit of the impugned measure at large exceeds the detriment visited upon the rights-holder."[42] Sometimes proportionality is inscribed into the national constitution. Section 1 of the Canadian Charter of Rights and Freedoms declares that constitutional rights and freedoms are "subject only to such reasonable limits prescribed by law as can be demonstrably justified in a free and democratic society." Accordingly, the Supreme Court of Canada has engaged in one or another form of proportional review when ruling on constitutional challenges to national and local laws. *Regina v. Keegstra et al.* (1990) decided whether a legislative provision prohibiting the "wilful promotion of hatred... towards any section of the public distinguished by colour, race, religion or ethnic origin" was "a reasonable limit on freedom of expression in a free and democratic society" or "proportional and appropriate to the ends of suppressing hate propaganda in order to maintain social harmony and individual dignity."[43] The judicial decision in that case sustained the law under constitutional attack. This outcome was not dictated by the particular method of constitutional interpretation. Justices in other countries using proportional review have struck down similar measures as excessive.[44] These different results highlight how proportionality is context related, flexible, and, some argue, more conducive to judge-made law.

Americans are more prone to vary the level of scrutiny when deciding whether government actions violate constitutional rights. In cases raising questions about the constitutional status of regulations on hate speech, the justices on the Supreme Court of United States often rely on a practice described as *definitional balancing*. They consider whether such laws engage in viewpoint or content discrimination. If a state law banning racial insults is interpreted as restricting the advocacy of particular positions, such as the claim that Jews control American banks (but not restricting the claim that Jews do not control American banks), the statute is unconstitutional. If, however, bans on insulting language are interpreted as neutral restrictions on all speakers, then the law may be subject only to a much weaker rationality test.[45]

Constitutional debates over religious freedom provide a particularly good example of interpretive similarities and differences among nations throughout the world. All constitutional democracies guarantee the free exercise of religion. At least at the turn of the twenty-first century, all forbid government from directly interfering with religious belief. Legislatures in liberal constitutional regimes may not criminalize Islam or Mormonism per se. Constitutional democracies differ, however, on whether government officials may pass secular laws that burden religious practice. Consider controversies over whether school dress codes may forbid girls from wearing religiously mandated head scarves in classrooms. Constitutional courts in Germany have declared such practices unconstitutional. Similar rules remain good law in France. Constitutional authorities in the United States insist that laws not explicitly discriminating against religion are constitutional.[46] Constitutional authorities in Germany and the European Court of Human Rights demand that government provide strong justifications for laws that inhibit religious practice.[47] These differences may be rooted in distinctive constitutional purposes. Gary Jacobsohn explains how divergent constitutional understandings of religious freedom are consequences of constitutional efforts to disestablish a previously established religion (India), maintain an established religion (Israel), or prevent any religion from becoming established (United States).[48] Paradoxically, constitutional democracies with established religions may be more tolerant of minority religions than states committed to "no-establishment" principles. Whereas Muslim tribunals in Israel or India are officially recognized and enjoy certain jurisdictional autonomy, they do not enjoy such statutory recognition and jurisdictional autonomy in the United States—a polity committed to a more assimilative notion of religious freedom.[49]

2.4 Comparative Constitutional Authority

The past half-century has witnessed a global explosion of judicial power as well as a global explosion of constitutionalism. Many new constitutions explicitly empower national courts to declare laws unconstitutional and settle constitutional disputes. Article 134 of the Italian constitution pronounces, "The Constitutional Court shall decide... on disputes concerning the constitutional legitimacy of laws and acts having the force of law, adopted by the State and the Regions." Courts in other constitutional democracies have successfully asserted the right to declare laws unconstitutional. The Basic Laws of Israel do not expressly vest the national judiciary with the power to strike down laws, but *United Mizrahi Bank v. Migdal Cooperative Village* (1995) treated those provisions as judicially enforceable. For the first time in Israeli history, the Supreme Court of Israel voided a parliamentary law, one that limited the rights of banks to collect certain debts. Constitutional courts throughout the world are declaring more laws unconstitutional and are declaring more politically important laws unconstitutional. Paraphrasing Tocqueville's famous aphorism about the United

States, Ran Hirschl observes that after the "constitutional revolution of 1992" in Israel "there is scarcely a public policy question that does not sooner or later turn into a judicial question."[50] The Hungarian Constitutional Court was been the most powerful governing institution in the nation during the first decade of the twenty-first century, issuing thousands of rulings and declaring numerous state laws unconstitutional.[51] Other constitutional courts have set out the conditions under which provinces may secede from the nation, laid out the rules for making new constitutions, determined the result of national elections, established the conditions for citizenship, and outlawed various political parties.[52]

A form of judicial review even seems to be taking root in the United Kingdom, one of the last bastions of legislative supremacy. One study found increased agreement in Great Britain that "judges are presumed to have the authority to develop judicial notions of justice and fairness, and to impose those limits on governmental actors in ways that may be contrary to Parliament's expressed intent."[53] Most English justices claim that they are be bound by "an abstracted and generalized notion of parliamentary intent," but this "intent" is often inconsistent with statutory texts and legislative history. In *Anisminic Ltd. v. Foreign Compensation Commission* (1969), the House of Lords reversed an administration ruling, casting aside legislation declaring that commission decisions "shall not be called in question in any court of law." The law was not struck down but was "creatively" interpreted. Parliament would have included "something much more specific than th[at] bald statement," Lord Reid dubiously insisted, if the national legislature had really intended to foreclose judicial reconsideration of an incorrect administrative decision.[54]

Constitutional dialogues between justices and other governing officials in foreign constitutional democracies exhibit several differences from practice in the United States. Many nations have distinctive constitutional courts whose jurisdiction is limited to constitutional issues. In the United States, traffic courts, in theory, may declare speed traps unconstitutional. The Supreme Court, if vested with jurisdiction by Congress, may adjudicate many complaints about parking tickets. In France, constitutional questions are adjudicated only by a special constitutional court. That tribunal may adjudicate only constitutional questions. Justices in most constitutional democracies do not have life tenure and are often selected by persons other than the nation's chief executive. The Constitution of Italy establishes a constitutional court that "consists of fifteen justices; one third being appointed by the president, one third by parliament in joint session, and one third by ordinary and administrative supreme courts." Those selected must be justices on other courts, full professors of law, or lawyers with more than twenty years' experience. All serve for nine years and cannot be reappointed. Constitutional rules for bringing constitutional disputes before judicial authorities vary significantly. India permits persons to initiate a lawsuit if they object on constitutional grounds to government action that might harm someone. Some European countries permit strong legislative minorities to refer bills to the national judiciary for constitutional evaluation before those proposals become law. This constitutional practice is known as abstract judicial review. Were Americans to adopt abstract review, opponents of limits on political contributions could compel a judicial ruling on proposed legislation restricting campaign finance before those measures became binding federal law.

A new commonwealth model of constitutionalism is emerging in many regimes that reject judicial supremacy while vesting courts with substantial power to base decisions on constitutional norms. Justices engaged in this weaker form of judicial review have broad power to "interpret legislation to make it consistent with constitutional norms." Statutes prohibiting persons from "disturbing the peace" are not understood as permitting the police to arrest political dissidents who inveigh against the alleged evils of the government. When courts declare legislation unconstitutional, they either may not order that their decision be enforced or "the legislature may respond by reinstating the original legislation by some means other than a cumbersome constitutional amendment."[55] The Canadian Charter of Rights and Freedoms includes a provision known as the "notwithstanding clause," which states that "Parliament...may expressly declare in an Act of Parliament...that the Act or a provision thereof shall operate notwithstanding" a judicial declaration that the measure is unconstitutional. Such legislative declarations remain good law for five years and may be reenacted. Were the United States to adopt this practice, Congress could reinstate the ban on flag burning declared unconstitutional in *United States v. Eichman* (1990). Whether this form of weak judicial review is viable in the long run is not yet clear. Some commentators claim that weak judicial review in the United States evolved into stronger forms of judicial review. Other constitutional democracies at the turn of the twenty-first century are witnessing the same tendency for shared constitutional authority to mutate into judicial supremacy.[56]

Comparative analysis suggests that how constitutional authority is allocated in a regime often determines governmental capacity to implement constitutional commitments and decisions. Professor Leslie Goldstein of the University of Delaware claims that the strong veto powers given to nations in the European Union help explain why contemporary decisions by the European Court of Justice limiting the power of nation states provoke less resistance to judicial authority than the analogous decisions before the Civil War by the Supreme Court of the United States that were routinely ignored by local officials. Unlike nineteenth-century (or contemporary) Virginia and Ohio, contemporary France and Italy have the power to prevent objectionable measures from becoming European Union law. Hence, while individual American states may vigorously oppose national policy, most European policies enjoy at least tepid support in all major states. Local units that have the power to veto hostile measures, Goldstein's study concludes, are less likely to resist judicial enforcement of whatever measures are legislatively adopted.[57] Mark Tushnet finds that the weak forms of judicial review discussed in the previous paragraphs may be the "best institutional mechanism for enforcing all fundamental rights" because that practice permits constructive dialogues between justices and elected officials over how constitutional commitments should be achieved. Again, sharing constitutional authority fosters cooperative relationships between the officials responsible for making and the officials responsible for implementing constitutional decisions. "Ongoing bargaining" between the Hungarian Constitutional Court and state legislature initially smoothed the transition from communism to a market economy.[58] By declaring that the Irish legislature was not fulfilling constitutional responsibilities to handicapped children, the Supreme Court of Ireland may have successfully pressured elected officials to pass ameliorative measures.[59]

The political construction of judicial power is another fruitful avenue for comparative analysis that informs American constitutionalism. Comparative constitutionalists rarely make statements analogous to "*Marbury v. Madison* established judicial review." Their explanations of judicial review in new constitutional regimes focus on decisions made by elected officials. Tom Ginsburg's study of Mongolia, South Korea, and Taiwan explores why "judicial review makes sense from the perspective of those who write the constitution." In his view:

> The answer has to do with the time horizons of those politicians drafting the constitution. If they foresee themselves in power after the constitution is passed, they are likely to design institutions that allow them to govern without encumbrance. On the other hand, if they foresee themselves losing in postconstitutional elections, they may seek to entrench judicial review as a form of political insurance. Even if they lose the election, they will be able to have some access to a forum in which to challenge the legislature. I argue that the particular institutional design of the constitutional court will tend to reflect the interests of powerful politicians at the time of drafting, with optimistic politicians preferring less vigorous and powerful courts so they can govern without constraint.[60]

Commentators observe a similar phenomenon in the United States. Judicial empowerment takes place when elected officials believe that courts will facilitate their political interests. Congress expanded federal jurisdiction in 1875 and 1891 to ensure that the lame duck Republican Party majority in Congress would continue exercising influence in the federal judiciary.[61] Jack Balkin and Sandy Levinson claim that the George W. Bush administration engaged in a similar "partisan entrenchment" strategy, appointing young movement conservatives to the federal courts who will exercise judicial power long after that coalition lost control of the federal government.[62] Politics matters even when politicians do not directly empower courts. Ginsburg points out, "The more diffused politics are, the more space courts have in which to operate."[63] Just as courts in a foreign country are able to exercise more power when no consensus exists among elected officials, so such decisions as *Dred Scott v. Sandford, Brown v. Board of Education,* and *Roe v. Wade* were in part consequences of legislative paralysis on slavery, segregation, and abortion.[64]

Comparative constitutionalists debate the practical consequences of constitutionalization and the increased empowerment of judiciaries. Conventional wisdom regards judicial review under a written constitution as a vital means for protecting vulnerable minorities. Ronald Dworkin urged the United Kingdom to ratify a judicially enforceable Bill of Rights that he believed would secure such values as "individual privacy and dignity, and freedom of speech and conscience."[65] Hirschl's *hegemonic preservation thesis*[66] suggests the contrary. He insists that judicial review throughout the world is primarily sponsored by elected officials and interest groups fearful of losing political power. "When their policy preferences have been, or are likely to be, increasingly challenged in majoritarian decision-making arenas," Hirschl observes, "elites that possess disproportionate access to, and influence over, the legal arena may initiate a constitutional entrenchment of rights and judicial review in order to transfer power to supreme courts."[67] Fulfilling this constitutional mission, courts are more likely to declare unconstitutional legislation that limits liberties exercised by the politically powerful than to protect powerless minorities. Hirschl's study of comparative constitutional law in action "contrast[s] the limited impact of constitutionalization on enhancing the life conditions of the have-nots with its significant contribution to the removal of so-called market rigidities and the promotion of economic liberties."[68] Other scholars believe that constitutionalism promotes greater social equality than Hirschl concedes. Women, in particular, may find the judiciary a friendly haven. Had Hirschl "defined progressive change more broadly ... to include challenges to the unequal distribution of power and resources on the basis of gender and efforts to alter patterns of gender inequality in institutions of civil society," Linda McClain and James Fleming assert, "we might find that constitutionalization and judicial review in the four countries he analyzes have been instrumental in bringing about some progressive social change."[69] Hirschl's more recent work accepts some of this critique. In particular, he notes the tendency of courts in constitutional theocracies to support the most secular interpretation of constitutional norms.[70]

American constitutionalism has experienced similar disputes over the practical consequences of empowering justices as constitutional authorities. No agreement exists on whether judicial review in the United States tends to promote liberal property rights, political and social equality for vulnerable populations, or only the idiosyncratic values of whatever justices happen to be on the bench at a particular time. Some commentators agree with Hirschl's assessment that courts tend to favor the interests of the propertied class. Many populists and progressives at the turn of the twentieth century insisted that the "plutocratic majority in the Senate" guaranteed the appointment of federal judges sympathetic to "the 'safe, sane and sound' predominance of wealth."[71] Other commentators insist that the federal courts have the potential to play leadership roles in progressive politics. In their view, such decisions as *Brown v. Board of Education* demonstrate that Justices have special capacities to "listen for voices from the margins."[72] A third line of commentary suggests that the influence of the Supreme Court on American constitutional politics has been ideologically erratic throughout history. "Judicial review," a leading critic states, "basically amounts to noise around zero," offering "essentially random changes, sometimes good and sometimes bad, to what the political system produces."[73]

2.5 Comparative Constitutional Change

Formal, semiformal, and informal constitutional changes take place in all liberal constitutional democracies. All constitutions specify procedures for amending the constitutional text. Most include the procedures for ratification. Official decisions in all countries clarify constitutional powers, rights, processes, and limitations. Many controversially challenge previous constitutional understandings. Justices in New Zealand and Canada helped redefine the constitutional rights of indigenous peoples.[74] Constitutional commentators in Australia sound quite American when complaining about judicial decisions they believe inconsistent with the powers originally vested in that country's administrative agencies.[75] Informal constitutional changes often generate more formal constitutional reforms. Shifts in the balance of power between Ashkenazi and Sephardic Jews help explain the increased prominence of the Ashkenazi-dominated Israeli judiciary.[76] The rise of civil liberties groups with the resources necessary to influence official decision-making is responsible for increased constitutional attention throughout the world to such concerns as free speech and religious liberty. Most constitutions do not recognize secession rights.[77] Canada is an important exception. The Supreme Court of that nation has interpreted the Canadian Constitution as permitting Quebec to secede should certain conditions be met.[78]

Provisions for ratifying constitutions throughout the world aim at legitimating constitutional rule, but countries use different procedures to achieve that goal.[79] Democratic constitutions have been drafted by an elected convention, the national legislature, or a constitutional court. They may be ratified by a national convention, the national legislature, or a national convention as well as by subnational units. Different regimes have insisted on pluralities, majorities, or supermajorities. The Constitution of Iraq was drafted by an interim legislature and approved by a popular referendum. To secure broad national support from both Sunni and Shiite factions, the ratification procedure required that the constitution not obtain less than one-third of the popular vote in three or more provinces. In some cases, most notably Japan after World War Two, a democratic constitution may be imposed on a people after their military defeat.

The constitutional amendment process exhibits similar variation. Most countries (and states) mandate more majoritarian procedures than the United States. The Constitution of Ireland, a somewhat typical example, requires that amendments first be approved by both houses of the national legislature and then submitted to the people in a popular referendum. Some constitutions limit legitimate amendments. Article 79 of the Basic Law for the Federal Republic of Germany states, "Amendments to this Basic Law affecting the division of the Federation into Länder, their participation on principle in the legislative process, or the principles laid down in Articles 1 and 20 shall be inadmissible." This provision entrenches the German equivalent of the Bill of Rights (Articles 1–20) and German federalism. An amendment to the German constitution may not empower government to prohibit flag burning if that form of political protest is presently constitutionally protected. As noted in Chapter 6, courts in Germany and other nations have struck down constitutional amendments believed inconsistent with the fundamental principles underlying the constitutional order.

The Constitution of the United States has outlasted numerous constitutions, including the constitutions of many constitutional democracies. Americans have had the same foundational text for more than 220 years. This is particularly remarkable given that the average national constitution lasts seventeen years. Constitutional failures are particularly common in authoritarian regimes. Still, most constitutional democracies change constitutions with some frequency. The Netherlands replaced constitutions wholesale in 1972 and 1983 and then substantially revised the constitutional text in each succeeding decade. The French sometimes joke that their constitution cannot be found in libraries that do not have an extensive periodical collection.

Preliminary research on the comparative constitutional experience suggests several reasons why the Constitution of the United States has endured for such a long period.[80] Constitutional change in liberal democracies tends to be a consequence of exogenous shocks. Liberal constitutions are abandoned only after "some cataclysmic situation such as revolution, world war, the withdrawal of empire, civil war, or the threat of imminent breakup."[81] The post–World War Two French constitution did not survive the end of colonialization. The 1997 Constitution of Thailand was the victim of a military coup. With the exception of the Civil War, Americans either have not experienced analogous crises or their experience was far less traumatic than that of other constitutional regimes. Many

European countries adopted new constitutions after the devastation wrecked by the First and Second World Wars. Neither conflict disrupted the home front in the United States to remotely the same degree. Enduring constitutions transcend the politics of the day. Authoritarian constitutions come and go with the changing of a dictatorship. The Dominican Republic is the present world leader, with twenty-nine constitutions since 1844. Constitutions that embody the vision of only one political party may not survive the collapse of that coalition. Taiwan substantially revised constitutional procedures during the 1990s after the Kuomintang, which had ruled that island since 1947, lost control of the government. The Constitution of the United States, by comparison, is better designed to transcend partisan and sectional divides. Article VII's requirement of a fairly inclusive ratification process ensured that, after the process was successful, the Constitution was supported by a broad spectrum of politically active citizens during the early Republic. The emergence of such prominent Federalists in the 1780s as Alexander Hamilton and James Madison as leaders of the opposing parties during the 1790s enabled political divisions in the United States to be over the meaning rather than about the merits of the Constitution. Some evidence suggests that enduring constitutions provide fairly specific details about the structure of governing institutions while being sufficiently flexible to incorporate the numerous informal constitutional changes that take place in any regime over time. The United States Constitution seems to incorporate the appropriate mix of detail and elasticity. American state constitutions, which often spell out the minutiae of governance, lack the flexibility conducive to a long shelf life. Government under the Articles of Confederation collapsed, in part, because the framers were too circumspect, failing to provide for an executive or judicial branch.

The virtues of this longevity are contested. Chapter 3 details that deeply entrenched constitutions have benefits and costs. Entrenchment prevents governing officials from unduly manipulating elections but may inhibit responses to social change. No good study exists on whether constitutional democracies that every twenty or thirty years formally change constitutions are better or worse governed than constitutional regimes that maintain the original constitutional structure for generations. That the Dutch and French more frequently adjust fundamental constitutional norms than Americans may be a sign of greater political instability in those regimes or their greater willingness to rethink fundamental governing institutions in light of experience and changing political circumstances.

2.6 Informing American Constitutionalism

Comparative constitutional perspectives inform domestic constitutional analysis in several ways. Americans have historically looked abroad to discover what their Constitution is not. Constitutional decision-makers often interpret constitutional provisions by contrasting practice in the United States with practice in other countries. Analysis of gun rights in Europe may reveal why the distinctive American fear of standing armies underlies a proper appreciation of the rights protected by the Second Amendment. Americans less often look abroad to discover what their Constitution is. To the extent constitutional protections for religious freedom or private property are best interpreted as guarantees for basic human liberties, however, then decisions handed down by constitutional decision-makers in countries similarly committed to basic human liberties might inform analysis of the First and Fifth Amendments. Whether and how comparative perspectives should influence American constitutionalism depends in part on whether Americans are constituted by a historical commitment to a distinctive set of rights or whether they are constituted by a distinctive historical commitment to universal human rights.

Constitutional arguments in the United States often and without controversy contrast domestic norms with foreign practices. The precise distinctions between American constitutionalism and other constitutional regimes are contestable, but general agreement exists that pointing to possible divergences is a legitimate method for interpreting or construing such provisions as the free exercise or commerce clauses. Madison employed this logic when explaining why the Sedition Act of 1798 was unconstitutional. That measure, which prohibited "false, scandalous, and malicious" criticisms of the federal government, was consistent with English common law at the time the Constitution was ratified. Political commentary in eighteenth-century England could not be subject to advance censorship or prior restraint, but government officials were free to punish speech for any reason after publication. Madison's claim that the First Amendment provided greater protection to speech rights than the common law appealed to "the essential difference between the British government and the American constitutions." Free speech law in England reflected the English commitment to Parliamentary supremacy. He stated:

> In the British government the danger of encroachments on the rights of the people, is understood to be confined to the executive magistrate. The representatives of the people in the legislature, are not only exempt themselves, from distrust, but are considered as sufficient guardians of the rights of their constituents against the danger from the executive.... Under such a government as this, an exemption of the press from previous restraint by licensers appointed by the king, is all the freedom that can be secured to it.

American free speech law, by comparison, was rooted in a national commitment to popular sovereignty that entailed restrictions on both executive and legislative censorship. Madison continued:

> In the United States, the case is altogether different. The people, not the government, possess the absolute sovereignty. The legislature, no less than the executive, is under limitations of power.... Hence, in the United States, the great and essential rights of the people are secured against legislative, as well as against executive ambition.... This security of the freedom of the press requires, that it should be exempt, not only from previous restraint by the executive, as in Great Britain, but from legislative restraint also; and this exemption, to be effectual, must be an exemption not only from the previous inspection of licensers, but from the subsequent penalty of laws.[82]

Constitutional arguments during World War Two and the Cold War emphasized differences between democratic and totalitarian regimes. "Precisely because they provide a sharp idea of what the U.S. does *not* stand for," Kim Lane Scheppele details, "Nazi Germany and the Soviet Union became irresistible points of reference."[83] Justice Black engaged in aversive constitutionalism when declaring that a coerced confession violated the Fifth and Fourteenth Amendments. His opinion in *Ashcraft v. Tennessee* (1944) compared the United States favorably with "certain foreign nations...which convict individuals with testimony obtained by police organizations possessed of an unrestrained power to seize persons suspected of crimes against the state, hold them in secret custody, and wring from them confessions by physical or mental torture."[84] Justice Jackson in 1943 spoke of the "fast failing efforts of our present totalitarian enemies" when insisting that Americans not "coerce uniformity of sentiment" by requiring public school students to salute the flag.[85]

Whether constitutional authorities should make positive use of foreign constitutional practices is more controversial. This constitutional borrowing, in sharp contrast to aversive constitutionalism, interprets or construes constitutional provisions by examining similarities between the United States and other constitutional democracies. Justice Kennedy ignited the contemporary debate over the place of comparative constitutionalism in American law when in *Lawrence v. Texas* (2003) he commented on European constitutional decisions striking down bans on sodomy. The majority opinions in *Bowers v. Hardwick* (1986) had pointed to the universal condemnation of homosexual behavior when sustaining a Georgia ban on such conduct. Kennedy looked abroad to refute that claim. He wrote:

> Almost five years before *Bowers* was decided the European Court of Human Rights considered a case with parallels to *Bowers* and to

today's case. An adult male resident in Northern Ireland alleged he was a practicing homosexual who desired to engage in consensual homosexual conduct.... The court held that the laws proscribing the conduct were invalid under the European Convention on Human Rights.... Authoritative in all countries that are members of the Council of Europe (21 nations then, 45 nations now), the decision is at odds with the premise in *Bowers* that the claim put forward was insubstantial in our Western civilization.[86]

While this passage might be read as merely refuting claims that *Bowers* was consistent with universal practice, Kennedy sometimes uses comparative constitutional practice as evidence of the contemporary standards he believes relevant to interpreting such provisions as the "cruel and unusual punishment" clause of the Eighth Amendment. When ruling in *Roper v. Simmons* (2005) that states could not constitutionally execute persons whose crimes were committed before they turned eighteen, he stated:

Our determination that the death penalty is disproportionate punishment for offenders under 18 finds confirmation in the stark reality that the United States is the only country in the world that continues to give official sanction to the juvenile death penalty. This reality does not become controlling, for the task of interpreting the Eighth Amendment remains our responsibility. Yet at least from the time of the Court's decision in *Trop* [*v. Dulles* (1958)], the Court has referred to the laws of other countries and to international authorities as instructive for its interpretation of the Eighth Amendment's prohibition of "cruel and unusual punishments."[87]

Justice Scalia vehemently objected to this use of comparative sources. His dissent in *Roper* declared, "The basic premise of the Court's argument—that American law should conform to the laws of the rest of the world—ought to be rejected out of hand." He added, "It is beyond comprehension why we should look" for American "standards of decency" to countries with "a legal, political, and social culture quite different from our own."[88]

Justice Scalia's claim that the American constitutional order is unique is at the heart of the debate over whether legitimate methods of constitutional decision-making in the United States may seek to align American practice with constitutional practices abroad. Critics of citations to comparative constitutional sources believe that substantial differences exist between the American and every other constitutional regime and that these differences powerfully counsel against any foreign constitutional borrowing. As Scalia has claimed in public debate:

> We don't have the same moral and legal framework as the rest of the world, and never have. If you told the framers of the Constitution that we're to be just like Europe, they would have been appalled. And if you read the *Federalist Papers,* they are full of statements that make very clear the framers didn't have a whole lot of respect for many of the rules in European countries. Madison...speaks contemptuously of the countries on continental Europe, "who are afraid to let their people bear arms."[89]

Those who champion increased reference to comparative sources believe that they help inform constitutional judgment on universal constitutional problems. Comparative constitutional law, Justice Stephen Breyer maintains, is relevant to constitutional decision-making because cases in foreign countries "sometimes involve a human being working as a judge concerned with a legal problem, often similar to problems that arise here, which problem involves the application of a legal text, often similar to the text of our own Constitution, seeking to protect certain basic human rights, often similar to the rights that our own Constitution seeks to protect."[90]

Participants in the controversy over foreign citations have different understandings of constitutionalism, constitutional purposes, and the best methods for discerning the meaning of constitutional provisions. Scalia and his supporters insist that the constitutional commitment to the rule of law entails a commitment to interpreting constitutional provisions by taking into account their distinctive histories. Free speech decisions in other countries, they point out, cast little if any light on the original meaning of the First Amendment or enduring practice in the United States. From this interpretive perspective, comparative constitutional citations at most point to differences between the American constitutional experience and the experience of other constitutional regimes. If, as everyone agrees, American sovereignty would be violated by permitting the Swedish legislature to make laws for the United States, then Swedish constitutional decisions can hardly count as authoritative precedents in American courts. Breyer and his supporters maintain that the constitutional commitment to "securing the blessings of liberty" entails a commitment to interpreting constitutional provisions by taking into account our best understanding of universal human rights. The growing consensus in the democratic world that certain crimes should not be punished by death, from this perspective, is evidence about what constitutes cruel and unusual punishment under the Eighth Amendment. American sovereignty is maintained because the duty to examine any global consensus is derived from the Constitution of the United States, not from some commitment external to American constitutionalism.

This controversy is unlikely to end in the foreseeable future. As Americans and American constitutional authorities become more familiar with comparative constitutional law sources, they are more likely to consider citing them and perhaps even relying on them when they make decisions. Some distinctions between American constitutionalism and foreign constitutional regimes may blur and others sharpen when constitutional authorities self-consciously confront the variety of constitutional practices in foreign nations. Optimists hope that comparative constitutional sources will become a legal vehicle for improved understandings of the American constitutional regime. Comparatively informed citizens may reflect more seriously on the unique and universal elements of constitutionalism in the United States. Pessimists fear that those materials will prove yet another device for interjecting policy preferences into constitutional law. Comparatively informed constitutional decision-makers may use their knowledge primarily to litter their opinions with citations to the foreign practices that are consistent with their preexisting political commitments.

3. A Higher Authority? International Law and the Constitution

International law purports to have a higher status than the constitutional law of any country. International tribunals frequently condemn nations as well as political leaders and their subordinates for violating the law of nations and fundamental human rights, even when the challenged actions were legal under domestic law. Adolph Eichmann was executed for his role in the Holocaust despite clear evidence that law in Nazi Germany permitted shipping Jewish residents to concentration camps. The United States promotes and assists these efforts to sanction governments and persons responsible for atrocities. Americans played central roles during the Nuremberg Trials, prosecuting prominent Nazi officials for waging aggressive war, committing war crimes, and perpetrating crimes against humanity. Americans encouraged the Iraqi government to try Saddam Hussein for genocide. When affirming the death sentence in that case, the Iraqi High Tribunal affirmed the higher law status of international norms. Under "international penal law," the legal opinion declared, "no government has the right to grant immunity to its officials for committing crimes against humanity or ethnic massacres."[91]

Treaties are the primary source of contemporary international law. For those who missed out on mandatory instruction in Latin or wish to impress friends and neighbors with their erudition, the proper phrase used by diplomats is *pacta sunt servanda*. Under the law of nations, agreements must be honored. The United States has a legal obligation to adhere to the Geneva Convention because the Senate ratified that accord. This duty is rooted in constitutional as well as international norms. Article VI states that "all treaties made ... under the Authority of the United States shall be the supreme Law of the Land." Treaties under international and constitutional law bind only signatory nations. The United States, after rejecting membership in the League of Nations, had no duty of any kind to participate in that body or adhere to its decrees.

Customary practice is the other source of international law. The law of nations at the time the Constitution was ratified consisted of understandings about the way civilized nations behaved. International law was regarded as "the system of right and justice that ought to prevail between nations and sovereign states."[92] Spies could be hung, eighteenth-century statesmen agreed, but captured soldiers who wore the uniform of their country were to be detained and then released when hostilities had ended. Legal authorities determine customary international law by looking for "a general and consistent practice of states followed by them from a sense of legal obligation."[93] Thomas Jefferson thought the "principles of the law of nations" could be ascertained by examining "the Declarations, Stipulations and Practices of every civilized nation."[94] Customary international law, in theory, binds all political regimes, with or without their consent. Nations have an obligation to obey the law of nations because these practices are rooted in principles of justice thought to be universal. International law, Supreme Court Justice Joseph Story stated, is "deduced by correct reasoning from the rights and duties of nations, and the nature of legal obligations."[95]

Determining the law of nations is often difficult. The practices of civilized nations is hardly a clear standard, given normative controversies over what practices are civilized and considerable variation in national behaviors. Americans who agree that governing officials are legally obligated to obey international law frequently dispute the substantive content of those norms. Consider the controversies that arose during the Civil War and the contemporary war on terrorism over the use of military tribunals. President Abraham Lincoln responded to the attack on Fort Sumter by ordering a naval blockade of southern ports. Whether this was a constitutional exercise of the president's Article II powers, Justice Robert Grier's majority opinion in *The Prize Cases* (1862) asserted, depended on whether under international law the United States was at war. He wrote, "The right of prize and capture has its origin in the '*jus belli*', and is governed and adjudged under the law of nations." After analyzing both international law and the origins of the Civil War, Grier concluded that President Lincoln had acted consistently with the law of nations and, therefore, consistently with his constitutional powers. In his view, "the President had a right, *jure belli*, to institute a blockade of ports in possession of the States in rebellion, which neutrals are bound to regard."[96] Justice Nelson's dissent agreed that international law determined the scope of executive authority. He insisted that the law of nations did not acknowledge the presidential power to recognize a state of war before hostilities were declared by the national legislature. "The President does not possess the power under the Constitution to declare war or recognize its existence within the meaning of the law of nations," Nelson stated, "which carries with it belligerent rights, and thus change the country and all its citizens from a state of peace to a state of war." In his view, because "this power belongs exclusively to the Congress of the United States,...the President had no power to set on foot a blockade under the law of nations."[97] A similar dispute over international law broke out more than 140 years later, after President George—W. Bush declared he would convene a military tribunal to try suspected terrorists for conspiracy. Federal law permitted the use of military tribunals to try war crimes, but no law specified whether conspiracy was such an offense. Supreme Court justices in *Hamdan v. Rumsfeld* (2006) agreed that this was a matter determined by international law. As in the *Prize Cases,* justices who agreed on the authority of international law disputed the relevant law of nations. Justice Stevens's majority opinion rejected presidential power. He emphasized that the crime of conspiracy "does not appear in either the Geneva Conventions or the Hague Conventions—the major treaties on the law of war."[98] Justice Clarence Thomas's dissent insisted that President Bush respected the law of nations. His opinion pointed to domestic and international practice as "establish[ing] that Hamdan's willful and knowing membership in al Qaeda is a war crime chargeable before a military commission."[99]

The Prize Cases and *Hamdan v. Rumsfeld* illustrate some dimensions of the complex relationships between American constitutionalism and international law. On one hand, all opinions in these cases recognized the ongoing American constitutional commitment to the law of nations. The framers acknowledged their national obligation to act consistently with international law. Governing institutions were designed to privilege the selection of persons steeped in the law of nations and were provided with powers thought sufficient to prevent states from violating international norms. Constitutional and statutory provisions for the past two hundred years have been routinely interpreted in light of the law of nations. On the other hand, all opinions in *The Prize Cases* and *Hamdan* regarded American constitutional authorities and American constitutional law as the highest legal authority within the American constitutional system. Constitutional commentators of all persuasions agree that Congress has the constitutional power to pass measures inconsistent with the law of nations, as long as such legislation is consistent with Article I. More important, Americans in practice determine for themselves the content of international law. The United States is committed to using military tribunals only when authorized

by international law, but Congress, the president, and the Supreme Court determine when for purposes of American constitutionalism international law permits military tribunals.

The relationship between constitutional law and customary international
law is particularly controversial. No agreement exists on whether customary
international law is legally binding in the United States in the absence of constitutional or statutory provisions incorporating some facet of the law of nations.
Federal courts presently treat international law as domestic law unless contro-
verted by statute. Some commentators would extend these decisions. They
maintain that customary international law is the law of the land under both
Article III and Article VI. Others insist that customary international law has
no legal status unless explicitly embodied in a federal law or treaty obligation.
At stake in what may appear technical legal issues, we shall see, is the extent
to which the United States has legal obligations to enforce and abide by what
members of the contemporary international community regard as fundamental
human rights.

3.1 Harmonic Convergence?

Political actors in the United States have historically regarded commitments
to American constitutionalism and international law as mutually reinforcing.
Members of the framing generation thought the obligation to respect international norms was an inherent responsibility of all sovereign nations. Justice
James Wilson in *Ware v. Hylton* (1796) proclaimed, "When the United States
declared their independence they were bound to receive the law of nations, in its
modern state of purity and refinement." John Jay agreed: "The Law of Nations
was part of the laws of this, and of every civilized nation."[100] Article I, Section
8 of the Constitution empowers Congress to "define and punish...Offences
against the Law of Nations." Alexander Hamilton extolled this power to "aid and
support" international law: "For want of this authority, the faith of the United
States may be broken, their reputation sullied, and their peace interrupted by
the negligence or misconception of any particular state."[101] Several prominent
framers insisted that international laws were higher authority than national laws.
The "law of nations," a Virginia Federalist maintained, is "superior to any act or
law of any nation."[102]

Presidents and other members of the executive branch defend American
actions abroad as dictated by or at least consistent with international law.
Woodrow Wilson in 1917 urged the Congress to declare war against a German
nation that had "put aside all restraints of law or of humanity" by using sub-
marines to attack passenger ships. This practice, he stated, threw "to the
winds all...respect for the understandings that were supposed to underlie the

intercourse of the world." American conduct during the forthcoming hostilities would respect the law of nations. Wilson promised to "observe with proud punctilio the principles of right and of fair play we profess to be fighting for."[103] Bush administration officials made similar claims when justifying interrogation practices during the war against terrorism. Efforts to extract information from detainees, Justice Department memos insisted, did not violate international bans on torture. In their view, any action inconsistent with some provisions of the Geneva Convention was consistent with "the right to self-defense... recognized under international law."[104]

General agreement exists among American constitutionalists that all forms of law in the United States should be construed when interpretively possible as conforming to the law of nations. Chief Justice Marshall's opinion in *Murray v. The Charming Betsy* (1804) declared, "An act of Congress ought never to be construed to violate the law of nations if any other possible construction remains." This dictum has remained good law for more than two hundred years.[105] The *Hamdan* opinions, discussed already, illustrate how justices use international law as a guide for interpreting federal statutes as well as constitutional provisions. Constitutional provisions are understood in light of their international law referents. The Supreme Court in *In re Baiz* (1890) claimed that the president's power under Article II to "receive ambassadors" was "descriptive of a class existing by the law of nations." The justices in *The Prize Cases,* discussed in the previous section, looked to international law for the standards that determined whether the United States was at war when President Lincoln ordered a blockade of Southern ports. Congress has interpreted the power to punish piracy vested by Article I as the power to punish what constitutes piracy under international law. Federal law forbids attacks on public ministers or persons with valid passports "in violation of the law of nations."

Customary international law in the United States is presently judicially enforceable, even in the absence of explicit federal regulations. This practice dates from at least the Spanish-American War. The Supreme Court in 1900 was asked to determine whether an American ship had legally captured the *Paquete Habana,* a private boat sailing under the Spanish flag. After noting that customary international law prohibited warring nations from interfering with "fishing vessels," the justices concluded that Americans who violated that rule of war necessarily violated unwritten American law. No federal statute was needed to incorporate the law of nations. Justice Horace Gray stated:

> International law is part of our law, and must be ascertained and administered by the courts of justice of appropriate jurisdiction as often as questions of right depending upon it are duly presented for their determination. For this purpose, where there is no treaty and no controlling

executive or legislative act or judicial decision, resort must be had to the customs and usages of civilized nations.[106]

Justice Souter in 2004 confirmed the continued vitality of *The Paquete Habana,* stating that "for two centuries we have affirmed that the domestic law of the United States recognizes the law of nations."[107]

3.2 Dissonance

Governing authorities in the United States may construe federal law in light of international law, but they must adhere to federal law in cases of clear conflict between domestic and international norms. As Justice Gray's comments in *The Paquete Habana* indicate, the Constitution authorizes Congress by statute to abrogate treaties and violate customary international law. Commentators who believe that the law of nations is the highest form of law in theory recognize that constitutional law is higher within the American constitutional order. "Every nation-state has the power—I do not say the right," a leading proponent of international human rights admits, "to violate international law and obligation."[108] Had Congress passed a law permitting the navy to seize Cuban fishing boats, all constitutional authorities in the United States would have ruled that the seizure of the *Paquete Habana* was legal. Whether a president may unilaterally abrogate treaties and violate customary international law is more controversial. The constitutional controversy that arose when President Carter announced that the United States would no longer honor a defense treaty with Taiwan has never been authoritatively settled. Constitutional decision-makers nevertheless agree that the rule "last in time, first in line" should be employed when deciding conflicts between international law and federal statutes. A more recent federal statute trumps an inherited rule of customary international law and existing treaty obligations, but a treaty ratified today trumps a federal statute passed yesterday.

Americans claim the right to interpret for themselves national rights and responsibilities under the law of nations. The governing officials in the United States responsible for assessing whether the *Paquete Habana* was seized consistently with international law were not bound by the international law doctrine of any other country or by rulings made by an international tribunal. "In the absence of special agreement," the *Restatement (Third) on Foreign Relations Law* states, "it is ordinarily for the United States to decide how it will carry out its international obligations."[109] This interpretive autonomy is particularly crucial, given the infrequency with which the United States—or any other nation— admits to violating the law of nations.

When the United States signs a treaty creating an international tribunal, Americans retain the right to determine whether that tribunal has correctly interpreted international law. The "interpretation of an international agreement by an international court," under American constitutional law, is entitled only to "respectful consideration."[110] Both the United States Supreme Court and George W. Bush rejected as binding international law a decision by the International Court of Justice holding that the Vienna Convention permitted aliens convicted of crimes to assert their rights under that treaty in a habeas corpus proceeding. American obligations under the Vienna Convention, any other treaty, or customary international law, such rulings as *Sanchez-Llamas v. Oregon* (2006) demonstrate, are ultimately for Americans to determine.

Decisions by international tribunals have no legal standing in the United States, unless American law vests those tribunals with the power to decide a question of international law for the United States.[111] Within the American constitutional system, appeals cannot be taken from the Supreme Court or a presidential decree to the International Court of Justice or the International Monetary Fund. Had an international court declared *The Prize Cases* or *Hamdan v. Rumsfeld* wrongly decided as a matter of international law, that verdict would have no legal status within the United States. Americans have no constitutional obligations to respect international decisions sanctioning the United States for violating the law of nations. Such verdicts may provide useful partisan fodder for American citizens opposed to the policy being condemned, but offensive policies will be reversed only if American authorities are convinced that the measures in question do violate American obligations under international law, conclude that reform is politically useful, or are defeated for reelection by candidates committed to respecting rulings made by international tribunals. Whether Americans should make every effort to comply with international tribunals is a controversial question of international politics. That the United States has no legal obligation to comply is a settled question of constitutional law.

3.3 Controversy

Vigorous disputes are presently taking place in the United States over the status of customary international law in the American constitutional regime. Both the law of nations and American constitutional law recognize treaties as voluntary obligations. As noted in the introduction to this section, international lawyers and American constitutionalists agree that the United States is legally obligated to adhere only to treaties ratified by the Senate. Customary international law principles, allegedly rooted in reason or natural law, purport to bind all nations. No provision in the Constitution, however, unambiguously incorporates the law of nations in its entirety. Some commentators assert that customary international law is part of the "laws of the United States" under both Article III and Article VI. If correct, then federal courts under Article III have the power to adjudicate lawsuits based entirely on customary international law, and under Article VI no state may violate customary international law. Not surprisingly, other commentators as strongly insist that "the Laws of the United States" refer only to federal laws passed by Congress and, perhaps, common law decisions made by federal judges.

Whether customary international law should have any special legal status in the American constitutional regime has recently become sharply contested. Opponents would abandon *The Pacquete Habana,* maintaining that incorporating customary international law violates principles of popular sovereignty. Two critics declare, "The modern position that CIL [customary international law] is federal common law is in tension with basic notions of American representative democracy." They point out that "when a federal court applies CIL as federal common law it is not applying law generated by U.S. lawmaking processes. Rather, it is applying law derived from the views and practices of the international community."[112] Those who insist customary international law is the law of the United States see the American polity as a crucial player in the international human rights regime. "The capacity of federal courts to incorporate customary international law into federal law," a prominent human rights advocate insists, "is absolutely critical to maintaining the coherence of federal law in areas of international concern." Otherwise, he continues, state governments would have "no domestic legal obligation to obey customary norms against genocide" in the absence of a treaty explicitly declaring those norms to be binding law.[113]

The changing nature of international law intensifies these controversies. The law of nations during the eighteenth century primarily elaborated relationships between different sovereignties. Such influential treatises as Vattel's *Law of Nations* were largely limited to matters of war and diplomacy. Such domestic matters as voting rights and religious freedom were for particular nations to decide for themselves. More contemporary commentators insist that the law of nations protects personal rights within nations. "How a state treats individual human beings," the prestigious American Law Institute maintains, "is a matter of international concern and proper subject for regulation by international law."[114] The Universal Declaration of Human Rights, which many international lawyers proclaim ought to be a prominent source for customary international law at present, declares that all human beings have rights to free exercise of religion, free speech, education, and some leisure time.

The debates over the constitutional status of customary international law presently raise vital questions about the significance of this increased international human rights focus for the American constitutional regime. Some legal activists maintain that Article III, by incorporating the law of nations, permits Congress to open federal courts to lawsuits by foreign citizens claiming human rights violations by the government of their home country. Relying on this logic, a federal judge permitted a Paraguayan citizen who asserted she was tortured by the Paraguayan government to sue for damages in the United States.[115] Other political activists insist that the supremacy clause prohibits state violations of customary international human rights law. Under this interpretation of the state obligation under Article VI to adhere to the laws of the land, many state executions are arguably unconstitutional because they are inconsistent with the increasingly anti-death-penalty stance of customary international law.[116] Needless to say, commentators who believe that customary international law has no special constitutional status object to such efforts as rooted in an "unwarranted assumption that all of international law must be incorporated into domestic law."[117]

3.4 Law and Politics

The gap between constitutional and international law in the United States has legal foundations. Some countries, Germany being a prominent example, explicitly incorporate a commitment to the law of nations in the constitutional text. Article 25 of the German constitution states, "The general rules of international law shall be an integral part of federal law." Customary international law "take[s] precedence over [federal] laws and directly create[s] rights and duties." The Constitution of the United States makes no such declaration. International law in the American constitutional system is a matter of interpretive presumptions and default rules. Legal provisions are interpreted as consistent with the law of nation when such a construction is possible. International law provides a standard for governance in the absence of other legal authority. Unlike Germany, some governing officials in the United States may act inconsistently with the law of nations, although the identity of those governing officials and the extent to which the Constitution sanctions actions inconsistent with international law are controversial.

Politics typically determines the extent of the gap between constitutional and international law. Partisan conflicts over international relations law in the United States are often between liberals, who believe that promoting international human rights should be a central theme of American foreign policy, and realists, who emphasize the role of self-interest in the international arena. Liberals favor constitutional practices, such as incorporating customary international law, that facilitate convergence between constitutional law and the law of nations. Realists insist that Americans and Americans alone determine the norms by which Americans are governed. Beneath the surface, attitudes toward international law do not seem motivated entirely by lofty principles on one hand and craven self-interest on the other. Most contemporary international liberals in the United States are political liberals domestically who believe that international norms at the turn of the twenty-first century are more congruent with their values and interests than are the norms formerly championed by George W. Bush administration. Liberal calls for a more universal constitutionalism, from this perspective, seem at least partly rooted in very particular policy commitments. Prominent international realists are often political conservatives who think George W. Bush and fellow conservatives in the states better protected such fundamental human rights as the right of a fetus to be born than does the international community. The conservative emphasis on particular American norms, therefore, is at least partly rooted in more universal values.

4. The Particular and Universal Revisited

The founding documents of American constitutionalism exhibit a tension between the universal and the particular. The Declaration of Independence declares, "We hold these truths to be self-evident." This language initially evokes a national commitment to timeless values, to a conception of justice recognized by all reasoning human beings. A more critical reading might observe that Jefferson states, "*We* hold these truths," not "These truths are self-evident." Perhaps the fundamental aspirations of American constitutionalism are perceived as self-evident only by Americans but are not axiomatic to other peoples. Being an American may entail a commitment to apple pie and free speech. Being a Fredonian may entail other commitments. The Preamble to the Constitution is similarly ambiguous. The framers stated their intention to "secure the Blessings of Liberty to ourselves and our Posterity." Who is included in "our Posterity" is not entirely clear. "Our Posterity" might be limited to future Americans; alternatively, the language of the Preamble might encompass all persons committed to the enduring principles set out in the Declaration of Independence.

This ambivalence has characterized American constitutionalism for more than two hundred years. Many important strands of constitutional practice promote universal norms. Americans have historically proclaimed a commitment to the law of nations. Chapter 4 points out how some prominent constitutional commentators interpret such language as the *freedom of speech* and *due process* as articulating aspirations to secure fundamental human rights. Other important strands of constitutional practice promote distinctive American values or interests. Constitutional rights provisions have never had the same scope when American officials act extraterritorially as they do within the United States. Many prominent originalists insist that the First Amendment should be interpreted consistently with the distinctive American understandings of the freedom of speech and due process at the time the Bill of Rights was ratified.

More often than not, American constitutionalists combine appeals to distinctive American concerns and more universalistic aspirations in ways that cannot be neatly distinguished. Consider recent debates in Congress over whether the Supreme Court should refer to constitutional practices in other countries when interpreting the meaning of the Constitution of the United States.[118] The House of Representatives in 2005 considered a resolution asserting that "judicial determinations regarding the meaning of the Constitution of the United States should not be based on judgments, laws, or pronouncements of foreign nations."[119] The congressman who sponsored the resolution claimed that foreign citations were "chipping away at our Nation's sovereignty and independence." These criticisms suggest a widespread understanding that American constitutional norms are peculiar to Americans. Other critics of foreign citations have more universalistic axes to grind. Representative Tom Feeney of Florida insisted that American exceptionalism was rooted in timeless values. He maintained that the Constitution of the United States protected "God-given rights" that "do[n't] change over time." Citations to constitutional practices in other countries, in his view, were rooted in little more than "fads . . . and opinion polls." Interpreting the Constitution of the United States only in light of distinctive American constitutional sources, from this perspective, secures the universalistic norms embodied in that text from the corrupting influence of the transient values that are presently being promulgated in other constitutional democracies. Progressives who champion comparative constitutional analysis as a means for determining the universalistic aspirations of the American constitutional regime exhibit similar ambivalence. Ken Kersch skeptically notes that liberal interest in foreign constitutional practices tends to be "particularly strong in areas of constitutional law that seemed to hold promise during the Warren and early Burger years, . . . but have since fallen upon hard times in the Reagan and Rehnquist years."[120] Unsurprisingly, justices in the United States who cite European decisions protecting gay rights and limiting capital punishment have not yet made constitutional use of Mary Ann Glendon's controversial assertion that American constitutional law would benefit from greater engagement with the more prolife orientation of most European constitutional orders.[121]

This tension between the universal and the particular is built into constitutionalism and into the American constitutional order. Liberal constitutionalism, as discussed in Chapter 2, emphasizes both the consent of a distinctive people and a commitment to the dignity of human beings. Consent is peculiar to a particular society. The framers believed the Constitution was binding law because a particular text was ratified by a particular people at a particular time. Neither natural law nor moral philosophy dictates that the chief executive will serve a four-year term or that the national legislature shall have power to create lower federal courts. These provisions are authoritative because they were agreed upon in 1789. The commitment to human dignity, by comparison, is common to all constitutional democracies. Abraham Lincoln could speak of the "Union" as the "last best hope of earth"[122] only on the assumption that American constitutional aspirations are shared by all decent human beings. Lincoln's determination to "assure freedom to the free"[123] was a commitment to guaranteeing fundamental human rights, not a dedication to liberties peculiar to Americans. Other aspects of constitutionalism and American constitutionalism exhibit the same tensions. Chapter 3 highlights how constitutions are both means for ensuring a particular people are well governed and vehicles for promoting national aspirations for justice. Chapter 4 details how methods of constitutional interpretation that look to distinctive American understandings of "free exercise of religion" at the time that constitutional provision was adapted uneasily coexist with methods of constitutional interpretation that assume the persons responsible for the Constitution meant to entrench fundamental human rights when they used the phrase "free exercise of religion."

The tension between the universal and particular norms of American constitutionalism is also built into the structure of governing institutions. Some institutions, most notably the House of Representatives, were designed to promote the particular interests Americans might have at a particular time. "Frequent elections," the framers agreed, would privilege the choice of representatives with the "immediate dependence on, and an intimate sympathy with, the people" necessary to ensure that the distinctive political concerns of various social groups at any particular time were given due weight in governmental deliberations.[124] Other governing institutions, most notably the Senate, were designed to secure more long-term interests and more universalistic values. *Federalist* 62 declares, "The necessity of a senate is not less indicated by the propensity of all single and numerous assemblies to yield to the impulse of sudden and violent passions, and to be seduced by factious leaders into intemperate and pernicious resolutions."[125] Senators who held office for six years were thought of as more likely than representatives elected every two years to pursue the permanent good of the community. The branch of government more committed to universalistic values, *Federalist* 62 declares, must "possess great firmness, and consequently ought to hold its authority by a tenure of considerable duration."[126] The president, the federal judiciary, and state governments were similarly thought to have distinctive perspectives on the universal and particular commitments of American constitutionalism that would be brought to bear on all matters of national importance. Life-tenured federal justices appointed by national officials would promote conformity with international law. A single president would more likely act decisively than a multimembered executive when protecting distinctive American interests abroad. One purpose of the separation of powers may be to make sure all these distinctive perspectives influence crucial foreign policy decisions.[127]

This effort to structure governing institutions suggests that constitutional politics, not constitutional law, provides the appropriate constitutional standards for thinking about the global dimensions of American constitutionalism. Constitutional provisions may not specify permanent or definitive answers to many important questions about the extraterritorial effect of constitutional limits on official actions, the constitutional status of customary international law, or the extent to which comparative constitutional practices are legitimate sources for interpreting the Constitution of the United States. Perhaps constructive dialogues among all affected governing institutions are constitutionally more important than specific legal resolutions. As Chapter 8 will detail, the constitutional system may be functioning properly as long as different institutions with different capacities and perspectives help shape decisions about the proper balance between what is universal and what is particular about American constitutional regime.

8

How Constitutions Work

1. Of Cheeseburgers and Constitutions

Popular American culture provides two methods for making cheeseburgers. The most common version can be purchased at McDonald's, Burger King, or other purveyors of fast food. Several pieces of cheese are placed on top of a ground beef patty. Patrons can easily identify by sight and by taste what part of the cheeseburger is the cheese and what part is the burger. The alternative cheeseburger is often whipped up on such popular cooking shows as *Iron Chef*. Ground beef, cheese, and a great many other ingredients commonly found in the kitchens of multibillionaires are first tossed into a very expensive food processor and then heated on a broiler especially designed by two generations of Cal Tech graduate students. Patrons cannot identify by sight or by taste what part of the cheeseburger is the cheese and what part is the burger. Nevertheless, the ingredients matter. How the fancy concoction tastes depends on the ratio of cheese to burger to other ingredients. Recipes matter as well. The Burger King cheeseburger tastes differently than the *Iron Chef* cheeseburger, even when both are prepared with identical ingredients.

Common constitutional conversations treat the constitutional relationship between law and politics as analogous to the relationship between the cheese and the burger at fast food restaurants. Law and politics are regarded as very distinctive enterprises. Politics is about the struggles between different interests. These interests may be self-serving or more altruistic. Some academics lobby for increased salaries; others fight to abolish capital punishment. Both preferences are treated as entirely independent of constitutional norms. Professors want more money so they can drive fancier cars. They oppose capital punishment because they believe state-mandated executions do not deter crime. These interests and values may influence how constitutional provisions are interpreted, but neither the Constitution nor constitutional practice cause people to want fancy cars or to oppose capital punishment. Constitutional law constrains these external interests and values. Constitutional decisions should be made on distinctive legal grounds, not on the basis of policy preferences. Whether capital punishment is constitutional depends on the proper interpretation of the Eighth Amendment, on the meaning of the words "cruel and unusual punishment," or on past precedents interpreting these words—not on the merits of the Kantian defense of the death penalty or, worse, which party won the last election.

We determine whether constitutions work, on the fast food model of constitutionalism, by assessing the extent to which distinctive legal considerations actually constrain politics. In a good constitutional order, people either act on law rather than on preferences or adhere to decrees handed down by an institution, such as the Supreme Court, that subordinates policy preferences to law. Presidents do not commit troops to battle, even when they believe doing so is vital to national security, when such decisions are inconsistent with the rules for using military force set out in the first two articles of the Constitution. Judges who believe capital punishment immoral or the condemned person innocent nevertheless do not halt executions when the death sentence was imposed consistently with the constitutional norms set out in the Bill of Rights.

Whether American politics is adequately constrained by constitutional norms is contestable. Judicial opinions and presidential decrees purport to be motivated entirely by law. Constitutional decision-makers claim that Article I compelled them to strike down federal bans on guns in schools (*United States v. Lopez* [1995]), and they must under the Fifth Amendment overturn criminal convictions when a prosecutor comments on the failure of the defendant to testify (*Griffin v. California* [1965]). Many political scientists challenge what they claim are self-serving pieties. A very prominent model of constitutional decision-making examines the impact of what the authors believe are distinctive legal variables and distinctive political variables. They find that politics in the form of policy preferences explains most constitutional decisions.[1] Justices decide what constitutes a cruel and unusual punishment by consulting their personal beliefs about punitive justice. They ignore constitutional text and precedent to the contrary. Constitutional law, at least the Burger King–McDonald's conception of constitutional law, does not matter much. The framers in 1787 apparently wasted a hot summer.

A New Introduction to American Constitutionalism presents an *Iron Chef* model of constitutionalism, one that treats the constitutional relationship between law and politics as more analogous to the relationship between the cheese and the burger at gourmet restaurants. Constitutions, an increasing number of scholars associated with the historical–institutionalist school of constitutional scholarship recognize, integrate legal and political norms in ways that blur sharp separations. Chapter 4 notes how widely accepted methods of constitutional interpretation permit, indeed, compel value voting. Much disagreement exists over which government actors should employ these methods for determining the meaning of constitutional provisions and the extent to which different constitutional provisions require value judgments. Still, a fair, though hardly perfect, consensus exists that some persons in some circumstances have a legal–constitutional obligation to be guided by what some political scientists describe as policy preferences about equality or cruelty when interpreting such phrases as *equal protection of the law* and *cruel and unusual punishment*. To the extent that the First Amendment requires judgments about the best philosophical meaning of free speech or should be interpreted in light of popular understandings about political dissent, constitutional opinions that cite John Stuart Mill's *On Liberty* and public opinion polls express both policy preferences and legal norms.

Other chapters point to different ways constitutions integrate law and politics. The discussions of constitutional purposes and the allocation of constitutional authority in Chapters 3 and 5 highlight how constitutions construct a political order. Articles I, II, and III provide norms for aggregating as well as constraining policy preferences. Constitutional rules for staffing government offices and making laws determine whose values and interests become the official constitutional law of the land. Such provisions protect the freedom of speech and facilitate economic prosperity by constructing politics in ways likely to create a political leadership committed to the freedom of speech and capable of identifying the commercial policies most likely to facilitate economic prosperity. Chapter 6 outlines how constitutions are themselves constructed by politics. Constitutions are created, changed, and abandoned by political processes that are in turn partly shaped by constitutional norms. The framers recognized that constitutional meanings would often be forged in ordinary politics. To once again quote James Madison on this subject: "All new laws, though penned with the greatest technical skill, and passed on the fullest and most mature deliberation, are considered as more or less obscure and equivocal, until their meaning be liquidated and ascertained by a series of particular discussions and adjudications."[2]

Presidents, members of Congress, justices, and the political activists who lead social movements often employ the same resources and tactics in the "particular discussions and adjudications" necessary for determining the meaning of open-ended constitutional provisions as they rely on during political struggles for national health care and political campaigns for the presidency. The politics of constitutional meaning (and health care) nevertheless is structured by processes designed by the constitutional text and constitutional precedent. Presidents wishing to overturn a judicial decision must follow the rules laid down in Article II for appointing justices or the rules laid down in Article V for passing a constitutional amendment (or perhaps the rules laid down in Article I for passing contrary legislation).

The Aristotelian conception of constitutionalism in Chapter 2 points to ways constitutions constitute politics. Contrary to many orthodox political science models, citizens do not develop values and interests independently from constitutional norms. Legal norms influence the values citizens hold and the interests they pursue in politics. Public school civics programs typically fashion citizens who perceive that their interests are best secured by constitutional norms and that those norms are consistent with their considered beliefs about a just policy. Such persons, when they vote or hold public office, often have no desire to act contrary to constitutional norms.[3]

Constitutions work by constraining, constructing, and constituting politics. Constitutions constrain politics when citizens and governing officials subordinate their policy preferences to constitutional norms. Constitutions construct politics when citizens and governing officials follow the rules that determine whose policy preferences and constitutional understandings at any time are the official law of the land. Constitutions constitute politics when citizens and elected officials are socialized in ways that lead them to internalize constitutional values and regard constitutional processes as the only legitimate means for resolving legal and policy disputes.

In healthy constitutional regimes, the constructive and constitutive functions of constitutions play a far greater role than the constraining function of constitutional norms. This has certainly been true in the United States for more than two hundred years. The common obsessive focus in too many textbooks and law review articles on constitutional constraints ignores alternative means by which the Constitution of the United States works to protect fundamental rights and limit government, disregards entirely how the Constitution of the United States promotes vital constitutional purposes that cannot be reduced to legal norms, and provides an impoverished account of the constitutional crises that have wracked American constitutionalism. Constitutional crises do not occur merely because people disagree, perhaps very strongly, about the meaning of constitutional provisions. Rather, serious crises are rooted in the constitutional failure to construct politics in ways that create tolerable solutions to constitutional disagreements or to constitute citizens willing to live within constitutional norms.

2. Constitutions as Constraining Politics

Constitutions are commonly regarded as constraints on ordinary politics. Government officials and citizens constantly face temptations to restrict religion, confiscate property, regulate purely local matters, or champion other policies that will have poor long-term social effects. Constitutions provide standards and institutions that help regimes overcome these incentives to maximize transient concerns. In some instances, political actors on their own reject otherwise desirable policy options that they believe are unconstitutional. President Madison vetoed an internal improvements bill he believed would promote desirable economic development because he believed Article I did not empower the national government to build roads.[4] Abraham Lincoln repeatedly insisted that he would respect every constitutional provision that protected slavery, including the obligation to return fugitive slaves to their owners.[5] More often, courts are understood as having the institutional independence from ordinary politics necessary for ensuring that constitutional norms trump policy preferences when the two conflict. The judicial majority in *Texas v. Johnson* (1989) ruled that constitutional protections for free speech did not permit popular majorities to prohibit flag burning. Justice Kennedy's concurring opinion made clear his personal disdain for behavior he thought constitutionally protected. "Sometimes we must make decisions we do not like," he wrote, "because they are right...in the sense that the law and the Constitution...compel the result."[6] A different judicial majority in *United States v. Lopez* (1995) ruled that national majorities could not prohibit guns in local schools. One suspects that the justices in the majority were motivated by a constitutional commitment to federalism rather than a desire to sanction weaponry in the classroom. Americans respect the rule of law, the argument goes, by adhering to Supreme Court decisions that are inconsistent with their nonconstitutional values, political interests, and policy preferences.

By entrenching and enforcing legal limits on government power, constitutions enable political regimes to achieve the various constitutional purposes set out in Chapter 3. Constitutional limits on otherwise legitimate policy preferences organize government, promote the rule of law, prevent self-dealing by politicians, facilitate credible commitments, foster national aspirations, and maintain the compromises necessary to preserve national union. Constitutional law is the primary means by which polities overcome temptations to sacrifice these enduring goods for mere short-term gains. Banning guns in schools, freeing fugitive slaves, and prohibiting flag burning often seem like attractive policy options. Nevertheless, regimes realize distinctive constitutional virtues only when governing officials and citizens follow constitutional norms when those norms conflict with their otherwise best-all-things-considered policy judgments. Returning fugitive slaves preserved the Union. The Supreme Court's decision in *Lopez* enabled local governments to take responsibility for local problems.

Chapter 4 provides substantial evidence that the Constitution of the United States significantly constrains politics. Governing officials and citizens often distinguish between constitutional commands and other sources of political judgment. To take an obvious example, proponents of having the president elected by a popular vote recognize that the Constitution mandates that successful candidates obtain an Electoral College majority. Benjamin Harrison, everyone agrees, won the presidential election in 1888, even though more people in the United States voted for Grover Cleveland. Americans often prove capable of acting on constitutional values when they perceive a conflict between those values and their policy preferences. Some Supreme Court justices who believe that capital punishment is morally wrong have felt constitutionally compelled to send condemned persons to the gallows. Justice Harry Blackmun in 1972 began an opinion supporting the constitutionality of a state-mandated execution by declaring, "I yield to no one in the depth of my distaste, antipathy, and, indeed, abhorrence, for the death penalty."[7] Al Gore abandoned his presidential campaign because he believed he had a constitutional obligation to honor a judicial ruling he believed to be constitutionally wrong. "While I strongly disagree with the court's decision," he told the American people the day after *Bush v. Gore* (2000) was handed down, "I accept it."[8]

Some commentators insist that these professions of constitutional fidelity mask more sophisticated policy preferences. Gore may have honored *Bush v. Gore* only because he had no chance of obtaining the presidency after the adverse judicial decision. Constitutional decision-makers who insist "the law is responsible for my decision" may be seeking to avoid being blamed personally for decisions the public finds distasteful.[9] Prominent political scientists insist that justices write opinions discussing precedent and other legal norms only because the public expects justices to follow precedent and other legal norms.[10] Legality apparently is a mere disguise that fools only the unwary law student and a few unsophisticated undergraduate professors.

The evidence better suggests naivety on the part of those who persistently claim that public commitments to constitutional norms (almost) always are sophisticated efforts to secure nonconstitutional values, interests, or policy preferences. Constitutional decision-makers do behave strategically. John Marshall almost certainly would have ordered Thomas Jefferson to deliver the judicial commission to William Marbury had he thought Congress would have supported that judicial decision. Nevertheless, much constitutionally constrained behavior, including the practice of providing legal justifications for decisions, cannot easily be explained away as strategic efforts to secure desired policies. Madison shortly before retiring from public office did not have strategic reasons for vetoing on constitutional grounds an internal improvements bill he thought good public policy. Blackmun was not conserving judicial power when he announced in a dissent that he believed capital punishment morally wrong but constitutionally permissible. Many Supreme Court decisions are unanimous or close to unanimous, even on matters on which reasonable people might have different policy preferences. Whether eight justices on the Supreme Court as a matter of policy would have permitted Fred Phelps and members of the Westboro Church to picket military funerals and chant antigay slogans is doubtful. First Amendment precedent probably best explains the 8–1 vote in *Snyder v. Phelps* (2011).[11]

Several difficulties beset claims that justices invoke law only to satisfy public demands for constitutional decisions based on distinctively legal criteria.
No evidence supports claims that ordinary citizens are more committed to
legality than justices or other authoritative constitutional decision-makers.
Just the opposite is more likely to be true, given that judges but not citizens
are socialized to think in legal terms, although this admitted hunch is neither
confirmed nor disconfirmed by the empirical evidence. Law matters even
when the influence of law on constitutional decision-making is somewhat
circuitous. If Citizen Mary favors judicial decisions based on precedent and
Judge John wishes only to please Citizen Mary, then Judge John will rely on
precedent when making judicial decisions. Similarly, if the public expects constitutional decisions based on law and Supreme Court justices wish to satisfy
public expectations, then constitutional decisions will be based on law. The
Constitution constrains justices who base their decisions partly on constitutional text, precedent, and history, no matter if their motive for following the
law is a desire to make the best legal decision, please the public, or go down in
history as a great justice.

Pervasive commitments to legality, we suspect, better account for both the
judicial willingness to subordinate policy preferences to some degree and public demands that constitutional decision-makers follow the law. Sociological
studies repeatedly conclude that naked self-interest does not explain why most
citizens most of the time are law abiding. People in no danger of being caught
do not trespass or shoplift. Most do not cheat on their taxes, even when they
believe government should lower their fiscal burden. Americans follow the
law, research suggests, because they respect the rule of law and think governing processes in the United States are basically fair. Tom Tyler points out, "To
the extent people perceive law enforcement officials as legitimate, they are significantly more willing to defer to individual authorities... and they are also
more likely to be in compliance with the law in general."[12] Justices and other
constitutional decision-makers seem no different from ordinary citizens. The
judicial tendency, all things being equal, to decide cases on the basis of law
may be no different from the judicial tendency, all things being equal, not to
litter. Constitutional decision-makers who think specific constitutional provisions or decisions unwise or unjust nevertheless believe that the Constitution
is the legitimate source of law in the United States and act accordingly. External
preferences influence decisions only when personal values or interests can be
incorporated by legal means. Ordinary citizens take every deduction that can
plausibly be justified by the tax code. Justices interpret ambiguous constitutional principles as consistent with their values, interests, and policy preferences. What judicial commitments to legality and legitimacy explain is why
constitutional decision-makers follow the Constitution when they conclude

clear constitutional commands cannot be reconciled with what they believe to be good policy.

The Constitution's capacity to constrain policy choices should not be exaggerated. On numerous issues, ranging from abortion and gay marriage to presidential power and the status of international law in American courts, constitutional judgments tend to reflect political judgments. Persons who are politically prochoice think *Roe v. Wade* (1973) should not be overruled. Prolife advocates think that abortion is a moral evil and that constitutional decisions protecting that right are legal abominations. Whether one thinks the George W. Bush administration behaved constitutionally during the war against terror largely depends on whether one thinks the Bush administration behaved properly. The future of capital punishment in the United States will depend as much on elections and judicial nominations as the constitutional text. Constitutional arguments against the Affordable Care Act of 2010 emerged seemingly out of thin air in response to strong Republican Party policy objections to that measure.

The persons responsible for the Constitution recognized that constitutions as devices for constraining politics have only a limited capacity to secure vital constitutional purposes. In sharp contrast to many contemporary constitutional theorists, the leading participants in the drafting and ratification debates often harped on the inadequacies of what they referred to as *parchment barriers*. Roger Sherman declared, "No bill of rights ever yet bound the supreme power longer than the honey moon of a new married couple, unless the rulers were interested in preserving the rights."[13] The contemporary constitutional law course, which emphasizes how judicial review constrains policy choices, is largely tangential to the ways the framers expected American constitutionalism to function. That class is too often limited to analyses of a few constitutional provisions, most notably the due process clause of the Fourteenth Amendment. Little attention is paid to such structural provisions of the Constitution as those mandating state equality in the Senate or a life-tenured federal judiciary. The framers thought that such provisions served vital constitutional purposes but advanced constitutional goals by constructing rather than constraining politics.

3. Constitutions as Constructing Politics

The Constitution of the United States constructs a political order expected to produce deliberative policy choices that appeal to broad segments of the population and do not violate fundamental rights. The Constitution works by aggregating existing interests, values, and policy preferences in ways that privilege

constitutionally desirable outcomes. Some constitutional processes, most notably judicial review, are primarily designed to ensure that constitutional limits on
government are respected in practice. Others, most notably the system for electing the president, are primarily designed to ensure that constitutional powers
are exercised in ways likely to secure such constitutional purposes as domestic
peace and commercial prosperity.

3.1 Protecting Rights through Institutional Design

The framers sought to minimize the potential for abusive government practices
through institutional design, not parchment barriers. "All observations founded
upon the danger of usurpation," *Federalist* 31 states, "ought to be referred to the
composition and structure of the government, not to the nature or extent of its
powers."[14] This emphasis on the constructive functions of rules for staffing government offices and rules for making laws explains why many framers thought a
Bill of Rights unimportant. If government institutions were designed correctly,
they claimed, persons in power would lack the incentives or capacity to violate
fundamental freedoms. When, at the drafting convention, Madison attempted
to "introduce the checks...for the safety of a minority in danger of oppression
from an unjust and interested majority," he proposed a national veto on state
legislation rather than specific limits on government power. Forty years after
ratification, Madison reminded delegates to the Virginia State Constitutional
Convention that "the only effectual safeguard to the rights of the minority, must
be laid in such a basis and structure of the Government itself."[15] His less than
inspiring speech proposing that Congress adopt the Bill of Rights described
constitutional protections for individual liberties as "neither improper nor altogether useless."[16]

Madison in *Federalist* 10 explained why he thought well-designed constitutional processes better protect rights than explicit constitutional constraints. He
was convinced that small republics could not adequately protect the freedom of
religion and other essential liberties. In such polities, Madison insisted, majority
factions easily formed and tyrannized the minority, no matter what the language
in the national constitution. Majority rule enabled the religious sect that enjoyed
the support of two-thirds of the population to violate the rights of the religious
sect that enjoyed the support of the other third. Madison stated:

> The smaller the society, the fewer probably will be the distinct par-
> ties and interests, the fewer the distinct parties and interests, the more
> frequently will a majority be found of the same party; and the smaller
> the number of individuals composing a majority, and the smaller the

compass within which they are placed, the more easily will they concert and execute their plans for oppression.[17]

Politics would take a different course in larger republics. In such polities, Madison believed, no religious sect enjoyed majority support. Hence, any political effort aimed at securing the hegemony of particular religious beliefs would be defeated by a united coalition of rival religious believers. The only policy that Madison thought could gain majority support in regimes where the largest religious sect enjoyed, at most, the support of a quarter of the voting population was one that respected the religious liberties of all. He wrote:

> Extend the sphere and you take in a greater variety of parties and inter-ests; you make it less probable that a majority of the whole will have a common motive to invade the rights of other citizens; or if such a com-mon motive exists, it will be more difficult for all who feel it to discover their own strength and act in unison with each other.[18]

If Madison was correct in his assumptions, then specific constitutional protec-tions for the freedom of religion were useless or unnecessary. Popular majori-ties in small republics would ignore parchment declarations about free exercise. Popular majorities in the large republic did not have the practical capacity to violate rights of religious conscience. The constitution of such a regime did not need a free exercise or establishment clause because national politics was con-structed in ways that privileged the selection of policies that protected religious freedom.

Persons who believe Madison's assumptions are wrong cannot avoid thinking about how constitutions construct politics when designing better constitutional safeguards for religious freedom and other liberties. One possible objection to *Federalist* 10 is that Protestants in 1787 were a national majority fully capable of uniting to oppress Catholics and non-Christians. Consider two schemes for reducing the possibility of such behavior. The first replaces Madison's central-izing ambitions with extreme decentralization. Religious liberty is protected in such a regime through a multiplicity of religious communities, each of which is governed exclusively by the local majority. People who object to the laws of Anatevka, Pennsylvania, which require that all residents keep kosher, are free to relocate five miles north to the town controlled by a Catholic majority, seven miles west to the Episcopalian regime, or six miles southeast to a village run by atheist elders. A few towns respect religious diversity. People are free to practice their religion in such a regime, because they can legally move to a community in which their religious practices are legal. The second scheme is a constitutional provision protecting religious liberty enforced by a life-tenured judiciary. When elected officials attempt to enforce a religious orthodoxy, federal justices declare their schemes unconstitutional. This more legal process for protecting the rights of conscience is nevertheless as rooted in a theory of constitutional politics as Madison's theory in *Federalist* 10 or the more decentralized scheme previously discussed. The judicial review strategy for protecting religious freedom works only when constitutional politics inhibits the formation of a judicial majority committed to Justice Joseph Story's proposition that the "real object" of constitutional protections for religious liberty "was, not to countenance, much less advance Mahometanism, or Judaism, or infidelity, by prostrating Christianity; but to exclude all rivalry among Christian sects."[19] The constitutional processes for staffing the federal bench must be designed to prevent in practice officials elected by a Protestant majority from appointing justices committed to Protestant religious hegemony. Alternatively, life tenure and the process of judicial deliberation must consistently induce Protestant justices to become more committed to the freedom of all religious believers once they join the bench. The large republic and judicial review, this analysis points out, yoke a commitment to particular constitutional constraints to a theory about the constitution design most likely to implement those constraints. Both rely on empirical assumptions about the political behavior of numerous political actors, and both protect rights only to the extent that these empirical assumptions are accurate.

Throughout American history, political coalitions have sought to fashion a constitutional politics that privileges their distinctive constitutional visions. Jacksonians before the Civil War sought to secure the constitutional rights of slaveholders by restructuring the federal judiciary so that a majority of the justices on the Supreme Court would hail from the South.[20] Shortly after gaining a national majority in 1860, Republicans secured a federal court system more friendly to northern constitutional commitments by restructuring the federal judiciary so that eight of the ten justices would hail from the free states.[21] The Civil Rights Act of 1866 adopted a different scheme for constructing a rights-protecting constitutional politics by declaring that "all persons...shall have the same right...to make and enforce contracts, to sue, be parties, give evidence, and to the full and equal benefit of all laws and proceedings for the security of persons and property as is enjoyed by white citizens."[22] This statutory requirement that governing officials provide all persons the same bundle of rights as white persons, Reconstruction Republicans thought, would practically guarantee a very robust set of rights. As Justice Robert Jackson later asserted:

> There is no more effective practical guaranty against arbitrary and unreasonable government than to require that the principles of law which officials would impose upon a minority must be imposed generally. Conversely, nothing opens the door to arbitrary action so effectively as

to allow those officials to pick and choose only a few to whom they will apply legislation and thus to escape the political retribution that might be visited upon them if larger numbers were affected.[23]

Jury trials are another means by which the Constitution constructs a politics that privileges particular liberties. The jury trial during the Revolutionary Era was a vehicle for preventing the enforcement of laws most people thought violated fundamental rights or vital interests. Whether instructed to or not, juries tended to acquit people accused of crime when they believed the act in question ought to have been legal. John Peter Zenger in 1735 was not convicted of seditious libel, even though the evidence quite clearly demonstrated that Zenger had published unlawful criticisms of royal officials in the New York. Jury nullification, refusing for political reasons to convict an obviously guilty defendant, constrained governing officials from violating speech and other popular rights. No specific constitutional declaration was necessary. Government is adequately constrained, proponents of jury trials insisted, when decisions about popular rights are made by members of the local community acting on the basis of their interests, values, or political preferences and not by a judge appointed by a faraway monarch or president.[24] Had Zenger criticized a popular political figure, of course, he might have suffered a different fate. Jury trials, judicial review, and every other constitutional decision-making process privilege only some rights claims.

Constitutions do rely on parchment barriers when constructing politics. The Sixth Amendment's decree that "in all criminal trials, the accused shall enjoy the right to a speedy and public trial, by an impartial jury of the State and district wherein the crime shall have been committed" is as much a paper guarantee as the First Amendment's promise that "Congress shall make no law respecting an establishment of a religion." Constitutions can construct politics, for this reason, only if constitutions constrain politics. Persons in power opposed to state equality in the Senate or jury trials must be constrained by these constitutional norms when governing. Political tyrants bent on destroying constitutional government are likely to ignore both constitutional procedures and constitutional rights.

Constitutional provisions that construct politics may nevertheless provide better and more secure foundations for certain rights than constitutional provisions that constrain politics. Most constitutional provisions that construct politics are quite specific. The meanings of the provisions providing for equal state representation in the Senate and a life-tenured judiciary are for the most part uncontroversial. Usurpation cannot take place subtly, by interpretation. Political leaders opposed to state equality in the Senate must announce their unconstitutional designs openly. They cannot plausibly assert that California is really seven states and so warrants fourteen senators. Most constitutional provisions that constrain politics are more open to interpretation. Bitter disputes take place over what constitutionally constitutes interstate commerce and over the constitutional meaning of free speech. Usurpations may be more insidious. Politicians bent on suppressing political dissent might not have to suspend the First Amendment. They might plausibly claim that their political opponents are inciting criminal conduct or intentionally lying about political developments.

Consider, in this light, the most likely way the Constitution would prevent a local prosecutor in a college town from enforcing a law that mandated life in prison for using soft drugs. A fair probability exists that the prosecutor could make a plausible constitutional argument that such a sentence is not cruel and unusual punishment. The Supreme Court's decision in *Harmelin v. Michigan* (1991), sustaining a life sentence imposed for possessing 650 grams of cocaine, provides a solid precedential foundation for this legal claim. Juries in college towns, however, are likely to be unwilling to impose such a sentence. Prosecutors are also unlikely to be able to make plausible arguments that drug cases do not constitutionally require jury trials. Of course, some possibility of conviction exists, even in very liberal communities. Nevertheless, the right to a jury trial seems more difficult to interpret away and a better bulwark against government oppression in this instance than the substantive guarantee that government shall not impose cruel and unusual punishments.

3.2 Constitutional Design and Constitutional Purposes

Well-designed constitutional institutions privilege policies that are just, consensual, intelligent and protect vital interests. *Federalist* 10 insists that factions bent on denying religious freedom will not come to power in large republics. Legislation that must pass both houses of Congress, must be signed by the president, and must be sustained by the federal judiciary is far more likely than legislation passed by simple majorities to provide broadly accepted solutions to national problems. The framers thought the constitutional system for selecting the president would facilitate the choice of a person who would use military force sparingly and wisely. The Senate was designed to provide vital protections for small-state interests.

The design of governing institutions is particularly important for securing constitutional purposes that require government choices among competing policies, none of which are prohibited by the constitutional text. Governing officials are constitutionally charged with the responsibility for protecting the United States from foreign invasion, maintaining domestic peace, and promoting economic prosperity. Constraints on constitutional powers play, at most, a minor role in achieving these ends. Future policymakers must be given substantial leeway to respond to the events, often unforeseen, of their time. Hamilton in *Federalist* 23 insisted that the national power to provide for the "common defense...ought to exist without limitation, because it is impossible to foresee or define the extent and variety of national exigencies, or the correspondent extent and variety of the means which may be necessary to satisfy them."[25] The framers, aware that they could not predict in advance what regulations of interstate commerce might best grow the economy, recognized the importance of establishing a process for governing in which the best commercial policies are likely to be identified and chosen. When creating that process, they avoided hortatory provisions mandating that government officials be virtuous and intelligent. We can no more specify by constitutional decree that a democratically elected member of the House of Representatives master the complexities of a modern economy than we could by contract require you or me to play correctly a Beethoven piano concerto. The talent may simply be lacking. Successful constitutions, the founding generations understood, must instead construct politics in ways that maximize the probability that persons who understand economics make economic policy.

The Constitution of the United States contains many features and provisions aimed at securing intelligent policymaking with broad appeal that accommodates crucial constituencies. The framers designed constitutional rules for office holding that they maintained would guarantee to the extent consistent with a republican form of government that persons of exceptional ability would hold public office. Elections in large voting districts would "center on men who possess the most attractive merit and the most diffusive and established characters."[26] Relatively long terms of office promote political stability and allow officials to develop expertise on national problems. Other constitutional rules provide important constituencies with the power necessary to protect their interests. The Senate is the most obvious example of an institution designed to accommodate crucial power holders whose support was necessary for the survival of the Union. The original constitutional protections for slavery are a less obvious instance of the institutional means by which the framers sought to facilitate compromise and promote consensus. Under the assumption, erroneous as events proved, that the Senate would typically have a free-state majority and the House would typically have a slave-state majority, the persons responsible for the Constitution believed that they had created a lawmaking process that prevented proposals from becoming national law unless they enjoyed substantial support in both the free and slave states.[27]

The structure of governing institutions provides particularly valuable constitutional protections when important social groups cannot be sure how their interests, values, and policy preferences will best be secured over time. Consider constitution-making in a seven-person food cooperative. Members of the cooperative are aware that their tastes in food, the price of desired items, the money they can spend on food, and political attitudes toward food may quickly change in surprising ways. Specific rules such as "ice cream for dessert three times a week" and "no produce from companies that employ left handed cashiers" may prove inadequate or even counterproductive should various interests and values associated with meals evolve. An alternative solution is to establish procedures for making decisions, such as requiring that a random and rotating group of three persons approve the menus and food purchases each week. Such practices might provide better protections for fluctuating values and interests than fixed rules that often become outdated. Cheesecake can easily be substituted for ice cream when prices or tastes change. Members can adjust their diets after unanticipated weight losses and gains without going through the typically difficult process of amending basic rules. Another advantage of this procedural scheme is that persons may trade less vital for more vital interests. Political liberals attempting to lose weight might agree to an occasional cheesecake in return for an agreement to buy only fair trade coffee.

The Great Compromise at the Constitutional Convention had a structure similar to this proposed constitution for a college student food cooperative. Representatives from low-population states feared a constitution that would privilege the interests of high population states. Such delegates as Roger Sherman of Connecticut and William Patterson of New Jersey could not predict in advance the form such hegemony might take. The large states might agree on tax policies that oppressed the small states, favor large state ports, or adopt any of a nearly infinite number of practices that would skew the benefits of Union to the most populous regions. Faced with these uncertainties, small-state representatives opted for a procedural protection, state equality in the Senate. Once that scheme was accepted, small states no longer had to anticipate all possible threats to their values and interests. Assuming the Senate functioned as expected, Connecticut, Delaware, and their allies would have the political power necessary to veto all measures perceived as providing disproportionate benefits to the large states.

When constitutions properly construct politics, constitutional ends may be served even when crucial constitutional actors are often not self-consciously constrained by constitutional norms.[28] Well-designed constitutional rules for staffing the government and constitutional rules for making laws provide sufficient incentives for the self-interested behaviors that promote constitutional purposes. Rights are secured by giving the rights holders veto powers rather than by explicitly forbidding government from passing oppressive laws. Consider Madison's analysis of the constitutional means for maintaining the separation of powers. In his view, *parchment barriers* would not suffice. Elected officials hungry for power would not be constrained by mere textual limits. Instead, Madison insisted, politics had to be structured in ways that preserved the equilibrium among governing institutions. Each branch of government would be given powers sufficient to resist encroachments by other branches but not adequate for unilateral domination. Madison wrote:

> To what expedient shall we finally resort, for maintaining in practice the necessary partition of power among the several departments, as laid down in the Constitution? The only answer that can be given is, that as all these exterior provisions are found to be inadequate, the defect must be supplied, by so contriving the interior structure of the government as that its several constituent parts may, by their mutual relations, be the means of keeping each other in their proper places.[29]

The resulting Constitution attempts to maintain the balance of power between governing institutions by preventing any branch of government from reducing the salaries of another branch, by minimizing the influence of one branch on the selection or retention of members of another branch, and by giving each elected branch important checks on the operation of other elected branches. This scheme does not require governing officials to be motivated by a desire to maintain the constitutional separation of powers, except insofar as they perceive the constitutional separation of powers to be the best means to secure their political interests. All Madison believed necessary was that governing officials be motivated by the desire to preserve their power and the power of their office: "Ambition must be made to counteract ambition. The interest of the man must be connected with the constitutional rights of the place."[30] Presidents may dream of military glory, but they cannot constitutionally invade a foreign country until Congress declares war and, more important (particularly in the nineteenth century), allocates the funds necessary to raise an army capable of such an invasion.

3.3 Law, Politics, and Constitutional Design

This focus on constitutional design abandons conventional distinctions between law and politics. When studying how constitutions constrain politics, scholars assess whether law influences how particular officials vote on constitutional matters. That approach makes little sense when studying how constitutions construct politics. Constitutional institutions aggregate various preferences or provide political actors with incentives to pursue some paths rather than others. Studies of constitutional design investigate whether structuring governmental institutions in particular ways influences policy and constitutional outcomes. More emphasis is placed on who makes decisions, how those officials are selected, and how their votes are aggregated than on what motivates a particular decision-maker. Constitutions influence political decisions by vesting John but not Mary with power—whether John and Mary when making decisions rely on law, policy preferences, or some combination of the two. Constitutional design also influences political decisions by providing government officials with different incentives. John will vote differently if he is practically compelled by constitutional rules to compromise with Mary than if the constitutional rules permit him to make the decision he thinks best. Constitutional rules that vest federal courts with the power to strike down death penalty statutes passed by the Alabama legislature affect outcomes in part because federal justices as a group are more opposed to state executions that most legislators in the Deep South and in part because federal justices, unlike state legislators, do not have to worry about being reelected. Concerns with constitution design also extent the scope of constitutional analysis. The Constitution constructs all political decisions, not just those concerned with constitutional law. How government officials are selected and make rules influences the interpretation of the Sixth Amendment, the speed limit on interstate highways, relationships with Finland, and the federal tax code. When considering how constitutions construct politics, the law–policy distinction obscures how policy is a means toward securing those vital constitutional ends that do not directly involve constitutional rights or other constitutional limits on government power.

The way constitutions construct politics matters. House and Senate majorities propose different schemes for distributing federal funds, even when members of both institutions act primarily on policy preferences, because the Constitution mandates that House seats be allocated by population and Senate seats be allocated by state.[31] Change the structure of the national legislature and the federal government will make different spending policies. New York City will almost certainly receive far more transportation funds and Boise, Montana, less, should the United States adopted an English-style parliamentary system. Constitutionally mandated judicial review influences public policy, no matter what the basis for particular judicial votes. Even if conventional wisdom is wrong in thinking that justices have a greater propensity for relying on legal factors than elected officials, the high probability exists that, because the constitutional rules for staffing the federal judiciary are different from the constitutional rules for staffing other governing institutions, the judicial majority at any given time is likely to have a somewhat different constitutional vision and policy preferences from the rest of the political system. The Constitution influenced the abolition of Jim Crow and legalization of abortion by vesting at least some policymaking power on those matters in federal justices, who in 1954 and 1973, respectively, were more inclined to favor racial equality and prochoice policies than the average elected official.

The Whig Party's failure to achieve their programmatic goals in the decades before the Civil War highlights how the constitutional rules for making policy influence what proposals become laws. Henry Clay, Daniel Webster, and other members of that coalition favored a national bank, federally sponsored internal improvements, and a high tariff. Jacksonian Democrats believed these measures bad policy. Many insisted that Whig proposals were unconstitutional. From 1836 until 1850, both parties received approximately the same share of the national vote. One might predict from these election returns that Whig policies would be the official law of the land approximately half the time or that approximately half the Whig program would be the law at any time. In fact, Whigs during the Jacksonian era never achieved any of their goals. The reason was simple. Closely divided elections under the constitutional rules for staffing the national government consistently generated divided government. For the Whigs to enact their program, they had to enjoy majorities in both houses of Congress and to control the presidency. Jacksonians needed to control only one elected branch of the national government to prevent Whig proposals from being law. The Constitution hardly provided neutral rules for regulating political struggles between Whigs who promoted activist government and Jacksonians who favored construing constitutional powers narrowly. When the Whigs controlled the presidency, Congress did not pass their preferred legislation. When Whigs controlled Congress, Jacksonian presidents vetoed the national bank, internal improvement, and tariff bills. Constitutional politics was constructed so that a relatively even split in the national vote provided a lopsided advantage for Jacksonian constitutional visions and notions of good public policy.

How constitutions are interpreted depends on how constitutional authority is allocated. Governing institutions in the United States represent different interests and are staffed by persons with different capacities. Change the institution making the constitutional decision, the manner in which members of that institution are selected, or the rules by which that institution makes decisions and official constitutional law will change. Vesting juries with power will protect popular criticisms of government while weakening the rights of unpopular dissenters. The lawyers who staff the federal court system are more likely than ordinary citizens who vote for the president to be concerned with procedural protections for persons accused of crime. Elected officials may be more sensitive than justices to the harms caused by obscenity or unregulated hate speech. A Senate whose members are selected by state legislators may be more prone to find Tenth Amendment limitations on federal power than a Senate whose members are selected by popular vote.

The Constitution of the United States has hardly mattered in the ways Federalists anticipated in 1787. Most framers intended an aristocratic republic in which ordinary people would defer to the superior governing abilities of a (largely) landed elite. Every framer who lived to see the Jacksonian Revolution was disgusted by that populist turn in American constitutional politics.[32] The persons who framed the post–Civil War Amendments thought they were empowering a Congress with a permanent Northern majority. That majority soon lost interest in the rights of persons of color. When the Fourteenth Amendment's aspiration for racial equality was revitalized after World War Two, the federal judiciary played a far greater leadership role than intended by Republicans in the Reconstruction Congress. Political parties have significantly undermined the institutional protections for the separation of powers by giving many members of the national legislature partisan incentives to stomach, if not facilitate, aggrandized presidential powers.[33]

The American two-party system may be the best illustration of how the Constitution was intended to and does structure all of American politics. The framers believed that the large republic would prevent the rise of a two-party system. That was the central argument of Madison's *Federalist* 10. The Constitution, had the opposite effect. The system for electing the president, particularly after passage of the Twelfth Amendment, encouraged the formation of two mass parties structured in ways to best capture the presidency. Popular voting for the Senate, combined with federal laws mandating single-member districts for members of the House, provide further incentives for a two-party system. Mark Tushnet notes, "In single-member districts with winner-take-all rules only two candidates have a realistic possibility of winning." More generally, Tushnet details the various ways political party decisions must take into account the ways the Constitution structures politics. He points out:

> [The Constitution] creates the structure within which our parties operate. The United States has a system in which the president and members of Congress are elected separately, in contrast to a parliamentary system in which the prime minister is chosen by elected party officials. It has a federal system in which political parties are organized on the state level, and state political parties join forces for presidential political campaigns, after which they revert to their focus. In short, the Constitution matters because political parties matter, and the Constitution has some influence on the way parties operate.[34]

Contemporary American two-party politics may explain, for example, why the Democratic Party has a strong prochoice platform and the Republican Party has a strong prolife platform, but no party adopts the more moderate position favored by a plurality of citizens. Thus, contemporary two-party politics highlights how the Constitution of the United States constructs politics, even if not always as intended by the framers.

The Electoral College provides another particularly good example of how the Constitution's influence on political activity has evolved over time. The persons responsible for the Constitution thought the Electoral College would privilege particularly worthy candidates for the presidency and, perhaps, increase the influence of slaveholders on presidential elections. The Electoral College in the twenty-first century serves none of these functions. Instead, the constitutional system for electing the chief executive explains why contemporary candidates make frequent campaign visits to Ohio and Florida but do not hold major October rallies in New York City, Chicago, or Los Angeles. The Constitution "works" in presidential election seasons by providing incentives for parties to give greater weight to the interests and values of swing-state voters than those of voters in perceived safe states, even populous safe states. Change the system for electing the president, and candidates for the presidency will allocate their time and money differently, make more proposals that appeal to urban voters, and, if elected, govern differently.

4. Constitutions as Constituting Politics

Constitutional rules are constitutive. They shape as well as constrain values, interests, and policy preferences. Constitutions constitute politics by helping fashion a distinctive people who think constitutional norms are valuable and behave in constitutionally appropriate ways. Americans to a considerable extent have been created in the image of the Constitution of the United States. Through a combination of indoctrination, socialization, and experience, most have over time internalized fundamental constitutional norms. Citizens experience commitments to democratic elections and property rights as good, natural, or matters of common sense, not as constitutional limits on their values, interests, and policy preferences.

Constitutions or constitutional amendments constitute by initiating a chain of events that buttresses popular support for textual norms. Consider how the constitutional ban on religious establishments has almost certainly increased the percentage of Americans who oppose on moral and policy grounds state support for any particular religious sect:

1. The constitutional ban on establishment encourages immigrants from foreign countries who oppose establishments.
2. Public school teachers who emphasize the virtues of the constitutional ban on establishments foster attitudes that lead their students to prefer religious denominations committed to the separation of church and state.
3. Religious denominations that depend on state establishments do not thrive when denied state support.

4. The combination of 2 and 3 increases the number of citizens whose religious training reinforces the constitutional ban on state support for any particular religious sect.
5. In order to attract or retain members, religious denominations that initially favored state support over time adjust their religious doctrines to conform to the constitutional ban on establishments.[35]

To the extent any of these propositions are true, and most seem to fit the American experience,[36] the constitutional ban on establishments has prevented government from supporting any particular religious sect as much by creating a popular consensus against such establishments as by constraining the preferences of those Americans who favor establishments.

4.1 The Constitutional Politics of Preference Formation

Professor Harold Hill understood that politics is as much about creating new as satisfying existing interests, values, and preferences. He convinced the citizens of River City, Iowa, that they had an unrequited need for a boys' band by explaining how a previously uncontroversial pool table threatened the town with imminent moral disaster. Proponents of the new institutionalism in political science recognize that plots analogous to *The Music Man* are a staple of democratic politics. "Politics," they insist, "involves ongoing efforts to persuade others ... that they should think of themselves and their interests differently than they do."[37] Political leaders do not take people as they are. James March and Johan Olsen note how "preferences and meanings develop in politics"[38] and are not simply givens that candidates for political office and political movements must satisfy. Following the example of Professor Hill, political entrepreneurs employ rhetorical strategies that they hope will inspire citizens to see themselves and their community in ways that support particular political agendas. Rogers Smith observes, "Aspirants to power require a population to lead that imagines itself to be a 'people', ... and they need a people that imagines itself in ways that make leadership by those aspirants appropriate."[39] Advertising agencies that routinely induce desires for light beer, designer jeans, and big cars during election season attempt to induce commitments to more funding for the arts, lower taxes on oil refineries, and war heroes as political leaders. While some commercials appeal to existing preferences, others may try to convince people that they have an unrecognized need to have brighter teeth or to join a crusade that will restore morality to their community.

The Lincoln–Douglas debates are the most famous instance of political leaders striving for power by shaping political preferences. Douglas encouraged members of the audience in towns across 1858 Illinois to understand themselves as united by a common racial characteristic. His speech in the fifth debate asserted, "This government was made by our fathers on the white basis. It was made by white men for the benefit of white men and their posterity forever, and was intended to be administered by white men in all time to come."[40] Lincoln's rhetorical strategy sought to fashion an American identity rooted in a common commitment to human equality. His response to Douglas in the fifth debate stated:

> Judge Douglas, and whoever like him teaches that the negro has no share, humble though it may be, in the Declaration of Independence, is going back to the era of our liberty and independence, and, so far as in him lies, muzzling the cannon that thunders its annual joyous return;…that he is blowing out the moral lights around us, when he contends that whoever wants slaves has a right to hold them; that he is penetrating, so far as lies in his power, the human soul, and eradicating the light of reason and the love of liberty.…[41]

Most persons watching the debate valued both their race and the Declaration of Independence. The political struggle between Lincoln and Douglas was over which candidate could more effectively mobilize the political identity that supported their claim to leadership. Both candidates, Lincoln in particular, were seeking to transform the values and interests that motivated political action and were not simply appealing to a set of fixed political preferences.

Constitutions and laws play important roles in the process by which citizens develop politically salient interests, values, and policy preferences. Fundamental laws and constitutional decisions fashion political identities, shape national aspirations, stimulate commitments to certain rights and political processes, and teach people what demands may be made of government. Political leaders aware of the constitutive function of constitutions seek constitutional practices that induce their followers to internalize fundamental constitutional norms. Specific constitutional limits on government, Madison and other framers thought, did more to educate the public about fundamental rights than to provide legal grounds for constraining political behavior.

Constitutions shape political identities. Beau Breslin notes how foundational texts "creat[e]…a new political community, with a new conception of citizenship."[42] The first words of the Preamble to the Constitution are "We the People of the United States." This identity did not exist twenty years previously. The language of the Fourteenth Amendment suggests that one's identity as an American is more important than one's identity as a citizen of particular state. Lincoln referred to the powerful influence that national identities have on behavior when his first inaugural closed by invoking "the mystic chords of memory, stretching from every battle-field, and patriot grave, to every living heart and hearthstone, all over this broad land."[43] This common nationality "will yet swell the chorus of the Union," Lincoln hoped, because persons considering secession would in the long run be motivated more by their identity as Americans than by their sectional grievances. Men and women who think of themselves as Americans engage in behavior as trivial as cheering for the US Olympic basketball team and as profound as volunteering for dangerous missions as members of the United States Armed Forces.

Constitutional identities have content. To be an American is not simply to share civic space with other persons who think of themselves as Americans but to share common interests, values, and preferences. The Preamble describes a constitutional commitment to "secur[ing] the blessings of liberty." At Gettysburg, Abraham Lincoln insisted that Americans were constitutionally "dedicated to the proposition that all men are created equal." These aspirational claims when first articulated often do not describe actual values. Many constitutions have a "militant" aspect. They are means for transforming the identities and commitments of a particular people. Gary Jacobsohn details how the Constitution of India is rooted in an "ameliorative aspiration...to diminish the social significance of caste."[44] Lincoln believed that the original constitutional commitment to equality was similarly forward looking. He asserted in 1857:

> [The authors of the Declaration of Independence] did not mean to assert the obvious untruth, that all were then actually enjoying that equality, nor yet, that they were about to confer it immediately upon them.... They meant simply to declare the *right*, so that the *enforcement* of it might follow as fast as circumstances should permit. They meant to set up a standard maxim for free society, which should be familiar to all, and revered by all; constantly looked to, constantly labored for, and even though never perfectly attained, constantly approximated, and thereby constantly spreading and deepening its influence, and augmenting the happiness and value of life to all people of all colors everywhere....[45]

Madison emphasized this constitutive function of constitutionalism when urging the First Congress to pass the Bill of Rights. A textual enumeration of certain principles, he declared, would "have a tendency to impress some degree of respect for them, to establish the public opinion in their favor, and rouse the attention of the whole community."[46] What became the First Amendment, in Madison's view, was as much an effort to induce commitments to the freedom of speech as an expression of existing commitments to expression rights. The future fourth president understood that textual proclamations about the freedom of speech would not by themselves adequately constrain or regulate political action. Constitutional texts more often educate than compel. Governing officials and citizens in a polity constitutionally dedicated to the freedom of expression would become convinced over time that the freedom of speech is both an intrinsic value and instrumental to achieving other interests or policy preferences. Americans, both Madison and Lincoln hoped, would be constituted rather than constrained by the principles set out in foundational texts.

Madison detailed another constitutive function of constitutionalism when rejecting Jeffersonian proposals for regular constitutional conventions. "Frequent appeals," he insisted, "would, in great measure, deprive the government of that veneration, which time bestows on everything, and without which perhaps the wisest and freest governments would not possess the requisite stability." Madison wanted to inculcate a "reverence for the laws" that would place "the prejudices of the community on [the] side" of constitutional practices.[47] A venerated constitution shapes rather than constrains interests, values, and policy preferences. If a venerated constitution prohibits government from interfering with the "obligations of contract," then citizens who revere the constitution are likely to conclude that government interference is not in the public interest. Constitutional naysayers exist in every generation, and events such as the electoral debacle of 1800 may demonstrate to even the most adoring constitutionalist that amendment is needed. Still, venerated constitutions create strong presumptions that constitutional rules are just and that constitutional processes are the best means for securing vital interests and fundamental rights. This powerful bias combined with the supermajority requirements for constitutional amendment, constitutional reformers of every generation have discovered, is almost impossible to overcome.

4.2 How Constitutions Influence Interests, Values, and Preferences

Constitutions fashion interests, values, and preferences through indoctrination, socialization, and experience. Children and immigrants are taught that constitutional norms are intrinsically good and responsible for a government that secures their fundamental rights and vital interests. Through basic socialization processes, many governing officials and citizens develop habits of thinking and speaking about social problems almost exclusively within constitutional categories. Constitutional laws, decisions, and practices induce people to have experiences that over time tend to align their values, interests, and policy preferences with those of the Constitution of the United States.

Elementary civics classes routinely indoctrinate constitutional values. Young Americans are taught that the Constitution mandates a sound democratic system of government and protects fundamental rights. Students learn that we should protect the freedom of speech because free speech is a fundamental right that serves their interests as individuals and is good for society. This is a far different account from what is often given for such rules as the prohibition on gum chewing in class. Teachers rarely explain why this edict is intrinsically good or serves more enlightened self-interest. That norm is typically taught simply as a constraint on what people might otherwise want to do. That children want to chew gum is unproblematic as long as they follow the rules. Young citizens at the turn of the twenty-first century, however, are expected to think racism immoral and not simply produce the appropriate answers on examinations.

The composition on why constitutional protections for freedom of speech or democracy are good is another manifestation of this indoctrination process. Unless advanced permission is clear, we do not recommend your essay on "The Right to Vote" be a polemic against republicanism or a diatribe on the baneful influence of the lower classes on elections. Students engage in a subtler form of this exercise when asked to compose an essay on whether colleges should regulate hate speech. "Correct" answers reconcile constitutional commitments to expression rights and equal protection. Wrong answers insist that one constitutional commitment is far more important than the other or, worse, deny that one constitutional commitment has any value at all.

Americans also internalize constitutional values simply by living in the United States. Common "experiences of law," analyses of "legal consciousness" point out, "become synthesized into a set of circulating, often taken-for-granted understandings and habits."[48] Persons who come of age in Massachusetts or Utah are likely to think natural a political system characterized by a bicameral legislature and a Bill of Rights that includes the right to counsel. Many think suspiciously foreign such notions as an elected federal judiciary or a constitutional right to employment. Americans are socialized to tolerate some religious and constitutional differences. Most are aware that constitutional "experts" dispute the meaning of the equal protection clause and whether the death penalty is cruel and unusual punishment. Citizens nevertheless recognize instinctively what is constitutionally off the wall. Even people with no training in constitutional interpretation "know" that only a crazy law professor might think Oedipus had a constitutional right to marry his mother.

Lawyers and other constitutional decision-makers are particularly prone to think almost exclusively in constitutional categories. Just as musicians instinctively read notes in light of their professional training, so persons with legal training habitually interpret social phenomenon in light of constitutional law. When a local community seeks to ban an obscene book, the legally minded immediately contemplate whether under *Miller v. California* (1973) the work has "serious literary, artistic, political, or scientific value." Many cannot take seriously radical feminist claims that pornography contributes to the subordination of women. "Well-trained" lawyers know that "under the First Amendment there is no such thing as a false idea."[49] Such socialization processes hardly produce absolute uniformity on constitutional matters. The prominent feminists who insist that pornography unconstitutionally degrades women have the same legal training as their critics.[50] Catharine MacKinnon and her political allies neverthe-less failed to gain broad support in the legal community for ordinances declaring pornography a form of sex discrimination in part because most legally minded persons in the United States reflexively think of the commitment to content neu-trality when faced with a First Amendment problem.

Americans often think within legal and constitutional categories even when they are not in the courtroom or directly addressing constitutional questions. Gordon Silverstein notes an American tendency toward "juridification," which he describes as "relying on legal process and legal arguments, using legal lan-guage, substituting or replacing ordinary policies with judicial decisions and legal formalisms," throughout the constitutional system.[51] Legality, Silverstein points out, is pervasive throughout the political system. Governing officials think and speak legally whether they are discussing the regulation of tobacco, considering whether to invade a foreign country, or determining the best means for congres-sional oversight of the bureaucracy. Nonlegal perspectives on social problems are more often not considered than consciously considered and rejected.

Political movements cannot escape the pull of this "constitutional conscious-ness." "Legal frameworks," Julie Novkov observes, "ha[ve] significant impacts upon the shape of ideologies emerging from controversial issues."[52] Consider the movement for abortion rights.[53] During the 1950s and 1960s, proponents of legal abortion based their arguments on the medical costs of illegal abor-tions, class disparities in access to medical care, and the need for zero population growth. *Roe v. Wade* vindicated a constitutional right to terminate a pregnancy but did so by conceptualizing the abortion right as inherent in the *choice* whether to become a parent and make other fundamental life decisions. Over time, partly as a result of this constitutional decision, abortion rights advocates began to con-ceive of themselves as prochoice, a term that does not appear to have had sub-stantial currency before *Roe*. Prochoice advocates championed policies that left family decisions to individuals. The connection between abortion and dispari-ties in class access to medical care became attenuated. The connection between abortion and zero population growth virtually disappeared.

Constitutions help socialize persons to make some, but not other, demands on government. Students hope to find good jobs and have romantic opportuni-ties. Most think the government bears some responsibility for their employment prospects. Elected officials, they believe, ought to create an economic climate in which jobs are plentiful (though they may dispute whether this requires regu-lation or deregulation). Few think government responsible for their romantic prospects. That is private. Young persons in other regimes have very different expectations of government. Quasi-public officials in traditional religious communities are often responsible for ensuring that eligible young people find appropriate mates, but friends and family are responsible for employment prospects. The daughters in *Fiddler on the Roof* sing "Matchmaker, matchmaker, make me a match," not "Bureaucrat, bureaucrat, find me a job." This difference in political expectations is partly rooted in constitutional law and practice. Americans expect that the federal government will promote commercial prosperity but not romantic attachments because Congress has powers that directly bear on the former but not the latter. Had the Bill of Rights included a right to state funding of dating services or such services been routinely provided by government throughout American history, Americans would presently make very different demands on elected officials.

Constitutions and laws also influence interests, values, and preferences by inducing people to have particular experiences. American movies from *The Defiant Ones* (Sidney Poitier and Tony Curtis as escaped prisoners chained to the other) and *Star Wars* (Harrison Ford and Carrie Fisher in the stereotypical love–hate relationship) routinely depict two persons who initially detest each other but, after being forced by circumstances to cooperate, develop mutual respect or love.[54] Similar preference-altering events regularly take place in constitutional politics. Most Northerners during the early 1860s were bitterly opposed to racial equality. As the war dragged on, Lincoln was forced to use African American troops to stave off possible defeat. The movie *Glory* accurately depicts how many white soldiers initially forced to fight alongside of former slaves soon abandoned their commitment to white supremacy. Friends and relatives at home received letters declaring, "You have no idea how my prejudices with regard to the negro troops have been dispelled by the battle the other day."[55] Northerners whose values had been shaped by being legally required to fight alongside African Americans returned home and helped ratify the Thirteenth, Fourteenth, and Fifteenth Amendments.

Affirmative action provides another instance of legal change inducing a preference change, which in turn influenced the content of constitutional law. Military and business leaders in 1978 were indifferent or opposed to race-conscious admissions policies. The American military did not participate when the Supreme Court in *Regents of the University of California v. Bakke* (1978) first considered whether public universities could give preferences to persons of color. The Chamber of Commerce submitted an amicus brief asserting that such racial preferences were inconsistent with the equal protection clause.[56] Twenty-five years later, American military and business leaders informed the Supreme Court that they favored a ruling sustaining the constitutionality of affirmative action programs.[57] During the interim period, the American military and most American businesses had adopted some form of affirmation action and found those programs important means for realizing institutional goals. Had *Bakke* completely outlawed such measures, American military and leaders would not have had that value-changing experience. These changed preferences and values, in turn, influenced the judicial decisions handed down in *Grutter v. Bollinger* (2003). Justice O'Connor's crucial opinion specifically pointed to the military and business experience with racial preferences as demonstrating why such policies should be maintained.[58]

Some constitutional indoctrination and socialization are inevitable. Teachers must teach something about the Constitution. Whatever they teach (tolerance, democracy, property rights) will privilege some political norms at the expense of others. Failing to teach anything about the Constitution inculcates beliefs that the Constitution is not particularly important or is a private matter analogous to religion. These problems cannot be resolved by exposing students to diverse perspectives on American constitutionalism. Given human capacities and scarce time, citizens can be exposed only to a limited number of constitutional viewpoints. What constitutes a diverse perspective on the Constitution is as controversial as what constitutes the best perspective on the Constitution. Ask five law professors to recommend the five best readings on the Constitution, insist the readings provide diverse perspectives, and you are likely to receive at least seven reading lists with little overlap.

Socialization and indoctrination become pernicious when they blind Americans to unjust policies or policies that subordinate various groups or classes. Even the briefest glance at American history reveals numerous instances when the constitutional culture masked racism, sexism, and other evils. Constitutional thought at the turn of the twentieth century emphasized the difference between legitimate racial distinctions and unconstitutional racial discriminations.[59] Working within these blinders, the judicial majority in *Plessy v. Ferguson* (1897) blithely contended that if "the enforced separation of the two races stamps the colored race with a badge of inferiority," the reason had nothing to do with segregation laws "but [was] solely because the colored race chooses to put that construction upon it." The common nineteenth-century notion that separate spheres were appropriate for men and women helps explain why justices who denied women the right to vote did not think they were creating second-class citizens. "The Constitution, when it conferred citizenship, did not necessarily confer the right of suffrage," Chief Justice Waite opined in *Minor v. Happersett* (1875). Some socialization processes encourage people to blame themselves or at least not blame government for what we now recognize are government-inflicted injuries. Gays and lesbians who were taught that homosexuality is a mental disease were often unable to conceive that state laws forbidding their employment might violate the equal protection clause.

While we might agree on particular past instances when thinking in constitutional categories facilitated injustice, present instances of subordination through indoctrination and socialization are controversial. Broad agreement exists that laws contribute to a socialization process in which people are likely to think the distribution of valuable goods and resources in society is fair or, if not fair, not the fault of government. Public school teachers engage in this practice when encouraging students to think that their bad grades reflect their abilities or effort, not a biased examination process. Whether grading and other practices are actually fair or merely fair from the narrow perspective of the governing class raises some of the most complex issues in American constitutionalism. Some critical race and feminist theorists insist that constitutional law continues to constitute politics in ways that disadvantage persons of color and women. An equal protection clause interpreted as requiring government officials to treat women and men with the same characteristics equally, they maintain, fosters a political environment in which both men and women devalue distinctive female characteristics. Unsurprisingly, other scholars insist that present equal protection law is fair and helps constitute citizens committed to gender equality. A constitutional law that emphasized distinctive gender characteristics, in their view, would socialize persons in ways conducive to subordination rather than equality.

The indoctrination, socialization, and experiential processes described in this section differ from the legitimating processes noted in Section 2 of this chapter. When the Constitution constrains behavior, people make decisions or act in ways they would otherwise think are wrong or mistaken because they believe they have an obligation to follow the law. Members of Congress who think the presidential veto undemocratic acknowledge that in the United States no bill may become law unless signed by the president (or passed by a supermajority of both the House and Senate). When the Constitution constitutes behavior, people do not experience this tension between the law and their other values, preferences, or interests. They regard the presidential veto as both the law of the land and as a desirable means for ensuring legislation in the national interest. We can nevertheless see the influence of constitutional norms, even when those norms seem identical to values or policy preferences. Americans think the presidential veto is valuable in part because they revere the Constitution and imagine that all constitutional processes serve valued purposes. In countries whose constitutions do not have a presidential veto, far more citizens are taught and believe that the presidential veto in other regimes interferes with the expression of majoritarian preferences.

4.3 Collapsing Law and Politics

Constitutions constitute a regime in which traditional distinctions between law and politics are confounded and collapsed. Americans do not have preferences that are distinctively political and preferences that are distinctively legal. The policy preferences and political values that help explain some legal decisions are typically partly consequences of other legal decisions. Two hundred years of judicial decisions declaring laws unconstitutional help explain the present American commitment to judicial review. *Brown v. Board of Education* (1954) and the Civil Rights Act of 1964 explain in part why most contemporary Americans abhor Jim Crow. Constitutional texts, decisions, and practices influence the demands persons make on government and their religious beliefs. The Congressional powers enumerated in Article I, Section 8 help explain why Americans believe government should grow the economy but not save souls. The establishment and free exercise clauses have fostered an environment more conducive to religious denominations that accept the separation of church and state than those committed to using the state as an instrument for jihad.

No human constitution constitutes automatons who think alike on every matter and confine themselves to purely legal considerations when making constitutional decisions. Constitutional politics in the United States is marked by important disagreements. Americans dispute whether the president may send troops into battle without congressional approval, whether a woman has the right to terminate her pregnancy, and whether Congress may require all persons to have health insurance. Political ideology and policy preferences help explain these differences. Conservatives favor a broader interpretation of gun rights and a narrower construction of the interstate commerce clause than liberals. Voting blocs on the Supreme Court remain fairly constant whether the issue is military tribunals in the war against terror or the exclusionary rule.

Constitutions constitute politics by reducing, cabining, and structuring these disagreements. The Thirteenth Amendment ended the legal controversy over whether Congress could constitutionally ban slavery in the territories and helped fashion a political environment in which, after a short period of time, few people thought slavery should be legal anywhere. Racial issues continued to wrack American politics after the Civil War, but the Reconstruction amendments changed the terrain on which such matters were contested. The justices in *Dred Scott v. Sandford* (1856) disputed whether African Americans could constitutionally be citizens of the United States. Thirty years later, the justices in *The Civil Rights Cases* (1883) disputed what rights African Americans enjoyed as citizens of the United States. *Brown v. Board of Education* and the Civil Rights Act of 1964 were part of the process that settled the constitutional status of segregation and raised new constitutional issues about the meaning of racial equality. Contemporary Americans when debating affirmative action argue over whether diversity is a compelling government interest that justifies race-conscious measures and whether a particular governmental program is a necessary means for securing diversity. These arguments are derived from such

Supreme Court decisions as *Regents of the Univ. of California v. Bakke* (1978) and *Grutter v. Bollinger* (2003) in which judicial majorities insisted that diversity is the only legitimate justification for race-conscious admissions policies at public universities. Liberals and conservatives continually dispute the meaning of racial equality, but the disputes they have and the terms of the debate are in large part determined by the constitutional text, constitutional decisions, and constitutional practice.

Constitutions constitute politics in ways that serve vital constitutional purposes. Texts, decisions, and practices that reduce, cabin, and structure disagreement make the political agenda manageable. Rather than repeatedly fight over basic questions of political structure, Americans take their presidential system for granted and focus their energies on what policies will promote national security or commercial prosperity.[60] Taking certain political questions off the table promotes political stability. Antebellum Americans maintained a precarious bond between the sections by forging a constitutional agreement that the federal government had no power to emancipate slaves in existing states.[61] This consensus limited political and legal debates over human bondage to such initially less explosive issues as the constitutional status of slavery in the territories and the rendition process for fugitive slaves. Constitutions fashion citizens committed to constitutional aspirations. Governing officials who are constitutionally required to explain why their actions respect the freedom of speech and religion are, in the long run, far more likely to respect those liberties than officials who do not have to justify important policies in light of those commitments.

5. The Self-Enforcing Constitution

The constraining, constructive, and constitutive functions of constitutionalism cast light on claims that the Constitution might be a "machine that runs of itself."[62] Well-designed constitutional values are secured by internal checks. Rather than constrain politics, constitutional values are insinuated into politics in ways that ensure their proper weight in political deliberation. Most governing officials and citizens in stable constitutional regimes internalize basic constitutional values. They regard such constitutional values as fair trial and such constitutional institutions as a life-tenured judiciary as intrinsic goods. People are socialized to make only the demands on constitutional institutions that constitutional institutions are designed to satisfy. Well-functioning constitutions generate governing officials who are extraordinarily committed to constitutional norms and establish governing practices that foster intelligent discussions about and solutions to public policy questions. When disputes over plausible interpretations arise, well-designed constitutional processes generate answers that most disputants acknowledge are fair and reasonable. Constitutions that so construct and constitute politics have no need for external institutions that constrain politics.[63]

The Supreme Court and the judicial system in general operate within, not outside of, constitutional politics. As Chapter 5 examines, judicial review is politically constructed. Justices are selected by elected officials, vested with jurisdiction to make constitutional decisions by elected officials, and their decrees are implemented by elected officials. Justices in such a regime can constrain politics in the traditionally prescribed manner only if most elected officials and their constituents have already internalized the relevant constraints or are practically compelled by the structure of constitutional politics to behave as if they have already internalized the relevant constraints. A constitutional system in which federal justices are chosen by elected officials who routinely ignore the Constitution is unlikely to generate an effective, rights-protecting Supreme Court.

Courts are distinctive. They are staffed differently than other governing institutions, and members are socialized differently. We should not be surprised when the judicial majority at any given time has a somewhat different perspective on constitutional issues than majorities in other government institutions. No good reason similarly exists for thinking a majority of the Senate at any given time will reach the same constitutional conclusions as a majority of the Federal Elections Commission. We are nevertheless likely to better understand the role of the judiciary or any other governing body by exploring how the Constitution constructs and constitutes that institution than by proclaiming on faith either that courts are the only governing institution constrained by the Constitution or that all governing officials act only on their policy preferences.

6. When Constitutions Do Not Work

Recurrent claims that Americans are experiencing a constitutional crisis provide a useful vehicle for thinking about how American constitutionalism works and may not work. Medical patients are in crisis when a vital organ is not or is in imminent danger of not properly functioning. Regimes are in crisis when the constitution is not or is in imminent danger of not properly constraining, constructing, or constituting politics. If constitutional regimes are constituted by a set of rules and principles, a set of institutions designed to implement those rules and principles, and citizens who must operate the institutions and be committed to the rules and principles, then the underlying cause of all constitutional crises may be a misalignment between constitutional norms, constitutional institutions, and constitutional citizens.

These constitutional crises take many forms. Prominent commentators often complain of a "crisis of constitutional fidelity" brought on "when important political actors [are] no longer willing to abide by existing constitutional arrangements or systematically contradict constitutional purposes."[64] Antislavery advocates in 1857 insisted that the Supreme Court undermined basic regime commitments to majority rule by manufacturing out of thin air a constitutional right to bring slaves into the territories. A different constitutional crisis occurs when important political actors are too faithful to the Constitution. "Fidelity to constitutional forms," Sandy Levinson and Jack Balkin note, may "lead to ruin or disaster."[65] James Buchanan failed to ward off secession in part because he believed the president was not constitutionally empowered to coerce the states that had left the Union. Contemporary presidents may be taking insufficient steps to prevent global warming because Congress has not passed the laws they believe necessary to prevent an environmental disaster. A third constitutional crisis occurs "when important political disputes cannot be resolved within the existing constitutional framework."[66] The most famous "operational crisis" in American history took place in 1860, when the slave states declared that they would not recognize as legitimate antislavery decisions made by the emerging national Republican Party majority. Stephen Elkin points to yet another form of constitutional crisis when changes in American political economy foster the sort of changes in the balance of political power that prevent constitutional institutions from promoting vital constitutional ends.[67] Northerners perceived such a crisis before the Civil War when they claimed slavery was being preserved and strengthened in the United States only because an increasingly powerful slave-holding class was exercising more control over the national government than the framers had intended. Elkin suggests that a related crisis is occurring today because American business has too much power over national policy and too short-term a vision of the national interest.[68]

Constitutional crises are shaped by the complex relationships between the constraining, constructive, and constitutive functions of constitutionalism. Some apparent crises of fidelity are rooted in deeper crises of constitutional politics or socialization. Seeming constitutional crises on one dimension of constitutionalism are sometimes a consequence of normal, healthy functioning in another dimension. The recent financial crisis illustrates how practices that do not appear to be constitutionally problematic when constitutions are understood as constraining politics are troubling when one considers the constructive or constitutive functions of constitutionalism.

Consider the common view that a constitutional crisis is taking place because Supreme Court justices are protecting (or not adequately protecting) abortion rights. This appears to be a crisis of constitutional fidelity (if you are pro-life). When justices substitute their policy preferences for constitutional law, the Constitution fails to constrain adequately crucial governing officials. This failing may be rooted in the construction of constitutional politics. When the Constitution is functioning properly, the federal courts should be staffed by the persons least likely to substitute their policy preferences for constitutional law. *Roe v. Wade* (1973) (or *Gonzales v. Carhart* [2007]), standing alone, does not demonstrate a design flaw. No institution functions perfectly. The present batch of justices may be mistaken on one matter or, alas, not be up to the two-hundred-year standard of probity set by their judicial ancestors. If, however, justices throughout history too frequently substitute their policy preferences for law, then we should blame the judicial selection process for continuous constitutional outrages. A strong case can be made that ongoing partisan struggles for control of national institutions privilege the selection of Supreme Court justices prone to substitute their policy preferences for the law. This crisis of constitutional politics, in turn, may have roots in a crisis of constitutional culture. One popular account of the increase in value voting insists that throughout much of the nineteenth century lawyers (and citizens) were socialized to regard the law as an intrinsic good. Supreme Court justices who received this education rarely thought about what constituted good policy when deciding cases, except in the rare instances when the political stakes were so high as to overwhelm judgment. For the last hundred years, lawyers have been trained to regard law as an instrument for good social policy. Justices socialized in this way interpret due process as mandating whatever they believe to be desirable values. The constitutional crisis responsible for *Roe* (or *Gonzales*) stems from the constitutional failure to generate a legal community sufficiently committed to the rule of law.[69] Correcting how the Constitution presently constructs and constitutes politics requires a considerable reworking of the constitutional rules for staffing the federal judiciary and wholesale changes in constitutional education. Providing better lectures to elected officials about their constitutional responsibilities and better arguments to justices about the proper meaning of the Fourteenth Amendment will be worthless until Americans make these broader institutional and cultural adjustments.

The common claim that recent exercises of presidential power (or recent efforts to limit presidential power) during the war against terrorism threaten a constitutional crisis illustrates different relationships between the ways constitutions constrain and construct politics. Presidents (or congressional majorities) may be flagrantly abusing their constitutional powers. If so, Americans are experiencing a crisis of constitutional fidelity. Many commentators, however, think that the Constitution is not entirely clear on the scope of presidential power, or at least on the legitimacy of presidential powers being exercised during the present war against terrorism. Given possible ambiguities, perhaps presidents and members of Congress opposed to exercises of presidential power may both be acting in good faith. This suggests an operational crisis. Larry Alexander and Fred Schauer provide one framework for thinking about operational crises when they insist that constitutions and constitutional institutions work by providing authoritative settlements to heated political disagreements.[70] The Constitution, in this view, may be failing to construct politics in ways that provide Americans with an authoritative account of presidential power or a means for obtaining an authoritative account. Future crises over presidential power will be averted only if a consensus is reached on what the president may do during the war against terror or on the particular institution vested with the authority to settle the relevant constitutional issues. Michael Seidman and Mariah Zeisberg challenge this view that unresolved constitutional disagreements are typically manifestations of a constitutional crisis. They contend that constitutions function best when certain vital issues are left unsettled, subject to ongoing democratic contestation.[71] What appear to be constitutional crises, in their view, are often healthy constitutional politics. Different persons with different values and different institutional perspectives are discussing and deliberating. The end result is constitutional decisions that are more intelligent, promote a greater range of values, and accommodate more people than would have been the case had the decision been entrusted to a particular constitutional decision-maker. We can, nevertheless, identify a different kind of operational crisis that may be afflicting American constitutionalism. In this view, the constitutional separation of powers often stimulates both the president and opposition leaders in Congress to intensify their demands. Partisan politics aggravates this tendency. Motivated primarily by felt needs to rally their political bases, neither Democrats nor Republicans have sufficient incentives to accommodate the legitimate constitutional perspectives offered by their partisan and institutional rivals. When government is divided, this constitutional politics generates stalemate or the unilateral imposition of presidential policy. When government is united, this constitutional politics generates extremism. If Americans are experiencing either of the operational crises described in this paragraph, then the underlying problem is the constitutional failure to construct politics in ways that provide governing officials with the necessary incentives to moderate their demands, take into account rival perspectives on the proper relationships between governing institutions, and amicably settle constitutional disputes. These constitutional failures can be cured only by formal, semiformal, or informal changes in constitutional processes, not by another set of lectures directed at the responsible governing officials.

The financial crisis the United States experienced at the end of the George W. Bush administration illustrates a subtler manifestation of a constitutional crisis. On a standard legal analysis, the events responsible for the bailout of many financial institutions were not constitutional at all. Governing officials may have made mistakes, but most constitutional thinkers believe that these were mistakes governing officials were constitutionally entitled to make. Article I, Section 8 gives Congress the power to regulate interstate commerce. The relevant provisions do not require Congress to regulate interstate commerce or the financial markets intelligently. Nevertheless, a deeper probe into the constructive and constitutive dimensions of constitutionalism illuminates possible regime failings. The persons responsible for the Constitution thought they had structured national institutions in ways that would privilege the selection of the persons most likely to make intelligent economic policy in the national interest. They may have succeeded. Perhaps the financial crisis was inevitable or not the fault of governing officials. On another view, the constitutional system for selecting economic planners is generating a far worse group of policymakers than would be the case had some alternative constitutional arrangements been in place. Perhaps the Constitution devolves too much power on a Congress whose members are too concerned with winning elections in the short-term to engage in efficient long-term planning (or too interested in securing nice jobs after retirement from politics to regulate appropriately). Perhaps the Constitution permits relatively unaccountable institutions like the Federal Reserve Board to make decisions that favor the interests of big banks rather than ordinary people. If either of these hypotheses is true, then Americans will experience inferior economic planning until the constitutional rules for making economic policy are changed.

The bailout and related events raise questions about the constitutive dimensions of constitutionalism. A failing education system may be generating voters incapable of selecting the best economic planners under any scheme consistent with constitutional democracy. The Constitution of the United States may have been designed for a people who consider a house to be primarily a place of residence. Such citizens make demands on government, such as police and fire services, that state and national institutions are well designed to satisfy. For many Americans at present, a house is as much an investment as a place of residence. Homeowners as investors demand government services different from homeowners as residents. Constitutional institutions may not be well suited to address those concerns. What Americans are experiencing may be a constitutional mismatch between their demands on government and government capacity to satisfy those demands. American constitutionalism may require a particular balance of power between persons who hold various amounts of property. Should that balance become skewed, constitutional institutions too dominated by wealthy interests may pay too little attention to the need for economic policies that preserve the strong middle class necessary for sustaining American constitutionalism or the same institutions too dominated by the propertyless may pay too little attention to the need to accommodate the business interests necessary for sustaining American constitutionalism.[72]

These ruminations on the present financial crisis provide yet another illustration that constitutions work to structure political outcomes on matters far removed from the traditional subjects of constitutional law. Economic policy in the United States is made by officials elected by or nominated according to the rules laid down in Article I and Article II. Constitutional texts, decisions, and practices determine how the legal and policy preferences of these economic planners are aggregated. Change the constitutional rules, this text chants over and over again, and the government of the United States would have made different economic policies and responded differently to the financial crises of the early twenty-first century. That most persons expected the federal government to alleviate the financial crisis is partly explained by a series of constitutional decisions that vested the national government with the responsibility for maintaining commercial prosperity. Had constitutional decision-makers in 1787 and 1937 insisted that government was responsible for saving souls rather than investments or that government was responsible for neither, public response at the turn of the twenty-first century to the collapse of various insurance and brokerage firms would have been quite different.

7. One Last Crisis

The United States may be experiencing a crisis of constitutional education. In classrooms, in media, and in popular culture, American constitutionalism is being reduced to American constitutional law—and a very narrow conception of American constitutional law at that. Students and citizens are being socialized to think that the only interesting constitutional questions are about the proper interpretation of a few constitutional provisions and that the Supreme Court is the only interesting constitutional institution. This preoccupation with determining whether the Supreme Court is correctly interpreting the Constitution may make some sense in law schools, although hardly any law school graduate practices constitutional law and those who practice constitutional law often do so as executive or legislative advisors. American constitutional education provides little of use to the greater number of American citizens who must understand and evaluate constitutional practices that often have little to do with adjudication.

The most fundamental questions of constitutionalism concern the nature and purposes of constitutions. American constitutional projects cannot be evaluated or assessed until citizens recognize what a constitution is, what purposes constitutions serve, and how constitutions serve those purposes. These considerations require the study of constitutionalism as political philosophy and institutional design. We cannot fully comprehend American constitutionalism unless we understand the extent to which American constitutionalism is committed to achieving universal ends or goods distinctive to Americans. These questions require far greater investigations into international and comparative law than traditional in the constitutional curriculum.

Americans lacking a broad foundation in basic constitutional theory will often fail to identify correctly the existence and causes of constitutional weaknesses and crises. Legalists who insist on a strict separation of law and politics too often scream "crisis" whenever the scent of value voting is in the air. Cynics who insist that law is politics with a few Latin words never perceive crises, even when legality breaks down completely. Neither recognize that constitutions are efforts to structure value voting. Rather than confine law and politics to separate spheres, constitutionalism channels values and interests toward desirable ends. Such constitutional provisions as Article I's requirement of state equality in the Senate or the life-tenured judiciary mandated by Article III work primarily by determining the extent to which different values, interests, and policy preferences influence official decisions. Constitutions more often fashion than constrain citizens. American identity is inextricably linked to the Declaration of Independence, the Constitution drafted in 1787, the Bill of Rights, and the post–Civil War amendments. Our interests, values, and policy preferences are partly constituted by our experiences living under the Constitution of the United States, even as those interests, values, and policy preferences partly construct the Constitution of the United States.

Whether American constitutionalism is in crisis, what the nature of that crisis might be, or the proper prescription are controversial. So is the constitutional right to abortion, the proper scope of presidential power during the war on terror, and the constitutional foundations, if any, of the financial crisis in the United States. The more crucial point is that students, scholars, and fellow citizens will best recognize, prevent, and alleviate any future constitutional crisis by developing a broader perspective on American constitutionalism. American constitutionalism is far more important and interesting than the study of the judicial essays in the *U.S. Reports*.

NOTES

Front Matter

1. Their seminal works in historical institutionalism include Rogers M. Smith, *Liberalism and American Constitutional Law* (Harvard University Press: Cambridge, MA, 1985); Rogers M. Smith, "Political Jurisprudence, the 'New Institutionalism,' and the Future of Public Law," 82 *American Political Science Review* 89 (1988); Keith E. Whittington, *Constitutional Construction: Divided Powers and Constitutional Meaning* (Harvard University Press: Cambridge, MA, 1999); Keith E. Whittington, "Once More unto the Breach: Postbehavioralist Approaches to Judicial Politics," 25 *Law and Social Inquiry* 601 (2000); Howard Gillman, *The Constitution Besieged: The Rise and Demise of Lochner Era Police Powers Jurisprudence* (Duke University Press: Durham, NC, 1993); Howard Gillman, "What's Law Got to Do with It? Judicial Behavioralists Test the 'Legal Model' of Judicial Review," 26 *Law and Social Inquiry* 465 (2001). Numerous other scholars have made important contributions to the historical institutionalist enterprise. I hope they are appropriately recognized in the acknowledgments and, more important, in the pages that follow.
2. See Keith E. Whittington, *Political Foundations of Judicial Supremacy: The Presidency, the Supreme Court, and Constitutional Leadership in U.S. History* (Princeton University Press: Princeton, NJ, 2007).
3. See Desmond S. King and Rogers M. Smith, *Still a House Divided: Race and Politics in Obama's America* (Princeton University Press: Princeton, NJ, 2011).
4. See Sanford Levinson, *Framed: America's 51 Constitutions and the Crisis of Governance* (Oxford University Press: New York, 2012).

Chapter 1

1. 5 *Journal of the Second Continental Congress* 342 (1776).
2. David McCullough, *John Adams* (Simon & Schuster: New York, 2001), p. 109.
3. *National Federation of Independent Business v. Sebelius*, 567 U.S. ____ (2012).
4. *West Virginia State Board of Education v. Barnette*, 319, U.S. 624, 638 (1943).
5. *West Virginia State Board of Education v. Barnette*, at 670 (Frankfurter, J., dissenting).
6. Laurence H. Tribe, "Taking Text and Structure Seriously: Reflections on Free-Form Method in Constitutional Interpretation," 108 *Harvard Law Review* 1223, 1302 (1995).
7. See Sanford Levinson, *Framed: America's 51 Constitutions and the Crisis of Government* (Oxford University Press: New York, 2012); Sanford Levinson, *Our Undemocratic Constitution: Where the Constitution Goes Wrong (and How We the People Can Correct It)* (Oxford University Press: New York, 2006).
8. 17 U.S. 316 (1819).
9. *McCulloch*, at 316, 401.
10. *McCulloch*, at 407.

11. Ibid.

12. *McCulloch,* at 415.

13. *McCulloch,* at 431.

14. *McCulloch,* at 403.

15. *McCulloch,* at 415.

16. *McCulloch,* at 401.

17. Ibid.

18. For an account of that impeachment process, see Keith E. Whittington, "Reconstructing the Federal Judiciary: The Chase Impeachment and the Constitution," 9 *Studies in American Political Development* 55 (1995).

19. Harry T. Edwards, "The Growing Disjunction between Legal Education and the Legal Profession," 91 *Michigan Law Review* 34, 35 (1992).

20. David Segal, "What They Don't Teach Law Students: Lawyering," *New York Times* (November 19, 2011).

21. Herbert Wechsler, "Toward Neutral Principles of Constitutional Law," 73 *Harvard Law Review* 1, 11 (1959).

22. Jeffrey A. Segal and Harold J. Spaeth, *The Supreme Court and the Attitudinal Model Revisited* (Cambridge University Press: New York, 2002), pp. 8, 26, 86.

23. "The Ratification of the Conventions of nine States shall be sufficient for the Establishment of this Constitution between the States so ratifying the Same."

24. "The Congress, whenever two thirds of both Houses shall deem it necessary, shall propose Amendments to this Constitution, or, on the Application of the Legislatures of two thirds of the several States, shall call a Convention for proposing Amendments, which, in either Case, shall be valid to all Intents and Purposes, as part of this Constitution, when ratified by the Legislatures of three fourths of the several States or by Conventions in three fourths thereof, as the one or the other Mode of Ratification may be proposed by the Congress."

25. See Levinson, *Undemocratic Constitution.*

26. See Mark A. Graber, *Dred Scott and the Problem of Constitutional Evil* (Cambridge University Press: New York, 2006).

27. See Daryl J. Levinson and Richard Pildes, "Separation of Parties, not Powers," 119 *Harvard Law Review* 2311 (2006).

28. Alexander M. Bickel, *The Least Dangerous Branch: The Supreme Court at the Bar of Politics* (Bobbs-Merrill Company, Inc.: Indianapolis, 1962), pp. 16–17.

29. See Mark A. Graber, "Constructing Judicial Review," 8 *Annuals Reviews in Political Science* 425 (2005).

30. Karl N. Llewellyn, "Some Realism about Realism—Responding to Dean Pound," 44 *Harvard Law Review* 1222, 1223 (1931).

Chapter 2

1. Antonin Scalia, "The Rule of Law as a Law of Rules," 56 *University of Chicago Law Review* 1175, 1187 (1989).

2. Howard Schweber, *The Language of Liberal Constitutionalism* (Cambridge University Press: New York, 2007), p. 2.

3. Giovanni Sartori, "Constitutionalism: A Preliminary Discussion," 56 *American Political Science Review* 853, 860 (1962).

4. T. H. Vance, ed., *Demosthenes: Against Meidias, Androtion, Aristocrates, Timocrates, Aristogeiton* (Harvard University Press: Cambridge, MA, 1956), p. 212.

5. Thomas Reed Powell, "The Logic and Rhetoric of Constitutional Law," 15 *Journal of Philosophy, Psychology, and Scientific Methods* 645, 647–648 (1918).

6. *Zorach v. Clauson,* 343 U.S. 306, 318 (1952).

7. Susan Moller Okin, *Justice, Gender, and the Family* (Basic Books: New York, 1991).

8. Aristotle, *Aristotle's Politics and Poetics* (translated by Benjamin Jowett and Thomas Twining) (Viking Press: New York, 1957), p. 46.

9. Plato, *The Republic* (translated by Benjamin Jowett) (Vintage Books: New York, 1991), pp. 186–91.

10. Aristotle, *Aristotle's Politics*, p. 3.
11. Aristotle, *The Nicomachean Ethics* (translated by David Ross) (Oxford University Press: New York, 1980), pp. 275–76.
12. Stephen L. Elkin, *Reconstructing the Commercial Republic: Constitutional Design after Madison* (University of Chicago Press: Chicago, 2006), p. 10.
13. Robert P. Kraynak, "Tocqueville's Constitutionalism," 87 *American Political Science Review* 1175, 1177 (1987).
14. Plato, *Republic*, p. 134.
15. Alexander Hamilton, James Madison, and John Jay, *The Federalist Papers* (edited by Lawrence Goldman) (Oxford University Press: New York, 2008), p. 53.
16. "Brutus," "To the Citizens of the State of New York, November 15, 1787," *The Complete Anti-Federalist* (Vol. 1) (edited by Herbert Storing) (University of Chicago Press: Chicago, 1981), p. 380.
17. Robert A. Dahl, *Democracy and Its Critics* (Yale University Press: New Haven, CT, 1989), p. 264.
18. *Dred Scott v. Sandford*, 60 U.S. 393, 412 (1856).
19. *Holy Trinity Church v. United States*, 143 U.S. 457, 470–71 (1892).
20. *Griswold v. Connecticut*, 381 U.S. 479, 486 (1965).
21. Abraham Lincoln, "'A House Divided': Speech at Springfield, Illinois," *The Collected Works of Abraham Lincoln* (Vol. 2) (edited by Roy P. Basler) (Rutgers University Press: New Brunswick, NJ, 1953), p. 461.
22. Hamilton et al., *Federalist Papers*, p. 15.
23. Rogers M. Smith, *Civic Ideals: Conflicting Visions of Citizenship in U.S. History* (Yale University Press: New Haven, CT, 1997).
24. Stephen A. Douglas, "Mr. Douglas's Speech: First Debate with Stephen A. Douglas at Ottawa, Illinois," *Collected Works of Abraham Lincoln* (Vol. 3) (edited by Roy P. Basler) (Rutgers University Press: New Brunswick, NJ, 1953), p. 9.
25. Smith, *Civic Ideals*, p. 489.
26. Mark Tushnet, *Taking the Constitution away from the Courts* (Princeton University Press: Princeton, NJ, 1999), p. 12.
27. John Dewey, *Democracy and Education* (Macmillan Company: New York, 1922), p. 101.
28. *The Civil Mission of Schools* (A report from the Carnegie Commission of New York and CIRCLE: The Center for Information and Research on Civic Learning and Engagement), http://www.carnegie.org/pdf/CivicMissionofSchools.pdf, p. 11.
29. See Ralph Lerner, "The Supreme Court as a Republican Schoolmaster," 1967 *The Supreme Court Review* 127 (1967).
30. Richard Delgado, "Words that Wound: A Tort Action for Racial Insults, Epithets, and Name Calling," *Words that Wound: Critical Race Theory, Assaultive Speech, and the First Amendment* (edited by Mari J. Matsuda, Charles R. Lawrence III, Richard Delgado, and Kimberle Williams Crenshaw) (Westview Press: Boulder, CO, 1993), p. 93.
31. Lee C. Bollinger, *The Tolerant Society* (Oxford University Press: New York, 1986), p. 10.
32. For a good analysis of constitutional ethics, see Keith E. Whittington, "On the Need for a Theory of Constitutional Ethics," 9 *The Good Society* 60 (2000).
33. Whittington, "Constitutional Ethics," pp. 60–66.
34. See Jeffrey K. Tulis, *The Rhetorical Presidency* (Princeton University Press: Princeton, NJ, 1987).
35. See Julie Novkov, *Racial Union: Law, Intimacy, and the White State in Alabama, 1865–1954* (University of Michigan Press: Ann Arbor, 2008).
36. Charles Howard McIlwain, *Constitutionalism: Ancient and Modern* (Lawbook Exchange, Ltd: Clark, NJ, 2005), p. 17.
37. McIlwain, *Constitutionalism: Ancient and Modern*, p. 11.
38. Ibid.
39. See Elizabeth Kelley Bauer, *Commentaries on the Constitution, 1790–1860* (Columbia University Press: New York, 1952), pp. 213, 254, 308.
40. Alexander Hamilton, *The Works of Alexander Hamilton* (edited by John C. Hamilton) (John P. Trow: New York, 1850), p. 322.

41. James Madison, *Letters and Other Writings of James Madison* (Vol. 4) (J. B. Lippincott & Co.: Philadelphia, 1967), p. 391.

42. Keith E. Whittington, *Constitutional Interpretation: Textual Meaning, Original Intent, and Judicial Review* (University Press of Kansas: Lawrence, 1999), p. 149.

43. Graber, *Dred Scott*, p. 223.

44. Randy E. Barnett, "An Originalism for Nonoriginalists," 45 *Loyola Law Review* 611, 629 (1999).

45. *Marbury v. Madison*, 5 U.S. 137, 178 (1803).

46. Chapter 5 discusses in some detail issues of constitutional authority.

47. E. P. Thompson, *Whigs and Hunters: The Origin and the Black Act* (Pantheon Books: New York, 1975), p. 266.

48. Frederick Schauer, *Playing by the Rules: A Philosophical Examination of Rule-Based Decision-Making in Law and in Life* (Oxford University Press: New York, 1991), p 77–78.

49. Ibid., pp. 136–37.

50. This paragraph summarizes Lon L. Fuller, *The Morality of Law* (revised edition) (Yale University Press: New Haven, CT, 1969), pp. 33–94.

51. Readers should determine whether the commitment to the rule of law entails additional standards or whether some might be safely subtracted.

52. See Lee Epstein, "Introduction to the Symposium," 2 *Perspectives on Politics* 757 (2004).

53. See James Madison, "To the House of Representatives of the United States," *The Mind of the Founder: Sources of the Political Thought of James Madison* (edited by Marvin Meyers) (Bobbs-Merrill Company, Inc.: Indianapolis, 1973), pp. 391–94.

54. "Virginia and Kentucky Resolutions of 1798," *American Constitutionalism: Structures of Government* (Vol. I) (edited by Howard Gillman, Mark A. Graber, and Keith E. Whittington) (Oxford University Press: New York, 2013), pp. 164–66.

55. Howard Gillman, "Preferred Freedoms: The Progressive Expansion of State Power and the Rise of Modern Civil Liberties Jurisprudence," 47 *Political Research Quarterly* 623 (1994).

56. "Essays of Brutus," *The Complete Anti-Federalist* (Vol. 1) (edited by Herbert J. Storing) (University of Chicago Press: Chicago, 1981), p. 421.

57. See Randy E. Barnett, *Restoring the Lost Constitution* (Princeton University Press: Princeton, NJ, 2004), pp. 274–76.

58. Joseph M. Lynch, *Negotiating the Constitution: The Earliest Debates over Original Intent* (Cornell University Press: Ithaca, NY, 1999), pp. 19–20.

59. Walter F. Murphy, James E. Fleming, Sotirios A. Barber, and Stephen Macedo, *American Constitutional Interpretation* (3rd ed.) (Foundation Press: New York, 2003), pp. 48–49.

60. Sartori, "Constitutionalism," p. 855.

61. See Ran Hirschl, *Constitutional Theocracy* (Harvard University Press: Cambridge, MA, 2010).

62. Thomas Jefferson, *The Portable Thomas Jefferson* (edited by Merrill D. Peterson) (Penguin Books: New York, 1975), p. 235.

63. "Positive rights" have two distinctive meanings in constitutional theory. The first, discussed already, are rights created by law, such as the right to swim in a public pool. The second, to be discussed shortly, are rights that require government action, such as the right to basic necessities.

64. Emily Zackin, *Looking for Rights in All the Wrong Places: Why State Constitutions Contain America's Positive Rights* (Princeton University Press: Princeton, NJ, 2013).

65. See especially, Smith, *Civil Ideals*.

66. Or perhaps in the 1960s, with the passage of the Civil Rights Act of 1964 and the Voting Rights Act of 1965.

67. This paragraph summarizes Peter E. Quint, "What Is a Twentieth-Century Constitution?" 67 *Maryland Law Review* 238 (2007).

68. Ibid., p. 243.

69. *Jackson v. City of Joliet*, 715 F.2d 1200, 1203 (7th Cir. 1983).

70. Sotirios A. Barber, *Welfare & the Constitution* (Princeton University Press: Princeton, NJ, 2003), pp. xiv–xv.

Chapter 3

1. Chapter 6 discusses whether entrenched constitutional provisions must be judicially enforceable.

2. E. P. Thompson, *Whigs and Hunters: The Origin and the Black Act* (Pantheon Books: New York, 1975), p. 266.

3. Walter F. Murphy, *Constitutional Democracy: Creating and Maintaining a Just Political Order* (Johns Hopkins University Press: Baltimore, MD, 2007), p. 16.

4. Although a pacifist might respond that violence in practice has no general tendency to promote human rights.

5. See Ran Hirschl, *Constitutional Theocracy* (Harvard University Press: Cambridge, MA, 2010).

6. See Melissa Schwartzberg, *Democracy and Legal Change* (Cambridge University Press: New York, 2007), pp. 31–70.

7. For an excellent critique of various arguments for entrenchment, see Schwartzberg, *Democracy and Legal Change*.

8. See Mary L. Dudziak, *Cold War Civil Rights: Race and the Image of American Democracy* (Princeton University Press: Princeton, NJ, 2000).

9. Stephen Holmes, "Precommitment and the Paradox of Democracy," *Constitutionalism and Democracy* (edited by Jon Elster and Rune Slagstad) (Cambridge University Press: New York, 1988), p. 237.

10. Howard Schweber, *The Language of Liberal Constitutionalism* (Cambridge University Press: New York, 2007).

11. Holmes, "Precommitment," p. 237.

12. Ibid., p. 231.

13. Ibid., p. 216.

14. Schwartzberg, *Democracy and Legal Change*, p. 2.

15. Douglas C. North and Barry R. Weingast, "Constitutions and Commitment: The Evolution of Institutions Governing Public Choice in Seventeenth-Century England," 49 *Journal of Economic History* 803, 803 (1989).

16. Charles A. Beard, *An Economic Interpretation of the Constitution of the United States* (Free Press: New York, 1986).

17. Robert Michels, *Political Parties: A Study of the Oligarchical Tendencies of Modern Democracy* (Hearst's International Library: New York, 1915), p. 377.

18. For a fascinating discussion of the consequences of constitutional provisions regulating legislative pay and pay raises, see Adrian Vermeule, *The System of the Constitution* (Oxford University Press: New York, 2011), pp. 106–15.

19. *Railway Express Agency v. New York*, 366 U.S. 106, 112–13 (1949) (Jackson, J., concurring).

20. North and Weingast, "Constitutions and Commitment," p. 829.

21. *Philadelphia v. New Jersey*, 437 U.S. 617 (1978); *Prigg v. Pennsylvania*, 41 U.S. 539 (1841).

22. Stephen L. Elkin, *Reconstructing the Commercial Republic: Constitutional Design after Madison* (University of Chicago Press: Chicago, 2006).

23. I confess to always having the temptation to respond to such pleas by declaring, "You're right. We do need a hit. And I was planning to ground out." Of course, I usually grounded out in those circumstances anyway.

24. Alexander Hamilton, James Madison, and John Jay, *The Federalist Papers* (edited by Lawrence Goldman) (Oxford University Press: New York, 2008), p. 282.

25. Ibid., p. 53.

26. Ibid., p. 353.

27. Elkin, *Reconstructing the Commercial Republic*, p. 35.

28. Hamilton et al., *Federalist Papers*, p. 306.

29. Ibid., p. 268.

30. Ibid., p. 234.

31. Thomas Paine, "Common Sense," *Tracts of the American Revolution, 1763–1776* (edited by Merrill Jensen) (Bobbs-Merrill Educational Publishing: Indianapolis), p. 441.

32. Antonin Scalia, *A Matter of Interpretation: Federal Courts and the Law* (Princeton University Press: Princeton, NJ, 1997), p. 40.
33. Tom Ginsburg, *Judicial Review in New Democracies: Constitutional Courts in Asian Cases* (Cambridge University Press: New York, 2003), p. 18.
34. Ran Hirschl, *Towards Juristocracy: The Origins and Consequences of the New Constitutionalism* (Harvard University Press: Cambridge, MA, 2004), p. 12.
35. Beard, *An An Economic Interpretation of the Constitution.*
36. Gordon S. Wood, *The Creation of the American Republic, 1776–1787* (W. W. Norton & Company: New York, 1969).
37. See Sidney M. Milkis, *Political Parties and Constitutional Government: Remaking American Democracy* (Johns Hopkins University Press: Baltimore, MD, 1999), pp. 3–4.
38. *Annals of Congress,* 1st Cong., 1st Sess, p. 453.
39. Abraham Lincoln, "'A House Divided': Speech at Springfield, Illinois," *The Collected Works of Abraham Lincoln* (Vol. 2) (edited by Roy P. Basler) (Rutgers University Press: New Brunswick, NJ, 1953), p. 406.
40. Jack M. Balkin, *Constitutional Redemption: Political Faith in an Unjust World* (Harvard University Press; Cambridge, MA, 2011), pp. 120–21.
41. Sotirios A. Barber, *The Constitution of Judicial Power* (Johns Hopkins University Press: Baltimore, MD, 1993), p. 110.
42. *Dred Scott v. Sandford,* 60 U.S. 393, 490 (1856) (Daniel, J. concurring), emphasis in original.
43. Rogers M. Smith, *Civil Ideals: Conflicting Visions of Citizenship in U.S. History* (Yale University Press: New Haven, CT, 1997), p. 1.
44. States receive a number of electoral votes equal to the number of their representatives in Congress. Before the 13th Amendment, slaves were counted as three-fifths of a person when determining a state's representation in the House of Representatives.
45. Arend Lijphart, *Patterns of Democracy: Government Forms and Performance in Thirty-Six Countries* (Yale University Press: New Haven, CT, 1999), p. 2.
46. Ibid., pp. 32–33.
47. Wood, *Creation,* p. 584 (quoting Benjamin Franklin).
48. Hamilton et al., *Federalist Papers,* p. 175.
49. Ibid., p. 179.
50. Ibid., p. 271.
51. See Mark A. Graber, "Redeeming and Living with Evil," 71 *Maryland Law Review* 1073, 1081–85 (2012).
52. Stephen A. Douglas, "Mr. Douglas's Reply," *The Collected Works of Abraham Lincoln* (Vol. 3) (edited by Roy P. Basler) (Rutgers University Press: New Brunswick, NJ, 1953), p. 241.
53. For a slightly different account of early liberal purposes, see Rogers M. Smith, *Liberalism and American Constitutional Law* (Harvard University Press: Cambridge, MA, 1985), pp. 18–35.
54. Alexander Hamilton is the exception that proves this rule.
55. James Madison, "Vices of the Political System of the U.S.," *Letters and Other Writings of James Madison* (Vol. I) (J.B. Lippincott: Philadelphia, PA, 1867), pp. 321, 325.
56. Lincoln, "'House Divided,'" p. 461.
57. Abraham Lincoln, "Address Delivered at the Dedication of the Cemetery at Gettysburg: Final Draft," *The Collected Works of Abraham Lincoln* (Vol. 7) (edited by Roy P. Basler) (Rutgers University Press: New Brunswick, NJ, 1953), p. 23.
58. Gary Wills, *Lincoln at Gettysburg: The Words that Re-made America* (Simon & Schuster: New York, 1992).
59. Akhil Reed Amar, *The Bill of Rights* (Yale University Press: New Haven, CT, 1998).
60. Mark A. Graber, *Dred Scott and the Problem of Constitutional Evil* (Cambridge University Press: New York, 2006), pp. 197–98.
61. Christopher L. Eisgruber, "The Fourteenth Amendment's Constitution," 69 *Southern California Law Review* 47, 48 (1995).
62. *Slaughter-House Cases,* 83 U.S. 36, 71 (1872).
63. Ibid. (Field, J., dissenting).

64. See John Hart Ely, *Democracy and Distrust: A Theory of Judicial Review* (Harvard University Press: Cambridge, MA, 1980), pp. 98–99.

65. John W. Burgess, *Recent Changes in American Constitutional Theory* (Columbia University Press: New York, 1923).

66. See Bruce Ackerman, *We the People: Foundations* (Harvard University Press: Cambridge, MA, 1991); Bruce Ackerman, "The Living Constitution," 120 *Harvard Law Review* 1737 (2007).

Chapter 4

1. Mark Tushnet, *Taking the Constitution away from the Courts* (Princeton University Press: Princeton, NJ, 1999), p. 95.

2. Alexander Hamilton, James Madison, and John Jay, *The Federalist Papers* (edited by Lawrence Goldman) (Oxford University Press: New York, 2008), p. 257.

3. Ibid., pp. 54–55.

4. See Howard Gillman, *The Constitution Besieged: The Rise and Demise of Lochner Era Police Powers Jurisprudence* (Duke University Press: Durham, NC, 1993).

5. See Daryl J. Levinson and Richard H. Pildes, "Separation of Parties, not Powers," 119 *Harvard Law Review* 2311 (2006).

6. Michael G. Kammen, *A Machine that Would Go by Itself: The Constitution in American Culture* (Knopf: New York, 1986).

7. Strict constructionists in the nineteenth century were committed to a narrow interpretation of government powers. The relationship between nineteenth- and twentieth-century strict constructionists is unclear. See Howard Gillman, Mark A. Graber, and Keith E. Whittington, *American Constitutionalism: Structures of Government* (Vol. 1) (Oxford University Press: New York, 2013), pp. 120–22.

8. E. E. Kensworthy, "Nixon Scores Indulgence," *New York Times*, November 3, 1968, p. 1.

9. *Trop v. Dulles*, 356 U.S. 86, 100 (1958).

10. Kensworthy, "Nixon," p. 1.

11. Raoul Berger, *Government by Judiciary: The Transformation of the Fourteenth Amendment* (Harvard University Press: Cambridge, MA, 1977), p. 244.

12. Robert H. Bork, *The Tempting of America: The Political Seduction of the Law* (Simon & Schuster Inc.: New York, 1990), pp. 76, 82.

13. Thomas C. Grey, "Do We Have an Unwritten Constitution?" 27 *Stanford Law Review* 703, 703 (1975).

14. Thomas C. Grey, "The Uses of an Unwritten Constitution," 64 *Chicago-Kent Law Review* 211, 220 (1988).

15. Ronald Dworkin, "Unenumerated Rights: Whether and How Roe Should Be Overruled," *The Bill of Rights in the Modern State* (edited by Geoffrey R. Stone, Richard A. Epstein, and Cass R. Sunstein) (University of Chicago Press: Chicago, 1992), p. 386.

16. See Keith E. Whittington, "The New Originalism," 2 *Georgetown Journal of Law and Public Policy* 599 (2004).

17. Hamilton et al., *Federalist Papers*, p. 177.

18. *Annals of Congress*, 1st Cong., 1st Sess. (1789), pp. 520–21.

19. Keith E. Whittington, *Constitutional Construction: Divided Powers and Constitutional Meaning* (Harvard University Press: Cambridge, MA, 1999), p. 6. For a related, but slightly different account of constitutional interpretation and construction, see Lawrence B. Solum, "The Interpretation-Construction Distinction," 27 *Constitutional Commentary* 95 (2010).

20. Whittington, *Constitutional Construction*, p. 6.

21. Ronald Dworkin, *Law's Empire* (Harvard University Press: Cambridge, MA, 1986), p. ix.

22. Dworkin, *Law's Empire*, p. 372.

23. There is no standard typology for constitutional arguments. For an important analysis of some forms, see Philip Bobbitt, *Constitutional Fate* (New York: Oxford University Press, 1982), 3–119.

24. *Adamson v. California*, 332 U.S. 46, 63 (1947) (Frankfurter, J., concurring).

25. Ibid., p. 64 (Frankfurter, J., concurring).

26. I am indebted to Howard Gillman for this point.

27. Joseph Story, *Commentaries on the Constitution of the United States* (Vol. 1) (Hillard, Gray: Boston, 1833), p. 391.

28. For historically oriented textualist approaches, see Antonin Scalia, *A Matter of Interpretation* (Princeton University Press: Princeton, NJ, 1997); Akhil Reed Amar, *The Bill of Rights* (Yale University Press: New Haven, CT, 1998).

29. Leslie Friedman Goldstein, *In Defense of the Text: Democracy and Constitutional Theory* (Rowman & Littlefield: Savage, MD, 1991), p. 3.

30. Akhil Reed Amar, "Intertextualism," 112 *Harvard Law Review* 747, 748 (1999).

31. Ibid., pp. 788–89.

32. Edmund Cahn, "Justice Black and First Amendment 'Absolutes': A Public Interview," 37 *New York University Law Review* 549, 553–54 (1962).

33. *Cohen v. California,* 403 U.S. 15, 25 (1971).

34. Ibid., p. 27 (Blackmun. J., dissenting).

35. Thomas Jefferson, "To William Johnson, Jun 12, 1823," *The Writings of Thomas Jefferson* (Vol. 10) (edited by Paul Leicester Ford) (G. P. Putnam and Sons: New York, 1899), p. 231.

36. Randy E. Barnett, *Restoring the Lost Constitution: The Presumption of Liberty* (Princeton University Press: Princeton, NJ, 2004), p. xiii.

37. *Morse v. Frederick,* 551 U.S. 393, 410–11 (2007) (Thomas, J., concurring).

38. Jack M. Balkin, "Original Meaning and Abortion," 24 *Constitutional Commentary* 293, 293 (2007). Balkin develops this position in Jack M. Balkin, *Living Originalism* (Harvard University Press: Cambridge, MA, 2011).

39. Balkin, "Original Meaning and Abortion," p. 293.

40. Different versions of originalism also raise questions of constitutional authority. Judges, on some views, may be better suited for both institutional and democratic reasons to determine practices and legal meanings when the First Amendment was ratified than to assess the best contemporary theory of free speech.

41. See Keith E. Whittington, "Dworkin's 'Originalism': The Role of Intentions in Constitutional Interpretation," 62 *Review of Politics* 197 (2000).

42. *State of Missouri v. Holland,* 252 U.S. 416, 433 (1920).

43. 343 U.S. 579, 610–13 (Frankfurter, J., concurring); 343 U.S. 579, 683–700 (Vinson, C. J., dissenting).

44. Andrew Jackson, "Veto Message," *A Compilation of the Messages and Papers of the Presidents, 1789–1897* (edited by James D. Richardson) (Government Printing Office: Washington, DC, 1896), pp. 581–82.

45. *Parents Involved in Community Schools v. Seattle School Dist. No. 1,* 551 U.S. 701, 746 (2007).

46. Ibid., p. 748 (Thomas, J., concurring).

47. Ibid., p. 803 (Breyer, J., dissenting).

48. Ibid., pp. 798–99 (Stevens, J., dissenting).

49. *Payne v. Tennessee,* 501 U.S. 808, 828 (1991).

50. *Hein v. Freedom from Religion Foundation, Inc.,* 551 U.S. 587, 628 (2007) (Scalia, J., concurring).

51. Charles L. Black Jr., *Structure and Relationship in Constitutional Law* (Louisiana State University Press: Baton Rouge, 1969), p. 7.

52. *McCulloch v. Maryland,* 17 U.S. 316, 431 (1819).

53. See "Statement on Signing the Energy Policy Act of 2005," 41 *Weekly Comp. Pres. Doc.* 1267 (Aug. 8, 2005).

54. See "Senate Signing Statements Hearing"(statement of Sen. Patrick Leahy, Ranking Member, S. Comm. on the Judiciary), available at http://judiciary.senate.gov/member_statement. cfm?id=1969&wit_id=2629.

55. The classic article is Herbert Wechsler, "The Political Safeguards of Federalism: The Role of the States in the Composition and Selection of the National Government," 54 *Columbia Law Review* 543 (1954).

56. *Garcia v. San Antonia Metropolitan Transit Authority,* 469 U.S. 528, 550–51 (1985).

57. Ibid., p. 565, n. 9 (Powell, J., dissenting).

58. *Terminiello v. City of Chicago,* 337 U.S. 1, 37 (1949).

59. 481 U.S. 279, 315–17 (1987).
60. *Webster v. Reproductive Health Services,* 492 U.S. 490, 557–58 (1989) (Blackmun, J., dissenting).
61. *Boumediene v. Bush,* 553 U.S. 723, 828 (2008) (Scalia, J., dissenting).
62. Ibid.
63. Alexander M. Bickel, *The Least Dangerous Branch: The Supreme Court at the Bar of Politics* (Bobbs-Merrill Company, Inc.: Indianapolis, 1962), pp. 111–98.
64. 262 U.S. 447, 487 (1923).
65. 323 U.S. 214, 244 (1944) (Jackson, J., dissenting).
66. 539 U.S. 558, 562 (2003).
67. William J. Brennan, "The Constitution of the United States: Contemporary Ratification," *South Texas Law Review* 27 (1986): 438.
68. *Grutter v. Bollinger,* 539 U.S. 306, 378 (2003) (Thomas, J., dissenting).
69. Dworkin, *Law's Empire,* p. 53.
70. Ronald Dworkin, *Taking Rights Seriously* (Harvard University Press: Cambridge, MA, 1978), p. 340.
71. *Griswold v. Connecticut,* 381 U.S. 479, 510 (1965) (Black, J., dissenting).
72. Antonin Scalia, "Originalism: The Lesser Evil," 57 *University of Cincinnati Law Review* 849, 864 (1987).
73. Ibid., p. 863.
74. Rogers M. Smith, "The Inherent Deceptiveness of Constitutional Discourse: A Diagnosis and Prescription," *Nomos XL: Integrity and Conscience* (edited by Ian Shapiro and Robert Adams) (New York University Press: New York, 1998), p. 239.
75. *I.N.S. v. Chadha,* 462 U.S. 919, 959 (1983).
76. Ibid., p. 973 (White, J., dissenting).
77. *Michael H. v. Gerald D.,* 491 U.S. 110, 127 n.6 (1989) (opinion of Scalia, J.).
78. Ibid., p. 141 (Brennan, J., dissenting).
79. Pamela S. Karlan and Daniel R. Ortiz, "Constitutional Farce," *Constitutional Stupidities, Constitutional Tragedies* (New York University Press: New York, 1998), p. 180.
80. Mark A. Graber, *Dred Scott and the Problem of Constitutional Evil* (Cambridge University Press: New York, 2006), pp. 15–89.
81. Jeffrey A. Segal, and Harold J. Spaeth, *The Supreme Court and the Attitudinal Model Revisited* (Cambridge University Press: Cambridge, 2002), pp. 86, 110.
82. Lee Epstein and Jack Knight, *The Choices Justices Make* (CQ Press: Washington DC, 1998), p. 23.
83. See Harold J. Spaeth and Jeffrey A. Segal, *Majority Rule or Minority Will: Adherence to Precedent on the U.S. Supreme Court* (Cambridge University Press: New York, 1999).
84. Lawrence Baum, *Justices and Their Audiences: A Perspective on Judicial Behavior* (Princeton University Press: Princeton, NJ, 2006).
85. See ibid., pp. 139–57.
86. Judges on inferior courts are the most important exception to this generalization. They are constrained to follow recent precedent because their decisions will otherwise be overruled by justices on higher courts.
87. Nathaniel Persily, Jack Citrin, and Patrick J. Egan, eds., *Public Opinion and Constitutional Controversy* (Oxford University Press: New York, 2008).
88. See Lee Epstein and Jeffrey A. Segal, *Advice and Consent: The Politics of Judicial Appointment* (Oxford University Press: New York, 2005).
89. Segal and Spaeth, *Attitudinal Model Revisited,* p. 433.
90. Ibid.
91. Abraham Lincoln, "First Inaugural Address," *The Collected Works of Abraham Lincoln* (Vol. 4) (edited by Roy P. Basler) (Rutgers University Press: New Brunswick, NJ, 1953), pp. 263–64.
92. See *Dennis v. United States,* 341 U.S. 494, 525–26 (1951) (Frankfurter, J., concurring); *West Virginia State Board of Education v. Barnette,* 319 U.S. 624, 646–47 (1943).
93. *Clinton v. Jones,* 520 U.S. 681 (1997).
94. *Planned Parenthood of Se. Pa. v. Casey,* 505 U.S. 833, 979 (1992) (Scalia, J., concurring in part and dissenting in part). For the rare opponents of *Roe* who thinks the Constitution prohibits

legal abortion, see David W. Louisell and John T. Noonan Jr., "Constitutional Balance," *The Morality of Abortion: Legal and Historical Perspectives* 200, 244–58 (edited by John T. Noonan Jr.) (Harvard University Press: Cambridge, MA, 1970), pp. 244–58.

95. *State Farm Mut. Auto. Ins. Co. v. Campbell,* 538 U.S. 408, 429 (2003) (Scalia, J., dissenting); *State Farm,* at 429–30 (Thomas, J., dissenting).

96. Frederick Schauer, "Foreword: The Court's Agenda—And the Nation's," 120 *Harvard Law Review* 4, 11 (2006).

97. Ibid., pp. 31–32.

98. Mark A. Graber, "Resolving Political Questions into Judicial Questions: Tocqueville's Thesis Revisited," 21 *Constitutional Commentary* 485 (2004).

99. Schauer, "Court's Agenda," p. 44.

100. David T. Canon, *Race, Redistricting, and Representation: The Unintended Consequences of Black Majority Districts* (University of Chicago Press: Chicago, 1999).

101. See Heather K. Gerken, "A Third Way for the Voting Rights Act: Section 5 and the Opt-In Approach," 106 *Columbia Law Review* 708, 712 (2006).

102. See *Shaw v. Reno,* 509 U.S. 630 (1993).

103. Howard Gillman, *The Constitution Besieged: The Rise and Demise of Lochner Era Police Powers Jurisprudence* (Duke University Press: Durham, NC, 1993), p. 199.

104. Thomas M. Keck, "Party, Policy, or Duty: Why Does the Supreme Court Invalidate Federal Statutes?" 101 *American Political Science Review* 321, 336 (2007).

105. See *Rubin v. Coors Brewing Co.,* 514 U.S. 476 (1995).

106. See, i.e., *Lorillard Tobacco Co. v. Reilly,* 533 U.S. 525 (2001).

107. See *Valentine v. Chrestensen,* 316 U.S. 52 (1942).

Chapter 5

1. Ronald Dworkin, *A Matter of Principle* (Harvard University Press: Cambridge, MA, 1985), p. 71.

2. Alexis de Tocqueville, *Democracy in America* (edited by Phillips Bradley & Francis Bowen) (translated by Henry Reeve) (Alfred A. Knopf, Inc.: New York, 1945), p. 280.

3. For a fascinating account of ways ordinary citizens participate in constitutional politics, see George Lovell, *This Is Not Civil Rights: Discovering Rights Talk in 1939 America* (University of Chicago Press: Chicago, 2012).

4. See Kevin J. McMahon, *Nixon's Court: His Challenge to Judicial Liberalism and Its Political Consequences* (University of Chicago Press: Chicago, 2011); Kevin J. McMahon, *Reconsidering Roosevelt on Race: How the Presidency Paved the Way to Brown* (University of Chicago Press: Chicago, 2003).

5. *Annals of Congress,* 7th Cong., 1st Sess., p. 179.

6. Abraham Lincoln, *The Collected Works of Abraham Lincoln* (Vol. 4) (edited by Roy P. Basler) (Rutgers University Press: New Brunswick, NJ, 1953), p. 268.

7. Alexander M. Bickel, *The Least Dangerous Branch* (Bobbs-Merrill: Indianapolis, 1962), pp. 16–23.

8. *Dennis v. United States,* 341 U.S. 494, 525 (1951)

9. *West Virginia State Board of Education v. Barnette,* 319 U.S. 624, 638 (1943).

10. *Chambers v. Florida,* 309 U.S. 227, 241 (1940).

11. *Colegrove v. Green,* 328 U.S. 549, 556 (1946).

12. Robert G. McCloskey, *The American Supreme Court* (4th ed.) (revised by Sanford Levinson) (University of Chicago Press: Chicago, 2005), pp. 250, 132–34.

13. *Baker v. Carr,* 369 U.S. 186, 226 (1962).

14. *Duncan v. Louisiana,* 391 U.S. 145, 170 (1968) (Black, J., concurring).

15. Robert H. Bork, "Neutral Principles and Some First Amendment Problems," 47 *Indiana Law Journal* 1, 3 (1971).

16. John O. McGinnis and Michael B. Rappaport, "Originalism and the Good Constitution," 98 *Georgetown Review* 1693 (2010).

17. Christopher L. Eisgruber, *Constitutional Self-Government* (Harvard University Press: Cambridge, MA, 2001), p. 64.

18. Louis Michael Seidman, *Our Unsettled Constitution: A New Defense of Constitutionalism and Judicial Review* (Yale University Press: New Haven, CT, 2001); Terri Peretti, *In Defense of a Political Court* (Princeton University Press: Princeton, NJ, 1999).
19. Bruce Ackerman, *We the People: Foundations* (Harvard University Press: Cambridge, MA, 1991).
20. *United States v. Carolene Products Co.,* 304 U.S. 144, 152–53 n. 4 (1938).
21. Ely, *Democracy and Distrust: A Theory of Judicial Review* (Harvard University Press: Cambridge, MA, 1980).
22. See Guido Calabresi, "The Supreme Court, 1990 Term—Foreword: Antidiscrimination and Constitutional Accountability (What the Bork-Brennan Debate Ignores)," 105 *Harvard Law Review* 80 (1991).
23. *Kelo v. City of New London,* 545 U.S. 469, 521–22 (2005).
24. Thomas M. Keck, *The Most Activist Supreme Court in History: The Road to Modern Judicial Conservatism* (University of Chicago Press: Chicago, 2004).
25. Michael J. Klarman, "Majoritarian Judicial Review: The Entrenchment Problem," 85 *Georgetown Law Journal* 491, 549 (1997).
26. See Christopher Wolfe, "The Rehnquist Court and 'Conservative Judicial Activism'," *That Eminent Tribunal* (edited by Christopher Wolfe) (Princeton University Press: Princeton, NJ, 2004); Lino Graglia, "The Myth of a Conservative Supreme Court: The October 2000 Term," 26 *Harvard Journal of Law and Public Policy* 281 (2003); Mark Tushnet, *Taking the Constitution away from the Courts* (Princeton University Press: Princeton, NJ, 2000).
27. See, i.e., Larry D. Kramer, *The People Themselves: Popular Constitutionalism and Judicial Review* (Oxford University Press: New York, 2004).
28. See, i.e., John O. McGinnis, "Reviving Tocqueville's America: The Rehnquist Court's Jurisprudence of Social Discovery," 90 *California Law Review* 485 (2002).
29. *Cooper v. Aaron,* 358 U.S. 1, 18 (1958).
30. *City of Boerne v. Flores,* 521 U.S. 507, 535 (1997).
31. Ronald Dworkin, *Freedom's Law: The Moral Reading of the American Constitution* (Harvard University Press: Cambridge, MA, 1996), pp. 7, 12.
32. *Marbury v. Madison,* 5 U.S. 137, 177 (1803).
33. *Boerne,* at 529.
34. Larry Alexander and Frederick Schauer, "On Extrajudicial Constitutional Interpretation," 110 *Harvard Law Review* 1359, 1359 (1997).
35. Dworkin, *Freedom's Law,* pp. 344–45.
36. Dworkin, *Matter of Principle,* p. 71.
37. Henry M. Hart Jr., "The Supreme Court, 1958 Term—Foreword: The Time Chart of the Justices," 73 *Harvard Law Review* 84, 99 (1959).
38. Frank Michelman, "Law's Republic," 97 *Yale Law Journal* 1493, 1537 (1988).
39. Abraham Lincoln, *Collected Works of Abraham Lincoln* (Vol. 3) (edited by Roy P. Basler) (Rutgers University Press: New Brunswick, NJ, 1953), p. 255.
40. For a discussion of the history and politics of departmentalism, see Keith E. Whittington, *Political Foundations of Judicial Supremacy: The Presidency, the Supreme Court and Constitutional Leadership in U.S. History* (Princeton University Press: Princeton, NJ, 2007).
41. Edwin Meese III, "The Law of the Constitution," 61 *Tulane Law Review* 979, 985 (1987).
42. See Sanford Levinson, "Could Meese Be Right This Time?" 61 *Tulane Law Review* 1071 (1987).
43. "Thomas Jefferson to Abigail Adams, September 11, 1804," *The Writings of Thomas Jefferson* (Vol. 8) (edited by Paul Leicester Ford) (G. P. Putnam's Sons: New York, 1897), p. 311.
44. James Madison, "To Mr. ___, 1834," *Letters of Other Writings of James Madison* (Vol. 4) (J. B. Lippincott: Philadelphia, 1867), p. 349.
45. Larry D. Kramer, "Popular Constitutionalism, Circa 2004," 92 *California Law Review* 959, 959 (2004).
46. Keith E. Whittington, "Extrajudicial Constitutional Interpretation: Three Objections and Responses," 80 *North Carolina Law Review* 773, 791 (2002).
47. For favorable reviews of congressional capacity to protect fundamental rights, see Rebecca F. Zietlow, *Enforcing Equality: Congress, the Constitution, and the Protection of Individual Rights*

(New York University Press: New York, 2006); Neal Devins and Keith Whittington, eds., *Congress and the Constitution* (Duke University Press: Durham, NC, 2005); Louis Fisher, *Religious Liberty in America: Political Safeguards* (University Press of Kansas: Lawrence, 2002).

48. Thomas Jefferson, "The Kentucky Resolutions," *The Portable Thomas Jefferson* (edited by Merrill D. Peterson) (Penguin Books: New York, 1975), p. 281.

49. John C. Calhoun, "Fort Hill Address," *The Nullification Era: A Documentary Record* (edited by William W. Freehling) (Harper & Row: New York, 1967), p. 144.

50. Oliver Wendell Holmes, "Law and the Court," *Collected Legal Papers* (Harcourt, Brace and Howe: New York, 1920), pp. 295–96.

51. *Annals of Congress*, 7th Cong., 1st Sess., p. 661.

52. Jeremy Waldron, *Law and Disagreement* (Oxford University Press: Oxford, 1999), p. 15.

53. Mark Tushnet, *Taking the Constitution Away from the Courts* (Princeton University Press: Princeton, NJ, 1999), p. 174.

54. William Blackstone, *Commentaries on the Laws of England* (Vol. 1) (University of Chicago Press: Chicago, 1979), pp. 90–91.

55. Ibid., p. 41.

56. Compare Ran Hirschl, *Towards Juristocracy: The Origins and Consequences of the New Constitutionalism* (Harvard University Press: Cambridge, MA, 2004) with Linda C. McClain and James E. Fleming, "Constitutionalism, Judicial Review, and Progressive Change," 84 *Texas Law Review* 433 (2005).

57. American Bar Association Task Force on Presidential Signing Statements and the Separation of Powers Doctrine, "Recommendation," available at http://www.abanet.org/op/signing-statements/aba_final_signing_statements_recommendation-report_7-24-06.pdf.

58. Saikrishna Bangalore Prakash, "The Executive's Duty to Disregard Unconstitutional Laws," 96 *Georgetown Law Journal* 1613, 1616–17 (2008).

59. Richard E. Neustadt, *Presidential Power and the Modern Presidents: The Politics of Leadership from Roosevelt to Reagan* (Free Press: New York, 1990), p. 29.

60. The wiggle word *normally* recognizes numerous exceptions and qualifications to this statement, most of which are covered in a standard course on civil procedure.

61. *Wiscart v. Dauchy*, 3 U.S. 321, 327 (1796).

62. James B. Thayer, "The Origin and Scope of the American Doctrine of Constitutional Law," 7 *Harvard Law Review* 129, 144 (1893).

63. See Keith E. Whittington, *Constitutional Interpretation: Textual Meaning, Original Intent, Judicial Review* (University of Kansas Press: Lawrence, 1999).

64. Lawrence Gene Sager, "Fair Measure: The Legal Status of Underenforced Constitutional Norms," 91 *Harvard Law Review* 1212 (1978).

65. See Mark Tushnet, *Weak Courts, Strong Rights: Judicial Review and Social Welfare Rights in Comparative Constitutional Law* (Princeton University Press: Princeton, NJ, 2007).

66. See *Rose v. Council for Better Education*, 790 S.W.2d 186 (Ky. 1989).

67. Cass R. Sunstein, "Foreword: Leaving Things Undecided," 110 *Harvard Law Review* 4, 7 (1996).

68. *Cooper v. Telfair*, 4 U.S. 14, 19 (1800) (Paterson, J., concurring).

69. See Keith Whittington, "The Road Not Taken: *Dred Scott*, Constitutional Law, and Political Questions," 63 *Journal of Politics* 365 (2001).

70. Alan M. Dershowitz, *The Best Defense* (Vintage Books: New York, 1983), pp. xxi–xxii.

71. This story is well told in Justin Crowe, *Building the Judiciary: Law, Courts, and the Politics of Institutional Development* (Princeton University Press: Princeton, NJ, 2012); Howard Gillman, "How Political Parties Can Use Courts to Advance Their Agendas: Federal Courts in the United States, 1875–1891," 96 *American Political Science Review* 511 (2002).

72. See Howard Gillman, "Party Politics and Constitutional Change: The Political Origins of Liberal Judicial Activism," *The Supreme Court and American Political Development* (University Press of Kansas: Lawrence, 2006); Lucas A. Powe Jr., *The Warren Court and American Politics* (Harvard University Press: Cambridge, MA, 2000).

73. See Susan E. Lawrence, *The Poor in Court: The Legal Services Program and Supreme Court Decision Making* (Princeton University Press: Princeton, NJ, 1990).

74. Tushnet, *Taking the Constitution*, pp. 173–74.

75. William G. Ross, *A Muted Fury: Populists, Progressives and Labor Unions Confront the Courts, 1890–1937* (Princeton University Press: Princeton, NJ, 1993).

76. See *Martin v. Hunter's Lessee,* 14 U.S. 304, 328–33 (1816); Akhil Reed Amar, "A Neo-Federalist View of Article III: Separating the Two Tiers of Federal Jurisdiction," 65 *Boston University Law Review* 205 (1985).

77. See Henry M. Hart Jr., "The Power of Congress to Limit the Jurisdiction of Federal Courts: An Exercise in Dialectic," 66 *Harvard Law Review* 1362 (1953).

78. See James S. Liebman and William F. Ryan, " 'Some Effectual Power': The Quantity and Quality of Decisionmaking Required of Article III Courts," 98 *Columbia Law Review* 696 (1998).

79. Whittington, *Political Foundations of Judicial Supremacy,* p. xi.

80. See George I. Lovell, *Legislative Deferrals: Statutory Ambiguity, Judicial Power, and American Democracy* (Cambridge University Press: New York, 2003).

81. Keith E. Whittington, "The Political Foundations of Judicial Supremacy," *Constitutional Politics: Essays on Constitution Making, Maintenance, and Change* (edited by Sotirios A. Barber and Robert P. George) (Princeton University Press: Princeton, NJ, 2001), pp. 261–97.

82. See especially Keith E. Whittington, "The New Originalism," 2 *Georgetown Journal of Law and Public Policy* 599 (2004).

83. Robert A. Dahl, "Decision-Making in a Democracy: The Supreme Court as a National Policy Maker," 6 *Journal of Public Law* 279, 291 (1957).

84. Benjamin N. Cardozo, *The Nature of the Judicial Process* (Yale University Press: New Haven, CT, 1921), p. 168.

85. See Wallace Mendelson, "*Dred Scott*'s Case—Reconsidered," 38 *Minnesota Law Review* 16, 20 (1953).

86. *Congressional Globe,* 31st Cong., 1 Sess., pp. 1154–55 (speech of Henry Clay).

87. John Hart Ely, "The Wages of Crying Wolf: A Comment on *Roe v. Wade,*" 82 *Yale Law Journal* 920, 947 (1973).

88. Powe, *Warren Court,* p. 492.

89. See McMahon, *Reconsidering Roosevelt on Race.*

90. Jack M. Balkin and Sanford Levinson, "Understanding the Constitutional Revolution," 87 *Virginia Law Review* 1045, 1066 (2001).

91. See Gillman, "How Political Parties Can Use Courts."

92. Ibid., p. 512.

93. Powe, *Warren Court,* p. 490.

94. See J. Mitchell Pickerill and Cornell W. Clayton, "The Rehnquist Court and the Political Dynamics of Federalism," 2 *Perspectives on Politics* 233 (2004); Keith E. Whittington, "Taking What They Give Us: Explaining the Court's Federalism Offensive," 51 *Duke Law Journal* 477 (October 2001).

95. Alexander Hamilton, James Madison, and John Jay, *The Federalist Papers* (edited by Lawrence Goldman) (Oxford University Press: New York, 2008), p. 380

96. Gerald N. Rosenberg, *The Hollow Hope: Can Courts Bring about Social Change?* (University of Chicago Press: Chicago, 1991), p. 337.

97. Ibid., p. 50.

98. Kenneth M. Dolbeare and Phillip E. Hammond, *The School Prayer Decisions: From Court Policy to Local Practice* (University of Chicago Press: Chicago, IL, 1971).

99. Rosenberg, *Hollow Hope,* p. 342.

100. Gerald N. Rosenberg, *The Hollow Hope: Can Courts Bring about Social Change?* (2d ed.) (University of Chicago Press: Chicago, 2008), pp. 369–92.

101. See Paul Frymer, *Black and Blue: African Americans, the Labor Movement, and the Decline of the Democratic Party* (Princeton University Press: Princeton, NJ, 2008).

102. Michael J. Klarman, *From Jim Crow to Civil Rights: The Supreme Court and the Struggle for Racial Equality* (Oxford University Press: New York, 2004).

103. Mark A. Graber, *Rethinking Abortion: Equal Choice, the Constitution, and Reproductive Politics* (Princeton University Press: Princeton, NJ, 1996), p. 124.

104. See Susan A. MacManus and Patricia A. Turner, "Litigation as a Budgetary Constraint: Problem Areas and Costs," 53 *Public Administration Review* 462 (1993).

105. Robert Post and Reva Siegel, "*Roe* Rage: Democratic Constitutionalism and Backlash," 42 *Harvard Civil Rights-Civil Liberties Law Review* 373, 376 (2007).
106. See Daniel R. Pinello, *America's Struggle for Same-Sex Marriage* (Cambridge University Press: New York, 2006).
107. Thomas Moylan Keck, *Judicial Politics in Polarized Times* (University of Chicago Press: Chicago, IL, 2014) (forthcoming).
108. Michael W. McCann, *Rights at Work: Pay Equity and the Politics of Legal Mobilization* (University of Chicago Press: Chicago, 1994).
109. Samuel Tyler, *Memoir of Roger Brooke Taney, LLD.* (John Murphy & Co.: Baltimore, MD, 1874), p. 384.
110. Powe, *Warren Court*, p. 72.
111. Some debate exists over the extent to which Franklin Roosevelt was a racial liberal or a president with a racially liberal Justice Department.
112. Whittington, *Political Foundations*, pp. 230–84.
113. Jacob S. Hacker and Paul Pierson, *Off Center: The Republican Revolution and the Erosion of American Democracy* (Yale University Press: New Haven, CT, 2005), p. 71.
114. George I. Lovell and Scott E. Lemieux, "Assessing Juristocracy: Are Judges Rulers or Agents?" 65 *Maryland Law Review* 100, 103 (2006).
115. See Frymer, *Black and Blue*; Gordon Silverstein, *Law's Allure: How Law Shapes, Constrains, Saves and Kills Politics* (Cambridge University Press: New York, 2009).

Chapter 6

1. See Mason Kalfus, "Comment: Why Time Limits on the Ratification of Constitutional Amendments Violate Article V," 66 *University of Chicago Law Review* 437 (1999).
2. *Coleman v. Miller*, 307 U.S. 433 (1939).
3. Stephen M. Griffin, "The Nominee Is…Article V," 12 *Constitutional Commentary* 171, 172 (1995).
4. Howard Gillman, *The Constitution Besieged: The Rise and Demise of Lochner Era Police Powers Jurisprudence* (Duke University Press: Durham, NC, 1993).
5. See Mark Silverstein, *Judicious Choices: The New Politics of Supreme Court Nominations* (W. W. Norton & Company: New York, 1994).
6. Akhil Reed Amar, "Amending the Constitution Outside Article V," 55 *University of Chicago Law Review* 1043, 1064–65 (1988).
7. Alexander Hamilton, James Madison, and John Jay, *The Federalist Papers* (edited by Lawrence Goldman) (Oxford University Press: New York, 2008), p. 198.
8. Alternatively, as happens in other regimes and during the American Civil War, those who oppose constitutional authority are slaughtered.
9. Consider the course of American politics had the surviving remnants of the Confederate Army in 1865 decided to engage in guerilla warfare rather than endorse the post–Civil War constitution. This may not be a hypothetical. A good case can be made that the post–Civil War amendments were not realized for more than 100 years because of violent white resistance during Reconstruction.
10. *Schneiderman v. United States*, 320 U.S. 118, 137 (1943).
11. Walter F. Murphy, *Constitutional Democracy: Creating and Maintaining a Just Political Order* (Johns Hopkins University Press: Baltimore, MD, 2007), p. 506.
12. Ibid., p. 503 (quoting *The SouthWest Case*, 1 BverfGE 14 [1951]).
13. Gary Jeffrey Jacobsohn, *The Wheel of Law: India's Secularism in Comparative Constitutional Context* (Princeton University Press: Princeton, NJ, 2003), p. 139.
14. 258 U.S. 130, 131–35 (1922) (argument of Thomas F. Cadwalader and William L. Marbury).
15. *Leser v. Garnett*, 258 U.S. 130, 136 (1922).
16. Ackerman's works making these claims include Bruce Ackerman, *We the People: Foundations* (Harvard University Press: Cambridge, MA, 1991); Bruce Ackerman, *The Failure of the Founding Fathers: Jefferson, Marshall, and the Rise of Presidential Democracy* (Harvard

University Press: Cambridge, MA, 2005); Bruce Ackerman, "The Living Constitution," 120 *Harvard Law Review* 1737 (2007).

17. Ackerman, *We the People*, pp. 266–67.

18. David R. Dow, "The Plain Meaning of Article V," *Responding to Imperfection: The Theory and Practice of Constitutional Amendment* (edited by Sanford Levinson) (Princeton University Press: Princeton, NJ, 1995).

19. See Barry Cushman, "Mr. Dooley and Mr. Gallup: Public Opinion and Constitutional Change in the 1930s," 50 *Buffalo Law Review* 7 (2002).

20. See Bruce Ackerman, "Transformative Appointments," 101 *Harvard Law Review* 1164 (1988).

21. *McCulloch v. Maryland*, 17 U.S. 316, 415 (1819).

22. *Texas v. White*, 74 U.S. 700, 724 (1868).

23. Thomas Jefferson, "To James Madison, September 6, 1789," *The Papers of Thomas Jefferson*, (Vol. 15) (edited by Julian P. Boyd) (Princeton University Press: Princeton, NJ, 1958), pp. 395–96.

24. "South Carolina Ordinance of Secession," *American Constitutionalism: Structures and Powers* (edited by Howard Gillman, Mark A. Graber and Keith E. Whittington) (Oxford University Press: New York, 2013).

25. Jefferson Davis, *The Rise and Fall of the Confederate Government* (Vol. 1) (D. Appleton and Company: New York, 1912), p. 184.

26. For the full text of Lincoln's first inaugural, see Abraham Lincoln, "First Inaugural Address–Final Text" *Collected Works of Abraham Lincoln* (Vol. 4) (edited by Roy P. Basler) (Rutgers University Press: New Brunswick, NJ, 1953), pp. 262–71.

27. Sanford Levinson, *Our Undemocratic Constitution: Where the Constitution Goes Wrong (and How We the People Can Correct It)* (Oxford University Press: New York, 2006), p. 6. See also Robert A. Dahl, *How Democratic Is the American Constitution?* (Yale University Press: New Haven, CT, 2002); Sanford Levinson, *Framed: America's 51 Constitutions and the Crisis of Governance* (Oxford University Press: New York, 2012).

28. Mark E. Brandon, *Free in the World: American Slavery and Constitutional Failure* (Princeton University Press: Princeton, NJ, 1998), p. 64.

29. Giovanni Sartori, "Constitutionalism: A Preliminary Discussion," 56 *American Political Science Review* 853, 861 (1962).

30. Hamilton et al., *Federalist Papers*, p. 251.

31. Thomas Jefferson, "Thomas Jefferson to Samuel Kercheval, June 12, 1816," *The Writings of Thomas Jefferson* (Vol. 10) (edited by Paul Leicester Ford) (G. P. Putnam's Sons: New York, 1899), p. 44.

32. Kathleen Sullivan, "What's Wrong with Constitutional Amendments?" *The New Federalist Papers: Essays in Defense of the Constitution* (W. W. Norton & Company: New York, 1997), pp. 63–64.

33. Levinson, *Our Undemocratic Constitution*, pp. 7, 160.

34. The material in this paragraph is taken from Donald S. Lutz, "Toward a Theory of Constitutional Amendment," *Responding to Imperfection*, pp. 266–67.

35. Good studies of state constitutionalism include John J. Dinan, *The American State Constitutional Tradition* (University Press of Kansas: Lawrence, 2006); G. Alan Tarr, *Understanding State Constitutions* (Princeton University Press: Princeton, NJ, 2000); James A. Gardner, *Interpreting State Constitutions: A Jurisprudence of Function in a Federal System* (University of Chicago Press: Chicago, 2005); Emily Zackin, *Looking for Rights in All the Wrong Places: Why State Constitutions Contain America's Positive Rights* (Princeton University Press: Princeton, NJ, 2013).

36. Lutz, "Toward a Theory," pp. 266–67.

37. Barry Friedman and Steven B. Smith, "The Sedimentary Constitution," 147 *University of Pennsylvania Law Review* 1, 6 (1998).

38. See Randall Kennedy, "Reconstruction and the Politics of Scholarship," 98 *Yale Law Journal* 521 (1989); Pamela Brandwein, *Reconstructing Reconstruction: The Supreme Court and the Production of Historical Truth* (Duke University Press: Durham, NC, 1999).

39. Chapter 5 discusses controversies over appropriate constitutional authorities.

40. Henry David Thoreau, *Civil Disobedience and Other Essays* (Dover Publications, Inc.: New York, 1993), p. 8.

41. *Debs v. United States*, 249 U.S. 211 (1919).

42. *Norton v. Shelby County*, 118 U.S. 425, 442 (1886).

43. *Linkletter v. Walker*, 381 U.S. 618, 624 (1985).

44. *Osborn v. Nicholson*, 80 U.S. 654 (1871).

45. *Linkletter v. Walker*.

46. Hamilton et al., *Federalist Papers*, p. 177.

47. James Madison, "Veto Message, January 30, 1815," in *A Compilation of the Messages and Papers of the Presidents* (Vol. 2) (edited by James D. Richardson) (Bureau of National Literature: New York, 1897), p. 540.

48. *Annals of Congress*, 1st Cong., 1st Sess., p. 520.

49. *Youngstown Sheet & Tube v. Sawyer*, 343 U.S. 579, 634 (1952) (Jackson, J., concurring).

50. *Brown v. Board of Education*, 347 U.S. 483, 489 (1954).

51. Alexander DeConde, *The Affair of Louisiana* (Scribner's: New York, 1976), p. 185.

52. Mark Tushnet, *Why the Constitution Matters* (Yale University Press: New Haven, CT, 2010), p. 7.

53. Abraham Lincoln, "Speech at Bloomington, Illinois" *Collected Works of Abraham Lincoln* (Vol. 2) (edited by Roy P. Basler) (Rutgers University Press: New Brunswick, NJ, 1953), p. 238.

54. See Keith E. Whittington, *Constitutional Construction: Divided Powers and Constitutional Meaning* (Harvard University Press: Cambridge, MA, 1999), pp. 72–112.

55. 505 U.S. 833, 866–67 (1992) (opinion of O'Connor, Kennedy, and Souter, J.J.).

56. *Casey*, at 995, 998 (Scalia, J., dissenting).

57. See H. Richard Uviller and William G. Merkel, *The Militia and the Right to Arms, or, How the Second Amendment Fell Silent* (Duke University Press: Durham, NC, 2002).

58. *Gibbons v. Ogden*, 22 U.S. 1, 194 (1824).

59. See Stephen L. Elkin, "The Constitutional Theory of the Commercial Republic," 69 *Fordham Law Review* 1933, 1943–49 (2001).

Chapter 7

1. *Ross v. McIntyre*, 140 U.S. 453, 454 (1891).

2. *Slaughter-House Cases*, 83 U.S. 36, 96 (1872) (Field, J., dissenting).

3. Louis Henkin, *Foreign Affairs and the U.S. Constitution* (2d ed.) (Oxford University Press: New York, 1996), p. 16.

4. John Yoo, *The Powers of War and Peace: The Constitution and Foreign Affairs after 9/11* (University of Chicago Press: Chicago, 2005), p. 19.

5. The discussion in this paragraph and the next relies heavily on *United States v. Curtiss-Wright Export Corporation*, 299 U.S. 304, 316, 318, 319 (1936).

6. Yoo, *Powers of War and Peace*, p. 18.

7. David J. Barron and Martin S. Lederman, "The Commander in Chief at the Lowest Ebb— Framing the Problem, Doctrine, and the Original Understanding," 121 *Harvard Law Review* 689, 802 (2008).

8. Gordon Silverstein, "Constitutional Contortion? Making Unfettered War Powers Compatible with Limited Government," 22 *Constitutional Commentary* 349, 361, 362 (2005).

9. Gordon Silverstein, *Imbalance of Power: Constitutional Interpretation and the Making of American Foreign Policy* (Oxford University Press: New York, 1997).

10. For a good discussion of these debates on the geographical scope of the Constitution, see Gerald L. Neuman, *Strangers to the Constitution: Immigrants, Borders, and Fundamental Law* (Princeton University Press: Princeton, NJ, 1996).

11. *Congressional Globe*, 30th Cong., 2nd Sess., App., pp. 272–73.

12. *Ross v. McIntyre*, at 454.

13. See *Downes v. Bidwell*, 182 U.S. 244 (1901); *Balzac v. Puerto Rico*, 258 U.S. 298 (1922).

14. *Boumediene v. Bush*, 555 U.S. 723, 766 (2008).

15. Ibid., p. 553.

16. *Reid v. Covert*, 351 U.S. 1 (1957).

17. *Johnson v. Eisentrager,* 339 U.S. 763 (1950).
18. *United States v. Verdugo-Urquidez,* 494 U.S. 259, 267 (1990).
19. Ibid., p. 288 (Brennan, J., dissenting).
20. *Missouri v. Holland,* 252 U.S. 416, 432–33 (1920).
21. Ibid., p. 433.
22. 23 *American Society of International Law Proceedings* 194, 195–96 (1929).
23. *De Geofroy v. Riggs,* 133 U.S. 258, 267 (1890).
24. Curtis A. Bradley, "The Treaty Power and American Federalism, Part II," 99 *Michigan Law Review* 98, 132 (2000).
25. *Foster v. Neilson,* 27 U.S. 253, 314 (1829).
26. David S. Law and Mila Versteeg, "The Declining Influence of the United States Constitution," 87 *New York University Law Review* 762, 769 (2012).
27. See generally, Mark Tushnet, "The Possibilities of Comparative Constitutional Law" 108 *Yale Law Journal* 1225 (1999).
28. *Palko v. Connecticut,* 203 U.S. 319, 326 (1938).
29. Donald S. Lutz, "Toward a Theory of Constitutional Amendment," *Responding to Imperfection: The Theory and Practice of Constitutional Amendment* (edited by Sanford Levinson) (Princeton University Press: Princeton, NJ, 1995), pp. 266–67.
30. See Ronald J. Krotoszynski Jr., *The First Amendment in Cross-Cultural Perspective: A Comprehensive Legal Analysis of the Freedom of Speech* (New York University Press: New York, 2006).
31. See Rogers M. Smith, *Liberalism and American Constitutional Law* (Harvard University Press: Cambridge, MA, 1985), pp. 18–35; Walter F. Murphy, *Constitutional Democracy: Creating and Maintaining a Just Political Order* (Johns Hopkins University Press: Baltimore, MD, 2007), p. 16.
32. Constitution of the Republic of South Africa, 1996, http://www.info.gov.za/documents/constitution/index.htm.
33. State constitutions in the United States are more hospitable to positive rights. See Emily Zackin, *Looking for Rights in All the Wrong Places: Why State Constitutions Contain America's Positive Rights* (Princeton University Press: Princeton, NJ, 2013).
34. Egypt Const. pt. I, art. 2. For a preliminary analysis of constitutional theocracy, see Ran Hirschl, *Constitutional Theocracy* (Harvard University Press: Cambridge, MA, 2010).
35. Gordon Silverstein, "Singapore: The Exception that Proves Rules Matter," *Rule by Law: The Politics of Courts in Authoritarian Regimes* (edited by Tom Ginsburg and Tamir Moustafa) (Cambridge University Press: New York, 2008).
36. Rogers Smith, *Civil Ideals* (Yale University Press: New Haven, CT, 1997), pp. 197–242.
37. See Gerald N. Rosenberg and John M. Williams, "Do Not Go Gently into that Good Right: The First Amendment in the High Court of Australia," 1997 *Supreme Court Review* 439 (1997).
38. See "Symposium on Constitutional Borrowing," 1 *International Journal of Constitutional Law* 181 (2003); Sujit Choudhry, ed., *The Migration of Constitutional Ideas* (Cambridge University Press: New York, 2006).
39. Jeffrey Goldsworthy, "Conclusions," *Interpreting Constitutions: A Comparative Study* (edited by Jeffrey Goldsworthy) (Oxford University Press: New York, 2006), p. 325.
40. Ibid., pp. 325–26.
41. Ibid., pp. 335–43.
42. Lorraine E. Weinrib, "The Postwar Paradigm and American Exceptionalism," *The Migration of Constitutional Ideas,* p. 97.
43. *Regina v. Keegstra,* 3 S.C.R. 697, 713, 759, 1990); *Regina,* at 848 (MaLachlin, J., dissenting).
44. See Michel Rosenfeld and Andras Sajo, "Spreading Liberal Constitutionalism: An Inquiry into the Fate of Free Speech Rights in New Democracies," *The Migration of Constitutional Ideas,* pp. 161–62.
45. See *R.A.V. v. City of St. Paul,* 505 U.S. 377 (1992).
46. *Employment Division v. Smith,* 494 U.S. 872 (1990).
47. *Rumpelkammer,* BVerfGE 24 (1968); *Kokkinakis v. Greece,* 17 EHRR 397 (1993).
48. Gary Jeffrey Jacobsohn, *The Wheel of Law: India's Secularism in Comparative Constitutional Context* (Princeton University Press: Princeton, NJ, 2003), pp. 49–50.

49. See ibid., pp. 57–72.
50. Ran Hirschl, *Towards Juristocracy: The Origins and Consequences of the New Constitutionalism* (Harvard University Press: Cambridge, MA, 2004), p. 74. This paragraph relies heavily on Hirschl's important study.
51. See Kim Lane Scheppele, "Guardians of the Constitution: Constitutional Court Presidents and the Struggle for the Rule of Law in Post-Soviet Europe," 154 *University of Pennsylvania Law Review* 1757, 1772–90 (2006).
52. See generally Ran Hirschl, "The Judicialization of Mega-Politics and the Rise of Political Courts," 11 *Annual Review of Political Science* 92 (2008).
53. Lori Ringhand, "Fig Leaves, Fairy Tales, and Constitutional Foundations: Debating Judicial Review in Britain," 43 *Columbia Journal of Transnational Law* 865, 896–97 (2005).
54. *Anisminic Ltd v. Foreign Compensation Commission*, 2 AC 147, 170 (1969) (opinion of Lord Reid).
55. Mark Tushnet, *Weak Courts, Strong Rights: Judicial Review and Social Welfare Rights in Comparative Constitutional Law* (Princeton University Press: Princeton, NJ, 2008), p. ix. See Steven Gardbaum, "The New Commonwealth Model of Constitutionalism," 49 *American Journal of Comparative Law* 707 (2001).
56. For the United States, see Larry D. Kramer, *The People Themselves: Popular Constitutionalism and Judicial Review* (Oxford University Press: New York, 2004); Keith E. Whittington, *Political Foundations of Judicial Supremacy: The Presidency, the Supreme Court, and Constitutional Leadership in U.S. History* (Princeton University Press: Princeton, NJ, 2007), pp. 230–84. For a comparative constitutional analysis, see Tushnet, *Weak Courts, Strong Rights*, pp. 43–76.
57. Leslie Friedman Goldstein, *Constituting Federal Sovereignty: The European Union in Comparative Context* (Johns Hopkins University Press: Baltimore, MD, 2001).
58. Tushnet, *Weak Courts, Strong Rights*, p. 228; Kim Lane Scheppele, "A Realpolitik Defense of Social Rights," 82 *Texas Law Review* 1921, 1935 (2004).
59. See Tushnet, *Weak Courts, Strong Rights*, pp. 239–41.
60. Tom Ginsburg, *Judicial Review in New Democracies: Constitutional Courts in Asian Cases* (Cambridge University Press: New York, 2003), p. 18.
61. Howard Gillman, "How Political Parties Can Use the Courts to Advance Their Agendas: Federal Courts in the United States, 1875–1891," 96 *American Political Science Review* 511 (2002).
62. Jack M. Balkin and Sanford Levinson, "Understanding the Constitutional Revolution," 87 *Virginia Law Review* 1045, 1066 (2001).
63. Ginsburg, *Judicial Review*, p. 18.
64. See Mark A. Graber, "The Non-Majoritarian Difficulty: Legislative Deference to the Judiciary," 7 *Studies in American Political Development* 35 (1993).
65. Ronald Dworkin, *A Bill of Rights for Britain* (Chatto and Windus: London, 1990), p. 1.
66. Hirschl, *Towards Juristocracy*, p. 11.
67. Ibid., p. 12.
68. Ibid., p. 14.
69. Linda C. McClain and James E. Fleming, "Constitutionalism, Judicial Review, and Progressive Change," 84 *Texas Law Review* 433, 435 (2005).
70. See Hirschl, *Constitutional Theocracy*.
71. Walter Clark, "Is the Supreme Court Constitutional?" 63 *Independent* 723, 726 (1907).
72. Frank Michelman, "Law's Republic," 97 *Yale Law Journal* 1493, 1537 (1988).
73. Mark Tushnet, *Taking the Constitution away from the Courts* (Princeton University Press: Princeton, NJ, 2000), p. 153.
74. See Hirschl, *Towards Juristocracy*, pp. 193–98.
75. See Jeffrey Goldsworthy, "Australia: Devotion to Legalism," *Interpreting Constitutions*, pp. 125–26.
76. See Hirschl, *Towards Juristocracy*, pp. 50–74.
77. See Charles R. Epp, *The Rights Revolution: Lawyers, Activists, and Supreme Courts in Comparative Perspective* (University of Chicago Press: Chicago, 1998).
78. Reference Re: Secession of Quebec, 2 S.C.R. 217 (1998).

79. The discussion in this paragraph and the next relies heavily on Donald S. Lutz, *Principles of Constitutional Design* (Cambridge University Press: New York, 2006).

80. The analysis of constitutional longevity in this and the preceding paragraph relies heavily on Tom Ginsburg, Zachary Elkins, and James Melton, *The Endurance of National Constitutions* (Cambridge University Press: New York, 2009).

81. Peter Russell, *Constitutional Odyssey: Can Canadians Become a Sovereign People?* (University of Toronto Press: Toronto, 1993), p. 106.

82. James Madison, *The Writings of James Madison* (Vol. 6) (edited by Gaillard Hunt) (G. P. Putnam's Sons: New York, 1906), pp. 386–87.

83. Kim Lane Scheppele, "Aspirational and Aversive Constitutionalism: The Case for Studying Cross-Constitutional Influence through Negative Models," 1 *International Journal of Constitutional Law* 296, 312 (2003).

84. 322 U.S. 143, 153 (1944). For other examples, see Scheppele, "Aspirational and Aversive Constitutionalism"; Richard Primus, "A Brooding Omnipresence: Totalitarianism in Postwar Constitutional Thought," 106 *Yale Law Journal* 423 (1996).

85. *West Virginia State Board of Education v. Barnette,* 319 U.S. 624, 640–41 (1943).

86. 539 U.S. 558, 573 (2003).

87. 543 U.S. 551, 575 (2005).

88. 543 U.S. 551, 624, 626–27 (2005) (Scalia, J., dissenting).

89. "A Conversation between U.S. Supreme Court Justices," 3 *International Journal of Constitutional Law* 519, 523 (2005).

90. Ibid.

91. Iraqi High Tribunal, 29/c/2006, p. 9.

92. Emmerich de Vattel, *Law of Nations* (edited by Joseph Chitty) (S. Sweet: London, 1834), p. viii.

93. *Restatement (Third) of the Foreign Relations Law of the United States* §102(2) (1987).

94. "Thomas Jefferson to Thomas Pinckney, May 7, 1793," *The Writings of Thomas Jefferson* (edited by Paul Leicester Ford) (G. P. Putnam's Sons: New York: 1895), p. 243.

95. *United States v. La Jeune Eugenie,* 26 F. Cas. 832, 846 (C.C.D. Mass. 1822).

96. *The Prize Cases,* 67 U.S. 635, 666, 671 (1862).

97. *The Prize Cases,* at 698 (Nelson, J., dissenting).

98. *Hamdan v. Rumsfeld,* 548 U.S. 557, 563 (2006).

99. *Hamdan v. Rumsfeld,* at 693 (Thomas, J., dissenting).

100. John Jay, "Charge to the Grand Juries by Chief Justice Jay," *The Correspondence and Public Papers of John Jay* (Vol. 3) (edited by Henry P. Johnston) (G. P. Putnam's Sons: New York, 1890), p. 393.

101. Alexander Hamilton, *The Papers of Alexander Hamilton* (Vol. 7) (Columbia University Press: New York, 1962), p. 424.

102. John P. Kaminski and Gaspare J. Saladino, eds., *The Documentary History of the Ratification of the Constitution* (Vol. 10) (Wisconsin Historical Society Press: Madison, 1993), p. 1383.

103. 55 *Congressional Record,* 65th Cong., 1st Sess., pp. 118–20 (1917).

104. Jay Bybee, "Memorandum for Alberto R. Gonzales, Counsel to the President" (August 1, 2002), p. 45 n. 26.

105. See *F. Hoffmann-La Roche Ltd. v. Empagran S.A.,* 542 U.S. 155, 164 (2004).

106. *The Paquette Habana,* 175 U.S. 677, 700 (1900).

107. *Sosa v. Alvarez-Machain,* 542 U.S. 692, 729 (2004).

108. Henkin, *Foreign Affairs and the Constitution,* p. 235.

109. *Restatement (Third) of Foreign Relations Law* § 111 cmt. h (1987).

110. *Sanchez-Llamas v. Oregon,* 548 U.S. 331, 355 (2006).

111. The extent to which Congress may authorize an international tribunal to make binding law for the United States is also constitutionally controversial. For a good discussion of some of the constitutional issues, see Curtis A. Bradley and Jack L. Goldsmith, *Foreign Relations Law: Cases and Materials* (Aspen Publishers: New York, 2003), pp. 359–73.

112. Curtis A. Bradley and Jack L. Goldsmith, "Customary International Law and Federal Common Law: A Critique of the Modern Position," 110 *Harvard Law Review* 815, 857 (1997).

113. Harold Hongju Koh, "Is International Law Really State Law?" 111 *Harvard Law Review* 1824, 1840 (1998).
114. *Restatement (Third) of Foreign Relations Law*, p. 144.
115. *Filartiga v. Pena-Irala*, 577 F. Supp. 860 (E.D.N.Y. 1984).
116. See Lea Brilmayer, "Federalism, State Authority, and the Preemptive Power of International Law," 1994 *Supreme Court Review* 295 (1994).
117. Curtis A. Bradley and Jack L. Goldsmith, "Federal Courts and the Incorporation of International Law," 111 *Harvard Law Review* 2260, 2261 (1998).
118. For that debate and the following quotations, see "Hearing before the Subcommittee on the Constitution," Committee of the Judiciary, House of Representatives, July 19, 2005, 109th Cong., 1st Sess.
119. Ibid.
120. Ken I. Kersch, *Constructing Civil Liberties: Discontinuities in the Development of American Constitutional Law* (Cambridge University Press: New York, 2004, p. 349).
121. Mary Ann Glendon, *Abortion and Divorce in the Western World: American Failures, European Challenges* (Harvard University Press: Cambridge, MA, 1987).
122. Abraham Lincoln, "Annual Message to Congress," *Collected Works of Abraham Lincoln* (Vol. 5) (edited by Roy P. Basler) (Rutgers University Press: New Brunswick, NJ, 1953), p. 537.
123. Ibid.
124. Alexander Hamilton, James Madison, and John Jay, *The Federalist Papers* (edited by Lawrence Goldman) (Oxford University Press: New York, 2008), p. 261.
125. Ibid., p. 306.
126. Ibid.
127. For an important discussion of many themes in this paragraph and the next, see Mariah Zeisberg, *War Powers: A Political Theory of Constitutional Judgment* (Princeton University Press: Princeton, NJ, 2013).

Chapter 8

1. The best-known political science model of this relationship between law and politics is Jeffrey A. Segal and Harold J. Spaeth, *The Supreme Court and the Attitudinal Model Revisited* (Cambridge University Press: New York, 2002).
2. Alexander Hamilton, James Madison, and John Jay, *The Federalist Papers* (edited by Lawrence Goldman) (Oxford University Press: New York, 2008), p. 177.
3. For the classic contemporary essay on politics as a struggle to create as well as satisfy values and interests, see Rogers M. Smith, "If Politics Matters: Implications for a New Institutionalism," 6 *Studies in American Political Development* 1 (1992).
4. See James Madison, "Veto Message," *A Compilation of the Messages and Papers of the Presidents* (Vol. 5) (edited by James D. Richardson) (Government Printing Office: Washington, DC, 1897), pp. 569–70.
5. See Abraham Lincoln, "Speech at Springfield, Illinois" *The Collected Works of Abraham Lincoln* (Vol. 2) (edited by Roy P. Basler) (Rutgers University Press: New Brunswick, NJ, 1953), p. 246; Abraham Lincoln, "Speech at Cincinnati, Ohio" *The Collected Works of Abraham Lincoln* (Vol. 3) (edited by Roy P. Basler) (Rutgers University Press: New Brunswick, NJ, 1953), p. 453.
6. *Texas v. Johnson*, 491 U.S. 397, 421 (1989) (Kennedy, J., concurring).
7. See *Furman v. Georgia*, 408 U.S. 238, 405 (1972) (Blackmun, J., dissenting). See *Furman*, at 375 (Burger, CJ, dissenting).
8. Al Gore, "Concession Speech," December 13, 2000, available at http://www.voxygen.net/cpa/speeches/goretxt.htm.
9. See Lawrence Baum, *Judge and Their Audiences: A Perspective on Judicial Behavior* (Princeton University Press: Princeton, NJ, 2006), pp. 104–5.
10. See Lee Epstein and Jack Knight, *The Choices Justices Make* (CQ Press: Washington, DC, 1998), p. 164.

11. This point is elaborated in Mark A. Graber, "Constitutional Law and American Politics," *The Oxford Handbook of Law and Politics* (edited by Keith E. Whittington, R. Daniel Kelemen, and Gregory A. Caldeira) (Oxford University Press: New York, 2010).

12. Tom R. Tyler, "Psychology and the Law," *The Oxford Handbook of Law and Politics*, p. 718.

13. Hamilton et al., *Federalist Papers*, p. 246; Merrill Jensen, ed., *The Documentary History of the Ratification of the Constitution by the States: Ratification of the Constitution by the States: Pennsylvania* (Vol. 2) (State Historical Society of Wisconsin: Madison, 1976), p. 433.

14. Hamilton et al., *Federalist Papers*, p. 150.

15. Max Farrand, ed., *The Records of the Federal Convention of 1787* (Vol. 1) (Yale University Press: New Haven, CT, 1937), p. 108; Charles A. Syndor, *The Development of Southern Sectionalism: 1819–1848* (Louisiana State University Press: Baton Rouge, 1968), p. 279.

16. *Annals of Congress*, 1st Cong, 1st Sess., p. 453.

17. Hamilton et al., *Federalist Papers*, p. 54.

18. Ibid.

19. Joseph Story, *Commentaries on the Constitution of the United States* (Carolina Academic Press: Durham, NC, 1987), p. 701.

20. Justin E. Crowe, "Westward Expansion, Preappointment Politics, and the Making of the Southern Slaveholding Supreme Court," 24 *Studies in American Political Development* 90 (2010).

21. 12 *U.S. Stat.* 576 (1862).

22. 14 *U.S. Stat.* 27 (1866).

23. *Railway Express Agency v. New York*, 366 U.S. 106, 112 (1949) (Jackson, J., concurring).

24. For a more general argument that most constitutional protections for persons accused of crime were originally thought to be means for protecting substantive liberties, see William J. Stuntz, "The Substantive Origins of Criminal Procedure," 105 *Yale Law Journal* 393 (1995). See also Kenneth Kersch, *Constructing Civil Liberties: Discontinuities in the Development of American Constitutional Law* (Cambridge University Press: New York, 2004), pp. 27–133.

25. Hamilton et al., *Federalist Papers*, p. 114.

26. Ibid., p. 53.

27. See Mark A. Graber, *Dred Scott and the Problem of Constitutional Evil* (Cambridge University Press: New York, 2006), pp. 101–6.

28. For a fascinating discussion of constitutional practices and invisible hands, see Adrian Vermeule, *The System of the Constitution* (Oxford University Press: New York, 2011), pp. 65–100.

29. Hamilton et al., *Federalist Papers*, p. 256.

30. Ibid., p. 257.

31. See Frances E. Lee and Bruce I. Oppenheimer, *Sizing Up the Senate: The Unequal Consequences of Equal Representation* (University of Chicago Press: Chicago, 1999).

32. Gordon Wood has developed this position at length. See Gordon S. Wood, *The Radicalism of the American Revolution* (Knopf: New York, 1992); Gordon S. Wood, *The Creation of the American Republic* (Norton: New York, 1969).

33. See Daryl J. Levinson and Richard H. Pildes, "Separation of Parties, not Powers," 119 *Harvard Law Review* 2311 (2006).

34. Mark Tushnet, *Why the Constitution Matters* (Yale University Press: New Haven, CT, 2010), pp. 38, 12–13.

35. For some evidence on this phenomenon, see Ran Hirschl, *Constitutional Theocracy* (Harvard University Press: Cambridge, MA, 2010).

36. See Stephen Feldman, *Don't Wish Me a Merry Christmas: A Critical History of the Separation of Church and State* (New York University Press: New York, 1996).

37. Smith, "If Politics Matters," p. 16.

38. James G. March and Johan P. Olsen, *Rediscovering Institutions: The Organizational Basis of Politics* (Free Press: New York, 1989), p. 163.

39. Rogers M. Smith, *Civic Ideals: Conflicting Visions of Citizenship in U.S. History* (Yale University Press: New Haven, CT, 1997), p. 6.

40. Abraham Lincoln, "First Debate with Stephen A. Douglas at Ottawa, Illinois," (Vol. 3) *The Collected Works*, p. 216 (quoting Stephen Douglas).
41. Ibid., p. 234.
42. Beau Breslin, *From Words to Worlds: Exploring Constitutional Functionality* (Johns Hopkins University Press: Baltimore, MD, 2009), p. 37.
43. Abraham Lincoln, "The First Inaugural–Final Text," *The Collected Works of Abraham Lincoln* (Vol. 4) (edited by Roy P. Basler) (Rutgers University Press: New Brunswick, NJ, 1953), p. 271.
44. Gary Jeffrey Jacobsohn, *The Wheel of Law: India's Secularism in Comparative Constitutional Context* (Princeton University Press: Princeton, NJ, 2003), p. 120. See generally, Gary Jeffrey Jacobsohn, *Constitutional Identity* (Harvard University Press: Cambridge, MA, 2010), pp. 213–70.
45. Abraham Lincoln, "Speech at Springfield, Illinois," (Vol. 2) *The Collected Works* p. 406.
46. *Annals of Congress*, 1st Cong., 1st Sess., p. 455.
47. Hamilton et al., *Federalist Papers*, p. 251.
48. Susan S. Silbey, "After Legal Consciousness," 1 *Annual Review of Law and Social Science* 323, 324 (2005)
49. *Gertz v. Robert Welch, Inc.*, 418 U.S. 323, 339 (1974).
50. The most prominent work in this genre is Catharine A. MacKinnon, *Only Words* (Harvard University Press: Cambridge, MA, 1993).
51. Gordon Silverstein, *Law's Allure: How Law Shapes, Constraints, Saves, and Kills Politics* (Cambridge University Press: New York, 2009), p. 5.
52. Julie Novkov, "Law and Political Ideologies," *The Oxford Handbook of Law and Politics*, p. 635.
53. The rest of this paragraph is based on Novkov, "Law and Political Ideologies," and Mary Ziegler, "The Framing of a Right to Choose: *Roe v. Wade* and the Change Debate on Abortion Law," 27 *Law and History Review* 281 (2009).
54. Abigail Graber, former film critic for the *Swarthmore Phoenix*, recommends *The Breakfast Club* (five teenagers from disparate high school cliques who hate each other trapped together in Saturday detention all come out dating one or the other or having earned newfound respect for each other), *The Parent Trap* (the girls hate each other at summer camp and then are forced to bunk together), and *Shrek* (Shrek hates Donkey, Fiona hates Shrek, they fight together, and everybody comes out happy). A different variation on this theme occurs when persons are forced by law to live in a certain place or perform a certain task they initially detest. The classic here is probably Goldie Hawn in *Private Benjamin*.
55. Philip A. Klinkner and Rogers M. Smith, *The Unsteady March: The Rise and Decline of Racial Equality in America* (University of Chicago Press: Chicago, IL, 1999), p. 62.
56. See *Brief of the Chamber of Commerce of the United States of America Amicus Curiae,* The Regents of the University of California v. Bakke, 438 U.S. 265 (August 6, 1977).
57. See *Consolidated Brief of Lt. Gen. Julius W. Becton, Jr., Adm. Dennis Blair, Maj. Gen. Charles Bolden, Hon. James M. Cannon, Lt. Gen. Daniel W. Christman, Gen. Wesley K. Clark, Sen. Max Cleland, Adm. Archie Clemins, Hon. William Cohen, Adm. William J. Crowe, Gen. Ronald R. Fogleman, Lt. Gen. Howard D. Graves, Gen. Joseph P. Hoar, Sen. Robert J. Kerrey et al. as Amici Curiae in Support of Respondents,* Grutter v. Bollinger, 539 U.S. 306 (February 21, 2003); *Brief for Amici Curiae 65 Leading American Businesses in Support of Respondents,* Grutter (February 18, 2003); *Brief of General Motors Corporation as Amicus Curiae in Support of Respondents,* Grutter (February 18, 2003).
58. *Grutter v. Bollinger,* 539 U.S. 306, 330–31 (2003).
59. See Gilbert Thomas Stephenson, *Race Distinctions in American Law* (D. Appleton and Company: New York, 1910).
60. Stephen Holmes, "Precommitment and the Paradox of Democracy," *Constitutionalism and Democracy* (edited by Jon Elster and Rune Slagstad) (Cambridge University Press: New York, 1988), p. 237.
61. See *Annals of Congress,* 1st Cong., 2nd Sess., p. 1474.
62. See Michael G. Kammen, *A Machine that Would Go of Itself: The Constitution in American Culture* (Knopf: New York, 1986).

63. For a related meditation on these matters, see Mark V. Tushnet, *Taking the Constitution away from the Courts* (Princeton University Press: Princeton, NJ, 1999), pp. 95–128.
64. Keith E. Whittington, "Yet Another Constitutional Crisis," 43 *William and Mary Law Review* 2093, 2109–10 (2002).
65. Sanford Levinson and Jack M. Balkin, "Constitutional Crises," 157 *University of Pennsylvania Law Review* 707, 714 (2009).
66. Whittington, "Yet Another Constitutional Crisis," p. 2101.
67. See Stephen L. Elkin, "Constitutional Collapse: The Faulty Founding," 18 *Good Society* 1 (2009).
68. Stephen L. Elkin, *Reconstructing the Commercial Republic: Constitutional Design after Madison* (University of Chicago Press: Chicago, 2006), pp. 60–65.
69. The previous summarizes Paul O. Carese, *The Cloaking of Power: Montesquieu, Blackstone, and the Rise of Judicial Activism* (University of Chicago Press: Chicago, 2003).
70. See Larry Alexander and Frederick Schauer, "On Extrajudicial Constitutional Interpretation," 110 *Harvard Law Review* 1359 (1997).
71. Louis Michael Seidman, *Our Unsettled Constitution: A New Defense of Constitutionalism and Judicial Review* (Yale University Press: New Haven, CT, 2001); Mariah Zeisberg, *War Powers: A Political Theory of Constitutional Judgment* (Princeton University Press: Princeton, NJ, 2013).
72. See Elkin, "Constitutional Collapse."

CASES

INDEX

by the people, 146
ratification, 141, 145–47
societal consensus, 156
state constitutionalism, 158–59
unconstitutional constitutional amendments, 148–50
Fortas, Abe, 135
Fourteenth Amendment. *See* due process clause
Fourth Amendment, 31, 33, 137, 162, 174, 178–79
France, 48, 51, 163, 181, 183, 187, 188, 189
Frankfurter, Felix, 3, 72–73, 94, 105, 106, 135
free speech, 2, 23, 71, 75, 77–78, 86, 107, 182, 198, 216
Friedman, Barry, 160
Fugitive Slave Acts of 1793 and 1850, 118
Fugitive Slave Clause, 58, 155, 160
Fuller, Lon, 30
fundamental law, 10, 24–28
    amendment process, reflection of fundamental or higher law status, 27
    American constitutionalism, thinking about basic constitutional questions, 10
    classical constitutionalism, contrasted, 25
    conflicts, 25
    enforceability and judicial review, 27–28
    higher law, 25–26
    last in time, first in line, 25
    liberal constitutionalism, protection of, 36–37
    partisan politics, 28
    popular elections as guarantee for fundamental rights, 37
    popular sovereignty and, relationship between, 138
    popular sovereignty and higher law, tensions between, 28
    ratification process, reflection of fundamental or higher law status, 27
    rule of law, commitment to, 29
    social contract theory, 26–27
    status, sources, 25–26
fundamental law and popular sovereignty, relationship between, 138

gay rights, 103, 109, 134, 173, 209, 239
    Defense of Marriage Act (DOMA), 103, 173
    homosexual activity/behavior, 70, 85, 103, 173, 196–97
    same-sex marriage, 28, 41, 70, 73–74, 89, 103, 123, 133, 141, 173, 219
gender discrimination, 160, 172, 191, 240. *See also* equal rights
Geneva Convention, 200, 201, 203
German nationals in custody of army after World War Two, 178
Germany, 11, 38–39, 46, 149, 183, 185, 187, 193, 207

Nazi Germany, 196, 199, 202
gerrymandering, 49, 134, 137
Gilded Age, 144
Gillman, Howard, 32n54, 33n55, 65n4, 67n7, 74n26, 97, 127n71, 128n72, 132n91, 143n4, 154n24, 190n61
Ginsburg, Ruth Bader, 34, 74, 89
Ginsburg, Tom, 55, 190–91
Glendon, Mary Ann, 209
global community, 184–85
global perspectives. *See* comparative constitutional authority, global perspectives
Goldstein, Leslie, 189–90
Goldsworthy, Jeffrey, 185–86
good constitutional law *vs.* good public policy, 3
good or legitimate constitutional politics, 3, 10
Gore, Al; 2000 national presidential election, 12–13, 91, 135, 217
governing officials in constitutional regimes, 14–15
Graber, Abigail, 238n54
Graber, Mark A., 11n26, 12n29, 26n43, 32n54, 60n51, 62n60, 67n7, 89n80, 96n98, 134n103, 154n24, 191n64, 217n11, 225n27
grand constitutional theory, 106–9
    development of, 108–9
    originalists and, 106–7
Gray, Horace, 203–4
Great Britain, 24, 57, 176, 188, 196
Great Compromise at Constitutional Convention, 226
Great Society, 69, 105, 130, 139, 168
Greenhouse, Linda, 91
Grey, Thomas, 68
Grier, Robert, 200
Guantanamo Bay, 84, 178
Guaranty Clause, 106, 122
gun control and handgun policies, 3, 72, 81, 123–24, 195, 213, 216

Hague Conventions, 201
Hamilton, Alexander, 21, 26, 53, 132–33, 162, 194, 198, 202, 224–25
    Federalist 23, 225
    Federalist 78, 132–33
handgun policies and gun control, 3, 72, 81, 123–24, 195, 213, 216
Harlan, John, 76, 85
Harrison, Benjamin, 216
Hart, Henry M., Jr., 113, 129n77
Hill, Harold, 232
Hirschl, Ran, 36n61, 41n5, 55, 120n56, 184n34, 188, 191–92, 232n35
historical-institutionalist American constitutional theory, 12–13

Madison, James
  comparative constitutional change, 194–96
  constitutional improvements and change, 60,
      145–46, 156–58, 162–63, 194–96, 214
  constitutional interpretation, 65, 69, 116
  elections and Article I, 19, 52–53, 56
  Federalist 10, 52, 169, 220–22, 224, 230
  Federalist 31, 220
  Federalist 37, 59, 69
  Federalist 51, 12
  Federalist 62, 53, 210
  formal constitutional change, dispute with
      Jefferson, 156–58
  freedom of speech, 234–35
  fundamental right, educating the public, 233
  internal improvements bill, 215, 217
  liberal constitutionalism, 37
  limited government, 32
  national aspirations and slavery, 59
  national bank, 7
  protection of rights, institutional design,
      220–22
  ratification, 145–46
  separation of powers, 226–27
  social contract theory, 26
  state laws, injustice of, 61
  two-party system, 230
Magna Carta (1215), 24, 36
Marbury, William L., 150, 217
March, James, 232
marriage
  Defense of Marriage Act (DOMA), 103, 173
  interracial marriage, 135, 164, 173
  same-sex marriage, 28, 41, 70, 73–74, 89, 103,
      123, 133, 141, 173, 219
Marshall, John, 4–10, 27, 81, 102, 112, 115, 121,
      132, 153, 180, 203, 217
Marshall, Thurgood, 93, 130
McClain, Linda, 120n56, 191
McCloskey, Robert, 106
McCulloch, James, 4
McGinnis, John O., 106, 109n28
McIlwain, Charles, 24–25
McLean, John, 135
Meese, Edwin III, 76, 114
Michels, Robert, 49
Miers, Harriet, 137
Mill, John Stuart, 214
Miller, Samuel F., 62, 160
Miranda rights, 127
Missouri Compromise, 166, 168, 170
modern constitutionalism, 14, 24–37
  commitment to rule of law, 29
  constitutional clauses, generally, 28
  contemporary constitutionalism, distinctions,
      38–39
  fundamental law, 24–28

generally, 24
liberal constitutionalism, 35–37
limited government, 32–35
partisan politics, 28
popular sovereignty and constitutionalism,
    28
ratification process, reflection of fundamental
    or higher law status, 27
rule of law, 29–32
Monroe, James, 9, 154
moral and policy considerations, constitutional
    arguments, 73
Murphy, Frank, 148–49
Murphy, Walter, 35, 41, 149

national aspirations, 56–58
  constitutional insurance and, differences, 57
  entrenched commitments, 56
  entrenched constitutional aspirations, 57–58
National Association for Advancement of
    Colored People (NAACP), 134
national banks, 4–10, 79, 120, 132, 163, 229
national identity, 21–22
natural rights, 36
nature of the constitution, 5–6
Nazi Germany, 196, 199
necessary and proper clause, 5–7, 75
necessary concomitant of nationality, 177
Nelson, Samuel, 201
New Deal, 12, 23, 105, 130–31, 132, 136,
    151–53, 168
Nineteenth Amendment, 63, 143, 150
Nixon, Richard M., 67, 102, 123
North, Douglas, 48, 50
Novkov, Julie, 23n35, 237
Nuremberg Trials, 199

Obama, Barack, 28, 100, 103, 138
O'Connor, Sandra Day, 109, 126, 167, 239
Okin, Susan, 17
Olsen, Johan, 232
originalism/originalist arguments, 76–78
  abstract clauses, 77–78
  proponents of, 77
  purpose, 87
original jurisdiction, 128
original purposes, 60–61
"Our posterity," 41, 208

pacta sunt servanda, 199–200
Paine, Thomas, 54, 163
parchment barriers, 219, 223, 226
Paterson, William, 125, 226
pattern of authority, 103–4
Peretti, Terri, 107
Phelps, Fred, 217
Philadelphia Convention, 35–36, 59, 157